Great American
Nature Writing

Great American
NATURE
WRITING

Selected and with Commentary by

JOSEPH WOOD KRUTCH

Decorations by Rudolf Freund

WILLIAM SLOANE ASSOCIATES

First Printing

Typography and format designed by
LEONARD W. BLIZARD

TO
Marcel and Celestine

There are some who can live without wild things, and some who cannot . . . wild things were taken for granted until progress began to do away with them. Now we face the question whether a still higher "standard of living" is worth its cost in things natural, wild, and free. For us of the minority the opportunity to see geese is more important than television, and the chance to find a pasqueflower is a right as inalienable as free speech.

These wild things, I admit, had little human value until mechanization assured us a good breakfast, and until science disclosed the drama of where they come from and how they live. The whole conflict thus boils down to a question of degree. We of the minority see a law of diminishing returns in progress; our opponents do not.

ALDO LEOPOLD: *A Sand County Almanac*

Contents

PROLOGUE

THOREAU AND THE THOREAUISTS

ESCAPE FROM THE COMMONPLACE

LIVES OF THE HUNTED

SMALL DEER

TWO LEGS TOO MANY

MAJESTY OF THE INANIMATE

MYSTERY OF CREATION

POSTSCRIPT

Great American
Nature Writing

NOTE

For the purpose of this anthology the term American is interpreted to include not only Canadians (who are certainly Americans) but also the Englishman Ernest Thompson Seton who was long a resident on this continent. For the inclusion of G. Murray Levick's piece on the habits of penguins there is, I am afraid, no formal excuse, since the author is British not American. However, because I was interested in a genre which is quite international and could find no American piece which so well represents one kind of subject matter and approach, I offer his essay in the conviction that no one who reads it will regret its inclusion.

J. W. K.

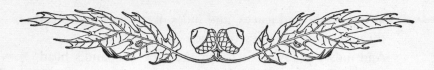

Prologue

STEPHEN LEACOCK once remarked that our ancestors were too busy clearing the forests to find time to take exercise. In a somewhat similar sense it may be assumed that primitive man was not interested in nature. But it would also appear that he had hardly got himself urbanized before he began, in imagination at least, to return to it.

No doubt there is some truth in the oft-repeated assertions that Petrarch was the first man to climb a mountain for the view; that the dweller in the medieval city preferred what we should call intolerable overcrowding; and that, as Macaulay pointed out, men do not begin to admire wild mountains until danger ceases to press upon them in their daily life. But it is equally true that the legend of a golden age when man lived in harmony with nature seems to be almost as old as civilization itself. Moschus and Bion idealized the shepherd's life. Virgil wrote about the delights of the country less like a farmer than like a city man who retires to a weekend estate. And in imperial Rome the literary cult of the simple life had reached a point where Juvenal could satirize it in the lines which Dryden magnificently translated:

> In Saturn's reign, at Nature's early birth,
> There was that thing called Chastity on earth;
> When in a narrow cave, their common shade,
> The sheep, the shepherds, and their gods were laid;

When reeds, and leaves, and hides of beasts were spread
By mountain huswifes for their homely bed,
And mossy pillows raised, for the rude husband's head.
Unlike the niceness of our modern dames,
(Affected nymphs with new affected names,)
The Cynthias and the Lesbias of our years,
Who for a sparrow's death dissolve in tears;
Those first unpolished matrons, big and bold,
Gave suck to infants of gigantic mold;
Rough as their savage lords who ranged the wood,
And fat with acorns belched their windy food.

Obviously, then, much nature writing of today springs from impulses almost as old as Western culture. To claim for it absolute originality of either feeling or expression would be foolish. The fact remains, nevertheless, that there is a recognizable genre of belles-lettres whose remoter history seems hardly to go back beyond the end of the seventeenth century, and much of that writing does define attitudes to some extent novel—in their emphases at least. There is in it some feeling for nature which is not quite that of the ancients nor that of the Romantics.

The intention of the present anthology is to reprint certain pieces of excellent American writing which are related to one another because, for all their diversity, they exhibit this feeling which is recognizably modern. There is no desire to strain the point, but the collection is not random. It excludes accounts of discovery, exploration, and adventure, insofar as they are that and nothing more. It excludes also both purely subjective musing on one hand, and purely objective scientific observation on the other. Thus it attempts by example to define a genre which has, perhaps, not been so clearly recognized as it might be.

There is a vast body of scholarly writings devoted to the analysis of what is loosely called "the appreciation of nature" as a literary phenomenon. But such writing concerns itself largely with poetry and other traditional forms of belles-lettres, especially during the Romantic revival. It generally pays but scant attention to "nature writing" as an emergent literary form struggling for its own independence.

Histories of English literature frequently mention *The Compleat Angler* and *The Natural History of Selborne* as somehow sufficiently novel in form and spirit to make them almost unique in their time. Similar histories of American literature generally devote considerably more space to Thoreau, in whom they recognize another uniqueness. Sometimes, indeed, they acknowledge him as the immediate begetter of the whole subsequent school. But there does not seem to have been before the present day any group of writers closely comparable to that which includes, for example, William Beebe, Gustav Eckstein, Donald Culross Peattie, Julian Huxley, and scores of others who produce a flood of widely read books neither purely scientific nor easily placeable in any of the traditional departments of belles-lettres.

What is new in them is certainly not the impulse to escape the complexities of civilization nor the desire to celebrate the soothing or inspirational effects of natural scenery. Neither is it an interest in natural history as such, for natural history was already a science in Aristotle's time. Yet there is some element of novelty. Either something new has been added, some new point of view introduced, or some new synthesis made. Thoreau was not merely following in the footsteps of Aristotle and Gilbert White any more than he was merely following in those of Wordsworth. And if it is true, not only that Thoreau was the most original of the modern nature writers, but also that nearly everyone who has come after has learned something from him, then it ought to be possible to put one's finger upon some aspect of his uniqueness.

Perhaps no man before him had ever taken quite so literally the term "fellow creatures," and perhaps that is one of the most significant things about him. When he spoke of having "a little fishy friend in the pond"; when he held interviews with a woodchuck, or hoped that one of his games had taught the fox something, he was expressing in his own special, humorous way a sense of intimacy and of fellowship to some degree novel. Insofar as it was simply an outpouring of love, the banal analogy would be, of course, St. Francis. But there is an intellectual difference which is of some importance. Thoreau could feel as he did, not so much because he was tender toward inferior creatures as because he did not think of them as inferior; because he had none of that sense of superiority or even separateness which is the inevitable result of any philosophy or any religion which attributes to man a qualitative uniqueness, and therefore inevitably suggests that all other living things exist for him. St. Francis preached to the birds; many moderns have hoped, on the contrary, that the birds would preach to them.

Many writers later than Thoreau—some of them far more scientific than he in training and temperament—have expressed his attitude in terms less humorous as well as less emotional, but they too have insisted upon looking at nature from some point of view common to all its creatures rather than from that of man's own special desires and purposes. And it may be that one distinguishing characteristic of the nature writings of our time, one common to Thoreau and the whole school, is the result of just this sense of oneness, this conviction that we are all, as it were, in the same boat.

It would be absurd, of course, to suggest that no one before Thoreau's time had ever, to some extent, anticipated this attitude or to some extent given expression to it. A Christian work sometimes attributed to St. Augustine supplied one volume of the austere Cambridge *Natural History* with a very appropriate motto which may be translated thus: "He created in heaven the angels and in the earth, worms; nor was He superior in the one case or inferior in the other. If no other hands but His could create the angels, neither could any other create the worms." And it can hardly be said that whoever wrote that sentence failed to share the conviction that the wonder of man is no greater than the wonder of all living things.

But the seed of such an idea does not find its most congenial soil in a mind which continues to insist, as the orthodox Christians did, upon some absolute uniqueness in man, and refuses to admit that he is really continuous with the rest of nature. Even Thoreau could not have written as he did had he not been the inheritor of the whole intellectual revolution which had been in progress since the Renaissance, and which was finally, just after his own time, to convince Westerners that they were the grandsons of the ape at least as truly as they were the sons of God.

No doubt, then, Thoreau was less fundamentally original than he himself supposed. Insofar as he was original in any absolute sense, the originality consisted in the extent to which he succeeded in giving highly personal expression to an attitude which history had made possible. But he is well enough known to be immediately used in raising a central question: By what series of steps had it become possible for a man to write as Thoreau wrote and to be read as sympathetically as he has been read? There is involved a question of what he knew; a question of the emotional attitudes he took toward that knowledge; and finally the question of the literary form which he employed in setting all these things forth.

I I

In the light of these questions let us consider Thoreau first in contrast with those writers about plants and animals whom he least resembles—namely, some of the popular authors of the Middle Ages. So far as the pure science of natural history was concerned, it had been carried little beyond the point at which Aristotle and Pliny had left it, and if even they did not always successfully distinguish between fact and fable, their remote followers added many fables but few facts. Nevertheless, what interfered most decisively with the development of the feeling for nature as such was less the paucity of facts than the strength of theological notions which served to discourage certain kinds of wonder by supplying ready answers to every question concerning the *why* of the universe outside man. The sun was put in the heavens to give light by day, and the moon to give light by night. Sun or moon may also declare the glory of God and so, for that matter, may the lamb. But the most obvious reason for the existence of them all is the meat which the last supplies for man's consumption, and the light which the other two supply him to eat it by.

Both histories of science and histories of literature have frequently emphasized the resulting fact that most medieval writing about nature seems to us remote and merely quaint. This is less because of how little, comparatively speaking, its authors knew than because of their attitude toward the nature of evidence on the one hand and toward the purpose of knowledge on the other. The more learned among them might revere Aristotle and, later, learn something from the Orient. But what at least the general public found most to its taste was contained in the various versions of *Physiologus*, the popular compilations of unnatural history drawn from an accumulated stock of misinformation, but offering both an abundance of wonders and an almost inexhaustible store of morals to be drawn from them. Such writings seem to us absurd not primarily because their compilers knew so much that was not true and so little that was, but because the whole tendency of their thinking was anthropocentric and teleological.

They never for a moment doubted that the right question to ask was the question, "What practical use or what moral instruction did God intend to provide for me when he created this creature or that?" And they were so sure of the rightness of the question that once they had heard a satisfactory answer they seldom doubted its correctness or felt the impulse to investigate it. If few ever troubled to see whether or not the toad, "ugly and venomous, wears yet a precious jewel in his head," that was simply because it seemed to them so inherently probable that he did. What reason other than the desire to teach man a useful lesson could God possibly have had for cluttering his beautiful earth with creatures so repulsive?

Here is a bit about the whale, translated from an Anglo-Saxon version of *Physiologus*, and therefore one of the very first writings in English about natural history:

"His appearance is like that of a rough boulder, so that seamen imagine they are going upon an island, and moor their high-prowed ship with cables to that false land, make fast the ocean coursers at the seas end, and boldly climb up on that island; the vessels stand by the beach, enringed by the flood. The weary-hearted sailors then encamp, dreading not of peril. . . . On the island they start a fire, kindle a mounting flame. Now when the cunning plotter feels that the seamen are firmly established upon him, and have settled down to enjoy the weather, the great ocean beast sinks without warning. . . .

"Such is the way of demons, the worst of devils; they spend their lives outwitting men by their secret power."

Those who read with delight this tale of a whale were obviously not deficient in that sense of wonder which has sometimes been cited as one of the distinguishing characteristics of Thoreau and of many subsequent writers. In that respect they were perhaps closer than some later anatomists and taxonomists to the spirit of Thoreau, as well as to that of Julian Huxley or Gustav Eckstein. But they obviously had neither a sense of fact nor, above all, a sense of the wonder of fact; no suspicion that the study of nature might do more than supply confirmation and illustration. The whale is important because he illustrates the ways of demons. The natural world could teach nothing radically new. It was merely a collection of metaphors and fables ingeniously repeating in figurative language the truths already known from authority. On occasion, to be sure, it might propound riddles to tempt the ingenuity of man, as in the case of the toad and his jewel. But the answer, when found, would always be one consonant with what was already known. Nothing really new would ever be discovered. The meaning of the universe, the proper place of man in it, was already known, completely and finally.

This does not mean that the medieval writer had lost the power of observation. It means at most that he had relatively little respect for it; that it seemed to him a crude instrument; and that when he used it he was, at best, indulging in a mere whim. Consider, for example, the case of Bartholomew Anglicanus, the monk whose encyclopedia, *De Proprieteribus Rerum*, was compiled in the thirteenth century and translated into wonderful English in the fourteenth. In its own time it was held in the highest respect, and today it is regarded as a monument of medieval literature. A great many of its entries are devoted to animals, real or fabulous, concerning which, for the most part, the author recounts what he has read in other equally ill-informed books. It tells us, for example, about the crocodile, who weeps after he has killed a man, and about the elephant, who is captured by cutting down the tree against which he has leaned to sleep. But the modern reader who turns its pages may have the good luck to fall upon a few items—one, for instance, on the dog and another on the cat—which leap up from the page because they are so obviously the product of original observation, and because the author's real delight in what he has seen for himself still shines through.

"Of The Cat: He is a full lecherous beast in youth, swift, pliant, and merry, and leapeth and rusheth on everything that is to fore him: and is led by a straw, and playeth therewith: and is a right heavy beast in age and full sleepy, and lieth slyly in wait for mice: and is aware where they be more by smell than by sight, and hunteth and rusheth on them in privy places: and when he taketh a mouse, he playeth therewith, and eateth him after the play. In time of love is hard fighting for wives, and one scratcheth and rendeth the other grievously with biting and with claws. And he maketh a ruthful noise and ghastful, when one proffereth to fight with another: and unneth is hurt when he is thrown down off an high place. And when he hath a fair skin, he is as it were proud thereof, and goeth fast about: and when his skin is burnt, then he bideth at home, and is oft for his fair skin taken of the skinner, and slain and flayed."

Obviously Bartholomew knew cats. He drew of them a generic portrait which in some respects suggests the famous animal portraits of Buffon, and which in some respects is superior to them. But it is not only knowledge which shines through his lines. Wonder may be largely absent, for Bartholomew had, perhaps, no sense that the cat is as wonderful as the dragon—to which he devoted a fuller account—would be if the dragon had ever existed. He was, nevertheless, capable of feeling and capable of communicating an emotion in which Buffon was notably deficient, but which every good modern writer about nature must to some extent exhibit—namely, love.

Bartholomew may or may not have "liked cats" in the vulgar meaning of that phrase. He may or he may not have kept pets or fed the birds. But in one of the truest senses of the word he must have loved the cat, since only love could so sharpen the observation, so wing the words which he chose in order to re-create the cat's whole being. For once he was describing something whose most important meaning was itself; which existed and which ought to exist in its own right; which was not useful to man, either directly or as an allegory, but was quite simply its own excuse for being.

From that passage it is hardly a step to the finest of Chaucer's little pictures of barnyard life or of the cat which had to be lifted from the best chair before the monk sat down. Yet in all the *De Proprieteribus Rerum* there are only one or two other examples of anything so genuine or so telling. The man who wrote them might have left an account of the sights and sounds and smells of the medieval world the like of which nowhere exists. He might have drawn to the life both the men and the beasts among whom he lived. But no doubt he would have regarded the task as unworthy; and perhaps, when he permitted himself to describe the dog and the cat, he did so with a certain sense of being truant. They lacked dignity; they lacked importance. The whale and the fabulous dragon were far more profitable and instructive.

Obviously Bartholomew was, in some sense of the term, a "nature writer." The animal kingdom was one of his principal subjects, and he wrote about it with an enthusiasm which suggests a general interest in that subject itself. He was not incapable of observation, and not incapable of love. But observation remained a method only occasionally employed, and love an emotion perhaps hardly recognized for what it was. He differs from the modern nature writer not only because he had fewer facts at his disposal, but because he was apparently less aware of what a fact was or why it was important. He differs also in a possibly more significant way because he could not rationalize, or perhaps even respect, the love which went out from him toward the dog and the cat. If he had read Thomas Aquinas he would probably have accepted the Thomistic doctrine that although cruelty to animals is a sin, it is so not because it results in pain to the animals (which have no souls), but because it may lead to similar cruelty toward men.

III

From *Physiologus* to Bartholomew is obviously one step. What is the next? The answer which the history of science gives seems to be that it was a new sense of fact and of the importance of fact in both botany and zoology. Such a sense of fact began to manifest itself in natural history long before any new emotional attitude toward our fellow creatures began to appear.

Botany was, of course, a branch of medicine. Its purpose was purely the recognition of plants useful to man. Insofar as it was scientific it was based largely on the work of the second-century Greek botanist Dioscorides, whose description of the

Mediterranean flora offered many puzzles to the collectors in northern Europe: They were loath to suppose that there were any plants in their region unknown to so great an authority. But about the middle of the fifteenth century a change began to come over the herbals. There was less stress on the mandrake and other miraculous plants; less concern with the doctrine of signatures, that characteristically medieval theory that God has indicated by the shape of the leaves or the root what a given plant is good for; more pictures and descriptions of plants actually seen and realistically delineated.

In zoology, the change is even more striking, thanks perhaps to the existence of a man of individual genius—Konrad von Gesner, who published in the sixteenth century his *Historia Animalia*. Its intention was to depict as completely as possible the beasts of the field, and to display the variety of life for some purpose which included more than merely the practical on the one hand, or the homiletic on the other. Gesner included, to be sure, a number of fabulous beasts; in some cases because he had no reason to doubt that they existed; in others because, although their existence seemed improbable to him, the reader would expect to find them and might be indulged in his expectation if suitably warned, as Gesner sometimes warned him, that they were probably mere creatures of fancy.

After Gesner, the science of natural history advanced by leaps and bounds. Soon men were not only looking at plants and animals, but peering at them with fanatical attention through the newly perfected lenses. In seventeenth-century Italy, Malpighi dissected the silkworm to learn the secrets of its spinneret; in Holland, Swammerdam ruined his health to observe and draw in incredible detail the anatomy of insects. In seventeenth-century Holland also, the industrious dilettante, Leeuwenhoek, peeked at all sorts of strange things through the lenses he ground himself, and discovered the existence of bacteria.

In London, the Royal Society, strangest of the Merry Monarch's whims, constituted itself a clearinghouse for discoveries both trivial and important. But its constitution definitely repudiated any interest in what some scientists had already begun to despise as the merely literary, and the danger now was, not that man should lack a sense of fact, but that he should lack everything else; that scientific knowledge should become merely a body of information, some of it curious and some of practical usefulness, but completely remote from his emotional life.

Yet even before the Royal Society was founded, one English man of letters—Sir Thomas Browne—felt the new urgency of fact, despite both his reverence for ancient authorities and his interest in cultivating his own unique literary style. In 1646 he published his *Pseudodoxia Epidemica; or Vulgar Errors*, in which he canvassed the opinions of the learned in support of various dubious theories and then boldly challenged them in the light of reason or experience. A great many of the epidemic false opinions which he considered had to do with natural history; and here, for instance, is a part of what he had to say about the fire-resisting salamander which had got itself so firmly entrenched in art as well as in literature:

"That a Salamander is able to live in flames, to endure and put out fire, is an assertion not only of great antiquity, but confirmed by frequent, and not contemptible testimony. The Egyptians have drawn it in their Hieroglyphics; Aristotle seemeth to embrace it; more plainly Nicander, Sarenus Sammonicus, Aelian, and Pliny, who assigns the cause of this effect: An Animal (saith he) so cold that it extinguisheth fire like Ice. . . .

"The ground of this opinion might be some sensible resistance of fire observed in the Salamander: which being, as Galen determineth, cold in the fourth, and moist in the third degree, and having also a mucus humidity above and under the skin, by virtue whereof it may a while endure the flame: which being consumed, it can resist no more. . . . And therefore some truth we allow in the tradition: truth according unto Galen, that it may for a time resist a flame, or as Scaliger avers, extinguish or put out a coal: for thus much many humid bodies perform: but that it perseveres and lives in that distructive element, is a fallacious enlargement."

I V

If one is interested, as we are here, not in the history of science itself, but in the development of a certain emotional attitude toward the world which science reveals, one cannot hope to follow that development by confining oneself to the conventional outlines of either the history of science or the history of literature. Familiar facts from both will appear in unfamiliar light. Leading ideas seem to turn up as often in the writings of theologians and philosophers as in those of the scientist or the poet. Minor figures take on unwonted importance and certain heroes of science—notably Francis Bacon and René Descartes—assume the role of villains.

As for Bacon, there is dispute concerning his importance even among the historians of pure science, and from our point of view his one work addressed to the general public, the unfinished *New Atlantis*, points in the wrong direction. Bacon saw science, or "the new learning" as it was then called, as something whose promise was primarily utilitarian, and the Utopia which he attempts to describe is almost purely what we should dub "technological." Its inhabitants, taking their orthodox and perfunctory religion from revelation, study the laws of the physical universe in order that they may increase their comfort and their wealth. By no stretch of the imagination can they be considered lovers of nature, and from the nature lover's point of view Bacon is almost Philistine.

Even more startling is the case of another hero of science. René Descartes, blessed or cursed with one of the most original and active intelligences the world has ever known, was certainly no Philistine. Of him Wordsworth might have said with almost equal propriety what he did say of Newton—that his was "a mind forever voyaging through strange seas of thought, alone." Mathematician, philosopher, and student of natural science, he was determined not only to know and to systematize but also to understand. Few men have ever left a deeper or more enduring mark upon the history of thought.

Nevertheless, Descartes' intellectual character included two tendencies which make a singularly dangerous combination—absolute skepticism concerning whatever comes from tradition, authority, or mere common sense, along with an absolute trust in the conclusions of pure reason. By the latter he was led to the astonishing conclusion that all the animals except man are mere machines without feeling and without consciousness.

Awareness, he argued, is a function of the soul, and since the soul is the possession of man alone, only man can reason and only man can feel. The instinctive behavior of the animal is not analogous to human habits but to merely physical laws. A dog is not glad when he wags his tail nor in pain when he screams since he operates "like a watch." He seems to us to be experiencing joy or agony only because the soul which we possess would experience those emotions if the mechanism of our bodies led us to react physically as a dog does at the sight of an old friend or at the rending of a limb. As Nicolas de Malebranche, one of Descartes' disciples, put it in 1678, the animals "eat without pleasure, they cry without pain, they grow without knowing it; they desire nothing, they fear nothing, they know nothing."

Now the folly of the foolish is more than likely to begin and end with the circle of the few who are in some way dependent upon them. But the folly of the wise can have consequences beyond measure. Descartes, a wise and good man, very nearly shut the gates of mercy, if not on mankind, then at least on everything that was not man. For a generation, thinking men were divided between those who accepted and those who did not accept the Cartesian theory of the animal constitution. Because of his authority, or more terribly yet, because of the greatness of mind which had won him that authority, sensible men turned their backs upon their good sense; and in the laboratories of virtuosi bone and flesh were cut and torn, sometimes for no purpose other than to marvel at how convincingly a mere machine could simulate suffering.

Perhaps never before in the history of the world had cruelty been so ingeniously taught or fellow creatures so effectively deprived of their last defense—the pity that "springeth soon in gentle hearts," and which may, indeed, at last appear even in those not gentle. The man of the earlier Renaissance could be both refinedly cruel and coarsely brutal. We may shudder to think of what went on in the bear rings that stood almost side by side with Shakespeare's theaters. But the spectators knew that the bear was suffering, and sooner or later some among them would protest and rebel. But how can cruelty be protested against if cruelty can be proved by pure reason neither to exist nor to be possible? In the laboratories sensible men did not say, "Obviously this creature on the table bleeds when he is cut and suffers when he screams." They said instead, "How wonderful is reason, and how doubly wonderful is that reasoner who can prove that what so convincingly *seems* cannot possibly *be.*"

The license which it gave to cruelty was not the only or perhaps even the most important of the effects of Cartesianism. Growing interest in and familiarity with the world of plants and animals might tend to provoke the sense that all life is one, and that we share it with other creatures no less wonderful than we. Descartes would persuade us, on the contrary, that these others are far less "fellow creatures" than the Western world had ever before believed them to be. The assumption that man alone has a soul may be ancient enough, but no such consequences of that assumption had usually been drawn. The Old Testament itself warns that a man may be judged by the treatment he accords to his beasts. A Christian writer could say, as Descartes could not, that God's power was displayed no less in the creation of a worm than in the creation of a man. In the older view, immortality might be impossible for the soulless—and so might reason. Both might be exclusive possessions of man and the angels. But it remained for Descartes to deprive the beasts of sentience itself. No other view had ever made man quite so lonely in the universe. He alone among created things was not a machine. Nothing else could rejoice or suffer with him. The earth which he inhabited was, in effect, as alien and as dead as the moon itself.

Fortunately, not all philosophers and scientists accepted the Cartesian doctrine. In England the "Cambridge Platonists" Cudworth and More set themselves against it. So, too, did Roger Boyle, of the Royal Society, and the microscopist Hook. Had it not been rejected before too long by the common sense of mankind, the eighteenth century could not have become, as it did, pre-eminently a period during which, in countless ways, men felt themselves drawn more and more to the contemplation of the whole spectacle of nature. But it was a near thing.

Literary historians sometimes write as though "nature" were the exclusive possession of Romantic writers, and as though "the appreciation of nature" meant only the development of a certain kind of poetic sensibility whose history is traceable from James Thomson to Wordsworth. But the eighteenth century was the first century during which some knowledge of natural history became almost an inevitable part of the cultivated man's equipment. So pre-eminently literary a figure as Samuel Johnson could discourse on the differences between the oviparous and the viviparous; a popular magazine could, as a matter of course, publish, along with literary and historical articles, a long illustrated account of the life history of the honeybee. Before the century was over Buffon's sumptuous *Natural History*, perhaps in the English translation, was a normal part of a gentleman's library; and Goldsmith, looking for possible hack work, could undertake to compile a natural history.

Perhaps even more important from our special standpoint is the fact that an enlightened man could include within the

scope of his understanding of the world some rational view of
man as a part of nature, and of the proper relationship between
him and the rest of created things. Not only would he know
certain facts about plant and animal life, as surely as Shakespeare's contemporaries knew certain fables like those of the mandrake and the toad; he would also, whether he happened to be
Christian or deist, have some definite general ideas concerning
God's purpose in creating the infinite variety of the natural
world, of which the boundless profusion was beginning to be
better and better known.

Thus, long before the Romantic poets had made the appreciation of nature a touchstone of sensibility, the eighteenth-century
gentleman of an older school was familiar, at least through his
Pope, with the assumption that man's place is *in* nature rather
than apart from it. He probably knew by heart many of the
crucial passages of *An Essay on Man,* in the course of which
Pope hammers home in epigrammatic couplets the fundamental
premise that the universe is not to be understood unless it can be
seen from the point of view of the whole, rather than from that
of man's own particular needs or desires.

> Has God, thou fool! work'd solely for thy good,
> Thy joy, thy pastime, thy attire, thy food?
> Who for thy table feeds the wanton fawn,
> For him as kindly spread the flow'ry lawn:
> Is it for thee the lark ascends and sings?
> Joy tunes his voice, joy elevates his wings.
> Is it for thee the linnet pours his throat?
> Loves of his own and raptures swell the note.
> The bounding steed you pompously bestride,
> Shares with his lord the pleasure and the pride. . .
> Know, Nature's children all divide her care;
> The fur that warms a monarch, warm'd a bear.
> While Man exclaims, "See all things for my use!"

"See man for mine!" replies a pamper'd goose:
And just as short of reason he must fall,
Who thinks all made for one, not one for all.

The feeling of this passage is obviously far closer to that
of a paragraph in Thoreau or William Beebe than it is to that
of either the Cartesian or the pure laboratory scientist of the
early eighteenth century, or of any other time. Pope was, of
course, merely formulating for his contemporaries something
which they were ready to accept, and he is quoted here only to
illustrate what by his time could be felt.

But how had the possibility of such an attitude come about?
What had generated this conviction which is at the opposite
extreme from any which Cartesianism could have produced? It
has been reiterated countless times since by innumerable writers
down to those of our own day, many of whom seem to be re-
discovering it for themselves. Thus John Muir can devote several pages of *The Story of My Youth* to expounding what is in
effect a prose version of Pope's couplets, and Ezra Pound can
translate the same thought into the idiom of his controversial
Pisan Cantos in the passage which begins: "The ant's a centaur
in his dragon world. . . ."

But there was a time when the attitude really was new.

V

Someday, perhaps, some historian of ideas will trace in detail the history of the attitude. But for the purpose of the present
sketch it is not difficult to see from the sampling of certain well-
known works how novel ideas of nature were beginning to
emerge.

Pope acknowledged his friend St. John Bolingbroke as his
teacher, but historians dismiss Bolingbroke as a mere superficial
rephraser of themes which he had borrowed from Leibnitz and
the Earl of Shaftesbury. Moreover, and so far as our special

interests are concerned, it may be well to look, not at the comprehensive philosophers, but at a popular book widely read by Pope's contemporaries. It is specifically concerned with natural history and hence, more directly than *An Essay on Man*, related to the evolution of nature writing.

Its author, John Ray, was a clergyman, a naturalist, and a member of the Royal Society. He was well read both in natural science and in the liberal theology of his time. Like Gilbert White, nearly a century later, he supplemented his studies with observation in the fields and woods near his home; he made contributions to official science; and shortly before the eighteenth century began, he published (in 1691) a book entitled *The Wisdom of God Manifest in the Works of the Creation*.

Anyone brought up, as thousands now living were, on the Reverend Woods's *Natural History* will recognize the approach implied in Ray's title, but his is not from any point of view a contemptible book; and it possesses for us a very special importance in the fact that it seems to have remained for at least three-quarters of a century the most widely read work of its kind. A twelfth edition was published as late as 1759, and though the history of such popular books is often obscure, it seems probable that it, more than any other work, served to fill its special purpose and to give the ordinary eighteenth-century reader his notions of the scope and meaning of natural history. What did he learn from it and in what direction did it lead him?

Ray was not, any more than Pope, an original thinker in these respects. Unlike Pope, however, he was more Christian than deist, and the general ideas which he transmitted were those of the liberal theologians rather than those of the secular metaphysicians. But there was much on which the two might have agreed and Ray was far more interested than Pope in pursuing and encouraging scientific observations of nature.

So far as the purely scientific aspects of his popularization are concerned, he was pretty well up to date both in his facts and in his interpretation of them. He recognized and cited the greats of his time; he also recognized what were the crucial scientific problems; and he almost invariably put himself on that side of a given argument which time has favored. He is, of course, anti-Cartesian, and though anxious to illustrate God's wisdom, he rejects as mere fable the already obsolete doctrine of signatures. More important, he rejects also the theory of spontaneous generation, marshaling effectively the arguments against an erroneous belief not to be finally disposed of for more than a century and a half after his time. Thus Ray's readers got from him a view of the state of the biological sciences which it would not be unfair to compare with what readers of our day get from H. G. Wells's *The Science of Life*.

Most important of all, from our point of view, is the fact that they got also the intellectual basis for a new feeling for nature. To put it briefly, God's wisdom is manifest, not so much in the adaptation of nature to men's needs as in her adaptation to her own. We have, so Ray implies, learned to use the natural world as no doubt God intended that we should. But the other living things are fulfilling themselves, not merely serving us, and the greatest profit we can draw from them is often the contemplation of this fact. Thoreau's pronouncement, made in a college essay, that "the world is more beautiful than convenient, more to be enjoyed than to be used" would not look out of place in Ray's own text.

The student of theology and of philosophy, as such, will discover his leading ideas in the philosophical and theological writings of certain of his immediate predecessors. He himself quotes from two of them—Henry More's *Antidote to Atheism* and the Bishop of Chester's *Treatise of Natural Religion*. But More was a Platonist whose treatise is almost wholly abstract; and the Bishop of Chester, though he cites specific examples, keeps his emphasis pretty steadily where one would expect to find it—namely, on Christian apologetics. The importance of Ray from our point of view is in part that he was a popularizer, but in perhaps even greater part that he managed, despite the implications of his title, a shift of emphasis. His point seems to be hardly more that nature manifests God's wisdom than it is that this fact furnishes a motive—gives, if you like, an excuse—for the study of Nature herself.

"Let us then consider the Works of God, and observe the Operations of his Hands: Let us take Notice of, and admire, his infinite Wisdom and Goodness in the Formation of them: No Creature in the Sublunary World is capable of so doing, besides Man, and yet we are deficient herein: We content ourselves with the Knowledge of the Tongues, or a little Skill in Philology, or History perhaps, and Antiquity, and neglect that which to me seems more material, I mean, Natural History, and the Works of the Creation. . . .

"Let it not suffice us to be Book-learn'd, to read what others have written, and to take upon Trust more Falsehood than Truth; but let us ourselves examine Things as we have Opportunity, and converse with Nature as well as Books. Let us endeavour to promote and increase this Knowledge, and make new Discoveries, not so much distrusting our own Parts, or despairing of our own Abilities, as to think that our Industry can add nothing to the Invention of our Ancestors, or correct any of their Mistakes. Let us not think that the Bounds of Science are fix'd, like *Hercules's* Pillars, and inscrib'd with a *Ne plus ultra*; let us not think we have done when we have learn'd what they have deliver'd to us: The Treasures of Nature are inexhaustible; here is Employment enough for the vastest Parts, the most indefatigable Industries, the happiest Opportunities, the most prolix and undisturb'd Vacancies. . . .

"Much might be done, would we but endeavour; and nothing is insuperable to Pains and Patience. I know that a new Study at first seems very vast, intricate, and difficult; but after a little Resolution and Progress, after a Man becomes a little acquainted, as I may so say, with it, his Understanding is wonderfully clear'd up and enlarg'd, the Difficulties vanish, and the Thing grows easy and familiar. And for our Encouragement in this Study, observe what the Psalmist saith, Psal. cxi.2. *The Works of the Lord are great, sought out of all them that have Pleasure therein.*

" . . . It is a general receiv'd Opinion, that all this visible World was created for Man; that Man is the End of the Creation; as if there were no other End of any Creature, but some Way or other to be serviceable to Man. This Opinion is as old as *Tully:* For, saith he, in his Second Book, *De Nat. Deorum, Principio ipse Mundus Deorum hominumque causa factus est: Quaeque in eo sunt omnia ea parata ad ructum hominum & inventa sunt.* But tho' this be vulgarly received, yet wise Men now-a-days think otherwise. Dr. *Moore* affirms, *That Creatures are made to enjoy themselves as well as to serve us; and that it is a gross Piece of Ignorance and Rusticity to think otherwise.* And in another Place: *This comes only of Pride and Ignorance, or a haughty Presumption; because we are encouraged to believe that in some Sense all Things are made for Man, therefore to think that they are not at all made for themselves. But he that pronounceth this, is ignorant of the Nature of Man, and the Knowledge of Things: For if a good Man be merciful to his Beast, then surely a good God is bountiful and benign, and takes Pleasure that all his Creatures enjoy themselves, that have Life and Sense, and are capable of Enjoyment.*"

V I

To stress in this particular connection the importance of Ray's book, or rather the importance of the attitude which it represented and helped to popularize, is not to deny the even greater importance, on another level, of the thinkers from whom he borrowed. They were as well known and as indispensable to Ray as the scientific workers from whom he drew most of his facts, and it is perhaps a paradox that the theologians contributed almost as much as scientific investigators to the modern feeling for nature. Many scientists were either philosophically neutral or tended, as the physiologist Grassenti did, in the direction of mechanism. But the theologians, upon whom natural fact had been thrust whether they wanted it or not, gave Nature a new emotional meaning in the course of their efforts to give her a religious one.

Any really adequate history of the feeling for nature as it manifests itself in the works of the nature writers would certainly have to devote no little attention to the encouragement which the new attitude got from the natural theologians of the seventeenth century, when what we still call the conflict between science and religion really began in earnest. It would have to point out that what the increasing authority in natural science actually did was not so much to put the defenders of theism to rout as to make them shift the emphasis of their argument and to modify the character of religious feeling. Without a glance at theology we cannot understand clearly how liberal religion made its contribution to nature writing. What the new learning did was to weaken one of the arguments for the existence of God, but to strengthen enormously another.

Insofar as it established a reign of law throughout the universe, science left less and less place for the operation of what theologians call "special providence." The constant intervention of God was no longer necessary to keep the stars in their courses or to will the fall of the sparrow. His existence was not demonstrated by a continuous succession of miracles, since the universe seemed quite capable of running itself. But if God was not at every moment manifesting himself, science itself was increasing the impressiveness of what is called the "argument from design."

That argument was, to be sure, not new. But the more science revealed the incredible complexity of nature's interrelations, the more difficult it was for the atheist to make credible the ancient Lucretian reliance upon chance to explain the universe. In our day the argument from design has been vulgarized into the familiar "the existence of a watch implies the existence of a watchmaker"; but to the seventeenth century, just becoming aware of nature's intricate arrangement, it was felt with a new force. The theologian could urge the wavering to peer through the microscope at the insect's anatomy in the full assurance that the observer must conclude that what he saw there could not merely have happened. He might end as a deist rather than specifically as a Christian, but he was not likely to find atheism tenable.

Such is, indeed, the foundation of the position taken by both the Christian Ray and the deist Pope. "Presume not God to scan" the latter warned his reader. But the corollary is, "presume not either to doubt his existence." Tradition may be dubious and metaphysics a mere spider's web, but the universe did not merely happen. Discard the absurd delusion that nature is explicable in terms of merely human needs. But contemplate also its infinite variety with delight and with wonder. Take your place in nature and rejoice that it is one vast fellowship; that man now has his being, not in the center of a vast machine, but simply as a member of a society every other member of which is, like him, alive, sentient, and capable to some extent of participating in experiences like his own.

It is also a very significant fact that Pope was among the first to put on record a direct concern with the whole question of cruelty to animals; and in his case what we would now call a "humane" attitude was not merely a sporadic revulsion against a specific brutality, but an organized and persistent interest. That fact is itself enough to indicate that the feeling for nature present in *An Essay on Man* is not merely a matter of literary convention or of abstract argument. It indicates that Pope's attitude has some real connection with nature writing, though by no stretching of the terms could *An Essay on Man* be included among the examples of that genre.

Ray's *Wisdom of God* is less remote from it, but even his is not a "nature book" in the sense that *The Natural History of Selborne* is. Not even to the limited extent of Gilbert White's book does it anticipate the form and method of a Thoreau, a John Muir, or a William Beebe. And it does not do so for the simple reason that, for all its incidental illustrations, its form is the form of a treatise, and it *argues* for more than it *exemplifies* an attitude toward nature.

VII

None of the works so far mentioned is, to put the fact in a different way, an out-of-doors book. Neither, for that matter, is any except *An Essay on Man* belles-lettres. The rest are scientific, philosophical, or theological. They are not literature by primary intention, nor do they seek by literary means to communicate the personal experience of living in contact with the natural world. Thoreau once complained that he knew no book which would tell him how to pass an afternoon, and none of these attempts to do so. The kind of writing of which Thoreau is perhaps still the greatest exemplar may have become possible partly because of attitudes which Ray and Pope helped to formulate, but it is not *like* their writing. Only literary artists with the artist's determination to communicate personal experience could create the genre; though such artists would have to absorb part of what the scientist and philosopher were teaching before the literature which they created could be tinged, as it had to be, with science.

Without that tinge of science, and without the new intimacy with other living things which this science and the new philosophy produced, it would not have been possible to escape—as it seems to me the Elizabethans, including even Shakespeare, did not usually escape—from the tendency to see nature merely in terms of decoration, as a sort of stage-set against which man plays out his dramas, rather than as something in which he participates. Shakespeare saw the world as beautiful, but there is comparatively little evidence that he ever either dreamed of thoughts too deep for tears to be found in a primrose, or felt more than occasionally anything approaching fellowship with creatures other than man. And this I say despite the fact that a few passages may be cited in rebuttal—as for example the one from *Measure for Measure* in which Isabella, somewhat preciously (and no doubt quite erroneously), declares:

> And the poor beetle, that we tread upon,
> In corporal sufferance finds a pang as great
> As when a giant dies.

In the history of English belles-lettres, Izaak Walton's *The Compleat Angler* is commonly cited as the first nature book vaguely belonging to the genre which we have been trying to define. Unquestionably it is belles-lettres; unquestionably, pre-eminently even, it is an out-of-doors book. Moreover, purely literary students struggling with the attempt to establish some sort of continuity for the tradition of nature as one of the themes of English literature like to cite its author as a figure of the greatest significance. But that is possible only if one is thinking of nature writing as a form rather than as the expression of an attitude, for in certain important respects Walton is further from Thoreau than John Ray is.

The Compleat Angler is, to be sure, an informal account of one man's journeyings afield. It tells you, if you like, how to spend an afternoon. There is in English no earlier well-known book which could be described in those terms, and the form may suggest Thoreau's *A Week on the Concord and Merrimack Rivers* or John Muir's *My First Winter in the Sierras*.

The resemblance is, nevertheless, extremely superficial. Walton was a sportsman who happened to have some literary gift, and some sensuous appreciation of the freshness of a spring morning or the brilliance of a summer noon. But in this particular book, at least, he is completely innocent of any tincture of any philosophy other than a vaguely Christian optimism. Certainly he reveals little feeling of fellowship with living creatures. Few commentators have failed to quote, either at its face value or with ironical implications, the famous passage in which the fisherman is advised to put the frog on his hook "as though you loved him."

But there are other even less ambiguous passages. One need consider, for example, only that in which the angler gleefully joins forces with the hunter to exterminate a nest of otters guilty of the crime of catching fish intended for man's delight, to realize how far Walton was from a desire to enter into, rather than merely to exploit, the natural world. He belongs hardly more than the big-game hunter of today among the lovers of nature.

Even among present-day writers there is, of course, a great deal of variation in the extent to which the attitude of the sportsman enters into their writing. Richard Jeffries and even John Burroughs used their guns with a cold freedom which would probably have cost them Thoreau's love. But no one can be called a nature writer rather than a sportsman to whom his fellow creatures are as consistently merely game as they are to Walton. And it is certainly no mere accident that the eighteenth century, which saw in England the popularization of natural history in contradistinction to the ancient fashion for mere hunting, should also be the century during which a conscious protest began to arise against that cruelty to animals which Shakespeare's contemporaries, for example, took for granted.

What Walton did have, and what the Augustan men of letters, including Pope, certainly lacked, was an intimate acquaintance with nature's actual phenomena. They had intellectual convictions which he probably did not share; but, unlike him, they were not out-of-doors men and—the conditions of Augustan literary society being what they were—could hardly have been.

In a passage like the following, Walton was not unaware of the pastoral tradition. One may be permitted to doubt that the milkmaid really sang Marlowe's *Passionate Shepherd*, or that her mother replied so patly with the answer to it. It is all rather too much like a court masque. But Walton did go afield and, despite the literary echoes, the little scene is mostly true to what he actually saw. It is in such passages that Walton is most truly a "nature writer."

"But turn out of the way a little, good scholar, towards yonder high hedge: We'll sit whilst this shower falls so gently upon the teeming earth, and gives a sweeter smell to the lovely flowers that adorn the verdant meadows.

"Look, under that broad beech tree I sat down when I was last this way fishing and the birds in the adjoining grove seemed to have a friendly contention with an echo, whose dead voice seemed to live in a hollow cave, near to the brow of that primrose hill; there I sat, viewing the silver streams glide silently towards their center, the tempestuous sea, yet sometimes opposed by rugged roots, and pebble stones, which broke their waves, and turned them into foam: and sometimes viewing the harmless lambs, some leaping securely in the cool shade, while others sported themselves in the cheerful sun; and others were craving comfort from the swollen udders of their bleeting dams. As thus I sat, these and other sights had so fully possessed my soul, that I thought as the poet has happily expressed it:

> I was for that time lifted above earth;
> And possessed joys not promis'd in my birth.

"As I left this place, and entered into the next field, a second pleasure entertained me, 'twas a handsome milkmaid, that had cast away all care, and sung like a nightengale; her voice was good, and the ditty fitted for it; 'twas the smooth song which was made by Kit Marlow, now at least fifty years ago; and the milkmaids mother sung an answer to it, which was made by Sir Walter Raleigh in his yonger days.

"They were old fashioned poetry, but choicely good, I think much better than is now the fashion in this critical age. Look yonder, on my word, yonder they be both a-milkin again: I will give her the chub, and persuade them to sing those two songs to us."

VIII

Many a sixteenth- and seventeenth-century man had, of course, wandered to far places and looked at wild scenes. Thanks to them the literature of travel and adventure was already extensive soon after the seventeenth century began. But that literature hardly concerns us directly, for it was even more clearly distinguishable than similar literature is today from "nature writing" as such. Its authors were soldiers, seamen, merchants, political adventurers, and occasionally mere dilettantes. But even when they were also to some extent naturalists they seldom exploited their feeling for nature in the fashion which peculiarly concerns this anthology. Some such feeling for it some of them must have had, because it is at times the only thing which would account for their activities. But like more recent writers, from the American William Bartram to Darwin himself, they made little effort to communicate the feeling which inspired them as distinguished from an account of the activities which it produced.

One must not, on the other hand, overlook entirely a minor genre which is another kind of nature writing. To the cultivated man of the late seventeenth and eighteenth centuries it was not the wilderness but the garden which symbolized the charm of nature as opposed to that of society. Insofar as there was at that time any literary tradition of prose in praise of country life, it was the tradition which concerned itself with the theme of retirement from the world, and which was, therefore, Horatian rather than either mystical or scientific.

The courtier disgusted with the court and the man of affairs disgusted with cities followed a pattern at least as old as the Roman Empire when they expressed a desire to withdraw to some little estate. But even when one is persuaded that the feeling was genuine, rather than merely an affectation consecrated by time, the desire for a *retreat* is more specific and real than any conception of a *life in nature* understandable in terms of a Thoreau or a W. H. Hudson. The ideal is an ideal of peace, rather than anything which suggests either communion with Nature or a determination to penetrate her secrets. Insofar as these men thought of nature as a "soothing presence," it was not of the nature of field and wood that they thought but of the nature, tamed and smiling, of the park, the flower garden, and, most often of all, the orchard. Yet of nature as something opposed to artificial civilization they were very much aware.

"I never had any other desire so strong, and so like to covetousness, as the one which I have had always, that I might be master at last of a small house and large garden, with very moderate conveniences joined to them, and there dedicate the remainder of my life only to the culture of them and study nature."

When Abraham Cowley wrote this sentence in the latter part of the seventeenth century, it was part of a letter acknowledging the dedication of John Evelyn's practical treatise, *Kalendrum Hortense*. As the Latin quotations which follow clearly indicate, Cowley was perfectly aware that he was expressing a sentiment which had the indispensable classical support. It is equally plain, however, that he was also feeling something for himself. Any modern reader is likely to recognize in his letter the tone of one kind of modern garden book, even though there is little or nothing to suggest even remotely the romantic or mystical elements which give the characteristic flavor to the modern nature lover. The latter usually thinks of himself as a gardener only secondarily, if at all, and he is likely to be most interested in what Nature has to offer when she is, as it were, on her own.

Cowley was not alone among his contemporaries in praising gardens. Sir Thomas Browne's *The Garden of Cyrus* is, as one would expect anything by the author to be, antiquarian and metaphysical, more concerned with the ancients and the quirks of his own baroque mind than with his reaction to nature. On the other hand, however, Sir William Temple's *Upon the Gardens of Epicurus; or Gardening in the Year 1685* seems to express more clearly and completely than any other seventeenth-century work what a cultivated gentleman thought of the place and function of the garden in civilization.

That function is, of course, first of all, practical. Before Sir William had finished his essay he had fulfilled the promise of his subtitle and given a summary account of the progress of practical gardening in England, laying great stress upon the fact that until quite recently most of the vegetables consumed there had been imported from Europe.

But the major part of the essay, written in elegant though straightforward prose which anticipated the Augustan ideal, was devoted to moral rather than utilitarian considerations. Life in the country—which was to say life in the garden—suggested to Temple the ideal of Epicurus, and that meant, most fundamentally, that the good life was the life led by those who had mastered the passions in retirement rather than attempted to gratify them through competition for the world's prizes. There was the inevitable polite bow in the direction of Christianity: "If we believe the Scripture, we must allow that God Almighty esteemed the life of man in a garden the happiest He could give him, or else He would not have placed Adam and Eve; that it was a state of innocence and pleasure; and that the life of husbandry and cities came after the Fall, with guilt and with labor." But Temple was above all a moralist. The strongest argument in favor of the garden lay in the fact that the wisest men of antiquity praised the withdrawal from business, rather than that they advocated the cultivation of a garden. And the emphasis was almost exclusively on this idea of withdrawal *from*. Nature herself does not furnish a subject for study or a theme for contemplation. She merely supplies a kind of soothing vacuum, a realm of peace which permits man to turn inward upon himself and to ponder the great abstract questions of wisdom and morality, concerning which Nature herself will have nothing to say.

Temple had no scientific interest in nature, except insofar as his concern with the practical methods of raising fruit or vegetables may be called that. Indeed, like many literary men of the time, he felt nothing but scorn for the pretentious folly of those in the grip of the new enthusiasm for the study of the laws of nature rather than the study of the moral law:

"As to that part of philosophy which is called natural, I know no end it can have, but that of either busying a man's brain to no purpose, or satisfying the vanities so natural to most men, of distinguishing themselves, by some way or other, from those that seem their equals by birth, and the common advantages of it . . . More than this I know no advantage mankind has gained by the progress of natural philosophy, during so many ages it has been invoked in the world, excepting always, and very justly, what we owe to mathematics."

Inevitably, therefore, there was not in Temple's essay the remotest hint of the new theology or of the conviction, so strongly expressed by his contemporary John Ray, that the wisdom of God might profitably be studied in his handiwork. It could never occur to Temple that man is merely one of the many living things, or that the human is in any way continuous with the natural. As a courtier glad to have retired from public affairs, he genuinely liked country life. He boasted that he had "passed five years without ever going once to town, though I am almost in sight of it, and have a house always ready to receive me." But Temple was a "nature writer" only insofar as this mere preference for the country over the city is a continuing theme in the literature which deals with country phenomena. Thoreau would have found country life as Temple understood it singularly vacuous, and there is a sense in which Alexander Pope was, at least by intellectual conviction, a nature lover while Temple was not.

Temple hardly recognized even the aesthetic as something separable from the utilitarian, or important in itself. "I will not enter upon any account of the flowers, having only pleased myself with seeing or smelling them, and not troubled myself with their care, which is more the ladies' part than the men's." The dream of self-sufficiency, the curious, haunting conviction that it would be well if each individual could owe his existence to himself alone rather than to society, he obviously felt dimly. But he was no mystic of any kind and a nature mystic least of all.

Even a generation later the Augustans, when they thought of

the country, thought usually of a "rural retreat"—preferably not too far into the suburbs, and carefully tamed. The garden and the grotto were still more artful than natural. It is ludicrous to think of Pope in connection with that love of wildness of which Thoreau made so much, and without which so much of the specifically modern feeling for nature is impossible. Yet before Pope's century was over, what is commonly called Romanticism was in full swing; and an enthusiasm for one kind of wildness, especially for the kind called "picturesque," was to be as fashionable as formalism had once been.

Less than a century after Temple had described what he called the "newest mode" for casting gardens "all into grass plots and gravel walks," gardening was likely to mean, as it did to Horace Walpole, what we call landscape gardening; and the effort became to create something which looked like nature as seen through the eyes of a Romantic painter. Moreover, this changing taste in gardens was only a minor and somewhat dandiacal expression of an increasing enthusiasm for wildness itself, an enthusiasm which readers are most familiar with as expressed in nature poetry, where the poet's taste runs the often-charted course from, let us say, the tameness of Andrew Marvell's ideal garden, "annihilating all that's made to a green thought in a green shade"; through the increasing concern of Thomson and Burns and Cowper for the actual country as such; and on into the late Romantic frenzy provoked by the contemplation of the violently untamable. It was such a frenzy that led Byron to express in the presence of a thunderstorm over the Alps a desire which would have seemed to Pope incomprehensibly "unnatural" in one of his most usual senses of the word:

> And this was in the night! Most glorious night
> Thou wert not made for slumber. Oh let me be
> A sharer in thy fierce and far delight,
> A portion of the tempest and of thee.

In many different ways the eighteenth century helped Nature to come into her own as a literary theme, and in this as in so many respects we have directly inherited more from this century than from any other. But few things are more important from the standpoint of the present discussion than the increasing interest in wild nature rather than tame. What did this new interest—the real bridge from Temple to Wordsworth—mean?

IX

Looking back upon it, Thomas Babington Macaulay attempted to explain the phenomenon with characteristic simplicity. One does not, he observed, begin to love "horrid" mountains until they no longer actually threaten one's safety, and the love of wild nature means merely that life has become very tame.

No doubt there is an important element of truth in this common-sense statement, and it explains equally well another aspect of Romanticism. Medieval castles become picturesque; Gothic architecture becomes imposing; and the whole past highly attractive, when there is no longer any chance that one will be compelled to live in a drafty castle or tremble in the face of the "superstition" which inspired the Gothic churches. Plumbing is unimportant only to those who have it as a matter of course.

But however true one may believe such explanations to be, the fact remains that it was not under any such form as this that the truth presented itself to those who found in mountain or castle the occasion for a new and tremendous emotional experience. Since all men live more intimately and significantly in the world as they feel it than in the world of what common-sense materialists call realities, one cannot possibly understand what we have inherited from early Romanticism by seeing only these so-called realities. From the standpoint of what concerns us, it is far less true to say that men began to love the wild because their physical surroundings had become tame than it is to say that it was because they had begun, for the first time, to understand what from the early eighteenth century on they were accustomed to call the "sublime."

To us that word is a common one, and we are aware of at least some vaguely defined area within which it is appropriate. We also probably know at least the title of Edmund Burke's once-famous treatise, *On the Sublime and Beautiful*. But we are not very aware of the sharp contrast once implied between the two nouns of his title. To us the sublime is likely to seem merely one variety of the beautiful, and that is partly because we have so completely assimilated the concept which the eighteenth century was struggling with. But for the man of that century the concept was crucial, and it is intimately connected with the new appreciation of nature untamed. The formal garden was beautiful. The mountain and forest were sublime.

Like most intellectual concepts, this one has a long history. Seventeenth-century literary critics got a hint of it from the work attributed to the late Greek rhetorician Longinus, and it served increasingly as a convenient defense of whatever in literature seemed to go beyond the reasonable, the orderly, the proper, the decorous, and the sensible. Shakespeare, for instance, obviously often overstepped the limits set by what pedants called "The Rules of Aristotle." But when they called him barbarous, his defenders could reply that he was, on the contrary, sublime. For sublimity soon came to mean that which produces an aesthetic effect which is the opposite of the calmly and regularly beautiful. Beauty is peaceful, coherent, rational, and soothing. The sublime surprises, excites, and disturbs because it is somehow beyond or above the merely rational. Inseparable from it is a feeling of mystery, even of fear. It must awaken "awe"—fear's aesthetic counterpart—and it is, therefore, most often to be discovered in connection with that which is vast, tumultuous, violent, and beyond the control of human rationality. Voltaire, one of the last proponents of pure rationality, suggested that his contemporaries should "cultivate their garden." It was the promise of the sublime which tempted them out of it.

With literary theory as such we have little concern, but the concept of wild nature as sublime plays in modern nature writing a role second only to that of fellowship with other living creatures, and in the nature writing of the eighteenth century it plays an even larger one. Whatever it was that drew the Romantics to the sea, the forest, and the mountains; whether they were, as Wordsworth thought, catching a glimpse of that being whose dwelling is the light in the setting sun; or whether, as Macaulay seems to suggest, they were merely bored by security; the fact remains that it was their delight in the sublime which seemed to them the motive.

In a forthcoming book Professor Marjorie Nicolson has traced, more completely than it has ever been traced before, the development of the eighteenth-century English writer's feeling for natural scenery, especially for its wilder aspects. As a sort of touchstone she employs the expressed attitude toward mountains, and the emotions which the sight of them generates. She finds, despite the often-cited example of Petrarch and a few others, that before the end of the seventeenth century mountains were usually merely "horrid"—which is to say tending to arouse horror. Only a hundred years later the all-but-inevitable cliché had come to be "sublime." And in that simple fact the whole outline of a revolution in feeling is suggested. John Muir would have been to some extent understandable in 1780; he would have been merely incomprehensible to most people a century earlier. Sir William Temple sought the calm orderliness of the garden in order that it might help him to find peace and to triumph over the passions. His descendants of three or four generations later sought in the mountains a new sense of mystery and a new excitement.

In the eighteenth century this pursuit of the sublime passed easily over into the merely fashionable cult of the picturesque— that adjective tending to mean not merely "like a picture," but like a particular kind of picture, especially the Romantic landscape. Pope had built a grotto, a kind of cozy garden retreat in which the order of art was at least as conspicuous as nature. Late eighteenth-century gentlemen, on the other hand, went in for elaborate landscaping which aimed to reproduce one of Salvator Rosa's pictures and to achieve a sort of well-disciplined wildness. It was said of the poet Shenstone that he was heard to whisper to a servant when unexpected visitors were announced: "Quick! go turn on the brook and give the hermit his beard."

Many great estates contained by this time elaborate artificial ruins, and in 1779 William Cowper, tongue in cheek, wrote how he had been to see "a fine piece of ruins, built by the late Lord Holland, at great expense." Next day the ruins themselves tumbled down, but Cowper comforts himself and the owner with a reflection: "Perhaps, therefore, it is still a ruin; and if it is, I would advise you by all means to visit it, as it must be much improved by this fortunate accident. It is hardly possible to put stones together with that air of wild and magnificent disorder which they are sure to acquire of their own accord."

How the labors of such dilettantes struck an observer notoriously resistant to both the newfangled "sublime" and to wild prospects themselves can be seen in the passage from Dr. Johnson's life of the same poet Shenstone mentioned above:

"Whether to plant a walk in undulating curves, and to place a bench at every turn where there is an object to catch the view; to make water run where it will be heard, and to stagnate where it will be seen; to leave intervals where the eye will be pleased, and to thicken the plantation where there is something to be hidden, demands any great powers of mind, I will not inquire. . . . But it must be at least confessed that to embellish the form of nature is an innocent amusement, and some praise must be allowed by the most supercilious observer to him who does best what such multitudes are contending to do well."

Perhaps those who are shocked at Johnson's insensibility to the charms of nature, as exhibited in the famous instance when he rebuked Boswell for describing as "an awful eminence" what Johnson preferred to call "a considerable protuberance," would do well to remember how much merely fashionable twaddle was being talked at the time and to consider the possibility that Johnson was less denying the beauties of nature than advising his interlocutor to "clear your mind of cant."

X

Miss Nicolson's account of the growth of interest in sublime landscapes is beautifully complete. Taken in connection with some further account of its foppish counterpart, the rage for picturesque gardens, it makes understandable one whole area of the "feeling for nature." But from our point of view one of the most striking things about the cults of the sublime and the picturesque is the fact that they account for the interest in wild scenery in terms almost exclusively literary or at least aesthetic, and that there seems little connection between this sort of love of nature and the other sort, with which we have been even more concerned.

Your lover of mountains may be attempting to establish some sort of communion with the forces which make them; may be communicating through them with Wordsworth's God. But his fellowship is directly with that force or that Being, and his interest in living creatures other than himself may be nil. His emotion may lead on to Wordsworth's pantheism, or on to the post-Romantic worship of violence and unreason for its own sake. But these emotions might have been generated without any influence from science, and they do not inevitably lead to a connection with that other sort of pantheistic identification with life which we found so important in Thoreau.

To say this is not to say that such connection has not sometimes—indeed, often—been made. Thoreau himself to some extent made it, for he was a lover of hills as well as of his fellow creatures. John Muir, though he seems to some extent a disciple of Thoreau, is first of all one who communes with the wilderness as a whole rather than with individual creatures. Indeed, one section of the present anthology is devoted to those who are more lovers of the sublime in nature than watchers of living things. Nevertheless, the two pursuits do have separate histories which more or less converge to become the history of what we have called "the nature writers"; and this commentary tends to put special emphasis upon the second, both because it has been less thoroughly investigated and because it is the newest element in modern nature writing. By what stages, we may ask, did men begin actually to feel that warm personal interest in living creatures to which the rational convictions of Ray and Pope must inevitably lead, but which the admirers of the sublime did not necessarily feel? How did the interest in fellow creatures as well as in mountains begin to exhibit itself?

Literary historians, generally concerned more with poetry than with prose, have sometimes noted in James Thomson, Thomas Gray, Cowper, and Burns not only their concern with the sublime, but also, and along with it, a certain kindly interest in animals, wild or domestic. Before that, even Herrick, the most genuinely bucolic of the earlier writers, composed his poem on the death of a sparrow with at least one eye on Catullus. And when the Augustans mentioned the beast, it was more likely than not to be merely an Aesopian symbol. Moreover, even Gray's goldfish, Cowper's spaniel, and Burns's field mouse were still used to point a moral, though they were obviously also described with an eye on the object and with some sense that they were interesting in themselves:

> Wee, sleekit, cowrin', tim'rous beastie
> O what a panic's in thy breastie . . .
>
> I'm truly sorry Man's dominion
> Has broken Nature's social union.

That famous phrase "social union" serves as a warning that even Burns's "nature" was not the nature of the scientist, nor even the nature of Pope's *An Essay on Man*. Burns's conception is not Pope's vision of the complicated system whose apparent cruelties and injustices are explicable only in terms of an ultimate good to the system as a whole. It is, instead, something easier and softer, something based on a wish rather than on observation, and in that definite sense, sentimental rather than realistic.

In other words, and like most of his poetical contemporaries, Burns was less interested in either the developing science of natural history, or in what Pope would have called "Reson," than he was in an intuition which seemed to tell him, as it was later to tell Wordsworth in much more confidently ringing terms, that what he *felt* about nature was *true* about nature.

Despite all his enthusiasm for nature and her sublimity, therefore, the eighteenth-century Romantic was not yet ready, was not even so nearly ready as Pope seems to have been, to base his love of Nature on the scientific view of her. Both the Romantic poet and the Romantic prose writer were moving away from the student of natural history, instead of converging with him toward some common ground. At the very height of the Romantic era, Keats thought that "all charms fly" at the touch of science; and Wordsworth, to whom nature was the only true teacher, expressed nevertheless his contempt for those who "peep and botanize." So far were the naturalist and the Romantic poet from understanding each other that, as we shall see when we come to it, the first great classic of English nature writing was almost Augustan rather than Romantic in its dry, sensible clarity, as well as in its determination to stick close to fact.

But the eighteenth century was not, as literary historians seem prone to suppose, merely the age of the Romantics. Quite as important from our standpoint is the fact that it was also the age of Linnaeus, whose *Systema Naturae* was world famous soon after its publication. Linnaeus' imagination had taken fire at the thought of the prodigious variety of living things the very existence of which was unknown to most human beings. His enthusiasm was contagious, and at the same time his easily mastered system of classification made it possible for even the amateur quickly to find his way among the genera and species without relying, as preceding botanists and zoologists had been compelled to rely, upon a brute memory which required a lifetime to stock. One English botanist, who had a vested interest in his subject, even went so far as to complain that Linnaeus had ruined botany (and zoology as well) by making it accessible to everyone. And make it accessible he certainly did.

As late as 1759 Samuel Johnson, still defending what had been the Augustan ideal, put into the mouth of Imlac in *Rasselas* the famous pronouncement: "the business of a poet is to examine, not the individual, but the species: to remark general properties and large appearances; he does not number the streaks of the tulip, or describe the different shades of the verdure of the forest." Every reader knows that Burns was soon to defy the dictum by writing, not about the mouse, but about a field mouse turned up while plowing, and that not long after Wordsworth was to specify "the lesser Celandine" when he addressed what an Augustan poet would have called merely "a flower." But students of literature do not so commonly know that even before Johnson's time, cultivated Englishmen who were often neither poets nor writers of any other kind were turning to the study of natural history as a science, were counting the stripes on a tulip and distinguishing one kind of mouse from another. They were eagerly buying not only books on ornithology, but also, as early as 1720, an illustrated *Natural History of English Insects*, which went into three editions in English as well as one in Latin. A *Method of Catching and Preserving Insects for Collections* may sound like the title of a modern handbook for the use of progressive schools, but it was published in the 1720's, and it preceded by a whole generation *The Natural History of Selborne*.

Exploring expeditions began now to include naturalists. At the same time stay-at-homes began to travel about extensively in their own fields and gardens, and Londoners to visit eagerly the collections of exotic beasts put on exhibition. The author of *An Elegy Written in a Country Churchyard* exhibited in his poetry a curious combination of fresh feeling about nature with a tendency to employ the generalizing vocabulary of the Augustans and to talk about "lowing herds" rather than about cows. But unlike most of the other Romantic poets he made natural history a hobby which he rode passionately for many years, and his interleaved copy of the *Systema Naturae* preserved careful notes of his own observations.

Cartesian science had been cruel; Linnaean science was inspired by love as much as by curiosity. And because of this fact, Linnaean science tended to support rather than run counter to a humane attitude toward animals which began to manifest itself strongly during the earliest years of the eighteenth century, and which was as radically new as any aspect of Romanticism.

XI

Even in the history of legislation one may see the tardy effects of this new sensibility.

Everyone knows Macaulay's paradox concerning the Puritans who forbade the fine old English sport of bull- and bearbaiting, not because it gave pain to the bear, but because it gave pleasure to the people. Yet even the Puritans could not wholly suppress the diversion which had been passionately defended by many of the learned (including members of the clergy) as a manly sport tending not only to make the spectators tough but also, what was quite as important, to make the meat of the baited bull tender. After the Restoration, bull- and bearbaiting, as well as all sorts of fantastic animal combats, became legal again and were often among the amusements provided for distinguished foreign visitors to the court.

Some of these foreigners left accounts indicating that they regarded the spectacles as indications that the English were an exceptionally savage people; but it was only during the eighteenth century that the sport lost caste so that it began to attract only the mob rather than the best people. And the law, as usual, lagged far behind enlightened public opinion. "Gardens" for blood sports were not legally abolished until 1835; and in general the laws were so slow in responding to the growing feeling against all forms of cruelty that "an act to prevent cruel and improper treatment of cattle," passed in 1822, created the first English law making the inhuman treatment of animals an offense *per se*. Up to that time such treatment had been punishable only if it depreciated the value of another's property, and as late as 1794 a judge had ruled that "in order to convict a man of barbarous treatment of a beast it should appear that he had malice towards the prosecutor" (i.e., the owner of the beast).*

But the law certainly did not represent the attitude of the cultivated classes. Almost a century before the judge assumed that animals as such had no rights, men of refinement had begun to assume that they did. *An Essay on Man* helped to popularize the conception of God as the ruler and protector of all creation, not merely of man; and the conception was not original with Pope, though Pope himself, as early as 1713, and thus long before *An Essay on Man* was written, had contributed to Steele's "Guardian" a paper on man's duty to inferior creatures, in which he argued that "the more entirely the inferior creation is submitted to our power, the more answerable we should seem for our mismanagement of it." And Pope's was only one of many such voices. In the *Spectator*, Addison, for instance, attacked Cartesianism not only as an intellectual doctrine, but went on to describe with horror the cruelties to which it led.

What this humanitarianism involved was a new concept of the origin and authority of moral feeling, a shift in emphasis away from either religious law and authority on one hand, or logic on the other, toward feeling and sensibility. The question was com-

---

*Most of these facts about the attitude of the law and public opinion will be found in *The Love of Animals and How It Grew* by Dix Harwood (Columbia University Press).

ing to be not so much what theologians could deduce from God's revealed word or what the philosopher could deduce from self-evident premises, as what refined and cultivated human nature found either attractive or revolting. Pope's famous

> Vice is a monster of so frightful mien
> As to be hated needs but to be seen

means not only that evil is recognized as such, but also that whatever a normal mind feels to be evil *is* evil, no matter what philosophy or theology may attempt to say. And men began to *feel* in their hearts that animals should be loved, not despised or tortured.

Throughout the century, and even down to the present day, the battle between those who appeal to law or reason and those who appeal to human feeling continues; but there is no doubt that from about 1700 on it has been humanitarianism which has tended to win the great causes. Slavery, for instance, was as ably defended as bearbaiting had been, both by abstract logic and by quotations from the Scripture. But its apologists were routed by those who *felt* that it was wrong. And the same thing may be said concerning the even larger and more abstract questions of eternal damnation and of salvation outside some particular church. Predestination and the doctrine of eternal punishment are now believed in by no more than a very small fraction of contemporary Europeans or Americans. But that is less because of any theological argument than because the doctrines seem to most people emotionally revolting.

Historians of ideas generally speak with scant respect of the writers who founded this English humanitarianism. They usually call it "sentimentalism," and they usually have for a Calvin, a Hobbes, or a Jonathan Edwards an intellectual respect they cannot feel for the "sentimentalists." But there is no denying the fact that it was these so-called sentimentalists who were responsible for changing the whole tone of moral feeling as well as for the later extravagances of what is properly called sentimentalism. Nor can there be any doubt of the further fact that they reinforced philosophical convictions about man's place in nature by enriching their emotional content.

In England the most widely read and influential, if not the most profound, of those who stressed the gentle heart was the Third Earl of Shaftesbury, whose *Characteristics of Men, Manners, Opinions, Times* was published in 1711, and exercised an influence far greater than the dimness of his present fame gives hint of. The showiness of Shaftesbury's style and a certain diffuse flabbiness in his writing have left him few admirers, but it has been maintained by respectable authority that he is the real father of eighteenth-century humanitarianism. And if that is putting it too strongly, then it is certainly true that no spokesman for the new attitude was more widely read. Moreover, Shaftesbury laid great stress upon the kind treatment of animals as evidence of the presence in any individual of the greatest of human virtues, pity.

The core of his doctrine is simply the conviction that a tendency to sympathize with others is as natural as any other human impulse; and that man is not, as Thomas Hobbes, the most influential philosopher of the century before, had maintained, an essentially self-regarding animal who can obey only two impulses—the impulse toward pleasure and the impulse toward that power which makes pleasure possible. To Shaftesbury it seemed that pity is the source of all virtue and that the tender heart capable of feeling it is of all human characteristics the one which ought most to be cultivated. He was among the first to see callousness as the most deadly of sins because it was the father of all others and among the first to maintain that a delight in human or animal manifestations of savagery is not the result of manliness, but of something radically corrupt and unnatural as well as evil.

If Shaftesbury had been alone in holding such opinions, one might be tempted to see in them only the product of his own rather morbid sensibility. But he was not alone, and it is interesting to note how the revolt against cruelty was so much in the atmosphere of the time as to make thinkers who agreed in little else agree in this. Bernard de Mandeville, whose *Fable of the Bees* was another speculative work once extremely influential, spoke in general for the tough-minded as against the tender-minded. His famous thesis that private vices turn into public benefits and that the welfare of the state is dependent upon these vices rather than upon any virtue in the individual, links him with Hobbes rather than with the new thinkers. Yet Mandeville was shocked by the slaughter of animals even for food. He thought the fact that slaughterhouses were removed as far as possible from the center of the community indicated "something like a consciousness of guilt," and discovered in that consciousness of guilt "some strong remains of primitive piety and innocence, which all the arbitrary power of custom, and the violence of luxury, have not yet been able to conquer." He, too, turned against what seems to have been the common enemy, Cartesianism. Speaking of the bludgeoned ox he asked: "When a creature has given such convincing and undeniable proofs of the terrors upon him, and the pains of agonies he feels, is there a follower of Descartes so inured to blood, as not to refute, by his commiseration, the philosophy of that vain reasoner?"

Throughout the whole century leading thinkers returned to themes like these. David Hume cited the behavior of animals to prove that they too were capable of sympathy. Adam Smith linked sympathy for the lower creatures to sympathy with our own kind. And Jeremy Bentham, pondering the philosophical basis of law and social institutions, treated "the rights of the animals" as something no less natural and inalienable than those of human beings. The question was, he said, not "Can they reason?" nor, "Can they talk?" but, "Can they suffer?" and at least in the case of Bentham we have to do not merely with an abstract conviction but with the fact that, as he said, "I love everything that has four legs."

If Bentham had not chosen to become the father of utilitarianism, he might have won a small place in history as one of the first of the articulate nature writers. He was no field naturalist, to be sure, but he kept pets, and he observed the domestic animals with a sharp and affectionate eye. Here is what the editor of his collected works has to say:

"Bentham was very fond of animals, particularly *pussies,* as he called them, 'when they had domestic virtues'; but he had no particular affection for the common race of *cats.* He had one, however, of which he used to boast that he had 'made a man of him,' and whom he was wont to invite to eat macaroni at his own table. This puss got knighted, and rejoiced in the name of Sir John Langborn. In his early days he was a frisky, inconsiderate, and, to say the truth, somewhat profligate gentleman; and had, according to the report of his patron, the habit of seducing light and giddy young ladies of his own race, into the garden of Queen's Square Place: but tired at last, like Solomon, of pleasures and vanities, he became sedate and thoughtful—took to the church, laid down his knightly title, and was installed as the Reverend John Langborn. He gradually obtained a great reputation for sanctity and learning, and a Doctor's degree was conferred upon him. When I knew him, in his declining days, he bore no other name than the Reverend Doctor John Langborn; and he was alike conspicuous for his gravity and philosophy. Great respect was invariably shown his reverence: and it was supposed he was not far off from a mitre, when old age interfered with his hopes and honours. He departed amidst the regrets of his many friends and was gathered to his fathers, and to eternal rest, in a cemetery in Milton's garden.

" 'I had a cat,' he said, 'at Hendon, which used to follow me about even in the street. George Wilson was very fond of animals too. I remember a cat following him as far as Staines. There was a beautiful pig at Hendon, which I used to rub with my stick. He loved to come and lie down to be rubbed, and took to following me like a dog.'

"The mice were encouraged by Bentham to play about in his

workshop. I remember, when one got among his papers, that he exclaimed, 'Ho! ho! here's a mouse at work; why won't he come into my lap?—but then I should be stroking him when I ought to be writing legislation, and that would not do.'

"One day while we were at dinner, mice had got, as they frequently did, into the drawers of the dinner table, and were making no small noise. 'O you rascals' exclaimed Bentham: 'there's an uproar among you. I'll tell puss of you'; and then added: 'I became once very intimate with a colony of mice. They used to run up my legs, and eat crumbs from my lap. I love everything that has four legs: so did George Wilson. We were fond of mice, and fond of cats; but it was difficult to reconcile the two affections.

" 'From my youth I was fond of cats—as I still am. I was once playing with one in my grandmother's room. I had heard the story of cats having nine lives, and being sure of falling on their legs; and I threw the cat out of the window on the grass-plot. When it fell, it turned toward me, looked in my face and mewed. "Poor thing!" I said, "thou art reproaching me with my unkindness." ' "

When Coleridge began the last stanza of *The Ancient Mariner* with a couplet:

> He prayeth best who loveth best
> All things both great and small

he was merely summing up a conclusion towards which a whole century had been tending. The road to Xanadu had passed through many places. Among them were both *An Essay on Man* and the *Characteristics* of Shaftesbury, both of which contributed also to the development of nature writing as well as to *The Ancient Mariner*.

XII

But what was nature writing like in the eighteenth century when natural history or natural scenery was the professed subject, rather than merely the occasion for themes used by the philosopher, the moralist, the poet, or the writer who chose any one of the conventional forms of belles-lettres?

One answer might be to glance at some of the books on natural history which appeared about this time. Another would be to note how frequently descriptions of rural life or of natural scenery, as well as references to animals—wild, tamed, and domestic—turned up in the correspondence of the great letter writers of the time.

Among these last, one will note that the young Thomas Gray, on the conventional grand tour with his worldly friend Horace Walpole, had less enthusiasm for the "antiquities," which had once been the principal sights, than he had for the Alps, which had previously been no more than a "horrid" barrier frightening the northern visitor who longed to visit the Italian cities. And of course there is William Cowper, who took refuge from worldliness and noise in a country clergyman's home. Cowper, being Methodist Christian rather than deist, had no doubt that the possession of a soul gave man rights which the animals did not have. "I allow," he wrote primly, "the life of an animal to be fairly taken away when it interferes either with the interest or convenience of man"—and that seems to afford a pretty wide license to those who interpret "interest" and "convenience" with sufficient liberalness. But it was Cowper's orthodoxy, not his natural temperament, which dictated those words, and he not only cherished his furred and his feathered pets but declared, of his delight in natural scenery, "My eyes drink the rivers as they flow." He was, moreover, capable of a passage like the following, which seems a prose anticipation of Keats's "The melody of earth is never dead":

"Now I sit with all the windows and the door wide open, and am regaled with the scent of every flower in a garden full of flowers. We keep no bees, but if I lived in a hive I should hardly hear more of their music. All the bees in the neighbourhood resort to a bed of mignonette opposite to the window, and pay me for the honey they get out of it by a hum, which, though rather monotonous, is as agreeable to my ear as the whistling of my linnets. All the sounds that nature utters are delightful—at least in this country. I should not perhaps find the roaring of lions in Africa, or of bears in Russia, very pleasing; but I know no beast in England whose voice I do not account musical, save and except always the braying of an ass. The notes of all our birds and fowls please me, without one exception. I should not, indeed, think of keeping a goose in a cage that I might hang him up in the parlour for the sake of his melody, but a goose upon a common, or in a farm-yard, is no bad performer; and as to insects, if the black beetle, and beetles indeed of all hues, will keep out of my way, I have no objection to any of the rest; on the contrary, in whatever key they sing, from the gnat's fine treble, to the bass of the humble bee, I admire them all. Seriously, however, it strikes me as a very observable instance of providential kindness to man, that such an exact accord has been contrived between his ear and the sound with which, at least in a rural situation, it is almost every moment visited. All the world is sensible of the uncomfortable effect that certain sounds have upon the nerves, and consequently upon the spirits:— and if a sinful world had been filled with such as would have curdled the blood, and have made the sense of hearing a perpetual inconvenience, I do not know that we should have had a right to complain. But now the fields, the woods, the gardens, have each their concert, and the ear of man if forever regaled by creatures who seem only to please themselves."

But perhaps it will be most enlightening to look a bit more carefully at two different works, one perhaps even more famous now than it was in its own time, the other once very popular but now almost forgotten. I choose Gilbert White's *The Natural History of Selborne*, which was the work of an amateur naturalist whose interest was fundamentally scientific; and then one of the various books of William Gilpin, a literary aesthete who sought among the mountains both the "sublime" and, more especially, its pale derivative, the "picturesque." White was a kind of Thoreau—if it is possible to imagine an eighteenth-century gentleman being at all like Thoreau while at the same time remaining so characteristically an eighteenth-century gentleman. Gilpin, if one must compare him to any American, was perhaps—but at an even greater distance—more of an eighteenth-century John Muir. Together they exhibit two characteristic forms of emergent nature writing.

In all the known outward events of his life Gilbert White was so typical of the whole class of eighteenth-century gentlemen that the biographical facts sound like a composite. His grandfather, also named Gilbert, had been vicar of the little village of Selborne, which lies in a corner of Hampshire some fifty miles—and they were then very long miles—southwest of London. Our Gilbert was born in the vicarage in 1720 and in due time he was sent to Oxford, where he got his degree, was appointed fellow shortly thereafter, and took the obligatory Holy Orders. He served for a time as curate at Old Alresford, but at the age of thirty-five he returned to his native village to spend the remaining thirty-eight years of his life there, pleasantly cut off by what he calls the "infamous roads" leading out of the region. He never married, never became officially the vicar of the village, and, so far as one can tell from his letters, took little or no interest in any of the world events of his time. Like Thoreau, he traveled about extensively in his own community and, like Thoreau, he was more interested in the fate of turtles than in the fate of empires. But unlike Thoreau, and in typical eighteenth-century fashion, he never attempted to make drama out of either of these facts.

No doubt Selborne was far less part of the great world than

Concord was, but White never either laments the fact or rejoices in it. He merely accepts isolation, and comments with dry humor on such cultural activities as were observable. "We have here this winter a weekly concert, consisting of first second fiddle, two ribianos, a bassoon, a hautboy, a violoncello, and a German flute; to the great annoyance of the neighboring pigs, which complain that their slumbers are interrupted and their teeth set on edge." Thoreau sought simplicity; White accepted a slightly more cozy simplicity with calm appreciation.

Since he did not publish his book until four years before his death, the world had had little occasion to notice him, and most of what is known is what he has told us himself. No picture of him is preserved, and when inquirers got around to question village survivors it did not appear that he had produced a very vivid impression. However, one anecdote reveals at least that rustics in his time had as vague an idea concerning the local fauna as they usually have today. An old woman remembered White as "a kindly old gentleman with very old-fashioned sayings. . . . He was very kind in giving presents to the poor, and used to keep a locust which crawled about his garden." Asked if it had not been a tortoise rather than a locust she replied: "Ah, that's what I meant."

After the fashion of the times, when men of similar interests met seldom and had fewer specialized publications than they have today, White corresponded with Thomas Pennant, author of *British Zoology*, and with the lawyer Daines Barrington, who was an amateur of both antiquities and natural history. A letter to Pennant describing the topography of Selborne, though apparently written without thought of publication, forms the first of the chapters (all in letter form) of White's book. As he explained in his "Advertisement," that book was conceived of as a new sort of local history. "The author . . . takes the liberty . . . of laying before the public his idea of parochial history, which, he thinks, ought to consist of natural productions and occurrences as well as antiquities." White did present just such a parochial natural history, though the passages most often quoted today are those in which he had to be the impersonal historian and become the retailer of anecdotes or personal observations.

Admirers of *The Natural History of Selborne* have made perhaps extravagant claims concerning its originality and influence. White has been described as "an almost unknown kind of man in his own day"; as the real father of the whole race of amateur scientific observers; and as, in some large sense, responsible for popularizing the discovery that the country gentleman can have some relation with his fellow creatures other than that of the mere huntsman. Moreover, and in order to heighten still further this importance, it has been said that "his age is one of an artificial character, when little interest was felt in natural objects."

All this is a good deal of an exaggeration. It was far from being true that in his lifetime "little real interest was felt in natural objects." As a matter of fact, from 1759 on, *The Annual Register*, that indispensable contemporary record of current events, devoted a section to natural history; and in 1763 a reviewer for the *Monthly Review* remarked in connection with John Hall's expensive three-volume *Natural History* that "Natural History is now, by a kind of national establishment, become the favorite study of the times." Unlike White, the poet Gray apparently did not correspond with others of similar interests; but as we have seen he did make a collection of insects and, like White, he also kept a calendar in which he recorded minute daily notes of the opening of flowers, the ripening of fruits, and the coming and going of birds, along with a great variety of miscellaneous observations. The fact that about the same time George Washington was making in his diaries similar, but characteristically briefer and more matter-of-fact entries probably means only that in either England or America a cultivated country gentleman was very likely to do so.

Thus Gilbert White's book owed its success and its lasting

reputation less to the fact that it was novel than to the fact that it wasn't. White did consciously, completely, and well what others had made some attempt to do. Certain of his observations are said to have made some slight contribution to scientific knowledge; from others he is said to have drawn erroneous conclusions. What is really important, however, is neither the novelty of the formal undertaking nor the new facts observed, but the flavor of his style and of his personality. For White was one of the first to communicate through words what many others were no doubt feeling. He combined with essentially scientific interests a certain human warmth. He did not, like many Romantics, merely muse about nature. He actually observed minutely the birds and the mammals; he took the trouble to know how they actually lived and acted. But he was not merely detached. He was curious about them as one is curious about fellow creatures, not as one is curious about a machine. Though he would never have used Thoreau's phrase, he was less interested in specimens than in what Thoreau called "little fishy friends."

And because, again like Thoreau, he wanted to know what nature was really like, he went even more persistently than Thoreau did to the scientists rather than to the poets or the mystics when he wished to supplement his own observations. He was enough of a man of his time to find the Sussex Downs "majestic" (i.e., "sublime"); but when he wanted to remind his readers that others had admired them too, he cited not the Romantic poets but Ray's *The Wisdom of God Manifest in the Works of the Creation*, which was by that time more than three-quarters of a century old. Besides the naturalists of his own country he knew also, among others, Réaumur, whose *Natural History of the Insects* anticipated by more than a hundred years the works of Henri Fabre, and was perhaps the first great classic to combine meticulous observation with a literary and dramatic sense of the special wonder which the life histories of insects provoked.

At the same time White was typically an eighteenth-century gentleman—which means that he was chary of "enthusiasm" and too much an amateur to devote himself to the systematic accumulation of purely scientific fact. What he sought was what his contemporaries were likely to call "rational amusement," and if the complete absence of anything remotely suggesting Romanticism makes him sometimes seem dry to modern readers, they will find, by way of compensation, certain typically eighteenth-century virtues. White can wonder though he cannot gush, and he can be dryly humorous as well. Wordsworth would probably have been offended, but Thoreau (who read White) was doubtless delighted by such a passage as the following:

". . . neither owls nor cuckoos keep to one note. A friend remarks that many (most) of his owls hoot in B flat: but that one went almost half a note below A. The pipe he tried their notes by was a common half-crown pitch-pipe, such as masters use for tuning of harpsichords; it was the common London pitch.

"A neighbour of mine, who is said to have a nice ear, remarks that the owls about this village hoot in three different keys, in G flat, or F sharp, in B flat and A flat. He heard two hooting to each other, the one in A flat, and the other in B flat. *Query*: Do these different notes proceed from different species, or only from various individuals? The same person finds upon trial that the note of the cuckoo (of which we have but one species) varies in different individuals; for, about Selborne wood, he found they were mostly in D: he heard two sing together, the one in D, the other in D sharp, who made a disagreeable concert: he afterwards heard one in D sharp, and about Wolmer-forest some in C. As to nightingales, he says that their notes are so short, and their transitions so rapid, that he cannot well ascertain their key. Perhaps in a cage, and in a room, their notes may be more distinguishable. This person has tried to settle the notes of a swift, and of several other small birds, but cannot bring them to any criterion."

It is only occasionally that White works up an incident into a set piece of quotable length, and his quality as a writer (not necessarily as an observer of nature) is probably best illustrated by some quotations from the famous history of his tortoise, successive installments of which appear from time to time through the letters:

"A land-tortoise, which has been kept for thirty years in a little walled court belonging to the house where I now am visiting, retires under ground about the middle of November, and comes forth again about the middle of April. When it first appears in the spring it discovers very little inclination towards food; but in the height of summer grows voracious: and then as the summer declines its appetite declines; so that for the last six weeks in autumn it hardly eats at all. Milky plants, such as lettuces, dandelions, sowthistles, are its favourite dish. In a neighbouring village one was kept till by tradition it was supposed to be an hundred years old. An instance of vast longevity in such a poor reptile!"

"On the first of November I remarked that the old tortoise, formerly mentioned, began first to dig the ground in order to the forming its hybernaculum, which it had fixed on just beside a great tuft of hepaticas. It scrapes out the ground with its forefeet, and throws it up over its back with its hind; but the motion of its legs is ridiculously slow, little exceeding the hour-hand of a clock; and suitable to the composure of an animal said to be a whole month in performing one feat of copulation. Nothing can be more assiduous than this creature night and day in scooping the earth, and forcing its great body into the cavity; but, as the noons of that season proved usually warm and sunny, it was continually interrupted, and called forth by the heat in the middle of the day; and though I continued there till the thirteenth of November, yet the work remained unfinished. Harsher weather, and frosty mornings, would have quickened its operations. No part of its behavior ever struck me more than the extreme timidity it always expresses with regard to rain; for though it has a shell that would secure it against the wheel of a loaded cart, yet does it discover as much solicitude about rain as a lady dressed in all her best attire, shuffling away on the first sprinklings, and running its head up in a corner. If attended to, it becomes an excellent weather-glass; for as sure as it walks elate, and as it were on tiptoe, feeding with great earnestness in a morning, so sure will it rain before night. It is totally a diurnal animal, and never pretends to stir after it becomes dark. The tortoise, like other reptiles, has an arbitrary stomach as well as lungs; and can refrain from eating as well as breathing for a great part of the year. When first awakened it eats nothing; nor again in the autumn before it retires: through the height of the summer it feeds voraciously, devouring all the food that comes in its way. I was much taken with its sagacity in discerning those that do it kind offices; for, as soon as the good old lady comes in sight who has waited on it for more than thirty years, it hobbles towards its benefactress with awkward alacrity; but remains inattentive to strangers. Thus not only *'the ox knoweth his owner, and the ass his master's crib,'* but the most abject reptile and torpid of beings distinguishes the hand that feeds it, and is touched with the feelings of gratitude!

"P.S. In about three days after I left Sussex the tortoise retired into the ground under the hepatica."

"The old Sussex tortoise, that I have mentioned to you so often, is become my property. I dug it out of its winter dormitory in March last, when it was enough awakened to express its resentments by hissing; and, packing it in a box with earth, carried it eighty miles in post-chaises. The rattle and hurry of the journey so perfectly roused it that, when I turned it out on a border, it walked twice down to the bottom of my garden; however, in the evening, the weather being cold, it buried itself in the loose mould, and continues still concealed.

"As it will be under my eye, I shall now have an opportunity of enlarging my observations on its mode of life, and propensities; and perceive already that, towards the time of coming forth, it opens a breathing place in the ground near its head, requiring, I conclude, a freer respiration, as it becomes more alive. This creature not only goes under the earth from the middle of November to the middle of April, but sleeps great part of the summer; for it goes to bed in the longest days at four in the afternoon, and often does not stir in the morning till late. Besides, it retires to rest for every shower; and does not move at all in wet days.

"When one reflects on the state of this strange being, it is a matter of wonder to find that Providence should bestow such a profusion of days, such a seeming waste of longevity, on a reptile that appears to relish it so little as to squander more than two-thirds of its existence in a joyless stupor, and be lost to all sensation for months together in this profoundest of slumbers."

As for William Gilpin, he has lasted much less well. Indeed, it is difficult to imagine anyone's reading him today for pleasure. Yet he wrote more; he had larger as well as different pretensions; and some half century after his first book he was still well enough known so that Thoreau in his search for some writing which would tell him "how to spend an afternoon" inevitably took Gilpin into consideration.

What makes Gilpin the perfect contrast and complement to White as an illustration of late eighteenth-century ways of writing about nature is the fact that though both might be called nature writers there is almost no overlapping of subject matter or angle of vision. White was a student of natural history who used the materials of science in the composition of a work which becomes belles-lettres because these materials, treated intimately rather than with complete detachment, take on emotional significance. Gilpin's interests were, on the other hand, almost purely aesthetic. Landscape, looked at as though it were a picture, was his theme. He had little or no feeling for animals— or even, one might say, for fields and woods—as living things.

They were spectacles which could delight the eye of a connoisseur, and it was the connoisseurs or would-be connoisseurs whom he addressed.

He made tours to the beauty spots of England, and in such books as *Observations on the River Wye* and *Observations of Cumberland and Westmoreland, Relative Chiefly to Picturesque Beauty* he provided guidebooks which analyzed the supposed excellence of various scenes much as one kind of art critic would analyze landscape painting.

Such books would have been unthinkable a century earlier, when the "Tours" of Defoe concerned themselves with towns and the roads between them, rather than with natural scenery; and took it for granted that the most beautiful and interesting towns were the newest, the most convenient, and the most bustling. Gilpin was a product of that new feeling for nature which the century developed, but he exhibited it in an attenuated, almost effeminate form. His relation was exclusively with the Romantics, not with the scientists, and his Romanticism was of the tamest sort. The picturesque rather than the sublime was his concern, and even the wildest scenery was to him less the living garment of God than simply an arrangement of colors, shades, lights, and shadows. He was just sufficiently touched by the faint suggestion of wildness to have some slight preference for the natural over the artificial, but he spoke with characteristic preciosity of "the embellished scene" (i.e., the landscaped estate) as one of the peculiar features of the English countryside, even though, as he warned, it was "oftener aimed at than attained."

At his best, Gilpin seldom achieved more than tepidity, and one short passage will be sufficient to illustrate his habitual and monotonous manner. Discussing the region of Keswick Lake he wrote:

"As the boundaries of this lake are more mountainous than those of Windermere; they, of course, afford more *romantic scenery*. But tho the whole shore, except the spot where we stood, is incircled with mountains; they rarely fall abruptly into the water; which is girt almost round by a margin of meadow —on the western shores especially. On the eastern, the mountains approach nearer the water; and in some parts fall perpendicularly into it. But as we stood viewing the lake from its northern shores, all these marginal parts were lost; and the mountains (tho in fact they describe a circle of twenty miles, which is double the circumference of the lake) appeared universally to rise from the water's edge. . . .

"The *front*-skreen (if we may so call a portion of a circular form,) is more formidable than either of the sides. But its line is less elegant than that of the eastern-skreen. The fall of Lodoar, which adorns that part of the lake, is an object of no consequence at the distance we now stood. But in our intended ride we proposed to take a nearer view of it.

"Of all the lakes in these romantic regions, the lake we are now examining seems to be most generally admired. It was once admirably characterized by an ingenious person who, on his first seeing it, cried out, *Here is beauty indeed—Beauty lying in the lap of Horrour!* We do not often find a happier illustration. Nothing conveys an idea of *beauty* more strongly than the lake; nor of *horrour* than the mountains; and the former *lying in the lap* of the latter expresses in a strong manner the mode of their combination. The late Dr. Brown, who was a man of taste, and had seen every part of this country, singled out the scenery of this lake for its peculiar beauty. And unquestionably it is, in many places, both beautiful and romantic; particularly along its eastern and southern shores: but to give it *pre-eminence* may be paying it perhaps as much too high a compliment; as it would be too rigorous to make any but a few comparative objections.

"In the first place, its form, which in appearance is circular, is less interesting, I think, than the winding sweep of Windermere, and some other lakes; which losing themselves in vast reaches behind some cape or promontory add to their other beauties, the varieties of distance and perspective. Some people object to this, as touching rather on the character of the river. But does that injure its beauty? And yet I believe there are very few rivers which form such reaches as those of Windermere. . . .

"But among the greatest objections to this lake is the abrupt and broken line in several of the mountains which compose its skreens (especially on the western and on part of the southern shore), which is more remarkable than on any of the other lakes. We have little of the easy sweep of a mountain-line: at least the cyc is hurt with too many tops of mountains, which injure the ideas of simplicity and grandeur. Great care therefore should be taken in selecting views of this lake."

Perhaps the most that could possibly be said of such a passage is simply that its author has at least found a way, good or bad, of writing about landscape, of taking certain aspects of nature as themselves the subject, and of writing with an eye actually on them. But the whole personality of the man is pretentiously trivial, and if White seemed in certain respects a belated Augustan, Gilpin seems a premature Victorian. His "Tours" are a great deal less like the writing of John Muir than they are like hundreds of books having such titles as "Along the Cote D'Azure with Pen and Pencil." In the hands of a man of genius Gilpin's method became the method of John Ruskin—but Ruskin was an art critic, not a nature writer.

The remarkable fact is, of course, not that Thoreau should have found something wanting in Gilpin, but that he should have found him interesting at all. The explanation probably is that there was so little else which even remotely suggested an enterprise like his own—the attempt, that is, to examine the phenomena of physical nature with an eye for objective fact, and also with sufficient imagination to discover the human significance of these phenomena.

The scientist sought fact for fact's sake; the Romantic was all too prone to neglect any fact except the fact of his inner consciousness. Thoreau knew both that the fact existed and that it could mean something—could, perhaps, mean almost everything—to the seeker for wisdom. He took Gilbert White for granted as a naturalist, but White was too dry to be inspiring, and he began to read Gilpin with an enthusiasm which passed rapidly over into irritation. Finally he put his finger squarely upon the basic, unexpressed presumption which made all such writing seem to him not only worthless but vicious. And when he did so he expressed, more clearly than he ever expressed elsewhere, an attitude which is responsible for a large part of his own uniqueness, and which is at the same time implicit in most modern nature writing insofar as it is significantly different from anything which came before.

In Thoreau's *Journal* the first mention of Gilpin is simply a quotation of the Englishman's definition of a copse—"composed of forest trees mixed with brushwood, which last is cut down periodically in twelve or fourteen years." This flat sentence set Thoreau to thinking about "the different places to which the walker resorts" and after a few sentences he is off, Gilpin completely forgotten, to write a series of paragraphs like nothing which anyone before him had ever written:

"It would be worth while to tell why a swamp pleases us. . . . Why the moaning of the storm gives me pleasure. . . . our spirits revive like lichens in the storm. There is something worth living for when we are resisted, threatened. . . . What would the days, what would our life, be worth if some nights were not dark as pitch—of darkness tangible, or that you can cut with a knife? How else could the light in the mind shine? How should we be conscious of the light of reason? If it were not for physical cold, how should we have discovered the warmth of the affections? I sometimes feel that I need to sit in a faraway cave through a three weeks' storm, cold and wet, to give a tone to my system. . . .

"Methinks, I would share every creature's suffering for the sake of its experience and joy. The song sparrow and the transient fox-colored sparrow—have they brought me no message this year? Do they go to lead heroic lives in Rupert's Land?

They are so small, I think their destinies must be large. Have I heard what this tiny passenger has to say, while it flits thus from tree to tree? Is not the coming of the fox-colored sparrow something more earnest and significant than I have dreamed of? Can I forgive myself if I let it go to Rupert's Land before I have appreciated it? God did not make this world in jest; no, nor in indifference. These migrating sparrows all bear messages that concern my life. . . . I see that the sparrow cheeps and flits and sings adequately to the great design of the universe; that man does not communicate with it, understand its language, because he is not at one with nature. I reproach myself because I have regarded with indifference the passage of birds; I have thought them no better than I. . . .

"I hear late to-night the unspeakable rain, mingled with rattling snow against the windows, preparing the ground for spring."

Next day, back to Gilpin's *Forest Scenery*, he finds it a pleasing book. Four months later: "I wish he would look at scenery sometimes not with the eye of an artist. It is all side screen and fore screens and near distances and broken grounds with him. However, his elegant moderation, his discrimination, and real interest in nature excuse many things." Then a year and a half after that the irritation comes to a head and, in a sudden burst of anger, Thoreau realizes not only what is wrong with Gilpin but also what is right about himself.

The occasion was a passage of finespun aesthetic argument about the nature of the picturesque, its relation to variety, and the reason why even a sleek, well-fed horse may be picturesque. "Though the horse, in a *rough* state . . . is more adapted to the pencil than when his sides shine with brushing, and high feeling; yet in this latter state also he is certainly a picturesque object. But it is not his smooth, and shining coat, that makes him so. It is the apparent interruption of that smoothness by a variety of shades, and colors, which produces the effect."

Suddenly Thoreau bursts out: "And this is the reason why

a pampered steed can be painted! Mark that there is not the slightest reference to the fact that this surface with its lights and shades, belongs to a horse and not to a bag of wind. The same reasoning would apply equally well to one of his hind quarters hung bottom upwards in a butcher's stall. Gilpin talked as if there was some fruit for the soul in mere physical light and shadow, as if, without the suggestion of a moral, they could give a man pleasure or pain!"

How stubbornly, so it seemed to Thoreau, men who actually did go to nature insisted, nevertheless, in finding some way of escaping from her. The scientist, bottling, studying, and classifying, tried to forget that his specimens had ever been alive; the Romantic—whom he knew best in Emerson and the other New England Transcendentalists—insisted on regarding these same living things as hieroglyphs or fables, to be interpreted only as emblems of man's own moral or political institutions. And now here was Gilpin wanting the painter to regard them as mere arrangements of light and shade. All these, he felt, are techniques, not for participating in Nature, but for separating oneself from her. Would no one ever understand that we are part of Nature, not merely observers of her; that everything which lives is in a fellowship with us; that only by feeling *with* them can we truly feel *about* them?

Thoreau also protested against the writers of monographs who described species without telling anything about their habits. But the protest was not merely a plea for life histories. What he wanted to say was that the way to profit from the existence of a fish, for example, was not to catch him like the sportsman; not to pickle him like the laboratory scientist; not to paint him like the artist; not even to moon over him like the Romantics. It must be to find, as he did, "a little fishy friend" in Walden Pond.

Sometimes Thoreau remembered that he went to nature "as one possessing the advantages of human culture, fresh from the society of men, but turned loose into the woods." He knew, that is to say, that his attitude was a good deal more than a merely primitive one. Even so, however, he hardly realized how complicated an intellectual history lay behind the possibility of his feeling as he did, of how many revolutions in the realm of science, philosophy, and sensibility he was the heir. He was achieving a new kind of pantheism, which took for granted both the deists' "Great Chain of Being" and the scientists' respect for stubborn fact.

XIII

So far as the a priori convictions implicit in the attitude of the modern nature writer are concerned, we have now traced very sketchily their progress from seventeenth-century theologians through those deistic philosophers whose ideas Alexander Pope popularized in England. We have also said something of the growth of interest in natural history. But before taking it too much for granted that some such attitude as Thoreau's was therefore inevitable, it should be remembered that the pantheists did not have it all their way. Men do not readily relinquish the assumption that the universe was made for them and that it can be explained only in terms of their needs. Thoreau's attitude represents a sort of ultimate democracy which proclaims that all living things, not merely all men, are born with an equal right to life, liberty, and the pursuit of happiness. And it is perhaps not an accident that the last classic writer on natural history whose tendency ran in a diametrically opposite direction should have been the official spokesman for the last great absolute monarch.

Only once in the *Journal*, and then only for a fact of nomenclature, does Thoreau mention Georges Louis Leclerc, Comte de Buffon. Yet Buffon, though he died more than twenty-five years before Thoreau was born, had been an often-quoted international authority, whose sumptuous *Histoire naturelle générale, et particulière* in forty-four volumes had made him unrivaled in the field. And if the authority of any one man could have successfully set itself against the whole tendency of two centuries, Buffon would have rendered forever impossible that kind of feeling for nature with which we are concerned. Great writer though he was in his own special way, he was almost totally without love for the creatures whom he described, not with the detachment of the pure scientist, but with the bias of an aristocrat.

Born in the minor nobility, Buffon had begun his career as a mathematician and a student of Leibnitz. Louis XV and the Pompadour, feeling that the court needed an official naturalist, picked him out to fill the role, and at the age of forty-two he published the first volume of what was planned as a general description of the whole natural world. Though it was, despite the help of various assistants, still incomplete when he died thirty-nine years later, he is said to have spent regularly eight hours a day at his writing desk—dressed always in the full court costume, including the inevitable ruffled sleeves, and with all his medals gleaming on his chest.

His task, in many ways a congenial one, was to write a courtly natural history. That meant, of course, an arresting style, and it meant also a cavalier disregard for such tiresome things as systematic classification, which he dismissed with the statement that all classifications were man-made because nature knew nothing but individuals. Being an official court writer meant, moreover, still more than this. It meant also that the order of nature must be found to be identical with the order of Bourbon society. There must be a Roi Soleil called man, and below him the other parts of an hierarchy extending from the "noble" animals down to the rabble—the members of which rabble, by the way, Buffon never got around to treating, despite his forty-four volumes. The noblest animals were naturally those which served man best and which he allowed to associate most intimately with him— exactly as the noblest men were those who approached most closely and with the greatest self-abnegation the King himself.

Inevitably, therefore, Buffon lauded the dog and vilified the cat. But the "noblest" of all animals was necessarily the horse. He was the first animal to be described, since the arrangement of the work is not from the lowest to the highest in point of physiological complexity, but from the "most noble" on down, as though this were not a natural history but an account of the aristocratic families of the world empire. Buffon is said to have regarded the portrait of the horse as his masterpiece and it begins thus:

"The most noble conquest which man has ever made is that of this proud and spirited animal who shares with him the fatigues of war and the glory of battle: as intrepid as his master, the horse perceives the danger and faces it; he accustoms himself to the sound of arms, he loves it, he seeks it out, he is inspired with the same ardor: he shares also man's pleasures; at the hunt, the tourney, the race course, he shines, he sparkles; but, as docile as he is courageous, he does not permit himself to be carried away by his fire, he knows how to restrain his movements: not only does he yield to the hand of him that guides him, he seems actually to consult his desires, and, always obedient to the impressions he receives from him, he hastens, he slows down, or he stops, and he acts only to give satisfaction: he is a creature who renounces his own self in order to exist only for the will of another and knows even how to anticipate it. He refuses nothing, exerts all his forces, surpasses himself, and even dies in order to obey the better."

Now as one kind of writing that is certainly superb. Insofar as Buffon survives, it is as a belletrist, especially as a maker of full-dress phrases. To him is attributed that commonplace of all debates about science and "values": "The purpose of [natural] philosophy is not to understand the *why* but the *how*." It was also he who first proclaimed that "The style is the man himself," and there is no better example than he of this truth. But his work is less important as science than as part of a struggle between two concepts of the meaning of nature and of man's relation to it. Buffon was a great defender of the ancient attempt to understand nature by reference to man's needs and desires.

In science he was sufficiently behind the times to champion the case for spontaneous generation which John Ray had taught the educated layman to reject almost a century earlier and which, even as Buffon wrote, was being more and more relegated to the position of a vulgar superstition. But from our point of view this scientific backwardness is less important than the fact that his whole view of man's place in nature was as much an anachronism as his belief in spontaneous generation or, even more significantly, as the political and social system of which he was a part.

For all his disclaimer of interest in the "why" of nature, Buffon obviously implies a very old-fashioned answer to that "why" when he calls the horse "noble" because he alone has caught man's enthusiasm for the most "noble" of activities—war—and because, like a fanatical courtier, he makes it his greatest glory to live only for and through his master.

Perhaps, however, the most striking illustration of Buffon's whole attitude toward the animal kingdom is afforded by certain remarks, probably intended to reflect especially upon his far greater but less fashionable contemporary, Réaumur:

"Is there, in fact, anything more gratuitous than this admiration for bees? What shall we think of the excess to which the details of these eulogies have been carried? For, in the end, a bee should not occupy more space in the head of a naturalist than it does in Nature; and this swarm of little beasts that have no other relation to us than to supply us with wax and honey."

"No other relation!" The whole significance of any creature, his only "natural importance" is his utility to man. Obviously no one who thought thus would be likely to learn anything *from* Nature no matter how much he might learn *about* her. And one need not wait for a Thoreau to criticize such an attitude. Buffon might have read in Pope's *Essay on Man:* "The fur that warms a monarch, warm'd a Bear!"

XIV

Charles Darwin published *The Origin of Species* in 1859 (some three years before Thoreau's death), and then crossed his t's with *The Descent of Man* twelve years later. This was science's official recognition of the fact that man is literally a part of nature. But there is a sense in which it might be truly said that Darwin's formulation was no more than one way of stating a conviction which had been growing during the two preceding centuries. In all probability his theory would never have occurred to him at all had he not been prepared to believe as a matter of inherent probability that man is merely the most highly organized of the animals. Certainly that theory would not have been so readily accepted if the public had not been similarly prepared. Thus there is a sense in which one may say that Darwinism is the effect rather than the cause of the convictions that it states.

Darwin's grandfather, Erasmus Darwin, had implied everything except a theory of the mechanism of evolution when he wrote in 1796 that the snout of the pig and the trunk of the elephant had "been gradually produced during the many generations by the perpetual endeavor of the creatures to supply the want of food and have been delivered to their posterity with constant improvement of them for the purposes required." But none of the tentative approaches to a theory of evolution, from that of the eccentric Lord Monboddo—who was convinced that sooner or later explorers would discover a missing link in the form of an aborigine with a tail—down through that of Darwin's most important predecessor, Lamarck, is as important as the atmosphere generated by the common-sense conviction that man is a part of nature and by the emotional willingness to accept that fact.

Shortly before Thoreau died he heard of *The Origin of Species* and expressed some mild interest in its theories, though it is not clear to what extent he really understood them. The matter is, however, of little importance because Thoreau's intuitions had already convinced him of the only fact which he could use in the development of his philosophy—the fact, that is to say, that man is somehow a part of nature, and that therefore only the emotional as well as the intellectual recognition of that fact can bring him spiritual or mental health. For him, the observation of Nature and the learning *from* her had become, not merely a way, but almost the only way of learning anything about either man or the universe in which he lives. Authority was gone; transcendental intuition was, so far as he was concerned, going. Nothing remained except the possibility of looking about him and of drawing what conclusions he could.

Insofar as the "feeling for nature" has undergone any important development since Thoreau's time, that development has come about through the influence of a science which was in its infancy when Thoreau came to his early death. The evolutionists had stressed the gross mechanical parallels between the human body and the animal. Since then, the biochemists have investigated the fundamental stuff of those bodies, and have discovered in protoplasm the chemical basis for the unity of all living things. They have pushed their search into the secrets of life until they have discovered its ultimate material embodiment in the colloid jelly, which is in itself the same, whether it be organized into an amoeba or a man. And that fact would, I suspect, have interested Thoreau more than the theory of evolution, partly because it makes all living things not merely related by remote descent, but essentially one, even now. Here, if you like, is the physical manifestation of the bond which he felt between himself and all other creatures, the physical aspect of that sense of kinship which made it possible to have a "little fishy friend" in Walden Pond. The fellowship he felt was the fellowship defined by protoplasm itself, which is the chemical embodiment of the world soul or, if one prefers, that aspect of the Great God Pan which can be perceived in a test tube.

Much nature writing today reflects more or less definitely this sense of identity, material as well as spiritual, with the fellow creatures which it studies and describes. It implies, if it does not state, a kind of pantheism in which the symbol of the unity of all living things is not an elusive spirit, but a definable material thing. Yet this definable material thing is also a symbol, and hence does not necessarily imply any thoroughgoing materialistic philosophy. It implies merely that life itself rather than something still more mysterious called the "cause of life" is the bond between fellow creatures.

Perhaps it is no accident that the best general statement of the "feeling for nature" in its most characteristic contemporary form should have been made by a writer who was first and foremost a great scientific observer. In an address to fellow scientists published in 1923, William Morton Wheeler, the greatest American authority on the social insects, protested against what he called "the dry rot of our academic biology," and he summed up his deepest conviction in a sentence to which Thoreau might have given hearty assent, and which may well stand as the simplest as well as the most forceful statement of the attitude with which this introduction has been chiefly concerned:

"Why animals and plants are as they are, we shall never know, of how they have come to what they are, our knowledge will always be extremely fragmentary because we are dealing only with the recent phases of an immense and complicated history, most of the records of which are lost beyond all chance of recovery, but that organisms are as they are, that apart from the members of our own species, they are our only companions in an infinite and unsympathetic waste of electrons, planets, nebulae and suns, is a perennial joy and consolation."

XV

The method of this prologue has been to make the history of nature writing in English chiefly the history of the approach to the attitude which Wheeler so eloquently formulated. To do so is obviously to single out one element in a very complex development and to confess to a somewhat one-sided view. It permits us to speak only in passing of some of the most persistent themes, like the search for peace, the dream of the golden age, and that whole nostalgia for a more primitive way of life which is no doubt central in such diverse phenomena as the boy's delight in playing Indian or the Rousseauistic conviction that man is evil only insofar as civilization has corrupted him.

One could, if one liked, make the Robinson Crusoe theme the center of a whole chapter in any complete history of the "return to nature." Defoe's matter-of-fact romance, which was one of the most often imitated as well as one of the most widely read of eighteenth-century books, is itself a kind of middle-class version of the golden age in which the dream of natural self-sufficiency is adapted to the ideals of that class by the insistence that the inhabitant of even the primitive paradise must bestir himself, instead of merely waiting for ripe fruit to fall. In such a view *Walden* itself would then become another expression of one of the most ancient of dreams, a manifestation of Crusoe-ism.

Even within the limitations of the special framework which we have chosen, many untouched aspects of the growth of "fellow feeling" might have been traced. Miss Nicolson, in the work previously cited, made the question whether a mountain was "horrid" or "sublime" a crucial test. Some future historian of ideas might well make a similar test by choosing some other pair of adjectives commonly applied to one of the animals not closely associated with man, and demonstrate how the attitude toward it changed also.

Shakespeare's toad, "ugly and venomous," might serve the purpose. For him, and doubtless for most of his contemporaries, toads seem to have been almost the type of what is disgusting in animate creation, just as mountains were the type of what was horrifying in the inanimate. He can think of nothing worse for one of the heroes in *Troilus and Cressida* to say than "I do hate a proud man, as I hate the engendering of toads."

But who today hates toads or feels any peculiar aversion to the thought of their "engendering"? As a matter of fact, pupils in progressive schools are sometimes taken to observe just that leisurely and rather unimpassioned performance. Most gardeners regard the toad as a pleasantly grotesque watchdog with a useful appetite for insects. Children's books generally represent him as "cute"—which is certainly almost at the opposite extreme from "ugly and venomous." Yet the remoter animals, especially no doubt the reptiles and the amphibia, were only slowly dissociated from their unflattering adjectives. Even Gilbert White can refer to the particular tortoise to which he was so much attached as "this vile reptile," though the choice of the adjective was certainly purely conventional and not at all expressive of his feeling.

Just when the change came about I do not know, but Sir Thomas Browne was in this respect far ahead of his time, and one passage from the *Religio Medici* will do more than merely illustrate the fact. It will also suggest that the reason for the change was something besides the mere realization that toads were not "venomous" and that they were useful. Toads ceased to be ugly and became, in some sense, beautiful, when the idea of beauty was enlarged to include whatever is innocently perfect in its own way; whatever realizes its own purpose and its own nature harmoniously and effectively, even though that nature and that purpose may be remote from the exclusively human. Sir Thomas was a functionalist ahead of his time when he wrote:

"I cannot tell by what logic we call a Toad, a Bear, or an Elephant ugly; they being created in those outward shapes and figures which best express the actions of their inward forms, and having passed that General Visitation of God, Who saw that all He had made was good, that is conformable to His Will, which abhors deformity, and is the rule of order and beauty. There is no deformity but in Monstrosity. . . . Nature hath made one World, and Art another. In brief, all things are artificial; for Nature is the Art of *God*."

Since we have not pretended to do much more than trace the development of one theme, let us conclude with a series of five illustrations of the different ways in which a single creature has been seen by five different writers.

For the first, the reader may turn back—if he has forgotten it—to page 58, where he will find Gilbert White's account of the pet tortoise whom he regards with that reasonable affection so characteristic of the eighteenth century, and whom he describes in so thoroughly unenthusiastic but "enlightened" a fashion.

For the second, let us take the Galapagos turtles as described by the great Darwin while still a young man, but already very much aware of his responsibility as a representative of science.*

"I will first describe the habits of the tortoise (*Testudo nigra*, formerly called *Indica*), which has been so frequently alluded to. These animals are found, I believe, on all the islands of the Archipelago; certainly on the greater number. They frequent in preference the high damp parts, but they likewise live in the lower and arid districts. I have already shown, from the numbers which have been caught in a single day, how very numerous they nust be. Some grow to an immense size. Mr. Lawson, an Englishman, and Vice-Governor of the colony, told us that he had seen several so large that it required six or eight men to lift them from the ground; and that some had afforded as much as two hundred pounds of meat. The old males are the largest, the females rarely growing to so great a size; the male

* From *The Voyage of the Beagle*, by Charles Darwin, Everyman's Library, published by E. P. Dutton & Co., Inc., New York. Published in England by J. M. Dent & Sons, Ltd., London. Reprinted by permission of the publishers.

can readily be distinguished from the female by the greater length of its tail. The tortoises which live on those islands where there is no water, or in the lower and arid parts of the others, feed chiefly on the succulent cactus. Those which frequent the higher and damp regions eat the leaves of various trees, a kind of berry (called *guayavita*) which is acid and austere, and likewise a pale green filamentous lichen (*Usnera plicata*), that hangs in tresses from the boughs of the trees.

"The tortoise is very fond of water, drinking large quantities, and wallowing in the mud. The larger islands alone possess springs, and these are always situated towards the central parts, and at a considerable height. The tortoises, therefore, which frequent the lower districts, when thirsty are obliged to travel from a long distance. Hence broad and well-beaten paths branch off in every direction from the wells down to the seacoast; and the Spaniards by following them up first discovered the watering places. When I landed at Chatham Island, I could not imagine what animal traveled so methodically along well-chosen tracks. Near the springs it was a curious spectacle to behold many of these huge creatures, one set eagerly traveling onwards with outstretched necks, and another set returning, after having drunk their fill. When the tortoise arrives at the spring, quite regardless of any spectator, he buries his head in the water above his eyes, and greedily swallows great mouthfuls, at the rate of about ten in a minute. The inhabitants say each animal stays three or four days in the neighborhood of the water, and then returns to the lower country; but they differ respecting the frequency of these visits. The animal probably regulates them according to the nature of the food on which it has lived. It is, however, certain that tortoises can subsist even on those islands where there is no other water than what falls during a few rainy days in the year.

"I believe it is well ascertained that the bladder of the frog acts as a reservoir for the moisture necessary to its existence. Such seems to be the case with the tortoise. For some time after a visit to the springs their urinary bladders are distended with fluid, which is said gradually to decrease in volume and to become less pure. The inhabitants, when walking in the lower district and overcome with thirst, often take advantage of this cirumstance, and drink the contents of the bladder if full. In one I saw killed, the fluid was quite limpid, and had only a very slightly bitter taste. The inhabitants, however, always first drink the water in the pericardium, which is described as being best.

"The tortoises, when purposely moving toward any point, travel by night and day, and arrive at their journey's end much sooner than would be expected. The inhabitants, from observing marked individuals, consider that they travel a distance of about eight miles in two or three days. One large tortoise which I watched walked at the rate of sixty yards in ten minutes, that is 360 yards in the hour, or four miles a day—allowing a little time for it to eat on the road. During the breeding season, when the male and female are together, the male utters a hoarse roar or bellowing which it is said can be heard at the distance of more than a hundred yards. The female never uses her voice, and the male only at these times; so that when the people hear this noise, they know that the two are together. They were at this time (October) laying their eggs. The female, where the soil is sandy, deposits them together and covers them up with sand; but where the ground is rocky she drops them indiscriminately in any hole. Mr. Bynoe found seven placed in a fissure. The egg is white and spherical; one which I measured was seven inches and three-eights in circumference, and therefore larger than a hen's egg. The young tortoises, as soon as they are hatched, fall a prey in great numbers to the carrion-feeding buzzard. The old ones seem generally to die from accidents, as from falling down precipices. At least, several of the inhabitants told me that they had never found one dead without some evident cause.

"The inhabitants believe that these animals are absolutely deaf; certainly they do not overhear a person walking close behind them. I was always amused when overtaking one of these great monsters, as it was quietly pacing along, to see how suddenly, the instant I passed, it would draw in its head and legs, and uttering a deep hiss fall to the ground with a heavy sound, as if struck dead. I frequently got on their backs, and then giving a few raps on the hinder part of their shells, they would rise up and walk away—but I found it very difficult to keep my balance. The flesh of this animal is largely employed, both fresh and salted; and a beautifully clear oil is prepared from the fat. When a tortoise is caught, the man makes a slit in the skin near its tail, so as to see inside its body, whether the fat under the dorsal plate is thick. If it is not, the animal is liberated; and it is said to recover soon from this strange operation. In order to secure the tortoises, it is not sufficient to turn them like turtles, for they are often able to get on their legs again.

"There can be little doubt that this tortoise is an aboriginal inhabitant of the Galapagos; for it is found on all, or nearly all, the islands, even on some of the smaller ones where there is no water. Had it been an imported species, this would hardly have been the case in a group which has been so little frequented. Moreover, the old Bucaniers found this tortoise in greater numbers even than at present. Wood and Rogers also, in 1708, say that it is the opinion of the Spaniards that it is found nowhere else in this quarter of the world. It is now widely distributed; but it may be questioned whether it is in any other place an aboriginal. The bones of a tortoise at Mauritius, associated with those of the extinct Dodo, have generally been considered as belonging to this tortoise. If this had been so, undoubtedly it must have been there indigenous; but M. Bibron informs me that he believes that it was distinct, as the species now living there certainly is."

A generation later, Thoreau meditates on the true meaning of turtles thus:

"How much lies quietly buried in the ground that we wot not of! We unconsciously step over the eggs of snapping turtles slowly hatching the summer through. Not only was the surface perfectly dry and trackless there, but blackberry vines had run over the spot where these eggs were buried and weeds had sprung up above. If Iliads are not composed in our day, snapping turtles are hatched and arrive at maturity. It already thrusts forth its tremendous head—for the first time in this sphere—and slowly moves from side to side—opening its small glistening eyes for the first time to the light—expressive of dull rage, as if it had endured the trials of this world for a century. When I behold this monster thus steadily advancing toward maturity, all nature abetting, I am convinced that there must be an irresistible necessity for mud turtles. With what tenacity Nature sticks to her idea! These eggs, not warm to the touch, buried in the ground, so slow to hatch, are like the seeds of vegetable life."

Thoreau's contemporary, Herman Melville, also contemplated turtles, not in Concord but on those same Galapagos Islands where Darwin had wondered at them in his own, different way. But Melville is neither a scientist nor, like Thoreau, one who believes that the key to the meaning of man may possibly be found in the larger world of nature. Melville is a moralist and a metaphysician. To him turtles are more emblems than natural facts, are almost what Emerson called hieroglyphics. Perhaps we should call what follows "The Turtle as Symbol."

"Concerning the peculiar reptile inhabitant of these wilds— whose presence gives the group its second Spanish name, Galapagos—concerning the tortoises found here, most mariners have long cherished a superstition, not more frightful than grotesque. They earnestly believe that all wicked sea officers, more especially commodores and captains, are at death (and in some cases before death) transformed into tortoises; thenceforth dwelling upon these hot aridities, sole solitary lords of Asphaltum.

"Doubtless, so quaintly dolorous a thought was originally inspired by the woebegone landscape itself; but more particularly, perhaps, by the tortoises. For apart from their strictly physical features, there is something strangely self-condemned in the appearance of these creatures. Lasting sorrow and penal hopelessness are in no animal form so suppliantly expressed as in theirs; while the thought of their wonderful longevity does not fail to enhance the impression.

"Nor even at the risk of meriting the charge of absurdly believing in enchantments can I restrain the admission that sometimes, even now, when leaving the crowded city to wander out July and August among the Adirondack Mountains, far from the influences of towns and proportionally nigh to the mysterious ones of nature; when at such times I sit me down in the mossy head of some deep-wooded gorge, surrounded by prostrate trunks of blasted pines and recall, as in a dream, my other and far-distant rovings in the baked heart of the charmed isles; and remember the sudden glimpses of dusky shells, and long languid necks protruded from the leafless thickets; and again have beheld the vitreous inland rocks worn down and grooved into deep ruts by ages and ages of the slow draggings of tortoises in quest of pools of scanty water; I can hardly resist the feeling that in my time I have indeed slept upon evilly enchanted ground.

"Some months before my first stepping ashore upon the group, my ship was cruising in its close vicinity. One noon we found ourselves off the South Head of Albemarle, and not very far from the land. Partly by way of freak, and partly by way of spying out so strange a country, a boat's crew was sent ashore with orders to see all they could and besides bring back whatever tortoises they could conveniently transport.

"It was after sunset when the adventurers returned. I looked down over the ship's high side as if looking down over the curb of a well, and dimly saw the damp boat deep in the sea with some unwonted weight. Ropes were dropped over, and presently three huge antediluvian-looking tortoises, after much straining, were landed on deck. They seemed hardly of the seed of earth. We had been broad upon the waters for five long months, a period amply sufficient to make all things of the land wear a fabulous hue to the dreamy mind. Had three Spanish custom-house officers boarded us then, it is not unlikely that I should have curiously stared at them, felt of them, and stroked them much as savages serve civilized guests. But instead of three customhouse officers, behold these really wondrous tortoises—none of your schoolboy mud turtles—but black as widow's weeds, heavy as chests of plate, with vast shells medallioned and orbed like shields, and dented and blistered like shields that have breasted a battle; shaggy, too, here and there, with dark green moss, and slimy with the spray of the sea. These mystic creatures, suddenly translated by night from unutterable solitudes to our peopled deck, affected me in a manner not easy to unfold. They seemed newly crawled forth from beneath the foundations of the world. Yea, they seemed the identical tortoises whereon the Hindoo plants this total sphere. With a lantern I inspected them more closely. Such worshipful venerableness of aspect! Such furry greenness mantling the rude peelings and healing the fissures of their shattered shells. I no more saw three tortoises. They expanded—became transfigured. I seemed to see three Roman Coliseums in magnificent decay.

"Ye oldest inhabitants of this or any other isle, said I, pray give me the freedom of your three-walled towns.

"The great feeling inspired by these creatures was that of age—dateless, indefinite endurance. And in fact that any other creature can live and breathe as long as the tortoise of the Encantadas I will not readily believe. Not to hint of their known capacity of sustaining life while going without food for an entire year, consider that impregnable armor of their living mail. What other bodily being possesses such a citadel wherein to resist the assaults of Time?

"As, lantern in hand, I scraped among the moss and beheld the ancient scars of bruises received in many a sullen fall among the marly mountains of the isle—scars strangely widened, swollen, half obliterate, and yet distorted like those sometimes found in the bark of very hoary trees—I seemed an antiquary of a geologist, studying the bird-tracks and ciphers upon the exhumed slates trod by incredible creatures whose very ghosts are now defunct.

"As I lay in my hammock that night, overhead I heard the slow weary draggings of the three ponderous strangers along the encumbered deck. Their stupidity or their resolution was so great that they never went aside for any impediment. One ceased his movements altogether just before the mid-watch. At sunrise I found him butted like a battering-ram against the immovable foot of the foremast, and still striving, tooth and nail, to force the impossible passage. That these tortoises are the victims of a penal, or malignant, or perhaps a downright diabolical enchanter, seems in nothing more likely than in that strange infatuation of hopeless toil which so often possesses them. I have known them in their journeyings ram themselves heroically against rocks, and long abide there, nudging, wriggling, wedging, in order to displace them, and so hold on their inflexible path. Their crowning curse is their drudging impulse to straightforwardness in a belittered world.

"Meeting with no such hindrance as their companion did, the other tortoises merely fell foul of small stumbling-blocks— buckets, blocks, and coils of rigging—and at times in the act of crawling over them would slip with an astounding rattle to the deck. Listening to these draggings and concussions, I thought me of the haunt from which they came: an isle full of metallic ravines and gulches, sunk bottomlessly into the hearts of splintered mountains, and covered for many miles with inextricable thickets. I then pictured these three straightforward monsters, century after century, writhing through the shades, grim as blacksmiths; crawling so slowly and ponderously, that not only did toadstools and all fungus things grow beneath their feet, but a sooty moss sprouted upon their backs. With them I lost myself in volcanic mazes; brushed away endless boughs of rotting thickets; till finally in a dream I found myself sitting crosslegged upon the foremost, a Brahmin similarly mounted upon either side, forming a tripod of foreheads which upheld the universal cope.

"Such was the wild nightmare begot by my first impression of the Encantadas tortoise. But next evening, strange to say, I sat down with my shipmates, and made a merry repast from tortoise steaks and tortoise stews; and supper over, out knife, and helped convert the three mighty concave shells into three fanciful soup-tureens, and polished the three flat yellowish calipees into three gorgeous salvers."

Our own age, like every other, has its own way of looking at nature. It has used turtles for purposes as different as those of D. H. Lawrence in his turtle poem or of Ogden Nash in his familiar verses. But it was inevitable that this age should also produce "The Sociological Turtle," which appears at the beginning of John Steinbeck's *The Grapes of Wrath.**

"The concrete highway was edged with a mat of tangled, broken, dry grass, and the grass heads were heavy with oat beards to catch on a dog's coat, and foxtails to tangle in a horse's fetlocks, and clover burrs to fasten in sheep's wool; sleeping life waiting to be spread and dispersed, every seed armed with an appliance of dispersal, twisting darts and parachutes for the wind, little spears and balls of tiny thorns, and all waiting for animals and for the wind, for a man's trouser cuff or the hem of a woman's skirt, all passive but armed with appliances of activity, still, but each possessed of the anlage of movement.

"The sun lay on the grass and warmed it, and in the shade under the grass the insects moved, ants and ant lions to set traps for them, grasshoppers to jump into the air and flick their yellow wings for a second, sow bugs like little armadillos, plodding restlessly on many tender feet. And over the grass at the roadside a

* From *The Grapes of Wrath*, by John Steinbeck, Copyright 1939 by John Steinbeck. Reprinted by permission of The Viking Press, Inc., New York, publishers.

land turtle crawled, turning aside for nothing, dragging his high-domed shell over the grass. His hard legs and yellow-nailed feet threshed slowly through the grass, not really walking, but boosting and dragging his shell along. The barley beards slid off his shell, and the clover burrs fell on him and rolled to the ground. His horny beak was partly open, and his fierce, humorous eyes, under brows like fingernails, stared straight ahead. He came over the grass leaving a beaten trail behind him, and the hill, which was the highway embankment, reared up ahead of him. For a moment he stopped, his head held high. He blinked and looked up and down. At last he started to climb the embankment. Front clawed feet reached forward but did not touch. The hind feet kicked his shell along, and it scraped on the grass, and on the gravel. As the embankment grew steeper and steeper, the more frantic were the efforts of the land turtle. Pushing hind legs strained and slipped, boosting the shell along, and the horny head protruded as far as the neck could stretch. Little by little the shell slid up the embankment until at last a parapet cut straight across its line of march, the shoulder of the road, a concrete wall four inches high. As though they worked independently the hind legs pushed the shell against the wall. The head upraised and peered over the wall to the broad smooth plain of cement. Now the hands, braced on top of the wall, strained and lifted, and the shell came slowly up and rested its front end on the wall. For a moment the turtle rested. A red ant ran into the shell, into the soft skin inside the shell, and suddenly head and legs snapped in, and the armored tail clamped in sideways. The red ant was crushed between body and legs. And one head of wild oats was clamped into the shell by a front leg. For a long moment the turtle lay still, and then the neck crept out and the old humorous frowning eyes looked about and the legs and tail came out. The back legs went to work, straining like elephant legs, and the shell tipped to an angle so that the front legs could not reach the level cement plain. But higher and higher the hind legs boosted it, until at last the center of balance was reached, the front tipped down, the front legs scratched at the pavement, and it was up. But the head of wild oats was held by its stem around the front legs.

"Now the going was easy, and all the legs worked, and the shell boosted along, waggling from side to side. A sedan driven by a forty-year-old woman approached. She saw the turtle and swung to the right, off the highway, the wheels screamed and a cloud of dust boiled up. Two wheels lifted for a moment and then settled. The car skidded back onto the road, and went on, but more slowly. The turtle had jerked into its shell, but now it hurried on, for the highway was burning hot.

"And now a light truck approached, and as it came near, the driver saw the turtle and swerved to hit it. His front wheel struck the edge of the shell, flipped the turtle like a tiddlywink, spun it like a coin, and rolled it off the highway. The truck went back to its course along the right side. Lying on its back, the turtle was tight in its shell for a long time. But at last its legs waved in the air, reaching for something to pull it over. Its front foot caught a piece of quartz and little by little the shell pulled over and flopped upright. The wild oat head fell out and three of the spearhead seeds stuck in the ground. And as the turtle crawled on down the embankment, its shell dragged dirt over the seeds. The turtle entered a dust road and jerked itself along, drawing a wavy shallow trench in the dust with its shell. The old humorous eyes looked ahead, and the horny beak opened a little. His yellow toe nails slipped a fraction in the dust."

Thoreau and the Thoreauists

O NE kind of nature writing does not replace another. Nearly every approach to the subject made by Europeans has been adopted by one American or another, and might be illustrated by a selection. However, the present anthology attempts nothing of the sort. It confines itself pretty closely to specimens of the special genre which the prologue attempted to define.

On occasion the definition has been stretched to its limit, but the aim is to include nothing which does not at least proceed on the assumption that nature is to be learned *from* as well as *about*. Neither the explorer nor the scientist is represented unless what he writes aims at more than merely an account of either his adventures or of the facts which he has accumulated. In each case it has been required of him that he be also something of a poet; that he enter into the nature which he describes; that he exhibit some sense of oneness with it.

No doubt the decision to begin with Thoreau is not absolutely inevitable. From earlier American writers one might select scattered passages which satisfy our requirement at least as well as certain of the passages included from certain of the later ones. But at least Thoreau was the first to propose to himself, consciously and clearly, the kind of enterprise with which we are especially concerned. Every subsequent writer had the opportunity to profit by his example, and a great many did so.

Logically, one must either begin with him or begin at the beginning—with the discovery of America. Sir Walter Raleigh commissioned a report on the natural resources of the new country, and Captain John Smith included a section on natural history in his *Map of Virginia* (1612). But the purpose of such accounts is severely practical, and so, essentially, is the fuller one in William Wood's *New England's Prospect* (1638)—which so saddened Thoreau with its reminder that the fauna of Massachusetts had once been far richer and far wilder than what Thoreau knew. For our purpose there would be no point even in listing the various early residents or visitors who paid greater or less attention to the botany or zoology of our continent.

More of a case might be made for William Bartram. He was a naturalist by profession; he had also at least enough of the philosopher's and the poet's vision to write what Wordsworth found it stimulating to read. In the introduction to his *Travels* (1791), he could include paragraphs like this:

"We admire the mechanism of a watch, and the fabric of a piece of brocade, as being the production of art; these merit our admiration, and must excite our esteem for the ingenious artist or modifier; but nature is the work of God omnipotent; and an elephant, nay even this world, is comparatively but a very minute part of his works. If then the visible, the mechanical part of the animal creation, the mere material part, is so admirably beautiful, harmonious, and incomprehensible, what must be the intellectual system? that inexpressibly more essential principle, which secretely operates within? that which animates the inimitable machines, which gives them motion, impowers them to act, speak, and perform, this must be divine and immortal!"

Nevertheless, the form of the body of his text is the conventional form of the travel journal, and Bartram never succeeded in expressing with any fullness the emotions which he no doubt felt.

Something of the same sort may be said of the ornithologist Alexander Wilson and even of Audubon himself. Wilson, who is sometimes credited with being the first American to popularize the study of bird life, wanted to be, literally, a poet and he wrote some unfortunately undistinguished verse. On the other hand, at least the best of his prose descriptions are enthusiastic and intimate. When he wrote, for instance, of the brown thrasher's song that it "conveys the sweet sensation of joy" and that "Heaven's abundance is, as it were, showering around us," many a present-day ornithologist would say he was well over the line separating science from the pathetic fallacy.

Nevertheless, Wilson was an ornithologist, not even secondarily a man of letters; and the case of Audubon is even more ambiguous. So great is the reverence in which his name is held that one must weigh carefully one's words in hinting that there was anything which he lacked. His passion for his subject was fanatically intense—as though he thought that to draw birds was the whole duty of man. Ornithology was a religion, a delirium, almost an insanity. Yet the fact that he could slaughter individuals wholesale and without a qualm; that he could shoot down a subject as though it were nothing *but* a subject seems to suggest one of the most important things about him.

Bernard Shaw's John Tanner, speaking of the temperament of the great artist, exclaims: "Perish a thousand women if only their deaths enable him to paint a finer picture or act a better Hamlet." Audubon was that kind of artist or, perhaps, that kind of scientist. One is tempted to say that it was the *spectacle* of birds and the *idea* of birds which fascinated him, and that he loved them more as one might love a work of art or a wonderful mechanism than as creatures with whose individual lives he was concerned.

Consider for example this passage from his account of the Mallard:

"The mallard, unlike the sea Ducks, is rarely seen on salt water, and—its course from the countries where it chiefly breeds is across the interior of the continent. From our great lakes, they spread along streams, betake themselves to ponds, wet meadows, submerged savannahs, and inland swamps, and are even found in the thick beech woods, in early autumn, and indeed long before the males have acquired the dark green color of the head. Many of them proceed beyond the limits of the United States.

"Be not startled, good reader, when I tell you that many of these Ducks are bred in the lakes near the Mississippi, nay even in some of the small ponds in the low lands or bottoms of the States of Kentucky, Indiana, and Illinois; for in many parts of those districts I have surprized the females on their eggs, have caught the young was cautiously and with anxiety leading them for greater safety to some stream, and have shot many a fat one before the poor thing could fly, and when it was so plump, tender and juicy, that I doubt whether you, like myself, would not much prefer them to the famed Canvass-backed Duck.

"Look at that Mallard as he floats on the lake; see his elevated head glittering with emerald-green, his amber eyes glancing in the light! Even at this distance, he has marked you and suspects that you bear no good will toward him, for he sees that you have a gun, and he has many a time been frightened by its report, or that of some other. The wary bird draws his feet under his body, springs upon them, opens his wings, and with loud quacks bids you farewell."

How keen was the eye of the man who wrote that! But how hard, one is tempted to say, was his heart!

So at least one imagines that Thoreau would have felt, and he might, indeed, have found Audubon's attitude toward the beauty of birds not unlike that of Gilpin toward the "picturesque" horse. When in 1854 Thoreau had "collected" a turtle for a Harvard scientist, he wrote that he had had "a murderer's experience in a degree." "I pray," he went on, "that I may walk more innocently and serenely through nature. No reasoning whatever reconciles me to this act."

Moreover, Thoreau's claim to be considered as the founder of a genre rests upon something besides the novelty, or at least the novel consistency, of his attitude toward "fellow" creatures. The form which his writing took was almost equally original. Neither *Walden* nor the *Journal* which he kept so assiduously is either "natural history" or "travel and description" in the ordinary meaning of the terms. A Bartram recounting his journeyings or a Wilson describing a bird may make *obiter dicta*; may, as it were, write reflections, meditations or even rhapsodies in the margin. But the center of their writing is the objective account; botany or ornithology is the ostensible subject. Thoreau, on the other hand, manages a shift of emphasis, and in so doing creates what is, in effect, a new form of nature writing. What is occasional and incidental in others is with him the main theme. His book is not "about" plants or animals or birds. It is about his relation with them; one may almost say about "himself in connection with nature."

Not every subsequent writer included in this anthology adopts his form. Many are closer in method to the pure scientist. But even among those, not a few show the influence of Thoreau's example; take advantage to some extent of the fact that he had demonstrated how the observer could be made effectively to play a role at least comparable in importance to that of the thing observed. And this is the final, if not the most important reason why it seems proper that Thoreau should begin the present anthology.

The majority of the quotations from him are from the *Journal*, which he began in 1837 when he was twenty years old and continued until a few months before his death. There are also passages from published work, but much of that also had first been written into the *Journal*, which was the day-by-day account of his surprisingly successful attempt to find for himself a happy way of living with nature. The first sentence—at least the first surviving sentence—of the *Journal* expresses a need for "a garret," and that may suggest that in Thoreau's case, as in the case of so many others, the impulse to get away from something preceded the drive to get *into* anything. But even if that is so, then at least Thoreau soon forgot the fact, and none of his characteristics is more nearly unique than his conviction that he, almost alone among men, had discovered how to live profitably and happily in nature.

Only a few of the selections presented deal directly with that criticism of society for which Thoreau is perhaps most often remembered today. Sometimes it seems to be almost forgotten that what he found wrong with life as it was commonly led was to him much less important than what he found right with life as he himself led it. He expressed the desire to make his writing more a record of what he loved than a record of what he hated, and it is his love that most of these selections express.

During his own lifetime Thoreau was not so very widely read and cannot be said to have founded a school. The best-known nature essayists contemporary with him—Thomas Wentworth Higginson and James Russell Lowell—are essentially genteel writers and Lowell's essay on Thoreau, one of the first general estimates to appear, seems definitely intended to discount its subject. Wild nature, so Lowell insisted, is well enough for a holiday, but a wise man will realize that civilization is his real business. He accused Thoreau of morbidity and warned against that extravagance which Thoreau himself valued so highly.

No second printing of *Walden* had been made during Thoreau's lifetime, but one was already preparing as he lay on his deathbed. His real fame was about to begin, and his influence lay heavy—heavier, indeed, than either seemed to realize—upon John Muir and John Burroughs, who were to be popular to an extent he had never been. It was they—especially Burroughs —who helped make out-of-door living an American cult, and I have ventured to call him and Muir "Thoreauists," though neither would have called himself quite that.

Muir, born in Scotland in 1838, was brought to a Wisconsin farm by his almost ferociously stern father. Through his own heroic efforts he managed to attend for a time the University of Wisconsin—where he was interested chiefly in geology and chemistry—until a passion for botany seized him, and he went on great foot-tours through the neighboring states and Canada. In 1867, while working in a wagon factory, he injured one of his eyes and resolved thereupon to devote his life, not to mechanics, which had always fascinated him, but "to the study of the inventions of God." He walked from Indiana to the Gulf of Mexico, keeping a naturalist-and-philosopher's diary as he went. Somewhat later he married; settled down to the business of fruit farming; and accumulated presently sufficient capital to support his two daughters, his wife, and himself while he indulged his passion for the wild regions of the West.

In *The Story of My Boyhood* (1913) he told how an awakening interest in animal life caused him to revolt against the thoughtless cruelty of those about him, and he wrote often of his fellow creatures. "When I was a boy in Scotland I was fond of everything that was wild, and all my life I've been growing fonder of wild places and wild creatures." Nevertheless, Muir seems to have been most deeply moved by, or perhaps most originally inspired by, what is called elsewhere in this volume the "Majesty of the Inanimate." Mountains, together with the forests which clothed them and the glaciers which moved down their ravines, were his special study. Like Thoreau in his later years, he realized that only a definite policy of conservation could save any part of our wilderness, and he began a campaign resulting in the Yosemite Park Act of 1890, which served, in turn, as a model for the successive acts establishing our National Parks.

Muir read Thoreau, of course, and Emerson as well. He could hardly have become what he did without the influence of both. But he was not primarily philosophical and his rather vague theisim is not quite identical with that of either Thoreau or Emerson; though, unlike his contemporary Burroughs, he definitely rejected mechanistic theories. The selection from his work here presented is taken from *My First Summer in the Sierra* (1911).

John Burroughs was born in Roxbury, Massachusetts, in 1837 —just one year before Muir. Even in boyhood he delighted to watch the birds of his neighborhood but he was also a pre-destined writer whose first gods were Wordsworth and Emerson. At the age of twenty-three he wrote his first Emersonian essay for the *Atlantic Monthly*. A few years later he went to Washington where he stayed for twenty years at a desk in the currency bureau. During that period he met and became close friends with Walt Whitman, of whom he said: "I loved him as I never loved any man—I owe more to him than to any other man in the world." Of *Walden* he said, on the contrary, that he met it early but that "I am not conscious of any great debt to Thoreau: I had begun to write upon out-door themes before his books fell into my hands, but he undoubtedly helped confirm me in my own direction."

Despite this somewhat grudging admission, Henry James, who in 1865 reviewed Burroughs' early book *Winter Sunshine*, called the author "a sort of reduced, but also more humorous, more available, and more sociable Thoreau." A present-day biographer concludes that "His debt to Thoreau was probably much greater than he was willing to acknowledge," and another student has pointed out both that Burroughs wrote three separate essays on the author of *Walden* and that Thoreau's name occurs elsewhere more than fifty times in Burroughs' work.

Perhaps the paradox is resolved by the fact that Burroughs was able to become the most popular of the nineteenth- and early twentieth-century American nature writers just because he rejected the more alarming aspects of Thoreau's attitudes and sought somehow to make an interest in nature and the out-of-doors compatible with what Thoreau had called "this trivial and bustling nineteenth century." It is true that in certain respects Burroughs was intransigent enough. As he grew old, official science interested him more and more; he leaned in the direction of a mechanistic interpretation of the universe; he rejected Whitman in a late essay and he declared himself ready to accept personal extinction. But in other ways he proclaimed a compromise with wildness, and at least a partial acceptance of some of the very aspects of modernity which offended Thoreau.

In the first place, nature as tamed by agriculture attracted him more than the wilderness. His famous rural retreat, "Slabsides," became a sort of place of pilgrimage for busy people who could thus pay their respects to a prophet who had become the official representative of nature. One can hardly imagine Thomas Edison and Henry Ford visiting Walden as they visited "Slabsides," and one is tempted to remember Samuel Butler's remark that the "vicar" of a church is so called because his parishioners pay him to be, vicariously, "good" for them. Burroughs was a convenient man to have for those who wanted someone to be natural for them.

With Theodore Roosevelt he joined in the war on "nature fakers," and in general he adopted a reassuring "no-nonsense" attitude toward those who might be regarded as either "fanatics" who wished to reject civilization, or "sentimentalists" who were repelled by the strenuously destructive life of his friend Roosevelt. The ordinary citizen could read Burroughs with full assurance that he would not be scolded as Thoreau would scold him.

From his very copious works a passage is selected from the volume called *Time and Change*.

Travel in Concord

—HENRY DAVID THOREAU

I think that no experience which I have today comes up to, or is comparable with the experiences of my boyhood. And not only this is true, but as far back as I can remember I have unconsciously referred to the experiences of a previous state of existence, "For life is a forgetting," etc. Formerly, methought, nature developed as I developed, and grew up with me. My life was ecstasy. In youth, before I lost any of my senses, I can remember that I was all alive, and inhabited my body with inexpressible satisfaction; both its weariness and its refreshment were sweet to me. This earth was the most glorious instrument, and I was audience to its strains. To have such sweet impressions made on us, such ecstasies begotten of the breezes! I can remember how I was astonished. I said to myself—I said to others—"There comes into my mind such an indescribable, infinite, all-absorbing, divine, heavenly pleasure, a sense of elevation and expansion, and [I] have had nought to do with it. I perceive that I am dealt with by superior powers. This is a pleasure, a joy, an existence which I have not procured myself. I speak as a witness on the stand, and tell what I have perceived." The morning and the evening were sweet to me, and I led a life aloof from society of men. I wondered if a mortal had ever known what I knew. I looked in books for some recognition of a kindred experience, but strange to say, I found none. Indeed, I was slow to discover that other men had had this experience, for it had been possible to read books and to associate with men on other grounds. The Maker of me was improving me. When I detected this interference I was profoundly moved. For years I marched as to a music in comparison with which the military music of the streets is noise and discord. I was daily intoxicated, and yet no man could call me intemperate. With all your science can you tell how it is, and whence it is that light comes into the soul?

There is little or nothing to be remembered written on the subject of getting an honest living. Neither the New Testament nor Poor Richard speaks to our condition. I cannot think of a single page which entertains, much less answers the questions which I put to myself on this subject. How to make the getting our living poetic! for if it is not poetic, it is not life but death that we get. Is it that men are too disgusted with their experience to speak of it? or that commonly they do not question the common modes? The most practically important of all questions, it seems to me, is how shall I get my living, and yet I find little or nothing said to the purpose in any book. Those who are living on the interest of money inherited, or dishonestly—i.e. by false methods—acquired, are of course incompetent to answer it. I consider that society with all its arts has done nothing for us in this respect. One would think from looking at literature that this question had never disturbed a solitary individual's musings. Cold and hunger seem more friendly to my nature than those methods which men have adopted and advise to ward them off. If it were not that I desire to do something here—accomplish some work—I should certainly prefer to suffer and die rather than be at the pains to get a living by the modes men propose.

While the Republic has already acquired a history world-wide, America is still unsettled and unexplored. Like the English in

New Holland, we live only on the shores of a continent even yet, and hardly know where the rivers come from which float our navy. The very timber and boards and shingles of which our houses are made grew but yesterday in a wilderness where the Indian still hunts and the moose runs wild. New York has her wilderness within her own borders; and though the sailors of Europe are familiar with the soundings of her Hudson, and Fulton long since invented the steamboat on its waters, an Indian is still necessary to guide her scientific men to its headwaters in the Adirondack country.

We have advanced by leaps to the Pacific, and left many a lesser Oregon and California unexplored behind us. Though the railroad and the telegraph have been established on the shores of Maine, the Indian still looks out from her interior mountains over all these to the sea. There stands the city of Bangor, fifty miles up the Penobscot, at the head of navigation for vessels of the largest class, the principal lumber depot on this continent, with a population of twelve thousand, like a star on the edge of night, still hewing at the forests of which it is built, already overflowing with the luxuries and refinement of Europe, and sending its vessels to Spain, to England, and to the West Indies for its groceries—and yet only a few axmen have gone "up river," into the howling wilderness which feeds it. The bear and deer are still found within its limits; and the moose, as he swims the Penobscot, is entangled amid its shipping, and taken by foreign sailors in its harbor. Twelve miles in the rear, twelve miles of railroad, are Orono and the Indian Island, the home of the Penobscot tribe; and then commence the batteau and the canoe, and the military road; and sixty miles above, the country is virtually unmapped and unexplored, and there still waves the virgin forest of the New World.

Maine, perhaps, will soon be where Massachusetts is. A good part of her territory is already as bare and commonplace as much of our neighborhood, and her villages generally are not so well shaded as ours.

Henry David Thoreau

And what are we coming to in our Middlesex towns? A bald, staring townhouse, or meetinghouse, and a bare liberty pole, as leafless as it is fruitless, for all I can see. We shall be obliged to import the timber for the last, hereafter, or splice such sticks as we have. And our ideas of liberty are equally mean with these. The very willow-rows lopped every three years for fuel or powder, and every sizable pine and oak, or other forest tree, cut down within the memory of man! As if individual speculators were to be allowed to export the clouds out of the sky, or the stars out of the firmament, one by one. We shall be reduced to gnaw the very crust of the earth for nutriment.

The kings of England formerly had their forests "to hold the king's game," for sport or food, sometimes destroying villages to create or extend them; and I think that they were impelled by a true instinct. Why should not we, who have renounced the king's authority, have our national preserves, where no villages need be destroyed, in which the bear and panther, and some even of the hunter race, may still exist, and not be "civilized off the face of the earth"—our forests, not to hold the king's game merely, but to hold and preserve the king himself also, the lord of creation—not for idle sport or food, but for inspiration and our own true recreation? Or shall we, like the villains, grub them all up, poaching on our own national domains?

Would it not be a luxury to stand up to one's chin in some retired swamp for a whole summer's day, scenting the sweet-fern and bilberry blows, and lulled by the minstrelsy of gnats and mosquitoes? . . . Say twelve hours of genial and familiar converse with the leopard frog. The sun to rise behind alder and dogwood, and climb buoyantly to his meridian of three hands' breadth, and finally sink to rest behind some bold western hummock. To hear the evening chant of the mosquito from a thousand green chapels, and the bittern begin to boom from his concealed fort like a sunset gun! Surely, one may as profitably be soaked in the juices of a marsh for one day, as pick his way dry-shod over sand. Cold and damp—are they not as rich experience as warmth and dryness?

Visited my nighthawk on her nest. Could hardly believe my eyes when I stood within seven feet and beheld her sitting on her eggs, her head to me. She looked so Saturnian, so one with the earth, so sphinx-like, a relic of the reign of Saturn which Jupiter did not destroy, a riddle that might well cause a man to go dash his head against a stone. It was not an actual living creature, far less a winged creature of the air, but a figure in stone or bronze, a fanciful production of art, like the gryphon or phoenix. In fact, with its breast toward me, and owing to its color or size no bill perceptible, it looked like the end [of] a brand, such as are common in a clearing, its breast mottled or alternately waved with dark brown and gray, its flat, grayish, weather-beaten crown, its eyes nearly closed, purposely, lest those bright beads should betray it, with the stony cunning of the sphinx. A fanciful work in bronze to ornament a mantel. It was enough to fill one with awe. The sight of this creature sitting on its eggs impressed me with the venerableness of the globe. There was nothing novel about it. All the while, this seemingly sleeping bronze sphinx, as motionless as the earth, was watching me with intense anxiety through those narrow slits in its eyelids. Another step, and it fluttered down the hill close to the ground, with a wabbling motion, as if touching the ground now with the tip of one wing, now with the other, so ten rods to the water, which [it] skimmed close over a few rods, then rose and soared in the air above me. Wonderful creature, which sits motionless on its eggs on the barest, most exposed hills, through pelting storms of rain or hail, as if it were a rock or a part of the earth itself, the outside of the globe, with its eyes shut and its wings folded, and, after the two days' storm, when you think it has become a fit symbol of the rheumatism, it suddenly rises into the air a bird, one of the most aerial, supple, and graceful of creatures, without stiffness in its wings or joints! It was a fit prelude to meeting Prometheus bound to his rock on Caucasus.

Suddenly, looking down the river, I saw a fox some sixty rods off, making across to the hills on my left. As the snow lay five inches deep, he made but slow progress, but it was no impediment to me. So, yielding to the instinct of the chase, I tossed my head aloft and bounded away, snuffing the air like a foxhound, and spurning the world and the Humane Society at each bound. It seemed the woods rang with the hunter's horn, and Diana and all the satyrs joined in the chase and cheered me on. Olympian and Elean youths were waving palms on the hills. In the meanwhile I gained rapidly on the fox; but he showed a remarkable presence of mind, for, instead of keeping up the face of the hill, which was steep and unwooded in that part, he kept along the slope in the direction of the forest, though he lost ground by it. Notwithstanding his fright, he took no step which was not beautiful. The course on his part was a series of most graceful curves. It was a sort of leopard canter, I should say, as if he were nowise impeded by the snow, but was husbanding his strength all the while. When he doubled I wheeled and cut him off, bounding with fresh vigor, and Antaeus-like, recovering my strength each time I touched the snow. Having got near enough for a fair view, just as he was slipping into the wood, I gracefully yielded him the palm. He ran as though there were not a bone in his back, occasionally dropping his muzzle to the snow for a rod or two, and then tossing his head aloft when satisfied of his course. When he came to a declivity he put his forefeet together and slid down it like a cat. He trod so softly that you could not have heard it from any nearness, and yet with such expression that it would not have been quite inaudible at any distance. So, hoping this experience would prove a useful lesson to him, I returned to the village by the highway of the river.

A neat herd of cows approached, of unusually fair proportions and smooth, clean skins, evidently petted by their owner, who must have carefully selected them. One more confiding heifer, the fairest of the herd, did by degrees approach as if to take some morsel from our hands, while our hearts leaped to our mouths with expectation and delight. She by degrees drew near with her fair limbs progressive, making pretense of browsing; nearer and nearer, till there was wafted toward us the bovine fragrance—cream of all the dairies that ever were or will be— and then she raised her gentle muzzle toward us, and snuffed an honest recognition within hand's reach. I saw 'twas possible for his herd to inspire with love the herdsman. She was as delicately featured as a hind. Her hide was mingled white and fawn-color, and on her muzzle's tip there was a white spot not bigger than a daisy, and on her side toward me the map of Asia plain to see.

Farewell, dear heifer! Though thou forgettest me, my prayer to heaven shall be that thou may'st not forget thyself. There was a whole bucolic in her snuff. I saw her name was Sumach. And by the kindred spots I knew her mother, more sedate and matronly, with full-grown bag; and on her sides was Asia, great and small, the plains of Tartary, even to the pole, while on her daughter it was Asia Minor. She not disposed to wanton with the herdsman.

And as I walked, she followed me, and took an apple from my hand, and seemed to care more for the hand than apple. So innocent a face as I have rarely seen on any creature, and I have looked in face of many heifers. And as she took the apple from my hand, I caught the apple of her eye. She smelled as sweet as the clethra blossom. There was no sinister expression. And for horns, though she had them, they were so well disposed in the right place, bent neither up nor down, I do not now remember she had any. No horn was held toward me.

A hen-hawk sails away from the wood southward. I get a very fair sight of it sailing overhead. What a perfectly regular and neat outline it presents! an easily recognized figure anywhere. Yet I never see it represented in any books. The exact correspondence of the marks on one side to those on the other, as the black or dark tip of one wing to the other, and the dark line midway the wing. I have no idea that one can get as correct an idea of the form and color of the under side of a hen-hawk's wings by spreading those of a dead specimen in his study as by looking up at a free and living hawk soaring above him in the fields. The penalty for obtaining a petty knowledge thus dishonestly is that it is less interesting to men generally, as it is less significant. Some, seeing and admiring the neat figure of the hawk sailing two or three hundred feet above their heads, wish to get nearer and hold it in their hands, perchance, not realizing that they can see it best at this distance, better now, perhaps, than ever they will again. What is an eagle in captivity!—screaming in a courtyard! I am not the wiser respecting eagles for having seen one there. I do not wish to know the length of its entrails.

I spend a considerable portion of my time observing the habits of the wild animals, my brute neighbors. By their various movements and migrations they fetch the year about to me. Very significant are the flight of geese and the migration of suckers, etc., etc. But when I consider that the nobler animals have been exterminated here—the cougar, panther, lynx, wolverine, wolf, bear, moose, deer, the beaver, the turkey, etc., etc.—I cannot but feel as if I lived in a tamed and, as it were, emasculated country. Would not the motions of those larger and wilder animals have been more significant still? Is it not a maimed and imperfect nature that I am conversant with? As if I were to study a tribe of Indians that had lost all its warriors. Do not the forest and the meadow now lack expression, now that I never see nor think of the moose with a lesser forest on his head in the one, nor of the beaver in the other? When I think what were the various sounds and notes, the migrations and works, and changes of fur and plumage which ushered in the spring and marked the other seasons of the year, I am reminded that this my life in nature, this particular round of natural phenomena which I call a year, is lamentably incomplete. I listen to [a] concert in which so many parts are wanting. The whole civilized country is to some extent turned into a city, and I am that citizen whom I pity. Many of those animal migrations and other phenomena by which the Indians marked the season are no longer to be observed. I seek acquaintance with Nature—to know her moods and manners. Primitive Nature is the most interesting to me. I take infinite pains to know all the phenomena of the spring, for instance, thinking that I have here the entire poem, and then, to my chagrin, I hear that it is but an imperfect copy that I possess and have read, that my ancestors have torn out many of the first leaves and grandest passages, and mutilated it in many places. I should not like to think that some demigod had come before me and picked out some of the best of the stars. I wish to know an entire heaven and an entire earth.

The simplest and most lumpish fungus has a peculiar interest to us, compared with a mere mass of earth, because it is so obviously organic and related to ourselves, however mute. It is the expression of an idea; growth according to a law; matter not dormant, not raw, but inspired, appropriated by spirit. If I take up a handful of earth, however separately interesting the particles may be, their relation to one another appears to be that of mere juxtaposition generally. I might have thrown them together thus. But the humblest fungus betrays a life akin to my own. It is a successful poem in its kind. There is suggested something superior to any particle of matter, in the idea or mind which uses and arranges the particles.

I cannot but see still in my mind's eye those little striped breams poised in Walden's glaucous water. They balance all the rest of the world in my estimation at present, for this is the bream that I have just found, and for the time I neglect all its brethren and am ready to kill the fatted calf on its account. For more than two centuries have men fished here, and have not distinguished this permanent settler of the township. It is not like a new bird, a transient visitor that may not be seen again for years, but there it dwells and has dwelt permanently, who can tell how long? When my eyes first rested on Walden the striped bream was poised in it, though I did not see it; and when Tahatawan paddled his canoe there. How wild it makes the pond and the township, to find a new fish in it! America renews her youth here. But in my account of this bream I cannot go a hair's breadth beyond the mere statement that it exists—the miracle of its existence, my contemporary and neighbor, yet so different from me! I can only poise my thought there by its side and try to think like a bream for a moment. I can only think of precious jewels, of music, poetry, beauty, and the mystery of life. I only see the bream in its orbit, as I see a star, but I care not to measure its distance or weight. The bream, appreciated, floats in the pond as the center of the system, another image of God. Its life no man can explain more than he can his own. I want you to perceive the mystery of the bream. I have a contemporary in Walden. It has fins where I have legs and arms. I have a friend among the fishes, at least a new acquaintance. Its character will interest me, I trust, not its clothes and anatomy. I do not want it to eat. Acquaintance with it is to make my life more rich and eventful. It is as if a poet or an anchorite had moved into the town, whom I can see from time to time and think of yet oftener. Perhaps there are a thousand of these striped bream which no one had thought of in that pond—not their mere impressions in stone, but in the full tide of the bream life.

Though science may sometimes compare herself to a child picking up pebbles on the seashore, that is a rare mood with her; ordinarily her practical belief is that it is only a few pebbles which are *not* known, weighed and measured. A new species of

fish signifies hardly more than a new name. See what is contributed in the scientific reports. One counts the fin rays; another measures the intestines; a third daguerreotypes a scale,
etc., etc.; otherwise there's nothing to be said. As if all but this
were done, and these were very rich and generous contributions
to science. Her votaries may be seen wandering along the shore
of the ocean of truth, with their backs to that ocean, ready to
seize on the shells which are cast up. You would say that the
scientific bodies were terribly put to it for objects and subjects.
A dead specimen of an animal, if it is only well preserved in
alcohol, is just as good for science as a living one preserved in
its native element.

What is the amount of my discovery to me? It is not that I
have got one in a bottle, that it has got a name in a book, but
that I have a little fishy friend in the pond. How was it when
the youth first discovered fishes? Was it the number of their fin
rays or their arrangement, or the place of the fish in some system
that made the boy dream of them? Is it these things that interest
mankind in the fish, the inhabitant of the water? No, but a faint
recognition of a living contemporary, a provoking mystery. One
boy thinks of fishes and goes a-fishing from the same motive that
his brother searches the poets for rare lines. It is the poetry of
fishes which is their chief use; their flesh is their lowest use.
The beauty of the fish, that is what it is best worth the while to
measure. Its place in our systems is of comparatively little importance. Generally the boy loses some of his perception and his
interest in the fish; he degenerates into a fisherman or an ichthy-
ologist.

Shad are still taken in the basin of Concord River, at Lowell,
where they are said to be a month earlier than the Merrimack
shad, on account of the warmth of the water. Still patiently,
almost pathetically, with instinct not to be discouraged, not to be
reasoned with, revisiting their old haunts, as if their stern fates
would relent, and still met by the Corporation with its dam.

Poor shad! where is thy redress? When Nature gave thee instinct, gave she thee the heart to bear thy fate? Still wandering the sea in thy scaly armor to inquire humbly at the mouths of rivers if man has perchance left them free for thee to enter. By countless shoals loitering uncertain meanwhile, merely stemming the tide there, in danger from sea foes in spite of thy bright armor, awaiting new instructions, until the sands, until the water itself, tell thee if it be so or not. Thus by whole migrating nations, full of instinct, which is thy faith, in this backward spring, turned adrift; and perchance knowest not where men do *not* dwell, where there are *not* factories, in these days. Armed with no sword, no electric shock, but mere shad, armed only with innocence and a just cause, with tender dumb mouth only forward, and scales easy to be detached.—I for one am with thee, and who knows what may avail a crowbar against that Billerica dam?—Not despairing when whole myriads have gone to feed those sea-monsters during thy suspense, but still brave, indifferent, on easy fin there, like shad reserved for higher destinies. Willing to be decimated for man's behoof after the spawning season. Away with the superficial and selfish phil-*anthropy* of men—who knows what admirable virtue of fishes may be below low-water mark, bearing up against a hard destiny, not admired by that fellow creature who alone can appreciate it! Who hears the fishes when they cry? It will not be forgotten by some memory that we were contemporaries. Thou shalt ere long have thy way up the rivers, up all the rivers of the globe, if I am not mistaken. Yea, even thy dull watery dream shall be more than realized. If it were not so, but thou wert to be overlooked at first and at last, then would not I take their heaven. Yes, I say so, who think I know better than thou canst. Keep a stiff fin, then, and stem all the tides thou mayst meet.

I thrive best on solitude. If I have had a companion only one day in a week—unless it were one or two I could name—I find that the value of the week to me has been seriously affected. It dissipates my days, and often it takes me another week to get over it. As the Esquimaux of Smith's Strait in North Greenland laughed when Kane warned them of their utter extermination, cut off as they were by ice on all sides from their race, unless they attempted in season to cross the glacier southward, so do I laugh when you tell me of the danger of impoverishing myself by isolation. It is here that the walrus and the seal, and the white bear, and the eider ducks and auks on which I batten, most abound.

A man asked me the other night whether such and such persons were not as happy as anybody; being conscious, as I perceived, of much unhappiness himself and not aspiring to much more than an animal content. "Why!" said I, speaking to his condition, "the stones are happy, Concord River is happy, and I am happy too. When I took up a fragment of a Walnut shell this morning, I saw by its very grain and composition, its form and color, etc., that it was made for happiness. The most brutish and inanimate objects that are made suggest an everlasting and thorough satisfaction; they are the homes of content. Wood, earth, mold, etc., exist for joy. Do you think that Concord River would have continued to flow these million of years by Clamshell Hill and round Hunt's Island, if it had not been happy—if it had been miserable in its channel, tired of existence, and cursing its Maker and the hour that it sprang?"

The catechism says that the chief end of man is to glorify God and enjoy him forever, which of course is applicable mainly to God as seen in his works. Yet the only account of its beautiful insects—butterflies, etc.—which God has made and set before us which the State ever thinks of spending any money on is the account of those which are injurious to vegetation! This is the way we glorify God and enjoy him forever. Come out here and behold a thousand painted butterflies and other beautiful insects which people the air; then go to the libraries and see what kind of prayer and glorification of God is there recorded. Massachusetts has published her report on "Insects Injurious to Vegetation," and our neighbor, the "Noxious Insects of New York." We have attended to the evil and said nothing about the good. This is looking a gift horse in the mouth with a vengeance. Children are attracted by the beauty of butterflies, but their parents and legislators deem it an idle pursuit. The parents remind me of the devil, but the children, of God. Though God may have pronounced his work good, we ask, "Is it not poisonous?"

Here have been three ultra-reformers, lecturers on Slavery, Temperance, the Church, etc., in and about our house and Mrs. Brooks's the last three or four days—A. D. Foss, once a Baptist minister in Hopkinton, N. H.; Loring Moody, a sort of traveling pattern-working chaplain; and H. C. Wright, who shocks all the old women with his infidel writings. Though Foss was a stranger to the others, you would have thought them old and familiar cronies. (They happened here together by accident.) They addressed each other constantly by their Christian names, and rubbed you continually with the greasy cheeks of their kindness. They would not keep their distance, but cuddle up and lie spoon-fashion with you, no matter how hot the weather nor how narrow the bed—chiefly——. I was awfully pestered with his benignity; feared I should get greased all over with it past restoration; tried to keep some starch in my clothes. He wrote a book called *A Kiss for a Blow*, and he behaved as if there were no alternative between these, or as if I had given him a blow. I would have preferred the blow, but he was bent on giving me the kiss, when there was neither quarrel nor agreement between us. I wanted that he should straighten his back, smooth out those ogling wrinkles of benignity about his eyes, and, with a healthy reserve, pronounce something in a downright manner. It was difficult to keep clear of his slimy benignity, with which he sought to cover you before he swallowed you and took you fairly into his bowels. It would have been far worse than the fate of

Jonah. I do not wish to get any nearer to a man's bowels than usual. They lick you as a cow her calf. They would fain wrap you about with their bowels. ——addressed me as "Henry" within one minute from the time I first laid eyes on him, and when I spoke, he said with drawling, sultry sympathy, "Henry, I know all you would say; I understand you perfectly; you need not explain anything to me;" and to another, "I am going to dive into Henry's inmost depths." I said, "I trust you will not strike your head against the bottom." He could tell in a dark room, with his eyes blinded and in perfect stillness, if there was one there whom he loved. One of the most attractive things about the flowers is their beautiful reserve.

This afternoon, being on Fair Haven Hill, I heard the sound of a saw, and soon after from the Cliff saw two men sawing down a noble pine beneath, about forty rods off. I resolved to watch it till it fell, the last of a dozen or more which were left when the forest was cut and for fifteen years have waved in solitary majesty over the sprout-land. I saw them like beavers or insects gnawing at the trunk of this noble tree, the diminutive manikins with their cross-cut saw which could scarcely span it. It towered up a hundred feet, as I afterward found by measurement, one of the tallest, probably, in the township and straight as an arrow, but slanting a little toward the hillside, its top seen against the frozen river and the hills of Conantum. I watch closely to see when it begins to move. Now the sawers stop, and with an ax open it a little on the side toward which it leans, that it may break the faster. And now their saw goes again. Now surely it is going; it is inclined one-quarter of the quadrant, and breathless, I expect its crashing fall. But no, I was mistaken; it has not moved an inch; it stands at the same angle as at first. It is fifteen minutes yet to its fall. Still its branches wave in the wind, as if it were destined to stand for a century, and the wind soughs through its needles as of yore; it is still a forest tree, the most

majestic tree that waves over Musketaquid. The silvery sheen
of the sunlight is reflected from its needles; it still affords an
inaccessible crotch for the squirrel's nest; not a lichen has
forsaken its mast-like stem, its raking mast—the hill is the
hulk. Now, now's the moment! The manikins at its
base are fleeing from their crime. They have dropped the
guilty saw and ax. How slowly and majestically it starts! as
if it were only swayed by a summer breeze, and would return
without a sigh to its location in the air. And now it fans the hillside with its fall; and it lies down to its bed in the valley, from
which it is never to rise, as softly as a feather, folding its green
mantle about it like a warrior, as if, tired of standing, it embraced
the earth with silent joy, returning its elements to the dust
again.

I went down and measured it. It was about four feet in
diameter where it was sawed, about one hundred feet long. Before I had reached it the axmen had already half divested it of
its branches. Its gracefully spreading top was a perfect wreck on
the hillside, as if it had been made of glass; and the tender cones
of one year's growth upon its summit appealed in vain and too
late to the mercy of the chopper. Already he has measured it
with his axe, and marked off the mill-logs it will make. And the
space it occupied in upper air is vacant for the next two centuries. It is lumber. He has laid waste the air. When the fish
hawk in the spring revisits the banks of the Musketaquid, he will
circle in vain to find his accustomed perch, and the hen-hawk
will mourn for the pines lofty enough to protect her brood. A
plant which it has taken two centuries to perfect, rising by slow
stages into the heavens, has this afternoon ceased to exist. Its
sapling top had expanded to this January thaw as the fore-
runner of summers to come. Why does not the village bell sound
a knell? I hear no knell tolled. I see no procession of mourners
in the streets, or the woodland aisles. The squirrel has leaped to

another tree; the hawk has circled farther off, and has now settled upon a new eyrie; but the woodman is preparing [to] lay his axe at the root of that also.

Today it snows again, covering the ground. To get the value of the storm we must be out a long time and travel far in it, so that it may fairly penetrate our skin, and we be, as it were, turned inside-out to it, and there be no part in us but is wet or weather-beaten—so that we become storm men instead of fair-weather men. Some men speak of having been wetted to the skin once as a memorable event in their lives, which, notwithstanding the croakers, they survived.

The snow is finally turned to a drenching rain.

Found amid the sphagnum on the dry bank on the south side of the Turnpike, just below Everett's meadow, a rare and re-markable fungus, such as I have heard of but never seen before. The whole height six and three-quarters inches, two-thirds of it being buried in the sphagnum. It may be divided into three parts, pileus, stem, and base—or scrotum, for it is a perfect phallus. One of those fungi named *impudicus*, I think. In all respects a most disgusting object, yet very suggestive.

It was as offensive to the eye as to the scent, the cap rapidly melting and defiling what it touched with a fetid, olivaceous, semiliquid matter. In an hour or two the plant scented the whole house, wherever placed, so that it could not be endured. I was afraid to sleep in my chamber, where it had lain, until the room had been well ventilated. It smelled like a dead rat in the ceiling, in all the ceilings of the house. Pray, what was Nature thinking of when she made this? She almost puts herself on a level with those who draw in privies.

The thin snow now driving from the north and lodging on my coat consists of those beautiful star crystals, not cottony and chubby spokes, as on the 13th December, but thin and partly transparent crystals. How full of the creative genius is the air in which these are generated! I should hardly admire more if real stars fell and lodged on my coat. Nature is full of genius, full of the divinity; so that not a snowflake escapes its fashioning hand.

A divinity must have stirred within them before the crystals did thus shoot and set. Wheels of the storm-chariots. The same law that shapes the earth-star shapes the snow-star. As surely as the petals of a flower are fixed, each of these countless snow-stars comes whirling to earth, pronouncing thus, with emphasis, the number six, Order, *kóomos.*

On the Saskatchewan, when no man of science is there to behold, still down they come, and not the less fulfill their destiny, perchance melt at once on the Indian's face. What a world we live in! where myriads of these little disks, so beautiful to the most prying eye, are whirled down on every traveler's coat, the observant and the unobservant, and on the restless squirrel's fur, and on the far-stretching fields and forests, the wooded dells, and the mountaintops. Far far away from the haunts of man, they roll down some little slope, fall over and come to their bearings, and melt or lose their beauty in the mass, ready anon to swell some little rill with their contribution, and so at last, the universal ocean from which they came. There they lie, like the wreck of chariot wheels after a battle in the skies. Meanwhile the meadow mouse shoves them aside in his gallery, the school-boy casts them in his snowball, or the woodman's sled glides smoothly over them, these glorious spangles, the sweeping of heaven's floor. And they all sing, melting as they sing of the mysteries of the number six—six, six, six, He takes up the water of the sea in his hand, leaving the salt; He disperses it in mist through the skies; He re-collects and sprinkles it like grain in six-rayed snowy stars over the earth, there to lie till He dissolves its bonds again.

Very little evidence of God or men did I see just then, and life not as rich and inviting an enterprise as it should be, when my attention was caught by a snowflake on my coat sleeve. It was one of those perfect, crystalline, star-shaped ones, six-rayed, like a flat wheel with six spokes, only the spokes were perfect little pine trees in shape, arranged around a central spangle. This little object, which, with many of its fellows, rested unmelting on my coat, so perfect and beautiful, reminded me that Nature had not lost her pristine vigor yet, and why should man lose heart? . . . I may say that the Maker of the world exhausts his skill with each snowflake and dewdrop that he sends down. We think that the one mechanically coheres, and that the other simply flows together and falls, but in truth they are the produce of *enthusiasm*, the children of an ecstasy, finished with the artist's utmost skill.

In the fall the loon (*Colymbus glacialis*) came, as usual, to moult and bathe in the pond, making the woods ring with his wild laughter before I had risen. At rumor of his arrival all the Mill-dam sportsmen are on the alert, in gigs and on foot, two-by-two and three-by-three, with patent rifles and conical balls and spyglasses. They come rustling through the woods like autumn leaves, at least ten men to one loon. Some station themselves on this side of the pond, some on that, for the poor bird cannot be omnipresent; if he dive here he must come up there. But now the kind October wind rises, rustling the leaves and rippling the surface of the water, so that no loon can be heard or seen, though his foes sweep the pond with spyglasses, and make the woods resound with their discharges. The waves generously rise and dash angrily, taking sides with all waterfowl, and our sportsmen must beat a retreat to town and shop and unfinished jobs. But they were too often successful. When I went to get a pail of water early in the morning I frequently saw this stately bird sailing out of my cove within a few rods. If I endeavored to overtake him in a boat, in order to see how he would maneuver, he would dive and be completely lost, so that I did not discover him again, sometimes, till the latter part of the day. But I was more than a match for him on the surface. He commonly went off in a rain.

As I was paddling along the north shore one very calm October afternoon—for such days especially they settle on to the lakes, like the milkweed down—having looked in vain over the pond for a loon, suddenly one sailing out from the shore toward the middle a few rods in front of me set up his wild laugh and betrayed himself. I pursued with a paddle and he dived, but when he came up I was nearer than before. He dived again, but I miscalculated the direction he would take, and we were fifty rods apart when he came to the surface this time, for I had helped to widen the interval; and again he laughed long and loud, and with more reason than before. He maneuvered so cunningly that I could not get within half-a-dozen rods of him. Each time, when he came to the surface, turning his head this way and that, he coolly surveyed the water and the land, and apparently chose his course so that he might come up where there was the widest expanse of water and at the greatest distance from the boat. It was surprising how quickly he made up his mind and put his resolve into execution. He led me at once to the widest part of the pond, and could not be driven from it. While he was thinking one thing in his brain, I was endeavoring to divine his thought in mine. It was a pretty game, played on the smooth surface of the pond, a man against a loon. Suddenly your adversary's checker disappears beneath the board, and the problem is to place yours nearest to where his will appear again. Sometimes he would come up unexpectedly on the opposite side of me, having apparently passed directly under the boat. So long-winded was he and so unweariable, that when he had swum farthest he would immediately plunge again, nevertheless; and then no wit could divine where in the deep pond, beneath the smooth surface, he might be speeding his way like a fish, for he had time and ability to visit the bottom of the pond in its deepest part. It is said that loons have been caught in the New

York lakes eighty feet beneath the surface, with hooks set for trout—though Walden is deeper than that. How surprised must the fishes be to see this ungainly visitor from another sphere speeding his way amid their schools! Yet he appeared to know his course as surely under water as on the surface, and swam much faster there. Once or twice I saw a ripple where he approached the surface, just put his head out to reconnoiter, and instantly dived again. I found that it was as well for me to rest on my oars and wait his reappearing, as to endeavor to calculate where he would rise; for again and again, when I was straining my eyes over the surface one way, I would suddenly be startled by his unearthly laugh behind me. But why, after displaying so much cunning, did he invariably betray himself the moment he came up, by that loud laugh? Did not his white breast enough betray him? He was indeed a silly loon, I thought. I could commonly hear the plash of the water when he came up, and so also detect him. But after an hour he seemed as fresh as ever, dived as willingly, and swam yet farther than at first. It was surprising to see how serenely he sailed off with unruffled breast when he came to the surface, doing all the work with his webbed feet beneath. His usual note was this demoniac laughter, yet somewhat like that of a waterfowl; but occasionally, when he had balked me most successfully and come up a long way off, he uttered a long-drawn unearthly howl, probably more like that of a wolf than any bird; as when a beast puts his muzzle to the ground and deliberately howls. This was his looning,—perhaps the wildest sound that is ever heard here, making the woods ring far and wide. I concluded that he laughed in derision of my efforts, confident of his own resources. Though the sky was by this time overcast, the pond was so smooth that I could see where he broke the surface when I did not hear him. His white breast, the stillness of the air, and the smoothness of the water were all against him. At length, having come up fifty rods off, he uttered one of those prolonged howls, as if calling on the god of loons to aid him, and immediately there came a wind from the east and rippled the surface, and filled the whole air with misty rain; and I was impressed as if it were the prayer of the loon answered, and his god was angry with me; and so I left him disappearing far away on the tumultuous surface.

As I turned round the corner of Hubbard's Grove, saw a woodchuck, the first of the season, in the middle of the field, six or seven rods from the fence which bounds the wood, and twenty rods distant. I ran along the fence and cut him off, or rather overtook him, though he started at the same time. When I was only a rod and a half off, he stopped, and I did the same; then he ran again, and I ran up within three feet of him, when he stopped again, the fence being between us. I squatted down and surveyed him at my leisure. His eyes were dull black and rather inobvious, with a faint chestnut (?) iris, with but little expression and that more of resignation than of anger. The general aspect was a coarse grayish brown, a sort of grisel (?). A lighter brown next the skin, then black or very dark brown and tipped with whitish rather loosely. The head between a squirrel and a bear, flat on the top and dark brown, and darker still or black on the tip of the nose. The whiskers black, two inches long. The ears very small and roundish, set far back and nearly buried in the fur. Black feet, with long and slender claws for digging. It appeared to tremble, or perchance shivered with cold. When I moved, it gritted its teeth quite loud, sometimes striking the under jaw against the other chatteringly, sometimes grinding one jaw on the other, yet as if more from instinct than anger. Whichever way I turned, that way it headed. I took a twig a foot long and touched its snout, at which it started forward and bit the stick, lessening the distance between us to two feet, and still it held all the ground it gained. I played with it tenderly awhile with the stick, trying to open its gritting jaws. Even its long incisors, two above and two below, were presented. But I thought it would go to sleep if I stayed long enough. It did not sit upright as sometimes, but *standing* on its forefeet with its

head down, i.e. half-sitting, half-standing. We sat looking at one
another about half an hour, till we began to feel mesmeric influences. When I was tired, I moved away, wishing to see him
run, but I could not start him. He would not stir as long as I was
looking at him or could see him. I walked round him; he turned
as fast and fronted me still. I sat down by his side within a foot.
I talked to him quasi forest lingo, baby talk, at any rate in a
conciliatory tone, and thought that I had some influence on
him. He gritted his teeth less. I chewed checkerberry leaves and
presented them to his nose at last without a grit; though I saw
that by so much gritting of the teeth he had worn them rapidly
and they were covered with a fine white powder, which, if you
measured it thus, would have made his anger terrible. He did
not mind any noise I might make. With a little stick I lifted one
of his paws to examine it, and held it up at pleasure. I turned
him over to see what color he was beneath (darker or more
purely brown), though he turned himself back again sooner than
I could have wished. His tail was also all brown, though not very
dark, rattail-like, with loose hairs standing out on all sides like
a caterpillar brush. He had a rather mild look. I spoke kindly to
him. I reached checkerberry leaves to his mouth. I stretched my
hands over him, though he turned up his head and still gritted a
little. I laid my hand on him, but immediately took it off again,
instinct not being wholly overcome. If I had had a few fresh
bean leaves, thus in advance of the season, I am sure I should
have tamed him completely. It was a frizzly tail. His is a humble,
terrestrial color like the partridge's, well concealed where dead
wiry grass rises above darker brown or chestnut dead leaves—a
modest color. If I had had some food, I should have ended with
stroking him at my leisure. Could easily have wrapped him in my
handkerchief. He was not fat nor particularly lean. I finally
had to leave him without seeing him move from the place. A
large, clumsy, burrowing squirrel. *Arctomys,* bear-mouse. I respect him as one of the natives. He lies there, by his color and
habits so naturalized amid the dry leaves, the withered grass,

and the bushes. A sound nap, too, he has enjoyed in his native fields, the past winter. I think I might learn some wisdom of him. His ancestors have lived here longer than mine. He is more thoroughly acclimated and naturalized than I. Bean leaves the red man raised for him, but he can do without them.

There is a period in the history of the individual, as of the race, when the hunters are the "best men," as the Algonquins called them. We cannot but pity the boy who has never fired a gun; he is no more humane, while his education has been sadly neglected. This was my answer with respect to those youths who were bent on this pursuit, trusting that they would soon outgrow it. No humane being, past the thoughtless age of boyhood, will wantonly murder any creature which holds its life by the same tenure that he does. The hare in its extremity cries like a child. I warn you, mothers, that my sympathies do not always make the usual phil-*anthropic* distinctions.

Such is oftenest the young man's introduction to the forest, and the most original part of himself. He goes thither at first as a hunter and fisher, until at last, if he has the seeds of a better life in him, he distinguishes his proper objects—as a poet or naturalist it may be—and leaves the gun and fish pole behind. The mass of men are still and always young in this respect. In some countries a hunting parson is no uncommon sight. Such a one might make a good shepherd's dog, but is far from being the Good Shepherd. I have been surprised to consider that the only obvious employment, except wood chopping, ice cutting, or the like business, which ever to my knowledge detained at Walden Pond for a whole half-day any of my fellow citizens, whether fathers or children of the town, with just one exception, was fishing. Commonly they did not think that they were lucky, or well paid for their time, unless they got a long string of fish, though they had the opportunity of seeing the pond all the while. They might go there a thousand times before the sediment of fishing would sink to the bottom and leave their purpose pure;

but no doubt such a clarifying process would be going on all the while. The Governor and his Council faintly remember the pond, for they went a-fishing there when they were boys; but now they are too old and dignified to go a-fishing, and so they know it no more forever. Yet even they expect to go to heaven at last. If the legislature regards it, it is chiefly to regulate the number of hooks to be used there; but they know nothing about the hook of hooks with which to angle for the pond itself, impaling the legislature for a bait. Thus, even in civilized communities, the embryo man passes through the hunter stage of development.

Who should come to my lodge this morning but a true Homeric or Paphlagonian man—he had so suitable and poetic a name that I am sorry I cannot print it here—a Canadian, a wood chopper and post maker, who can hole fifty posts in a day, who made his last supper on a woodchuck which his dog caught. He, too, has heard of Homer, and "if it were not for books," would "not know what to do rainy days," though perhaps he has not read one wholly through for many rainy seasons. A more simple and natural man it would be hard to find. Vice and disease, which cast such a somber moral hue over the world, seemed to have hardly any existence for him. He was about twenty-eight years old, and had left Canada and his father's house a dozen years before to work in the States, and earn money to buy a farm with at last, perhaps in his native country. He was cast in the coarsest mold; a stout but sluggish body, yet gracefully carried, with a thick sunburned neck, dark bushy hair, and dull, sleepy blue eyes, which were occasionally lit up with expression. He wore a flat gray cloth cap, a dingy wool-colored greatcoat, and cowhide boots. He was a great consumer of meat, usually carrying his dinner to his work a couple of miles past my house—for he chopped all summer—in a tin pail; cold meats, often cold woodchucks, and coffee in a stone bottle which dangled by a string from his belt; and sometimes he offered me a drink. He came along early, crossing my bean field, though without anxiety or haste to get to his work, such as Yankees exhibit. He wasn't a-going to hurt himself. He didn't care if he only earned his board. Frequently he would leave his dinner in the bushes, when his dog had caught a woodchuck by the way, and go back a mile and a half to dress it and leave it in the cellar of the house where he boarded, after deliberating first for half an hour whether he could not sink it in the pond safely till nightfall—loving to dwell long upon these themes. He would say, as he went by in the morning, "How thick the pigeons are! If working every day were not my trade, I could get all the meat I should want by hunting—pigeons, woodchucks, rabbits, partridges—by gosh! I could get all I should want for a week in one day."

He was a skillful chopper, and indulged in some flourishes and ornaments in his art. He cut his trees level and close to the ground, that the sprouts which came up afterward might be more vigorous, and a sled might slide over the stumps; and instead of leaving a whole tree to support his corded wood, he would pare it away to a slender stake or splinter which you could break off with your hand at last.

He interested me because he was so quiet and solitary and so happy withal; a well of good humor and contentment which overflowed at his eyes. His mirth was without alloy. Sometimes I saw him at his work in the woods, felling trees, and he would greet me with a laugh of inexpressible satisfaction, and a salutation in Canadian French, though he spoke English as well. When I approached him he would suspend his work, and with half-suppressed mirth lie along the trunk of a pine which he had felled, and peeling off the inner bark, roll it up into a ball and chew it while he laughed and talked. Such an exuberance of animal spirits had he that he sometimes tumbled down and rolled on the ground with laughter at anything which made him think and tickled him. Looking round upon the trees he would exclaim, "By George! I can enjoy myself well enough here chopping; I want no better sport." Sometimes, when at leisure, he amused himself all day in the woods with a pocket pistol, firing salutes to himself at regular intervals as he walked. In the winter he had a fire by which at noon he warmed his coffee in a kettle; and as he sat on a log to eat his dinner the chickadees would sometimes come round and alight on his arm and peck at the potato in his fingers; and he said that he "liked to have the little *fellers* about him."

In him the animal man chiefly was developed. In physical endurance and contentment he was cousin to the pine and the rock. I asked him once if he was not sometimes tired at night, after working all day; and he answered, with a sincere and serious look, "Gorrappit, I never was tired in my life." But the intellectual and what is called spiritual man in him were slumbering as in an infant. He had been instructed only in that innocent and ineffectual way in which the Catholic priests teach the aborigines, by which the pupil is never educated to the degree of consciousness, but only to the degree of trust and reverence; and a child is not made a man, but kept a child. When Nature made him, she gave him a strong body and contentment for his portion, and propped him on every side with reverence and reliance, that he might live out his threescore years and ten a child. He was so genuine and unsophisticated that no introduction would serve to introduce him, more than if you introduced a woodchuck to your neighbor. He had got to find him out as you did. He would not play any part. Men paid him wages for work, and so helped to feed and clothe him; but he never exchanged opinions with them. He was so simply and naturally humble—if he can be called humble who never aspires —that humility was no distinct quality in him, nor could he conceive of it. Wiser men were demigods to him. If you told him that such a one was coming, he did as if he thought that anything so grand would expect nothing of himself, but take all the responsibility on itself, and let him be forgotten still. He never heard the sound of praise. He particularly reverenced the writer and the preacher. Their performances were miracles. When I told

him that I wrote considerably, he thought for a long time that
it was merely the handwriting which I meant, for he could
write a remarkably good hand himself. I sometimes found the
name of his native parish handsomely written in the snow by
the highway, with the proper French accent, and knew that he
had passed. I asked him if he ever wished to write his thoughts.
He said that he had read and written letters for those who could
not, but he never tried to write thoughts—no, he could not, he
could not tell what to put first, it would kill him, and then there
was spelling to be attended to at the same time!

I never in all my walks came across a man engaged in so
simple and natural an occupation as building his house. We belong to the community. It is not the tailor alone who is the ninth
part of a man; it is as much the preacher, and the merchant,
and the farmer. Where is this division of labor to end? and what
object does it finally serve? No doubt another *may* also think of
me; but it is not therefore desirable that he should do so to the
exclusion of my thinking for myself.

A wise man is as unconscious of the movements in the body
politic as he is of the process of digestion and the circulation of
the blood in the natural body. These processes are *infra*-human.
I sometimes awake to a half-consciousness of these things going
on about me—as politics, society, business, etc., etc.—as a man
may become conscious of some of the processes of digestion, in
a morbid state, and so have the dyspepsia, as it is called. It appears to me that those things which most engage the attention
of men, as politics, for instance, are vital functions of human
society, it is true, but should [be] unconsciously performed,
like the vital functions of the natural body. It is as if a thinker
submitted himself to be rasped by the great gizzard of creation.
Politics is, as it were, the gizzard of society, full of grit and
gravel, and the two political parties are its two opposite halves,
which grind on each other. Not only individuals but states have
thus a confirmed dyspepsia, which expresses itself, you can

imagine by what sort of eloquence. Our life is not altogether a forgetting, but also, alas, to a great extent a remembering, of that which perchance we should never have been conscious of—the consciousness of what should not be permitted to disturb a man's waking hours. As for society, why should we not meet, not always as dyspeptics, but sometimes as eupeptics?

No true and absolute account of things—of the evening and the morning and all the phenomena between them—but ever a petty reference to man, to society, aye, often to Christianity. What these things are when men are asleep. I come from the funeral of mankind to attend to a natural phenomenon. The so much grander significance of any fact—of sun and moon and stars—when not referred to man and his needs but viewed absolutely! Sounds that are wafted from over the confines of time.

To such a pass our civilization and division of labor has come that A, a professional huckleberry picker, has hired B's field and, we will suppose, is now gathering the crop, perhaps with the aid of a patented machine; C, a professed cook, is superintending the cooking of a pudding made of some of the berries; while Professor D, for whom the pudding is intended, sits in his library writing a book—a work on the *Vocciniaceae*, of course. And now the result of this downward course will be seen in that book, which should be the ultimate fruit of the huckleberry field and account for the existence of the two professors who come between D and A. It will be worthless. There will be none of the spirit of the huckleberry in it. The reading of it will be a weariness to the flesh. To use a homely illustration, this is to save at the spile but waste at the bung. I believe in a different kind of division of labor, and that Professor D should divide himself between the library and the huckleberry field.

I left the woods for as good a reason as I went there. Perhaps it seemed to me that I had several more lives to live, and could not spare any more time for that one. It is remarkable how easily and insensibly we fall into a particular route, and make a beaten track for ourselves. I had not lived there a week before my feet wore a path from my door to the pond-side; and though it is five or six years since I trod it, it is still quite distinct. It is true, I fear, that others may have fallen into it, and so helped to keep it open. The surface of the earth is soft and impressible by the feet of men; and so with the paths which the mind travels. How worn and dusty, then, must be the highways of the world, how deep the ruts of tradition and conformity! I did not wish to take a cabin passage, but rather to go before the mast and on the deck of the world, for there I could best see the moonlight amid the mountains. I do not wish to go below now.

I know of no more startling development of the morality of trade and all the modes of getting a living, than the rush to California affords. Of what significance the philosophy, or poetry, or religion of a world that will rush to the lottery of California gold-digging on the receipt of the first news; to live by luck; to get the means of commanding the labor of others less lucky, i.e. of slaveholding, without contributing any value to society? And that is called enterprise, and the devil is only a little more enterprising! The philosophy and poetry and religion of such a mankind are not worth the dust of a puffball. The hog that *roots* his own living, and so makes manure, would be ashamed of such company. If I could command the wealth of all the worlds by lifting my finger, I would not pay such a price for it. It makes God to be a moneyed gentleman who scatters a handful of pennies in order to see mankind scramble for them. Going to California. It is only three thousand miles nearer to hell. I will resign my life sooner than live by luck. The world's raffle. A subsistence in the domains of nature a thing to be raffled for! No wonder that they gamble there. I never heard that they did anything else there. What a comment, what a satire, on our institutions! The conclusion will be that mankind will hang itself upon a tree. And who would interfere to cut it down. And have all the precepts in all the bibles taught men only this?

My First Summer in the Sierra

—JOHN MUIR

THROUGH THE FOOTHILLS WITH A FLOCK OF SHEEP

In the great Central Valley of California there are only two seasons—spring and summer. The spring begins with the first rainstorm, which usually falls in November. In a few months the wonderful flowery vegetation is in full bloom, and by the end of May it is dead and dry and crisp, as if every plant had been roasted in an oven.

Then the lolling, panting flocks and herds are driven to the high, cool, green pastures of the Sierra. I was longing for the mountains about this time, but money was scarce and I couldn't see how a bread supply was to be kept up. While I was anxiously brooding on the bread problem, so troublesome to wanderers, and trying to believe that I might learn to live like the wild animals, gleaning nourishment here and there from seeds, berries, etc., sauntering and climbing in joyful independence of money or baggage, Mr. Delaney, a sheep owner for whom I had worked a few weeks, called on me and offered to engage me to go with his shepherd and flock to the headwaters of the Merced and Tuolumne Rivers—the very region I had most in mind. I was in the mood to accept work of any kind that would take me into the mountains whose treasures I had tasted last summer in the Yosemite region. The flock, he explained, would be moved gradually higher through the successive forest belts as the snow melted, stopping for a few weeks at the best places we came to. These I thought would be good centers of observation from which I might be able to make many telling excursions within a radius of eight or ten miles of the camps to learn something of the plants, animals, and rocks; for he assured me that I should be left perfectly free to follow my studies. I judged, however, that I was in no way the right man for the place, and freely explained my shortcomings, confessing that I was wholly unacquainted with the topography of the upper mountains, the streams that would have to be crossed, and the wild sheep-eating animals, etc.; in short that, what with bears, coyotes, rivers, canyons, and thorny, bewildering chaparral. I feared that half or more of his flock would be lost. Fortunately these shortcomings seemed insignificant to Mr. Delaney. The main thing, he said, was to have a man about the camp whom he could trust to see that the shepherd did his duty; and he assured me that the difficulties that seemed so formidable at a distance would vanish as we went on, encouraging me further by saying that the shepherd would do all the herding; that I could study plants and rocks and scenery as much as I liked; and that he would himself accompany us to the first main camp and make occasional visits to our higher ones to replenish our store of provisions and see how we prospered. Therefore I concluded to go, though still fearing, when I saw the silly sheep bouncing one by one through the narrow gate of the home corral to be counted, that of the two thousand and fifty many would never return.

I was fortunate in getting a fine St. Bernard dog for a companion. His master, a hunter with whom I was slightly acquainted, came to me as soon as he heard that I was going to spend the summer in the Sierra and begged me to take his favorite dog, Carlo, with me, for he feared that if he were compelled to stay all summer on the plains the fierce heat might be the death of him. "I think I can trust you to be kind to him," he said, "and I am sure he will be good to you. He knows all about the mountain animals, will guard the camp, assist in managing the sheep, and in every way be found able and faithful." Carlo knew we were talking about him, watched our faces, and listened so attentively that I fancied he understood us. Calling him by name, I asked him if he was willing to go with me. He looked me in the face with eyes expressing wonderful intelligence, then turned to his master, and after permission was given by a wave of the hand toward me and a farewell patting caress, he quietly followed me as if he perfectly understood all that had been said and had known me always.

June 3, 1869. This morning provisions, camp-kettles, blankets, plant-press, etc., were packed on two horses, the flock headed for the tawny foothills, and away we sauntered in a cloud of dust; Mr. Delaney, bony and tall, with sharply hacked profile like Don Quixote, leading the pack-horses; Billy, the proud shepherd, a Chinaman and a Digger Indian to assist in driving for the first few days in the brushy foothills; and myself with notebook tied to my belt.

IN CAMP ON THE NORTH FORK OF THE MERCED

June 8. The sheep, now grassy and good-natured, slowly nibbled their way down into the valley of the North Fork of the Merced at the foot of Pilot Peak Ridge to the place selected by the Don for our first central camp, a picturesque hopper-shaped hollow formed by converging hill slopes at a bend of the river. Here racks for dishes and provisions were made in the shade of the riverbank trees, and beds of fern fronds, cedar plumes, and various flowers, each to the taste of its owner, and a corral back on the open flat for the wool.

June 9. How deep our sleep last night in the mountain's heart, beneath the trees and stars, hushed by solemn-sounding waterfalls and many small soothing voices in sweet accord whispering peace! And our first pure mountain day, warm, calm, cloudless —how immeasurable it seems, how serenely wild! I can scarcely remember its beginning. Along the river, over the hills, in the ground, in the sky, spring work is going on with joyful enthusiasm, new life, new beauty, unfolding, unrolling in glorious exuberant extravagance—new birds in their nests, new winged creatures in the air, and new leaves, new flowers, spreading, shining, rejoicing everywhere.

June 19. Pure sunshine all day. How beautiful a rock is made by leaf shadows! Those of the live oak are particularly clear and distinct, and beyond all art in grace and delicacy, now still as if painted on stone, now gliding softly as if afraid of noise, now dancing, waltzing in swift, merry swirls, or jumping on and off sunny rocks in quick dashes like wave embroidery on seashore cliffs. How true and substantial is this shadow beauty, and with what sublime extravagance is beauty thus multiplied! The big orange lilies are now arrayed in all their glory of leaf and flower. Noble plants, in perfect health, Nature's darlings.

June 20. Some of the silly sheep got caught fast in a tangle of chaparral this morning, like flies in a spider's web, and had to be helped out. Carlo found them and tried to drive them from the trap by the easiest way. How far above sheep are intelligent dogs! No friend and helper can be more affectionate and constant than Carlo. The noble St. Bernard is an honor to his race.

The air is distinctly fragrant with balsam and resin and mint —every breath of it a gift we may well thank God for. Who could ever guess that so rough a wilderness should yet be so fine, so full of good things. One seems to be in a majestic domed pavilion in which a grand play is being acted with scenery and music and incense—all the furniture and action so interesting we are in no danger of being called on to endure one dull moment. God himself seems to be always doing his best here, working like a man in a glow of enthusiasm.

June 23. Oh, these vast, calm, measureless mountain days, inciting at once to work and rest! Days in whose light everything seems equally divine, opening a thousand windows to show us God. Nevermore, however weary, should one faint by the way who gains the blessings of one mountain day; whatever his fate, long life, short life, stormy or calm, he is rich forever.

July 8. Now away we go toward the topmost mountains. Many still, small voices, as well as the noon thunder, are calling, "Come higher." Farewell, blessed dell, woods, gardens, streams, birds, squirrels, lizards, and a thousand others. Farewell. Farewell.

THE YOSEMITE

July 15. Followed the Mono Trail up the eastern rim of the basin nearly to its summit, then turned off southward to a small shallow valley that extends to the edge of the Yosemite, which we reached about noon, and encamped. After luncheon I made haste to high ground, and from the top of the ridge on the west side of Indian Canyon gained the noblest view of the summit peaks I have ever yet enjoyed. Nearly all the upper basin of the Merced was displayed, with its sublime domes and canyons, dark up-sweeping forests, and glorious array of white peaks deep in the sky, every feature glowing, radiating beauty that pours into our flesh and bones like heat rays from fire. Sunshine over all; no breath of wind to stir the brooding calm. Never before had I seen so glorious a landscape, so boundless an affluence of sublime mountain beauty. The most extravagant description I might give of this view to anyone who has not seen similar landscapes with his own eyes would not so much as hint its grandeur and the spiritual glow that covered it. I shouted and gesticulated in a wild burst of ecstasy, much to the astonishment of St. Bernard Carlo, who came running up to me, manifesting in his intelligent eyes a puzzled concern that was very ludicrous, which had the effect of bringing me to my senses. A brown bear, too, it would seem, had been a spectator of the show I had made of myself, for I had gone but a few yards when I started one from a thicket of brush. He evidently considered me dangerous, for he ran away very fast, tumbling over the tops of the tangled manzanita bushes in his haste. Carlo drew back, with his ears depressed as if afraid, and kept looking me in the face, as if expecting me to pursue and shoot, for he had seen many a bear battle in his day.

Following the ridge, which made a gradual descent to the south, I came at length to the brow of that massive cliff that stands between Indian Canyon and Yosemite Falls, and here the far-famed valley came suddenly into view throughout almost its whole extent. The noble walls—sculptured into endless variety of domes and gables, spires and battlements and plain mural precipices—all atremble with the thunder tones of the falling water. The level bottom seemed to be dressed like a garden— sunny meadows here and there, and groves of pine and oak; the river of Mercy sweeping in majesty through the midst of them and flashing back the sunbeams. The great Tissiack, or Half-Dome, rising at the upper end of the valley to a height of nearly a mile, is nobly proportioned and lifelike, the most impressive of all the rocks, holding the eye in devout admiration, calling it back again and again from falls or meadows, or even the mountains beyond—marvelous cliffs, marvelous in sheer dizzy depth and sculpture, types of endurance. Thousands of years have they stood in the sky exposed to rain, snow, frost, earthquake and avalanche, yet they still wear the bloom of youth.

July 19. Watching the daybreak and sunrise. The pale rose and purple sky changing softly to daffodil yellow and white, sunbeams pouring through the passes between the peaks and over the Yosemite domes, making their edges burn; the silver firs in the middle ground catching the glow on their spiry tops, and our camp grove fills and thrills with the glorious light. Everything awakening alert and joyful; the birds begin to stir and innumerable insect people. Deer quietly withdraw into leafy hiding-places in the chaparral; the dew vanishes, flowers spread their petals, every pulse beats high, every life cell rejoices, the very rocks seem to thrill with life. The whole landscape glows like a human face in a glory of enthusiasm, and the blue sky, pale around the horizon, bends peacefully down over all like one vast flower.

About noon, as usual, big bossy cumuli began to grow above the forest, and the rainstorm pouring from them is the most imposing I have yet seen. The silvery zigzag lightning lances are longer than usual, and the thunder gloriously impressive, keen, crashing, intensely concentrated, speaking with such tremendous energy it would seem that an entire mountain is being shattered at every stroke, but probably only a few trees are being shattered, many of which I have seen on my walks hereabouts strewing the ground. At last the clear ringing strokes are succeeded by deep low tones that grow gradually fainter as they roll afar into the recesses of the echoing mountains, where they seem to be welcomed home. Then another and another peal, or rather crashing, splintering stroke, follows in quick succession, perchance splitting some giant pine or fir from top to bottom into long rails and slivers, and scattering them to all points of the compass. Now comes the rain, with corresponding extravagant grandeur, covering the ground high and low with a sheet of flowing water, a transparent film fitted like a skin upon the rugged anatomy of the landscape, making the rocks glitter and glow, gathering in the ravines, flooding the streams, and making them shout and boom in reply to the thunder.

How interesting to trace the history of a single raindrop! It is not long, geologically speaking, as we have seen, since the first raindrops fell on the newborn leafless Sierra landscapes. How different the lot of these falling now! Happy the showers that fall on so fair a wilderness—scarce a single drop can fail to find a beautiful spot—on the tops of the peaks, on the shining glacier pavements, on the great smooth domes, on forests and gardens and brushy moraines, plashing, glinting, pattering, laving. Some go to the high snowy fountains to swell their well-saved stores; some into the lakes, washing the mountain windows, patting their smooth glassy levels, making dimples and bubbles and spray; some into the waterfalls and cascades, as if eager to join in their dance and song and beat their foam yet finer; good luck and good work for the happy mountain raindrops, each one of them a high waterfall in itself, descending from the cliffs and hollows of the clouds to the cliffs and hollows of the rocks, out of the sky-thunder into the thunder of the falling rivers. Some, falling on meadows and bogs, creep silently out of sight to the grass roots, hiding softly as in a nest, slipping, oozing hither, thither, seeking and finding their appointed work. Some, descending through the spires of the woods, sift spray through the shining needles, whispering peace and good cheer to each one of them. Some drops with happy aim glint on the sides of crystals— quartz, hornblende, garnet, zircon, tourmaline, feldspar—patter on grains of gold and heavy way-worn nuggets; some, with blunt plap-plap and low bass drumming, fall on the broad leaves of Veratrum, Saxifrage, Cypripedium. Some happy drops fall straight into the cups of flowers, kissing the lips of lilies. How far they have to go, how many cups to fill, great and small, cells too small to be seen, cups holding half a drop as well as lake basins between the hills, each replenished with equal care; every drop in all the blessed throng a silvery newborn star with lake and river, garden and grove, valley and mountain, all that the landscape holds reflected in its crystal depths, God's messenger, angel of love sent on its way with majesty and pomp and display of power that makes man's greatest shows ridiculous.

Now the storm is over, the sky is clear, the last rolling thunder-wave is spent on the peaks, and where are the raindrops now—what has become of all the shining throng? In winged vapor rising some are already hastening back to the sky, some have gone into the plants, creeping through invisible doors into the round rooms of cells, some are locked in crystals of ice, some in rock crystals, some in porous moraines to keep their small springs flowing, some have gone journeying on in the rivers to join the larger raindrop of the ocean. From form to form, beauty to beauty, ever changing, never resting, all are speeding on with love's enthusiasm, singing with the stars the eternal song of creation.

July 20. Fine calm morning; air tense and clear; not the slightest breeze astir; everything shining, the rocks with wet crystals, the plants with dew, each receiving its portion of irised dewdrops and sunshine like living creatures getting their breakfast, their dew manna coming down from the starry sky like swarms of smaller stars. How wondrous fine are the particles in showers of dew, thousands required for a single drop, growing in the dark as silently as the grass! What pains are taken to keep this wilderness in health—showers of snow, showers of rain, showers of dew, floods of light, floods of invisible vapor, clouds, winds, all sorts of weather, interaction of plant on plant, animal on animal, etc., beyond thought! How fine Nature's methods! How deeply with beauty is beauty overlaid! the ground covered with crystals, the crystals with mosses and lichens and low-spreading grasses and flowers, these with larger plant leaf over leaf with ever-changing color and form, the broad palms of the first outspread over these, the azure dome over all like a bell-flower, and star above star.

Yonder stands the South Dome, its crown high above our camp, though its base is four thousand feet below us; a most noble rock, it seems full of thought, clothed with living light, no sense of dead stone about it, all spiritualized, neither heavy-looking nor light, steadfast in serene strength like a god.

Our shepherd is a queer character and hard to place in this wilderness. His bed is a hollow made in red dry-rot punky dust beside a log which forms a portion of the south wall of the corral. Here he lies with his wonderful everlasting clothing on, wrapped in a red blanket, breathing not only the dust of the decayed wood but also that of the corral, as if determined to take ammoniacal snuff all night after chewing tobacco all day. Following the sheep he carries a heavy six-shooter swung from his belt on one side, and his luncheon on the other. The ancient cloth in which the meat, fresh from the frying pan, is tied, serves as a filter through which the clear fat and gravy juices drop down on his right hip and leg in clustering stalactites. This oleaginous formation is soon broken up, however, and diffused and rubbed evenly into his scanty apparel, by sitting down, rolling over, crossing his legs while resting on logs, etc., making shirt and trousers watertight and shiny. His trousers, in particular, have become so adhesive with the mixed fat and resin that pine needles, thin flakes and fibers of bark, hair, mica scales and minute grains of quartz, hornblende, etc., feathers, seed wings, moth and butterfly wings, legs and antennae of innumerable insects, or even whole insects such as the small beetles, moths and mosquitoes, with flower petals, pollen dust and indeed bits of all plants, animals, and minerals of the region adhere to them and are safely imbedded, so that though far from being a naturalist he collects fragmentary specimens of everything and becomes richer than he knows. His specimens are kept passably fresh, too, by the purity of the air and the resiny bituminous beds into which they are pressed. Man is a microcosm, at least our shepherd is, or rather his trousers. These precious overalls are never taken off, and nobody knows how old they are, though one may guess by their thickness and concentric structure. Instead of wearing thin they wear thick, and in their stratification have no small geological significance.

Besides herding the sheep, Billy is the butcher, while I have agreed to wash the few iron and tin utensils and make the bread. Then, these small duties done, by the time the sun is fairly above the mountaintops I am beyond the flock, free to rove and revel in the wilderness all the big immortal days.

Sketching on the North Dome. It commands views of nearly all the valley besides a few of the high mountains. I would fain draw everything in sight—rock, tree, and leaf. But little can I do beyond mere outlines—marks with meanings like words, readable only to myself—yet I sharpen my pencils and work on as if others might possibly be benefited. Whether these picture-sheets are to vanish like fallen leaves or go to friends like letters, matters not much; for little can they tell to those who have not themselves seen similar wildness, and like a language have learned it. No pain here, no dull empty hours, no fear of the past, no fear of the future. These blessed mountains are so compactly filled with God's beauty, no petty personal hope or experience has room to be. Drinking this champagne water is pure pleasure, so is breathing the living air, and every movement of limbs is pleasure, while the whole body seems to feel beauty when exposed to it as it feels the campfire or sunshine, entering not by the eyes alone, but equally through all one's flesh like radiant heat, making a passionate ecstatic pleasure-glow not explainable. One's body then seems homogeneous throughout, sound as a crystal.

Perched like a fly on this Yosemite dome, I gaze and sketch and bask, oftentimes settling down into dumb admiration without definite hope of ever learning much, yet with the longing, unresting effort that lies at the door of hope, humbly prostrate before the vast display of God's power, and eager to offer self-denial and renunciation with eternal toil to learn any lesson in the divine manuscript.

It is easier to feel than to realize, or in any way explain, Yosemite grandeur. The magnitudes of the rocks and trees and streams are so delicately harmonized they are mostly hidden. Sheer precipices three thousand feet high are fringed with tall trees growing close like grass on the brow of a lowland hill, and extending along the feet of these precipices a ribbon of meadow a mile wide and seven or eight long, that seems like a strip a farmer might mow in less than a day. Waterfalls, five hundred to one or two thousand feet high, are so subordinated to the mighty cliffs over which they pour that they seem like wisps of smoke, gentle as floating clouds, though their voices fill the valley and make the rocks tremble. The mountains, too, along the eastern sky, and the domes in front of them, and the succession of smooth rounded waves between, swelling higher, higher, with dark woods in their hollows, serene in massive exuberant bulk and beauty, tend yet more to hide the grandeur of the Yosemite temple and make it appear as a subdued subordinate feature of the vast harmonious landscape. Thus every attempt to appreciate any one feature is beaten down by the overwhelming influence of all the others. And, as if this were not enough, lo! in the sky arises another mountain range with topography as rugged and substantial-looking as the one beneath it—snowy peaks and domes and shadowy Yosemite valleys—another version of the snowy Sierra, a new creation heralded by a thunderstorm. How fiercely, devoutly wild is Nature in the midst of her beauty-loving tenderness!—painting lilies, watering them, caressing them with gentle hand, going from flower to flower like a gardener while building rock mountains and cloud mountains full of lightning and rain. Gladly we run for shelter beneath an overhanging cliff and examine the reassuring ferns and mosses, gentle love tokens growing in cracks and chinks. Daisies, too, and ivesias, confiding wild children of light, too small to fear. To these one's heart goes home, and the voices of the storm become gentle. Now the sun breaks forth and fragrant steam arises. The birds are out singing on the edges of the groves. The west is flaming in gold and purple, ready for the ceremony of the sunset, and back I go to camp with my notes and pictures, the best of them printed in my mind as dreams. A fruitful day, without measured beginning or ending. A terrestrial eternity. A gift of good God.

July 23. Another midday cloudland, displaying power and beauty that one never wearies in beholding, but hopelessly unsketchable and untellable. What can poor mortals say about clouds? While a description of their huge glowing domes and ridges, shadowy gulfs and canyons, and feather-edged ravines is being tried, they vanish, leaving no visible ruins. Nevertheless, these fleeting sky mountains are as substantial and significant as the more lasting upheavals of granite beneath them. Both alike are built up and die, and in God's calendar difference of duration is nothing. We can only dream about them in wondering, worshiping admiration, happier than we dare tell even to friends who see farthest in sympathy, glad to know that not a crystal or vapor particle of them, hard or soft, is lost; that they sink and vanish only to rise again and again in higher and higher beauty. As to our own work, duty, influence, etc., concerning which so much fussy pother is made, it will not fail of its due effect, though, like a lichen on a stone, we keep silent.

The Gospel of Nature

—JOHN BURROUGHS

The other day a clergyman who described himself as a preacher of the gospel of Christ wrote, asking me to come and talk to his people on the gospel of Nature. The request set me to thinking whether or not Nature has any gospel in the sense the clergyman had in mind, any message that is likely to be especially comforting to the average orthodox religious person. I suppose the parson wished me to tell his flock what I had found in Nature that was a strength or a solace to myself.

What had all my many years of journeyings to Nature yielded me that would supplement or reinforce the gospel he was preaching? Had the birds taught me any valuable lessons? Had the four-footed beasts? Had the insects? Had the flowers, the trees, the soil, the coming and the going of the seasons? Had I really found sermons in stones, books in running brooks and good in everything? Had the lilies of the field, that neither toil nor spin, and yet are more royally clad than Solomon in all his glory, helped me in any way to clothe myself with humility, with justice, with truthfulness?

It is not easy for one to say just what he owes to all these things. Natural influences work indirectly as well as directly; they work upon the subconscious, as well as upon the conscious, self. That I am a saner, healthier, more contented man, with truer standards of life for all my loiterings in the fields and woods, I am fully convinced.

That I am less social, less interested in my neighbors and in the body politic, more inclined to shirk civic and social responsibilities and to stop my ears against the brawling of the reformers, is perhaps equally true.

One thing is certain, in a hygienic way I owe much to my excursions to Nature. They have helped to clothe me with health, if not with humility; they have helped sharpen and attune all my senses; they have kept my eyes in such good trim that they have not failed me for one moment during all the seventy-five years I have had them; they have made my sense of smell so keen that I have much pleasure in the wild, open-air perfumes, especially in the spring—the delicate breath of the blooming elms and maples and willows, the breath of the woods, of the pasture, of the shore. This keen, healthy sense of smell has made me abhor tobacco and flee from close rooms, and put the stench of cities behind me. I fancy that this whole world of wild, natural perfumes is lost to the tobacco-user and to the city-dweller. Senses trained in the open air are in tune with open-air objects; they are quick, delicate, and discriminating. When I go to town, my ear suffers as well as my nose: the impact of the city upon my senses is hard and dissonant; the ear is stunned, the nose is outraged, and the eye is confused. When I come back, I go to Nature to be soothed and healed, and to have my senses put in tune once more. I know that, as a rule, country or farming folk are not remarkable for the delicacy of their senses, but this is owing mainly to the benumbing and brutalizing effect of continued hard labor. It is their minds more than their bodies that suffer.

When I have dwelt in cities the country was always nearby, and I used to get a bite of country soil at least once a week to keep my system normal.

Emerson says that "The day does not seem wholly profane in which we have given heed to some natural object." If Emerson had stopped to qualify his remark, he would have added, if we give heed to it in the right spirit, if we give heed to it as a nature-lover and truth-seeker. Nature-love as Emerson knew it, and as Wordsworth knew it, and as any of the choicer spirits of our time have known it, has distinctly a religious value. It does not come to a man or a woman who is wholly absorbed in selfish or worldly or material ends. Except ye become in a measure as little children, ye cannot enter the kingdom of Nature—as Audubon entered it, as Thoreau entered it, as Bryant and Amiel entered it, and as all those enter it who make it a resource in their lives and an instrument of their culture. The forms and creeds of religion change, but the sentiment of religion—the wonder and reverence and love we feel in the presence of the inscrutable universe—persist. Indeed, these seem to be renewing their life today in this growing love for all natural objects and in this increasing tenderness toward all forms of life. If we do not go to church as much as did our fathers, we go to the woods much more, and are much more inclined to make a temple of them than they were.

The lesson in running brooks is that motion is a great purifier and health producer. When the brook ceases to run, it soon stagnates. It keeps in touch with the great vital currents when it is in motion, and unites with other brooks to help make the river. In motion it soon leaves all mud and sediment behind. Do not proper work and the exercise of will power have the same effect upon our lives?

The other day in my walk I came upon a sap bucket that had been left standing by the maple tree all the spring and summer. What a bucketful of corruption was that, a mixture of sap and rain-water that had rotted, and smelled to heaven. Mice and birds and insects had been drowned in it, and added to its unsavory character. It was a bit of Nature cut off from the vitalizing and purifying chemistry of the whole. With what satisfaction I emptied it upon the ground while I held my nose and saw it filter into the turf, where I knew it was dying to go and where I knew every particle of the reeking, fetid fluid would soon be made sweet and wholesome again by the chemistry of the soil.

I am not always in sympathy with nature-study as pursued in the schools, as if this kingdom could be carried by assault. Such study is too cold, too special, too mechanical; it is likely to rub the bloom off Nature. It lacks soul and emotion; it misses the accessories of the open air and its exhilarations, the sky, the clouds, the landscape, and the currents of life that pulse everywhere.

I myself have never made a dead set at studying Nature with notebook and fieldglass in hand. I have rather visited with her. We have walked together or sat down together, and our intimacy grows with the seasons. What I have learned about her ways I have learned easily, almost unconsciously, while fishing or camping or idling about. My desultory habits have their disadvantages, no doubt, but they have their advantages also. A too-strenuous pursuit defeats itself. In the fields and woods more than anywhere else all things come to those who wait, because all things are on the move, and are sure sooner or later to come your way.

To absorb a thing is better than to learn it, and we absorb what we enjoy. We learn things at school, we absorb them in the fields and woods and on the farm. When we look upon Nature with fondness and appreciation she meets us halfway and takes a deeper hold upon us than when studiously conned. Hence I say the way of knowledge of Nature is the way of love and enjoyment, and is more surely found in the open air than in the schoolroom or the laboratory. The other day I saw a lot of college girls dissecting cats and making diagrams of the circulation and muscle attachments, and I thought it pretty poor business unless the girls were taking a course in comparative anatomy with a view to some occupation in life. What is the moral and intellectual value of this kind of knowledge to those girls? Biology is, no doubt, a great science in the hands of great men, but it is not for all. I myself have got along very well without it. I am sure I can learn more of what I want to know from a kitten on my knee than from the carcass of a cat in the laboratory. Darwin spent eight years dissecting barnacles; but he was Darwin, and did not stop at barnacles, as these college girls are pretty sure to stop at cats. He dissected and put together again in his mental laboratory the whole system of animal life, and the upshot of his work was a tremendous gain to our understanding of the universe.

I would rather see the girls in the fields and woods studying and enjoying living nature, training their eyes to see correctly and their hearts to respond intelligently. What is knowledge without enjoyment, without love? It is sympathy, appreciation, emotional experience, which refine and elevate and breathe into exact knowledge the breath of life. My own interest is in living nature as it moves and flourishes about me winter and summer.

I know it is one thing to go forth as a nature-lover, and quite another to go forth in a spirit of cold, calculating, exact science. I call myself a nature-lover and not a scientific naturalist. All that science has to tell me is welcome, is, indeed, eagerly sought for. I must know as well as feel. I am not merely contented, like Wordsworth's poet, to enjoy what others understand. I must understand also; but above all things, I must enjoy. How much of my enjoyment springs from my knowledge I do not know. The joy of knowing is very great; the delight of picking up the threads of meaning here and there, and following them through the maze of confusing facts, I know well. When I hear the woodpecker drumming on a dry limb in spring or the grouse drumming in the woods, and know what it is all for, why, that knowledge, I suppose, is part of my enjoyment. The other part is the associations that those sounds call up as voicing the arrival of spring; they are the drums that lead the joyous procession.

To enjoy understandingly, that, I fancy, is the great thing to be desired. When I see the large ichneumon fly, *Thalessa*, making a loop over her back with her long ovipositor and drilling a hole in the trunk of a tree, I do not fully appreciate the spectacle till I know she is feeling for the burrow of a tree borer, *Tremex*, upon the larvae of which her own young feed. She must survey her territory like an oil-digger and calculate where she is likely to strike oil, which in her case is the burrow of her host *Tremex*. There is a vast series of facts in natural history like this that are of little interest until we understand them. They are like the outside of a book which may attract us, but which can mean little to us until we have opened and perused its pages.

I certainly have found "good in everything"—in all natural processes and products—not the "good" of the Sunday-school books, but the good of natural law and order, the good of that system of things out of which we came and which is the source of our health and strength. It is good that fire should burn, even if it consumes your house; it is good that force should crush, even if it crushes you; it is good that rain should fall, even if it destroys your crops or floods your land. Plagues and pestilences attest the constancy of natural law. They set us to cleaning our streets and houses and to readjusting our relations to outward nature. Only in a live universe could disease and death prevail. Death is a phase of life, a redistributing of the type. Decay is another kind of growth.

Yes, good in everything, because law in everything, truth in everything, the sequence of cause and effect in everything, and it may all be good to me if on the right principles I relate my life to it. I can make the heat and the cold serve me, the winds and the floods, gravity and all the chemical and dynamical forces, serve me, if I take hold of them by the right handle. The bad in things arises from our abuse or misuse of them or from our wrong relations to them. A thing is good or bad according as it stands related to my constitution. We say the order of nature is rational; but is it not because our reason is the outcome of that order? Our well-being consists in learning it and in adjusting our lives to it. When we cross it or seek to contravene it, we are destroyed. But Nature in her universal procedures is not rational as I am rational when I weed my garden, prune my trees, select my seed or my stock, or arm myself with tools or weapons. In such matters I take a short cut to that which Nature reaches by a slow, roundabout, and wasteful process. How does she weed her garden? By the survival of the fittest. How does she select her breeding-stock? By the law of battle; the strongest rules. Hers, I repeat, is a slow and wasteful process. She fertilizes the soil by plowing in the crop. She cannot take a short cut. She assorts and arranges her goods by the law of the winds and the tides. She builds up with one hand and pulls down with the other. Man changes the conditions to suit the things. Nature changes the things to suit the conditions. She adapts the plant or the animal to its environment. She does not drain her marshes; she fills them up. Hers is the larger reason—the reason of the All. Man's reason introduces a new method; it cuts across, modifies, or abridges the order of Nature.

I do not see design in Nature in the old teleological sense; but I see everything working to its own proper end, and that end is foretold in the means. Things are not designed; things are begotten. It is as if the final plan of a man's house, after he had begun to build it, should be determined by the winds and the rains and the shape of the ground upon which it stands. The eye is begotten by those vibrations in the ether called light; the ear by those vibrations in the air called sound; the sense of smell by those emanations called odors. There are probably other vibrations and emanations that we have no senses for because our well-being does not demand them.

Yet I would not say that the study of Nature did not favor meekness or sobriety or gentleness or forgiveness or charity, because the great Nature students and prophets, like Darwin, would rise up and confound me. Certainly it favors seriousness, truthfulness, and simplicity of life; or, are only the serious and single-minded drawn to the study of Nature? I doubt very much if it favors devoutness or holiness, as those qualities are inculcated by the church, or any form of religious enthusiasm. Devoutness and holiness come of an attitude toward the universe that is in many ways incompatible with that implied by the pursuit of natural science. The joy of the Nature student like Darwin or any great naturalist is to know, to find out the reason of things and the meaning of things, to trace the footsteps of the creative energy; while the religious devotee is intent only upon losing himself in infinite being. True, there have been devout naturalists and men of science; but their devoutness did not date from their Nature studies, but from their training, or from the times in which they lived. Theology and science, it must be said, will not mingle much better than oil and water, and your devout scientist and devout Nature student lives in two separate compartments of his being at different times. Intercourse with Nature—I mean intellectual intercourse, not merely the emotional intercourse of the sailor or explorer or farmer—tends to beget a habit of mind the farthest possible removed from the myth-making, the vision-seeing, the voice-hearing habit and temper. In all matters relating to the visible, concrete universe it substitutes broad daylight for twilight; it supplants fear with curiosity; it overthrows superstition with fact; it blights credulity with the frost of skepticism. I say frost of skepticism advisedly. Skepticism is a much more healthful and robust habit of mind than the limp, pale-blooded, non-resisting habit that we call credulity.

There can be little doubt, I think, but that intercourse with Nature and a knowledge of her ways tends to simplicity of life. We come more and more to see through the follies and vanities of the world and to appreciate the real values. We load ourselves up with so many false burdens, our complex civilization breeds in us so many false or artificial wants, that we become separated from the real sources of our strength and health as by a gulf.

For my part, as I grow older I am more and more inclined to reduce my baggage, to lop off superfluities. I become more and more in love with simple things and simple folk—a small house, a hut in the woods, a tent on the shore. The show and splendor of great houses, elaborate furnishings, stately halls, oppress me, impose upon me. They fix the attention upon false values, they set up a false standard of beauty; they stand between me and the real feeders of character and thought. A man needs a good roof over his head winter and summer, and a good chimney and a big wood-pile in winter. The more open his four walls are, the more fresh air he will get, and the longer he will live.

Nature is not benevolent; Nature is just, gives pound for pound, measure for measure, makes no exceptions, never tempers her decrees with mercy, or winks at any infringement of her laws. And in the end is not this best? Could the universe be run as a charity or a benevolent institution, or as a poorhouse of the most approved pattern? Without this merciless justice, this irrefragable law, where should we have brought up long ago? It is a hard gospel; but rocks are hard too, yet they form the foundations of the hills.

Man introduces benevolence, mercy, altruism, into the world, and he pays the price in his added burdens; and he reaps his reward in the vast social and civic organizations that were impossible without these things.

Man has been man but a little while comparatively, less than one hour of the twenty-four of the vast geologic day; a few hours more and he will be gone; less than another geologic day like the past, and no doubt all life from the earth will be gone. What then? The game will be played over and over again in other worlds, without approaching any nearer the final end than we are now. There is no final end, as there was no absolute beginning, and can be none with the infinite.

Escape from the
Commonplace

WHEN James Boswell enthusiastically compared a Scottish harbor with the bay of Naples Dr. Johnson deflated him with too complete an agreement: "Water is much the same everywhere." This is only the obverse of Thoreau's conviction that no one need go further than the nearest field to escape from the World and to find the Universe. But not everyone can feel the truth of that tremendous proposition—until, at least, he has tried to find the unfamiliar away from his own doorstep.

The present section of this anthology is devoted to several accounts by men who have undertaken to escape from the commonplace and it is my fancy to arrange them in the order which will carry the reader from a city such as he may live in to, literally, the end of the world. Louis Halle follows the course of "Spring in Washington" and Edwin Way Teale describes in a chapter from his *Lost Woods* what he found without wandering far from the concrete. At the other extreme, Commander Richard Byrd fled on and on until he retired ultimately to a solitary hermitage under the ice very close to the South Pole itself. In between come some accounts of "escapes" by Lewis Gannett, to his "Cream Hill"; by "David Grayson" (the pseudonym of Ray Stannard Baker), who wandered on foot through his own countryside to find his "Adventures in Contentment"; and by Laura Lee Davidson, a Baltimore schoolteacher who passed "A Winter of Content" alone on a Canadian lake. Wandering farther afield, the adventurous Californian Caroline Mytinger, armed only with a tin of crayons, went "Headhunting in the Solomon Islands," and Vilhjalmur Stefansson found the delightful—to him—experiences described in *My Life with the Eskimo*. Some men find wildness in wild places; others, as Thoreau insisted, take it with them.

Spring in Washington

—LOUIS J. HALLE, JR.

Though they ransack the National Archives, historians to come will find no records of certain remarkable episodes and developments that took place in Washington during the first half of 1945. The government has no department that takes cognizance of life itself; it posts no watchers out of doors to sniff the wind and inform those within of eternity. That is volunteer work, good occupation for a man. It is not for government personnel, who are preoccupied with official transactions on paper. These are workers in the hive of our civilization, and the hive is their universe. They trouble themselves about the real universe, as Henry Adams puts it, "much as a hive of honey-bees troubles about the ocean, only as a region to be avoided."

To snatch the passing moment and examine it for signs of eternity is the noblest of occupations. It is Olympian. Therefore I undertook to be monitor of the Washington seasons, when the government was not looking. Though it was only for my own good, that is how the poorest of us may benefit the world.

Though the Lord created the world in seven days, its annual re-creation takes longer. In the week following January 28, the

From *Spring in Washington*, by Louis J. Halle, Jr., Copyright 1947 by Louis J. Halle, Jr. Published by William Sloane Associates, Inc., New York.

temperature remained in the teens. The next Sunday, February 4, a light breeze came from the south and again the morning sun shone through a haze—until midday. The afternoon brought rain, sleet, and hail from a darkened sky. My friend Og and I bicycled south, down the river to meet the spring. This was not altogether quixotic, for there were birds wintering at Mount Vernon that would not arrive in Washington until the spring migration brought them: towhees, red-bellied woodpeckers, and field sparrows. They were toeing the mark. In the blackened marshes between the airport and Alexandria, a flock of red-winged blackbirds were clearing their pipes but not yet singing. A flock of female redwings, not even clucking, landed in a tree by Roaches Run. At one point a song sparrow sang lustily. The forty-one species of birds that we counted that day, however, represented the wintering population, the base of departure from which we might measure the expected change of season.

At dawn the next day the pavements were glazed with frozen rain under low, solid clouds, but two or three cardinals sang tentatively and, for the first time this year, I heard a titmouse tirelessly calling *Peter, Peter, Peter.*

Sunday, February 25, the wind had gone around to the south and the sun shone through a haze. The first arrival of the year was a robin that flew over Rock Creek in the morning. On the uplands of Wellington, halfway between Alexandria and Mount Vernon, we came on the first flock of grackles, sauntering in black-and-purple elegance along the grass borders, perched on spires of cedar, or dragging their tails in labored flight. Their grating voices, all conversing together, were the voices of spring. Mourning doves, of which a scattered few had wintered, were suddenly common today. This was spring itself in its debut. These were the first arrivals of the first wave of migration. More came during the day, for on our return from Mount Vernon we found flocks of grackles where none had been in the morning and from Dyke to Washington the countryside was suddenly overrun with red-winged blackbirds. Against the reddening sky of evening, the blackbirds were flying, flock after flock, to roost in the big marshes.

Every morning now is a fresh wonder, no two quite the same. Thursday, March 1, a cloudless day, the west wind blowing easily across the city. By the time the sun rises now, about a quarter to eight, I am likely to be across the bridge and into Virginia, having myself arisen in the starlight. On a morning like this I have knotted a woolen scarf about my neck and tucked it into my jacket, for it is frosty and clear and the wind cuts. Looking across the river, I see the sun rise brilliantly between the silhouettes of the Monument and the Capitol dome, and feel its warm rays flash across the land at the same moment that the countryside about me is transformed into light and shadow. The trees at Roaches Run and the marsh grasses stand in relief, flooded by radiance from the horizon. All the birds are sparkling and ebullient in the sharp dawn. A redwing at the top of a tree is singing *conqueree-ee-ee,* shaking out his black-and-scarlet wings and spreading his tail at each utterance. Three grackles are clucking and grating to one another in the thicket. This is life beginning all over again, emerging from the darkness and damp into the new day. It is spring in microcosm. The tide is out, and where an area of marsh grass is exposed in the middle of the lagoon a great blue heron stands motionless. Another comes in from behind the island like a drifting feather, the sun illuminating it from below; drops its legs, uncurls its neck, and alights silently near the first. A horned grebe sits by its solitary self across the water. Two coots swim about the edge of the grasses, pumping their heads. I have already formed a nodding acquaintance with them.

Anyone could have recognized by Sunday, March 4, that spring was here, for the golden forsythia was suddenly in bloom along the Mount Vernon highway, and the lily of the valley in flower at the edge of the woods. It must have happened overnight, under the warm rain and the south wind. The woods and fields still stood in penciled outline, the trees mere skeletons against the sky, but the first touches of color that would at last fill the entire landscape had been applied. Half a dozen wood ducks had arrived at the Dyke marshes, and green-winged teal at Dyke and Four Mile Run. Four black vultures, ponderous and somber, circled over Mount Vernon, supplementing the eagles and turkey vultures that drifted across the sky. Down the wooded path bordering the marshes at Dyke we drove the first woodcock of the year, flushing it repeatedly. It would alight beyond the first bend in the path and wait for us to come up with it again, aberrant bird with misplaced eyes and disproportioned bill, waddling on uncertain feet, alert for flight. Then, with an explosive whistling of wings, flying jaggedly in a series of impulses, it would disappear around the next bend.

Below Mount Vernon on the wooded river shore, the first phoebe of the year, and it was only March 4. A migrating winter wren, a fox sparrow, and the first meadowlark singing. It was a month to the day since our first excursion downriver, and of the fifty-two species of birds that we counted ten were listed for the first time. Grackles, redwings, robins, and doves were now common to abundant everywhere.

In full sunlight, where the highway ran through deciduous woods on either hand, some strange bird with glowing wings or a great golden moth was weaving and circling, fluttering silently out over the highway, silently into the woods, back over the highway again. O beautiful, on wings through which the sun shines golden! Surely there never was such a creature alive! But it came close, fluttering and flittering in and out between us, and up close we saw what it was: a tawny-colored bat. Off into the woods at last, fluttering and dipping still, till we saw it no more.

A scientist later identified the apparition for me by my

description as the red bat, *Lasiurus borealis*; but with half a mind I was still disposed to believe we had seen—who knows what?

It is curious how the preoccupations of the hive fill us, driving out all memory of the universe into which we were born. Perhaps the whole human race may be said to suffer from amnesia, not knowing whence it came or why it finds itself here. But we inhabitants of the hive suffer from double amnesia, one case within another, and are removed one stage further from the ultimate reality in which we have our beginning and our end. We have forgotten that we live in the universe, and that our civilization itself is merely an elaboration of the palm-leaf hat that one of our ancestors tried on ten thousand years ago to ward off the sun, a more complicated and ample version that now not only wards off the sun but shuts out the view. We have lost ourselves within it. Yet some have told me, when I set out to have a look at the stars or to watch the migration of birds, that I was escaping reality! I judge that it is they who are escaping into the artificial problems of their workaday life. The tailor makes himself a prisoner in his own shop, and if you speak to him of other dimensions than those he knows in his trade he will not sleep nights. "To an amazing degree people's environment has come to consist of machines and man-made things, much as the environment of animals is made up of natural objects and growing things." I quote from the findings of the Harvard Committee appointed to study the problem of *General Education in a Free Society*, and which reported on the increasing difficulty of educating men for the universe.

I have looked through the Washington newspapers in season without finding any account of the arrival of ducks or the visitations of gulls, although they reported the visit of a French functionary and the return from her wintering grounds in the south of somebody's wife. It was all news of the hive, with not a word of events in the outside world. The magazines for sale on the stands and the new books displayed in the shops reflect this preoccupation. Our civilization, apparently, has become divorced from the universe and is feeding on itself.

This is equally apparent when you listen to our talk. Our society is made up of workers, not men. We are obsessed with the inadequacies of the hive, which does not support us to our satisfaction, and attribute these inadequacies to the shortcomings of our fellow workers. We are possessed by a sort of panic at finding ourselves dependent on one another. We are tormented by the fear of what might happen to us if our fellow workers should be negligent or ill-willed or simply too smart for us. Consequently, we clamor all together for a new ordering of matters, for new rules and new regulations and new restraints to secure us against one another. We find ourselves fettered by the chains we have designed for our fellows, and threatened with destruction by the weapons we have invented to destroy them; yet we do not, on that account, cease our frantic search for more binding fetters and more terrible engines of destruction.

Under the circumstances it is proper to wonder why our entrapped multitudes do not seek escape from the hive, once more asserting their individual independence as men. The door stands open on the outside world. I conclude that we have lost our knowledge of the outside world, and fear of the unknown is greater than that of any accustomed horror. I have seen a bird cowering in its cage when the door was opened for its escape.

You will find that any reference to the times when we men were not altogether dependent on our hive organization arouses a general revulsion among us. It appears that before our swarm took refuge in the hive it lived in darkness, that the only light shining in the world is the artificial light of the hive. Obsessed with fear at our dependence on one another, we are even more fearful of being dependent once more on ourselves. It is the nature of slavery to render its victims so abject that at last, fearing to be free, they multiply their own chains. You can liberate a freeman, but you cannot liberate a slave.

Louis J. Halle, Jr.

It follows that the training of a worker for the hive is something distinct from the education of a freeman for the universe. The purpose of education in a free society of men is to gain knowledge of the universe in which they live and their relation to it. To realize our independence we must know what we can about ourselves and about our outer environment. The laws of the universe are more important than the laws of society, the limits that it puts to man's action are the limits that count. Man learns to know the universe, and his place in it, from the accumulated experience and study of mankind, corroborated by his own observation. But the worker who has retreated into the hive can dispense with knowledge of it; all he needs is to master one of the technical skills required by the society. In return for performing one operation, the hive will feed him and shelter him for the duration of his life, and lay him away when he dies. The coal miner, the radio operator, and the file clerk need not understand the nature of a cow to consume their allotments of bottled milk. Because, in reading the newspapers, books, and magazines, I see that the majority favor the elimination of useless education and the provision, in its place, of more thorough training in the skills, I come to the gloomy conclusion that most of us have abandoned all desire to be free. We shall continue to sell our birthright for what we take to be the security of the hive until we have destroyed ourselves and it. When that time comes, perhaps the remnant of us, thrown unwillingly on the resources of our own manhood, will be able to make a fresh start.

Meanwhile, it is not likely that the newspapers will carry news from outside.

To the uneducated politician the goal of life is the advancement of his party, to the uneducated intellectual it is the advancement of his cause or the acceptance of his dogma. Each measures the world by his own shadow, overlooking the assistance he has from the sun in casting it. All these people are the victims of circumstances they cannot hope to understand, whether it is the American mechanic who shouts for democracy or the European barber who shouts for a dictator. In their somnambulism they are bound to the wheel of the immediate present, and will be freed only when education has awakened them to the breadth and scope of the universe they share in common.

The discovery of spring each year, after the winter's hibernation, is like a rediscovery of the universe. In my bleak winter quarters, preoccupied with the problems of the moment, I had forgotten the immeasurable richness and continuance of life. This recollected smell of fresh loam in my nostrils is the smell of eternity itself.

It was now almost two months since that bleak morning when the cardinal had reminded me that winter would not last forever; and now the forsythia was in bloom, the elms had flowered, along the river at dusk clouds of blackbirds traveled toward their roosting grounds in the big marshes, passing smaller clouds of starlings coming the other way to roost in the city. It was no longer a matter of listening for an isolated cardinal or song sparrow at dawn; for now, at dawn and dusk alike, and at intervals during the day, the robins stationed in the treetops filled the atmosphere with their uninterrupted caroling, *cheer-up cheery cheer-up cheery cheerily cheer-up* . . . , and then the rapid succession of call notes as if the birds were near to bursting with their passionate vitality. The earth had been filling with music, mourning doves consoling themselves in solitary places, whitethroats at the other end of the scale singing their equally slow and sad but ethereal songs, nuthatches barking or laughing at one another in the deep woods as they clung upside-down beneath branches or against the trunks, chickadees chattering softly or breaking into their high *dee-didee dee doo doo*, titmice inventing all sorts of surprising phrases now as a relief from their incessant *Peter, Peter, Peter* . . . , downy woodpeckers emitting their dwindling bursts of sound, the occasional mockingbird performing by himself as if to show the world that he could overmatch any one of these or all together. . . . In the marshes, still sere and gray, the blackbirds clucked and sang and the ducks had increased, while gulls swarmed in the river. . . .

With the unseasonable heat of the past few days, Act I was now complete. The stage was set, earlier than ever this year, for the main developments.

On June 8 I saw my last spring migrant, a blackpoll warbler, behind the Japanese Embassy. This sets the terminal date for spring in Washington, 1945. I went out again June 9 and for the first time since February found no migrant; only the resident breeding birds. The accomplished fact of a Washington summer lay before me. It was already an accustomed spectacle. Frost in the air and a lone cardinal trying out his voice in a naked tree seemed far away now.

Yet this was merely one tick of the great clock that ticks out eternity. For a few ticks I am here, uncomprehending, attempting to make some record or memorial of this eternal passage, like a traveler taking notes in a strange country through which he is being hurried on a schedule not of his making and for a purpose he does not understand. He knows only that he has been bustled blindfold onto this scene and that blindfold he will be bustled off it again in short order. Meanwhile, the spectacle itself is beautiful, immense, awe-inspiring. He thinks, in default of other guidance, he had better make a few hurried notes on it in his passage. This much he must attempt, leaving his notes behind as an acknowledgment of this strange hospitality and the gift of vision, and as a record by which other travelers may recognize their similar experience.

Natural History in Times Square

—EDWIN WAY TEALE

In the course of a single day, a quarter of a million people may pass through Times Square, in New York City. They pour out of the side-streets. They eddy around the bases of the sky-scrapers. They funnel downward into subways. Like a great heart, Times Square endlessly draws in this stream of human corpuscles and sends it flowing away again, year in and year out, all day long and far into the night.

Here, amid the throngs, the buses, the dodging taxicabs, the clanging streetcars; here, among the gaudy billboards and the glaring colors of the nighttime spectaculars; here, in this public and populous spot—fenced in by glass and brick, stone and asphalt, cement and steel—is a world so divorced from that of the open fields and woods that it seems impossible that the two should ever meet. A naturalist in Times Square seems almost as much out of place as a botanist in the stratosphere.

Yet, during the dozen years my life was spent in a New York office, when I was one of those whom Herman Melville describes in *Moby Dick* as "pent up in lath and plaster, tied to counters, nailed to benches, clinched to desks," I discovered—during odd and rare moments—surprising events in natural history taking place in the heart of the great city.

One October day, I was walking north on Seventh Avenue and came out into Times Square. From beyond the Hudson, the afternoon sun was lighting the skyscrapers. And all across the open space, against the high-piled background of the buildings, the air was filled with a silver, glinting shimmer. The fine silken threads of a gossamer shower were descending from the sky. Baby spiders, born in the New Jersey countryside, had ridden like dandelion seeds across the river and above the skyscrapers. Some of the threads of silk, that carried them aloft in the up-drafts, were less than 1/100,000th of an inch in thickness. In the dying breeze of late afternoon, the updrafts had ceased. The tiny aeronauts were descending slowly, the rays of the sun glinting on the threads as they turned in mid-air. Journey's end, for these spiders were amid the inhospitable concrete and asphalt of Times Square. Trusting themselves to the uncertainties of the breeze, the tiny spiders of autumn spread by such ballooning. Most of those that thus ride through the air alight in favorable homes; a few, less fortunate, descend into cities or stretches of water. Gossamer showers have been seen falling from the sky hundreds of miles at sea.

During years when the aphid population on Long Island farms is abnormally large, these plant lice are sometimes carried by the breeze and fall on New York City streets like green, living rain. Storms, on a more violent scale, also bring strange visitors to America's largest city. Sooty shearwaters, yellow-billed tropic birds and dovekies, those small web-footed divers of the Arctic seas, all have been carried ashore by the winds. One year, large numbers of exhausted dovekies were found resting in the city streets after a night when gale-winds blew from the east.

In his *The Book of British Waders*, Brian Vesey-Fitzgerald speaks of the wildness of the curlew's call. "That cry," he writes, "the high, forlorn double note from which the bird receives his name, is the spirit of the wildest wildness, whether you hear it above a populous city, or on heath, or down, or lonely shore or deserted estuary." For me, a wild bird's call takes on added, immeasurably added, wildness when heard amid the concentrated civilization of a great city.

Twice, in Times Square, I caught such a sound amid the traffic. One of these occasions was on a raw, gray midafternoon in March. Pedestrians were hurrying along the street with coat-collars turned up and the day-long twilight of the overcast sky had brought on office lights by three o'clock. Above the sound of taxicab wheels rushing through slush on the pavement, there came from high overhead a faint, raucous call. It brought back a vivid remembrance of that winter day in the Lost Woods. The call was the cawing of a crow.

Another time, in the brilliant sunshine of Indian Summer, I heard above the clatter and screech of Broadway traffic a sound that came like a breath from a lonely pine woods. It was the high, wild, rolling cry of a flicker. Rising and falling in its flight, the golden-winged woodpecker was passing over the skyscrapers, and the Grand-Canyon gulches between them, on its way to Bryant Park.

Only a few steps from the spot where I heard the flicker that day, a motorist had an adventure that gave him a surprise that he never forgot. It also demonstrated that, even in Times Square, Nature can be counted on for the unexpected. The driver had pulled up for a red traffic light and was just getting under way again when a brilliant-feathered cock pheasant fluttered down and struck the fender of his car. The bird was unhurt. A wild pheasant hunt ensued in the midst of this populous Crossroads of the World. The motorist finally retrieved the bird and turned it over to the American Society for the Prevention of Cruelty to Animals. How the cock pheasant reached Times Square remains a mystery to this day.

Other odd bird visitors to the great city include a horned owl that perched in a tree near City Hall; a glossy ibis, seen for weeks near Van Cortlandt Park; a red phalarope, one of the so-called "swimming snipe"; and a thrush that lived all winter in a florist's shop on Madison Avenue and flew away again when spring came. One autumn, a duck hawk stayed for weeks on the Paramount Building, high above Times Square, and preyed on the pigeons of the neighborhood. And across the East River in Brooklyn, a visiting hawk created a first-class mystery by snatching freshly killed chickens from a line in the rear of a restaurant.

During the migration season, birds of many kinds stop off in parks, back-yard gardens, and even on the window-ledges of skyscrapers. At the hanging gardens, high up on Radio City, an American bittern—a bird we associate with lonely marshlands or wild, boggy dells—settled down to rest one autumn as it was winging its way south over the miles of city buildings. For a quarter of an hour, this shy swampland wader perched there, high above the traffic, and then took off again. In one back-yard garden, in the heart of New York and not many blocks from Times Square, migration time brought such interesting visitors as a wood peewee, a scarlet tanager, a white-throated sparrow, a Baltimore oriole, a woodcock and a hermit thrush. A cardinal, one winter, attracted the attention of tens of thousands of people by feeding among the pigeons and sparrows in Bryant Park, one block to the east of Times Square.

Pigeons and sparrows are always present in Times Square. Probably the English sparrow population has decreased since the change from stables to garages. But the number of pigeons appears to remain about the same year after year. Every so often, one of these birds gets its picture in the papers. One had its leg set at Bellevue Hospital and was listed as a patient; another hatched out a brood of young on a window-ledge of a hospital maternity ward; a third, in the heart of a motorized city, produced a nest made largely of paper clips and rubber bands.

To one who grew up surrounded by wild birds, by flickers and orioles, brown thrashers and bluebirds, the tame and discolored pigeons of Times Square always seem a sorry lot. The only thrill they provide for me is when they shoot from building to building on a windy day, navigating with half-closed wings the aerial rapids and whirlpools of the city canyons. But even that drabbest of birds to the average person, an English sparrow, can become a fascinating personality if we grow to know it well enough.

Across from the American Museum of Natural History, I once encountered a fifteen-year-old boy who had made friends in a remarkable way with an English sparrow from Central Park. The sparrow slept each night on the top of a closet door in the boy's bedroom; it perched on his schoolbooks when he was studying; it flew up the sheer front of the apartment house in which the boy lived and entered the right window. It was never caged; it was free to come and go; but before dusk, it always returned to the apartment.

The boy, Bennett Rothenberg, found the sparrow as a baby in Central Park. He carried it home and installed it in an empty robin's nest in his room. With the aid of a medicine dropper and a pair of tweezers, he fed it at hourly intervals. On a diet of flies, bits of worms, water and pieces of egg-biscuit, it grew rapidly. A snobbish tilt of its beak when it had had enough food resulted in its name: Snobber. The boy taught Snobber to fly by placing it in low trees, offering it food and chirping to it. The sparrow learned to recognize his chirp and would fly 130 feet up to the apartment window when he called. To the uninitiated, all sparrows seem to chirp alike. But not to Bennett. He maintained he could recognize Snobber's chirp in a tree full of sparrows. And he could tell whether she was angry, curious or excited. When they started out together, Snobber often rode down the elevator on Bennett's shoulder. And when they returned, the sparrow would fly on ahead and then wait—like a dog—at the entrance of the apartment house for Bennett to cross the street.

In Central Park, on an August afternoon, one of the eminent ornithologists of the American Museum of Natural History—a scientist who had journeyed as far away as Equatorial Africa to observe bird life—was surprised to see something entirely new to his experience. A sparrow darted down from one of the park trees and, perching on a boy's shoulder, began to eat ice cream from a cone. The sparrow, of course, was Snobber and the boy was Bennett.

Ice cream, pieces of apple and small bits of candy were delicacies of which the bird was passionately fond. Boys in the neighborhood shared their candy and cones with her when she alighted on their shoulders. As soon as she saw a piece of candy, she began to chirp and flutter. Bennett and a companion sometimes played a game with her for five minutes at a time by tossing a piece of cellophane-covered candy back and forth. Like a kitten pursuing a ball, Snobber would shuttle swiftly from boy to boy in pursuit of the flying candy. Pedestrians near the museum were often surprised to have an English sparrow swoop down from a tree and try to alight on their shoulders. The reaction was varied. One woman jerked off a fur neckpiece and swung it around in the air like a lasso to ward off the supposed attack. An elderly gentleman became even more excited.

He was stout, nearsighted, and wearing a derby hat. He came down the street reading a newspaper held close to his face. In his left hand, he clutched an ice cream cone from which he absent-mindedly took a bite from time to time. Snobber was perched on the lower limb of a tree. She cocked her head as he went by; she had spotted the ice cream. Swooping down, she alighted on the cone and began nibbling away. Just then, the man put the cone to his mouth abstractedly to take another bite. The cone bit him, instead! Or, at least, that was the impression he got when Snobber pecked him on the lower lip. Unable to believe his eyes, he peered nearsightedly at the cone and the bird. Then he began to wave the cone in circles in the air. Like a pinwheel, the cone and the pursuing sparrow whirled above his head.

Seeing the commotion, Bennett ran across the street to explain and to catch Snobber. But in the process he accidentally knocked the cone from the man's hand. Thinking he was being set upon from the air and the ground simultaneously, the near-sighted gentleman clutched his newspaper in one hand and his derby in the other and sprinted down the street.

As long as Snobber was sleeping on the top of the closet door in his bedroom, Bennett told me, he didn't need any alarm clock. As soon as it was daylight, the sparrow was awake. Hopping down, she would perch on his head and begin tugging at individual hairs. If he failed to wake up, she often snuggled down near his neck for an additional nap, herself. If he disturbed her by moving in his sleep, she would give him a peck on the chest. As a consequence Bennett often kept moving farther and farther back until when he awoke he would be lying on the extreme edge and the sparrow would be occupying almost all the bed.

During a month that Bennett was away at a camp, one summer, Frank Olmedo, an elevator operator at the apartment house, cared for Snobber. The two became fast friends. After that, on rainy days, the sparrow made no effort to mount upward along the sheer cliff of brick and glass to Bennett's apartment-window. Instead, she rode up on the elevator! Flying in the front entrance of the apartment house, she would alight on Olmedo's shoulder. When they reached the eleventh floor, he would ring the bell at the apartment and, when the door opened, the sparrow would fly—like a homing pigeon—to the boy's bedroom.

Nearly 1,000 feet higher than the bedroom window that Snobber had learned to recognize, is the tip of the Empire State Building, only a few blocks to the south and east of Times Square. This highest peak on Manhattan's skyline, the loftiest building ever constructed by human hands, has revealed some surprising things about insect visitors to a great city. Alighting on the observation platform at the top of the Empire State Building have been a long list of six-legged creatures including such unexpected tourists from the country as assassin bugs, ichneumon-flies, ladybird beetles, lacewing flies and paper-making wasps. A radio technician, who was associated with pioneer television broadcasts made from the tower of the Empire State Building, once told me that as many as 100 praying mantises a week would alight there during certain periods of the autumn season.

The praying mantis—as long as your hand, green or brown, with forelegs that are kept folded as though in prayer when they are not in use—is one of the most striking visitors to come from the outer country into the congested areas of a metropolis. It always attracts special attention. I remember pushing my way into a crowd in Times Square, some years ago, and finding the center of attention—in this spot where the highest-priced billboards in the world were vying for attention and where the most publicized theatrical productions on earth offered their wares—was a praying mantis sitting up on a sparkplug!

Insects of other kinds also provide moments of diversion for the naturalist in Times Square. On August afternoons, I have seen dragonflies, slender-bodied and swift-winged, hovering and dipping over the shimmering black asphalt of Broadway. They were females, darting down just as they do in dropping their eggs, and, apparently, mistaking the black roadway for some dark river.

At the entrance of an alley, just off Times Square, I once saw a yellow-jacket wasp hunting for bits of meat and fruit at the rear of a restaurant. And nearby, on the sidewalk, there were the smashed remains of that spurned aristocrat among the insects, that despised cosmopolitan, the lowly cockroach.

The cockroach is unhonored and unsung. It walks about with downcast eyes. Its head hangs dejectedly between its knees. It lives on modest fare and in humble circumstances. It is drab-colored and inconspicuous. But don't let that Uriah Heep exterior fool you. For here you have Superbug, himself!

During 100,000,000 years, the cockroach has been a winner. Dinosaurs sent roaches scuttling up the trunks of prehistoric trees; but roaches lived to see these monsters disappear forever.

Great American Nature Writing

Before any bee or ant or butterfly appeared, cockroaches were holding their own, as they are today. Wherever food and warmth are found, there is a cockroach also. One species even lives so far north it dines on dried fish in the huts of the Laplanders.

If an inventor sat up nights trying to devise an indestructible bug, he would have a hard time outdoing the roach. Its seed-shaped body is smooth and waxed, as hard to hold as a slippery orange-pip. Its flat form permits it to squeeze into incredibly small cracks. Its nimble legs provide such speed and shiftiness that it could give pointers on openfield running to an All-American halfback. Delicate body hairs catch vibrations and warn of approaching danger and its long, slender antennae form a supersensitive nose for smelling hidden food. Its body is a living thermometer, reacting quickly to any changes in temperature and enabling it to select living quarters where the average warmth is between seventy and eighty degrees F. Break off a cockroach's leg and, if the insect has not reached its full size, another grows in its place. By sleeping daytimes and coming abroad at night, the roach avoids most of its natural enemies. So sensitive is its body to light and shade that a completely blinded cockroach will infallibly seek the dark.

In addition, a roach seems to have an internal anatomy as immune to stomach-ache as a concrete-mixer. Its jaws will tackle whitewash, grease, hair, paint, honey, beer, bedbugs, gold lettering on books, and watercolor paints as readily as they will meat and potatoes. A cockroach is an insect goat with a goat's appetite raised to the nth power. Moreover, its body requires so little oxygen that it can live for hours after all its breathing tubes have been sealed with paraffin. Roaches get along with about half as much blood, in relation to body weight, as humans require. Nitrogen is needed in the diet of other forms of life, but none is required by the adult cockroach.

Some years ago, an English entomologist, without giving his reasons, predicted that the cockroach is on its way out, that it is destined to become the dwindling remnant of a dying race.

Grave doubts will remain in the mind of anyone acquainted with the indestructible roach. It has survived so many vicissitudes in the past that it seems likely that, when the date of its projected end arrives, it will be discovered safe and sound, pointing its feelers at the nearest food. At least, as long as Times Square exists, this unappreciated and durable superbug is certain to be listed on any record of its permanent dwellers.

A transient that drifted by on black-and-orange wings, spending only a few minutes within reach of my eyes, gave me special delight one late-September afternoon. Caught up in the swift tide of hurrying, home-going workers, I was passing through Times Square when I recognized a friend of mine associated with far different surroundings. On a level with the open windows of the third floor of surrounding skyscrapers, above the tumult of buses and taxicabs, a Monarch butterfly sailed into view. It would give its wings a few quick flaps and then coast, teetering in the crosscurrents. When first I sighted it, it was sailing along Seventh Avenue, beneath the level of the great electric signs. It disappeared down Broadway. Deliberately, it was winging its way down the length of Manhattan island on its migration to the South.

One other recollection comes to mind, a remembrance of an evening a little later in the year. In the warm dusk, I was passing the rear of the Metropolitan Opera House, on Seventh Avenue, just below Times Square. A familiar song reached my ears. I stopped abruptly. The singer was no operatic tenor, no coloratura soprano. The stage from which the music came had no floodlights or scenery. The voice was small and shrill; the stage was a dark recess beneath discarded props stacked on the sidewalk. From these deep shadows came the creaking song of a field cricket. In the heart of that vast city, it was sendnig out its little melody just as, since time immemorial, other field crickets, amid country meadows and hedgerows, have produced this same simple refrain—one of the earliest love-songs of the world.

Weekend World

—LEWIS GANNETT

T he weekend world is a modern invention.

You didn't need a weekend to get to the country in Ezra's day; the country then reached right into the back yards of the cities—the cities, indeed, were mere villages. Cream Hill was sixty miles from Ezra's New Haven, but it was a three-day horseback ride—an expedition, not a weekend jaunt.

Nor was the modern weekend possible in the horse-and-buggy age. You couldn't park a horse and buggy in a shed beside the railroad station and expect to find them safe and sound if you returned five of six days later.

Summer vacations in my boyhood hadn't changed much since my father's boyhood fifty years before. They were middle-class affairs. All New England was spotted in those days with overgrown farmhouses converted into summer boarding houses. The farmer met you at the train, some time after the Fourth of July, and took you back to it, at the latest, just before Labor Day. In the intervening vacation time you used your legs if you wanted to get away from the croquet game on the lawn. Only rich people like Clarence Day's father, with money enough to maintain their

Lewis Gannett

own horses and coachmen, in those days had individual "places in the country."

The automobile has changed all that. It has made possible the itinerant vacations of today, the middle-class summer home, the workman's shack, the whole still-evolving weekend pattern. First it spilled the cities into the suburbs, and latterly it has been stretching the suburbs into the hinterlands. It is changing the American way of life. There must be millions of us in America today who live more or less on a weekend pattern.

Meanwhile, though the airplane has spanned the oceans and the poles, it has not yet learned to span the suburbs. The airplane is a convenient way to get to Los Angeles or Ireland, but for a man who just wants to get out of the city, it is no help at all. As a pattern of everyday living the air age is not yet here.

We didn't dream of a weekend world when we first went to Cream Hill. We were thinking, I suppose, in terms of my father's long ministerial vacations. Cream Hill was a place for the children during the City and Country School's long vacations. My wife and I both had full-time jobs; we took our vacations separately to space out the parent-child vacation period, and left Michael and Ruthy the rest of the time with the incomparable Lucille, who is now superintendent of a city play center. We used to drive to the city only twice in a season, and every trip was an ordeal. The roads were poorer, the Model T slower; what is today a two-and-a-half-hour drive then consumed at least five hours—often, with a meal or a flat tire on the way, six. Usually we traveled by train.

The all-year weekend pattern grew on us gradually. Small children are not natural weekenders. The same old drive, week after week, bores them. Curvy New England roads are hard on small stomachs; I shall not soon forget the time when Ruthy gurgled a signal to stop, and I didn't stop quite in time. It took weeks for the lower frame of that car window to dry out, and for months a good rain would remind us of it. And when

· 171 ·

Michael and Ruthy became bored in the back seat, they opened stimulating arguments which tended to develop into active physical combat. We racked our heads for games to keep them amused. It was Michael, however, who invented the sport which solved the problem of the weekend drive.

"Betcha I can make my Lifesaver last longer than yours," said Michael to Ruthy. I clocked them on the speedometer. Ruthy, of a more impatient nature, could hardly keep a Pep-o-Mint intact for three miles. Michael first set a par of five miles. Then he raised it to ten. Within two years of active training he worked up to a record of seventy miles. He would refuse to answer questions, lest speech jar his tongue and hasten the dissolution of his lozenge. For two full hours he would sit silent—and happy! —on the back seat, his dry tongue thrust out to keep the juices of his mouth from hastening dissolution. It was a triumph. Ruthy could never equal that record—nor could Ruth or I. And while Michael and Ruthy were developing techniques for making a Lifesaver last, Ruth and I were able to sit peacefully on the front seat, quietly talking to each other with no fear of combat in the rear.

Neither Michael nor Ruthy was a natural weekend gardener. In fact, I doubt that any child is. I have always suspected books that tell of "children's gardens." Gardening requires long-term imagination—months, often years, of waiting to see. Children want immediate results. Michael and Ruthy were willing to plant, but they never had much interest in any of the subsequent gardening processes until it came to harvesting. So, while Ruth and I spent our weekends gardening, Michael became a tree-house builder. Ruthy became a barn builder.

All this time the children were growing up. They went away to school and college; they had summer jobs, and, eventually, all-year jobs of their own. Occasionally they would bring gangs of their friends to Cream Hill, but our weekends became increasingly childless. The house ceased to be a "summer place" for children; without our quite realizing the change it became an all-year-round weekend home. Weekends long ago became more important to us than summers. The "summer place" idea is obsolete.

We grew older, too—it happens in the best of families—and the house seemed not only empty, but, to Ruth, the housekeeper, dismally big. At times Ruth wonders if some modern architect could not invent a collapsible house. She would like to wheel half our house off into the woods and fold and pack it away where it would not need dusting, but remain available when children and grandchildren arrive in mass.

Ruthy is herself a mother now, and Michael is a father, but Michael is in the Foreign Service and visits home are rare, and Ruthy's baby is not yet old enough to appreciate Midget Village. We hope—one can't help hoping—for a few summers of grandchildren. Sometimes, when Ruth isn't dreaming of collapsing the back wing of the house, she talks of building a little house for grandparents up the hill, leaving the big house to Michael or Ruthy and their growing tribe. It might happen. It probably won't. It isn't the American pattern. Americans move on, generation after generation. Americans seldom stay put.

My father was born on a street called Bumstead Place, in the heart of old Boston. Few who walk Tremont Street today know that Boston ever had a Bumstead Place; an office building covers its entire area. My mother was born in Altoona, Pennsylvania, a city she has not seen for more than sixty years. A garage stands on the site in Rochester, New York, where I was born. And the old New England summer boarding houses have given way to "hotels" and cabin clusters. Ruth's family is even more typical: her grandparents came from Kentucky, her mother was born in Indiana, her father in Missouri, she in California. The idea of a family home, persistent through the generations, despite the Currier and Ives calendars, is not a living authentic part of the American tradition.

The old Reed place on Cream Hill, in which, after the Reeds

moved out, the Bierces lived for twenty years, may, in another decade or two, come to be known as the old Gannett place. But the likelihood is that before many decades pass someone else will buy the old Gannett place, put in new bathrooms and shift the whole arrangement of the house, let the rock garden go to pot, and start a new pattern of Cream Hill life. The only thing I am sure about is that no one can foresee what Cream Hill will look like in 2050, or even in 1975.

Meanwhile, through a quarter-century of summer vacations and all-year weekends, Cream Hill has sustained, in many senses of the word, the Gannetts. Ruth and I had both drifted to New York City almost as instinctively as hummingbirds fly south in autumn, and we still love the big city. But it exhausts us. Puttering in the Cream Hill garden, cutting firewood, scything, are tiring too, but they tire different nerve-ends, and meanwhile they restore what the city frazzles. It is weekend country living which makes our mid-week city living feasible. The old fable of Antaeus and Mother Earth has modern meaning in our Cream Hill weekends. A man who never sees a bluebird only half lives.

We are no Thoreaus, seeking to escape the "slave economy" of the cities; we depend on the city for our livelihood. We are not escaping neighbors; we see more of our country neighbors, though they live miles from us, than we ever see of the mysterious non-neighbors who live in other houses on our city street. We are not fanatics of the homemade; we like fresh frozen peas in the winter better than home-canned string beans or slightly desiccated carrots from our own cellar. We have never made a cost accounting of our garden, and never will; we know it pays in deeper satisfactions than any profit or loss that could be reckoned in dollars and cents. We like to grow things, and to watch them grow. We also like the city's theaters; but we have never seen a play on Broadway more durably exciting than the drama of a robin's family growing up in a nest behind the bedroom shutter, a lady's-slipper unfolding from a bed of pine needles, or the calendar of flowers, from arbutus to fringed gentian.

Ours is a hybrid and ever-changing life pattern of city work and country weekends. We argue about it sometimes, and wonder if our weekend world is really mere escapism. We aren't sure. What we are sure about is that it works, and that we love it.

The Burden of the Valley of Vision

—DAVID GRAYSON

I came here eight years ago as the renter of this farm, of which soon afterward I became the owner. The time before that I like to forget. The chief impression it left upon my memory, now happily growing indistinct, is of being hurried faster than I could well travel. From the moment, as a boy of seventeen, I first began to pay my own way, my days were ordered by an inscrutable power which drove me hourly to my task. I was rarely allowed to look up or down, but always forward, toward that vague Success which we Americans love to glorify.

My senses, my nerves, even my muscles were continually strained to the utmost of attainment. If I loitered or paused by the wayside, as it seems natural for me to do, I soon heard the sharp crack of the lash. For many years—and I can say it truthfully—I never rested. I neither thought nor reflected. I had no pleasure, even though I pursued it fiercely during the brief respite of vacations. Through many feverish years I did not work; I merely produced.

The only real thing I did was to hurry as though every mo-

From *Adventures of David Grayson*, by David Grayson, Copyright 1925 by Doubleday & Company, Inc., Garden City, New York. Reprinted by permission of the publishers.

ment were my last; as though the world, which now seems so rich in everything, held only one prize which might be seized upon before I arrived. Since then I have tried to recall, like one who struggles to restore the visions of a fever, what it was that I ran to attain, or why I should have borne without rebellion such indignities to soul and body. That life seems now of all illusions the most distant and unreal. It is like the unguessed eternity before we are born; not of concern compared with that eternity upon which we are now embarked.

All these things happened in cities and among crowds. I like to forget them. They smack of that slavery of the spirit which is so much worse than any mere slavery of the body.

One day—it was in April, I remember, and the soft maples in the city park were just beginning to blossom—I stopped suddenly. I did not intend to stop. I confess in humiliation that it was no courage, no will of my own. I intended to go on toward Success; but Fate stopped me. It was as if I had been thrown violently from a moving planet; all the universe streamed around me and past me. It seemed to me that of all animate creation, I was the only thing that was still or silent. Until I stopped I had not known the pace I ran; and I had a vague sympathy and understanding, never felt before, for those who left the running. I lay prostrate with fever and close to death for weeks and watched the world go by: the dust, the noise, the very color of haste. The only sharp pang that I suffered was the feeling that I should be broken-hearted and that I was not; that I should care and that I did not. It was as though I had died and escaped all further responsibility. I even watched with dim equanimity my friends racing past me, panting as they ran. Some of them paused an instant to comfort me where I lay, but I could see that their minds were still upon the running and I was glad when they went away. I cannot tell with what weariness their haste oppressed me. As for them, they somehow blamed me for dropping out. I knew. Until we ourselves understand, we accept no excuse from the man who stops. While I felt it all, I was not bitter. I did not seem to care. I said to myself; "This is Unfitness. I survive no longer. So be it."

Thus I lay, and presently I began to hunger and thirst. Desire rose within me, the indescribable longing of the convalescent for the food of recovery. So I lay, questioning wearily what it was that I required. One morning I wakened with a strange, new joy in my soul. It came to me at that moment with indescribable poignancy, the thought of walking barefoot in cool, fresh plow furrows as I had once done when a boy. So vividly the memory came to me—the high airy world as it was at that moment, and the boy I was walking free in the furrows—that the weak tears filled my eyes, the first I had shed in many years. Then I thought of sitting in quiet thickets in old fence corners, the wood behind me rising still, cool, mysterious, and the fields in front stretching away in illimitable pleasantness. I thought of the good smell of cows at milking—you do not know, if you do not know!—I thought of the sights and sounds, the heat and sweat of the hay fields. I thought of a certain brook I knew when a boy that flowed among alders and wild parsnips, where I waded with a three-foot rod for trout. I thought of all these things as a man thinks of his first love. Oh, I craved the soil. I hungered and thirsted for the earth. I was greedy for growing things.

And thus, eight years ago, I came here like one sore-wounded creeping from the field of battle. I remember walking in the sunshine, weak yet, but curiously satisfied. I that was dead lived again. It came to me then with a curious certainty, not since so assuring, that I understood the chief marvel of nature hidden within the Story of the Resurrection, the marvel of plant and seed, father and son, the wonder of the seasons, the miracle of life. I, too, had died; I had lain long in darkness, and now I had risen again upon the sweet earth. And I possessed beyond others a knowledge of a former existence, which I knew, even then, I could never return to.

For a time, in the new life, I was happy to drunkenness—working, eating, sleeping. I was an animal again, let out to run in green pastures. I was glad of the sunrise and the sunset. I was glad at noon. It delighted me when my muscles ached with work and when, after supper, I could not keep my eyes open for sheer weariness. And sometimes I was awakened in the night out of a sound sleep—seemingly by the very silences—and lay in a sort of bodily comfort impossible to describe.

I did not want to feel or to think; I merely wanted to live. In the sun or the rain I wanted to go out and come in, and never again know the pain of the unquiet spirit. I looked forward to an awakening not without dread for we are as helpless before birth as in the presence of death.

But like all birth, it came, at last, suddenly. All that summer I had worked in a sort of animal content. Autumn had now come, late autumn, with coolness in the evening air. I was plowing in my upper field—not then mine in fact—and it was a soft afternoon with the earth turning up moist and fragrant. I had been walking the furrows all day long. I had taken note, as though my life depended upon it, of the occasional stones or roots in my field; I made sure of the adjustment of the harness; I drove with peculiar care to save the horses. With such simple details of the work in hand I had found it my joy to occupy my mind. Up to that moment the most important things in the world had seemed a straight furrow and well-turned corners—to me, then, a profound accomplishment.

I cannot well describe it, save by the analogy of an opening door somewhere within the house of my consciousness. I had been in the dark; I seemed to emerge. I had been bound down; I seemed to leap up—and with a marvelous sudden sense of freedom and joy.

I stopped there in my field and looked up. And it was as if I had never looked up before. I discovered another world. It had been there before, for long and long, but I had never seen nor felt it. All discoveries are made in that way; a man finds the new thing, not in nature but in himself.

It was as though, concerned with plow and harness and furrow, I had never known that the world had height or color or sweet sounds, or that there was *feeling* in a hillside. I forgot myself, or where I was. I stood a long time motionless. My dominant feeling, if I can at all express it, was of a strange new friendliness, a warmth, as though these hills, this field about me, the woods, had suddenly spoken to me and caressed me. It was as though I had been accepted in membership, as though I was now recognized, after long trial, as belonging here.

Across the town road which separates my farm from my nearest neighbor's, I saw a field, familiar, yet strangely new and unfamiliar, lying up to the setting sun, all red with autumn, above it the incalculable heights of the sky, blue, but not quite clear, owing to the Indian summer haze. I cannot convey the sweetness and softness of that landscape, the airiness of it, the mystery of it, as it came to me at that moment. It was as though, looking at an acquaintance long known, I should discover that I loved him. As I stood there I was conscious of the cool tang of burning leaves and brush heaps, the lazy smoke of which floated down the long valley and found me in my field, and finally I heard, as though the sounds were then made for the first time, all the vague murmurs of the countryside—a cowbell somewhere in the distance, the creak of a wagon, the blurred evening hum of birds, insects, frogs. So much it means for a man to stop and look up from his task. So I stood, and I looked up and down with a glow and a thrill which I cannot now look back upon without some envy and a little amusement at the very grandness and seriousness of it all. And I said aloud to myself: "I will be as broad as the earth. I will not be limited."

Thus I was born into the present world, and here I continue, not knowing what other world I may yet achieve. I do not know, but I wait in expectancy, keeping my furrows straight and my corners well turned. Since that day in the field, though my fences include no more acres, and I still plow my own fields, my real domain has expanded until I crop wide fields and take the profit of many curious pastures. From my farm I can see most of the world; and if I wait here long enough all people pass this way.

And I look out upon them not in the surroundings which they have chosen for themselves, but from the vantage ground of my familiar world. The symbols which meant so much in cities mean little here. Sometimes it seems to me as though I see men naked. They come and stand beside my oak, and the oak passes solemn judgment; they tread my furrows and the clods give silent evidence; they touch the the green blades of my corn, the corn whispers its sure conclusions. Stern judgments that will be deceived by no symbols!

Thus I have delighted, secretly, in calling myself an unlimited farmer, and I make this confession in answer to the inner and truthful demand of the soul that we are not, after all, the slaves of things, whether corn, or banknotes, or spindles; that we are not the used, but the users; that life is more than profit and loss. And so I shall expect that while I am talking farm some of you may be thinking of dry goods, banking, literature, carpentry, or whatnot. But if you can say, "I am an unlimited dry goods merchant; I am an unlimited carpenter," I will give you an old-fashioned country handshake, strong and warm. We are friends; our orbits coincide.

A Winter of Content

—LAURA LEE DAVIDSON

A small, rocky island in a lake, a canoe paddling away across the blue water, a woman standing on a narrow strip of beach, looking after it. I was the woman left on the shore; the canoe held my companions of the past summer; the island was to be my home until another summer should bring them back again.

There is no denying that I was frightened as I turned back along the trail toward the little house among the birches. It was hard work to keep from jumping into a boat and putting out after the canoe that was rounding the point and leaving me alone.

Little chilly fears laid icy fingers on the back of my neck. A shadow slipped between the trees; a sigh whispered among the leaves. I wanted to see all round me; I wanted to put my back against a wall. A little, grinning goblin of a misgiving stuck out an impudent tongue as it quoted some of the jeers of unsympathetic friends and relatives, who had derided my plan for borrowing the camp, when summer was gone, and staying on alone at the Lake of Many Islands.

"Good-by," had smiled my sister. "You say you mean to stay

From A Winter of Content, by Laura Lee Davidson, Copyright 1922 by Laura Lee Davidson. Published by Abingdon-Cokesbury Press, Nashville, Tennessee, and reprinted by permission of the author's estate.

a year, but you'll tire of solitude long before the winter. We'll see you back at Thanksgiving."

It was only mid-September, but I wanted to see her then at that very instant.

There had been a farewell dinner, the family assembled, to prophesy disaster.

"You'll freeze your nose and ears off," mourned a reassuring aunt.

In vain I reminded her that no inhabitant seen in five summers' sojourn at the lake had been without a nose or ears; all had had the requisite number of features, although some of those same features had withstood the cold of well-nigh a hundred winters. But she was not consoled, and continued to regard me so tearfully that I felt sure that she was bidding farewell to my nose.

"You'll break a leg and lie for days before anyone knows you are hurt," said Cousin John.

"You'll be snowed in and no one will find you until spring," said Brother Henry.

"You are a city woman and not strong. What do you know of a pioneer's life? It is the most foolish plan we ever heard of," chorused all.

Descending from prophecy to argument, they continued:

"Of course you will have a telephone."

"That I will not," I answered. "I have been jerked at the end of a telephone wire for years. I want rest."

"At least you will have a good dog. That will be some protection."

"A dog would drive away all the wild things. I want to study them," I objected.

"Then, for mercy's sake, find some other woman to stay there with you. Surely there is another lunatic willing to freeze to death on the precious island. You should have a companion, if only to send for help."

"I don't want a companion," I protested, tearfully. "I won't be responsible for another person's comfort or safety. I will do this thing alone or not at all."

"I am tired to death," I stormed. "I need rest for at least one year. I want to watch the procession of the seasons in some place that is not all paved streets, city smells and noise. Instead of the clang of car bells and the honk of automobile horns, I want to hear the winds sing across the ice fields, instead of the smell of asphalt and hot gasoline, I want the odor of wet earth in boggy places. I have loved the woods all my life; I long to see the year go round there just once before I die."

At which outburst they shrugged exasperated shoulders and were silent, but each one drew me aside, at parting, and pressed a gift into my hand.

"Be sure to let us know if anything goes wrong. Write to us if you need the least thing. Don't be ashamed to come back, if the experiment proves a failure"—and so on and so on, God bless them!

Of all this the bogey reminded me as he danced ahead up the winding trail.

The house looked lonely, even in the brightness of the late afternoon. I hurried supper, to be indoors before the twilight fell. Big Canadian hares hopped along the paths and sat at the kitchen door, their great eyes peering, long, furry ears alert, quivering noses pressed against the wire screen. Grouse pecked on the hillside, as tame as barnyard fowl. From the water came the evening call of the loons.

The scant meal finished, I ran across the platform from the kitchen to the main house and locked up. Somehow, I did not want any open doors behind me that evening. Then I loaded the pistol and laid it on a shelf at the head of the bed, along with the Bible and the Prayer Book. If any marauder could know how dreadfully afraid I am of that pistol, he would do his marauding with a quiet mind. I never expect to touch that weapon. It shall be cleaned and oiled when any of the men come over from the mainland, but handle it—never! I would not fire it for a kingdom.

While it was still light I climbed into bed, and lay down rigid, with tight-shut eyes, trying to pretend I did not hear all the rustling, creaking, snapping noises in the woods. Heavy animals pushed through the fallen leaves. Something that sounded as large as a moose went crashing through the dry bushes.

"A rabbit," I whispered to myself.

Creatures surely as large as bears rushed through the underbrush.

"Grouse," I tried to believe.

From the lake came stealthy sounds.

"Driftwood pounding against the rocks, not really oars," I murmured to my thumping heart.

Then light, pattering footsteps on the porch.

In desperation I raised my head and looked out. It was a little red fox, trotting busily along, snuffling softly as he went. I lay down and closed my eyes firmly, determined not to open them again no matter what might happen; then must have dozed, for suddenly I was aware of a light that flooded all the room.

There through the northeast window, large and round and beautiful, shone the moon, the great Moon of the Falling Leaves. It was like the sudden meeting with a friend, reassuring, comforting. A broad band of light lay across my breast like a kind arm thrown over me. The path of the moonbeams on the water seemed the road to some safe haven. With the moon's calm face looking in and the soft lapping of the waves as lullaby, I fell asleep—and lo! it was day.

The days are still warm, but autumn is surely here. The wasps are dying everywhere and lie in heaps on all the window-sills; the great water spiders have disappeared, and all day long the yellow leaves drift down silently, steadily, in the forests.

Wreaths of vapor hang over the trees, and every wind brings the pungent fall odor of distant forest fires. The hillsides are a blaze of color, with basswoods a beautiful butter-yellow; oaks, russet and maroon; and sugar maples, a flame of scarlet against the dark-green velvet of the cedars and hemlocks. Each birch stands forth, a slender Danaë, white feet in a drift of gold. The woods here on the island are thinning rapidly. All sorts of hidden dells and boulders are coming to light. Soon the whole island will lie open to the sight, and then there will no longer be anything mysterious about it.

At the approach of cold weather the small animals and the few birds that are left draw nearer to the house. Grouse are in all the paths, flying up everywhere. They rise with a thrashing, pounding noise and soar away over the bushes, to settle again only a little further on. Last evening, at twilight, two of them came on the porch, the little cock ruffling it bravely, wings dragging, fantail spread, ruff standing valiantly erect. A hen followed sedately at his heels. They are very pretty, about the size of bantam chickens. How I hope that I shall be here to see their young in the spring!

This afternoon a red squirrel came round the corner of the house and sat down, absent-mindedly, beside me on a bench. When he looked up and saw what he had done he gave a shriek and a bound and fled chattering off toward the sundial. But he will come back and will probably be darting into the house when he thinks my back is turned, for there is nothing half so impudent or so mischievous as the red squirrel. I am told that they do not "den in" as the chipmunks do.

The rabbits do their best to help me get rid of my stores. There are hundreds of them about. They sit under the bushes, peering out; they appear and disappear between the dry stalks of the brakes. At evening they come close to the house, and catch bits of bread and potatoes thrown to them, then sit in the paths munching contentedly. They are not rabbits, correctly speaking, but Canadian hares, with long brown fur, bulging black eyes, furry ears, fringed with black, and very long hind legs. One of them comes so close and seems so fearless that it should not be difficult to tame him. I have named him Peter. These hares turn snow-white in winter, I am told. Even now their coats are showing white where the winter coat is growing.

In the dusk the porcupines come pushing through the fallen leaves, snuffling and grunting. Away in the woods the bobcats scream and snarl.

Peter, the rabbit, spends most of his time at the door, waiting for a chance crust. He sits on his haunches, rocking gently back and forth, making a soft, little knocking noise on the porch floor. If I am late in coming out at mealtimes, he looks at me with so dignified an air of patient reproof that I feel quite apologetic for having kept him waiting. His meal finished, he washes his face and paws carefully, like a cat; then sits in the sun, eyes closed, forepaws tucked away under his breast and ears laid back along his shoulders. He is turning white very rapidly. At first, only his tail, feet, breast, and the ends of his ears were lightly powdered, but now he looks as if he had hopped into a pan of flour by mistake.

Other hares, now lean and wild, come out of the woods at dusk and try to share Peter's bread. But he turns on them fiercely, driving them back over the hill, with an angry noise, something between a squeal and a grunt. If anyone thinks a rabbit a meek, poor-spirited creature, he should see Peter when threatened with the loss of his dinner. Evidently, he believes that he has pre-empted this territory and all that goes here in the way of food, and he means to defend his claim.

Rufus, the red squirrel, torments Peter unmercifully, dashing across the ground under his nose and snatching the bread from between the rabbit's very teeth. He is there and away before the rabbit knows what has happened. Poor, slow little Peter stood these attacks in bewildered patience for a time; but now he has worked out a plan for getting even with the squirrel that serves him fairly well. He sits on his crust, drawing it out inch by inch from under him as he nibbles, but even at that Rufus gets about half. I am training the rabbit to take his food from my hand, for nothing thrown on the ground is safe for an instant from the little red-brown robber. It took some very patient sitting to overcome Peter's timidity, but after the first bit was taken the rest was easy. Now he comes fearlessly to me as soon as I appear.

The squirrel is growing very tame too, but he will never be as tranquil a companion as the rabbit. He lacks Bunny's repose of manner. He is sitting on the window-sill now, eating a bit of cold potato. He turns it round and round, nibbling at it daintily. Now and again he stops to lay a tiny paw on his heart—or is it his stomach? The area of his organs is very minute and it may be either.

There is something very flattering in the confidence of these little creatures of the island. How do they know that they may safely trust my kindness? How can they be sure that I will not betray them suddenly with trap or gun?

The rabbit came into the house yesterday, padding about noiselessly on his cushioned toes. He stopped at each chair and stood on his hind feet, resting his forepaws on the seat. He examined everything, ears wriggling, nose quivering, tail thumping on the carpet. Suddenly he discovered that the door had blown shut and then he went quite wild with fear. He was in a trap, he thought, and tore round and round the room, jumping against the windowpanes, dashing his head against the walls until I feared that he would injure himself before I could reach the door to open it. Poor little Peter, he is not valiant after all. He comes in still, but always keeps close to the door, and the way of escape must always be open.

The time of great winds has come, the heavy November gales that roar down the lakes, lashing the water into white-capped waves, dashing the driftwood against the rocks and decking the beaches with long wreaths of yellow foam. The swell is so strong and the waves so high that even the men do not care to venture out. When I must get over to Blake's farm I hug the shore of the island to the point, then dash across the channel between this land and his, and the wind turns my light skiff round and round before I can catch the lee again.

All night the house rocks and shivers and the trees creak, groan and crash down in the woods. I am afraid to walk the trails because of falling branches, for if I were struck down I should lie in the path for days and no one would know that I had been hurt.

These winds give the strangest effect of distant music. I am always thinking that I can almost hear the sound of trumpets, blowing far away.

Inside, the house is warm and comfortable, with its creamy yellow walls of unpainted wood, its many windows, its pictures, its books; but I am lonely; I cannot settle to any occupation. The constant roaring of the wind unnerves me, the gray, scudding clouds depress me. A hound on the shore bays and howls day and night. I have heard no human voice for more than a week.

Headhunting in the Solomon Islands

—CAROLINE MYTINGER

We had started out from the plantation house at a walk, but that was soon corrected. Even the normal Australian horse knows only two gaits, and there is nothing between a sleep-walk and a swoop. We took the plantation on the fly, branches flapping like banners, the colt running in wide, delighted circles, and my kangaroo staggering the course like the afternoon-of-a-faun. The flies held their cloud formation even at high speed, and far behind us, Friday, the carrier, ran holding onto his flower. It was like tearing up a boulder-strewn creek, for the clover was littered with fallen coconuts; by the time we reached the edge of the plantation our hands were raw from trying to keep our horses from making the trip on their chins. We were frothing like the animals—and this was still in the shade.

Now we came out on an upward-sloping expanse .of tiger grass. It was one of the few low growths we saw anywhere in the islands, only ten feet high, and revealing no trail whatsoever. The lead horse seemed to know the way, however, and plunged straight into the wilderness of grass. There was no shade here, nothing save the tassels hanging over our heads, and the tunnel was an inferno. Also, now at a walk, the flies settled down in earnest, finding our juices just as tasty as the horses' sores. Walking on my own feet is one of my phobias, but I felt so desperate that I very nearly did get off the heaving stead. I was saved from such an extremity just in time by our reaching the bush wall.

So far as we could see there was no opening of any trail into it. With the morning sun striking it, the façade was a solid mass with even the patterns swallowed up in the flat light. We followed along it for some distance, and then suddenly we saw the planter duck forward and he and his horse disappeared straight into the wall. Only an animal could have smelled out that trail. The opening was overgrown with a thin curtain of leaves, but just behind it was a dark tunnel exactly horse size. We lay over on our horses' necks and did not rise until the planter called, "All clear."

Everything was black at first, and there was the chill of a cave. "*Coo-oo-oo-ee!*" Margaret yipped—the Australian cowhand's "Whoopee"—and sure enough back came the hollow echo from somewhere far up ahead. Gradually our eyes became adjusted to the gloom, and then we pulled up, awed, enchanted. We *were* in a cave, a cave going up a hillside, complete with stalactites and stalagmites. The first astonishing thing was the missing jungle. There was no thicket, no underbrush, and not one robust green thing growing anywhere on the surface. There were just gigantic tree trunks spaced wide apart, rising absolutely straight and branchless to eighty or more feet above us. High up there they branched out into a solid ceiling of leaves through which came only a glimmer of light. It was like being under an enormous circus tent, with the roof hung with great leafless loops of vine rope. Below, knotted and twisting with the powerful roots of the trees that spread all over the surface, these vines crawled like strangling pythons up and around the trunks, growing into them, covering them in a network of thick arms. No wonder there were no low branches; only the very tops of the trees struggling toward the sun could hope to keep ahead of those writhing parasites.

Underfoot it was a labyrinth of huge aerial roots and black muck, drooling with centuries of undried rains, and the cold air was pungent with the odor of rotting leaves and wood. Some of the giants had fallen, yet there was no break in the leaf roof anywhere. How these mountain slopes reforest themselves is hard to explain. Only here and there stood a timid sapling, shooting up branchless and as straight as an arrow toward the feeble light above. At the very tip were a few transparent green leaves. But these were the only color throughout the great cave. The muck underfoot was a deep brown, almost black; the towering pillars of the trees were a cold gray with here and there patches of brown moss. Yet all through the forest was the curious green glow which is the peculiarity of the great forests, even the leafless redwoods. We should have missed our first island flower if the planter had not pointed it out. High up on the trunk of a tree was a tiny cluster of yellow and green, very pale. It looked like a butterfly, and it was an orchid. And it was consistent with the nature of these islands that the only place a fragile bud could survive to become a blossom was hidden away from the competition in the sunlight.

This was a great cavern in every respect except sound; here was none of the hush of the palm cathedral through the night. It was a Rackham haunted forest come alive. All the sounds of a birdhouse in the zoo, and of a madhouse; all the weird piping and wailing, croaking and lowing and sawing and thumping. Something cried like a child—and there was not a visible creature to make these sounds. Even the cockatoos of the plantation could not be seen, though we could hear their raucous screams above the tree roof. It is little wonder that the bushmen, living for centuries in this eerie gloom where the very air moans and cries so mysteriously, are animists.

But the singing close to our ears was made by no spirit. The air was filled with gloom-loving anopheles. We had left most of the flies behind in the bush wall tunnel, but now our tortured horses, ourselves included, were coated with blood-swollen mosquitoes. My kangaroo had long ago exhausted his adrenal glands and was now stumbling up over the high roots with his head hanging nearly to the ground. All the horses were heaving painfully from the incline, and were white with froth as if they had been cantering. It was sheer torture sitting on them and I was shivering with cold, so I got down with the idea of walking. What I did was mush, in the truest sense of the word, for the higher we climbed the deeper the muck and the higher the roots above the ground. I was panting and boiling (and back on my horse) before I had gone ten yards.

And now up on the horse I was immediately shivering again— and still hot. A storm was coming up. We could hear the roar of it over the treetops far away from us, and long before we felt the first gusts of wind. Like magic the clamor of spirits ceased. The distant roar swelled in volume, and then we were in the darkness of a moonless night. Wave on wave of wind passed over the roof and then finally the whirlwind hit. The sound has no parallel. It was howl, roar, and moan together but with unearthly volume. Man's instinctive fear may be that of being dropped, but certainly a good runner-up is the terror of having things dropped on him in the dark. Our roof split open in flashing gaps of light, showing briefly the vine ropes slashing about as if whipped by some mighty hand. Showers of leaves fell through the whitened air, and then dead limbs. The terrified colt dashed off into the dark and my own animal tore frantically at his bridle and then stood stiff with his flesh quivering. I expected him to bolt from under me. We were all off then, trying to find something to tie our horses to. Friday was useless. He would not come near the frantic animals.

Then came the rain. It came in a deafening roar and fell not in drops, but in streams from the high branches and vine loops, and in bucketfuls when the roof split open. The trunks of the trees were upright rivers gleaming white in the ripples, and our trail, what there had been of it, was a freshet pouring over already saturated earth. And all the while the roof was screaming and being pitched about by an icy wind which corrugated our wet hides.

And still I felt hot. Even while I was shaking with cold my nose was hot. Something had happened to the back of my neck; it felt as if it had been hit with a club. My eyeballs must be on rubber bands hitched to sore places in my brain, for every time I moved my eyes I could feel the stretch clear to the back of my skull. And my spine hurt and all my muscles and joints, and my skin felt raw and dry even while it was cold and wet. And I felt very tired and dizzy and hot and cold—and utterly miserable.

I had "it"—malaria.

My Life with the Eskimo

—VILHJALMUR STEFANSSON

It was at this time that I first became familiar with the psychology of seals. Arctic explorers of some experience have said in print that a white man may learn to hunt caribou as well as an Eskimo, but no white man can ever learn to hunt seals successfully on top of the Arctic spring ice. This is so far from being true in my experience that I should say it is much easier to stalk seals than it is to stalk caribou. All you have to know is one or two elementary facts about the seal's habits and mental processes. One day Dr. Anderson and I were out on the sea ice and happened to notice a seal basking in the sun. As a matter of scientific interest one of us watched him through the field glasses, while the other held a watch in one hand and a pencil in the other, and noted down the length of the naps the seal was taking between his short periods of wakefulness. Like other seals at this time of year, he was lying beside his hole, enjoying the warm sun. After each short nap he would raise his head about twelve inches above the level of the ice, take a survey of the horizon, and drop to sleep again. From his movements we took down the following series of observations:

AWAKE	ASLEEP	AWAKE	ASLEEP
5 seconds	70 seconds	4 seconds	20 seconds
2 "	10 "	5 "	30 "
10 "	10 "	2 "	5 "
1 "	30 "	3 "	18 "
8 "	2 "	5 "	90 "
7 "	7 "	2 "	60 "
8 "	48 "	3 "	4 "
2 "	15 "	4 "	48 "
6 "	45 "		

From this we deduced the interesting fact that the ratio of the lengths of his periods of wakefulness to those of his periods of sleep was as 1 : 6.6, and further, that the average length of his periods of wakefulness was 4.5 seconds, and the average length of his naps was 30.1 seconds.

Another day, watching another seal, we got the following results:

AWAKE	ASLEEP	AWAKE	ASLEEP
8 seconds	60 seconds	7 seconds	50 seconds
8 "	22 "	3 "	25 "
4 "	100 "	4 "	18 "
6 "	14 "	4 "	20 "

This seal was evidently somewhat more somnolent than the first, for his sleeping time was to his waking as 1 : 7.02. He was awake on an average 5.5 seconds at a time and his naps averaged 35.6 seconds each.

The whole principle of successfully stalking a seal is just in realizing from the first that he is bound to see you and that your only hope is in pretending that you also are a seal. If you act and look so as to convince him from the first that you are a brother seal, he will regard you with unconcern. To simulate a seal well enough to deceive a seal is not difficult, for, to begin with, we know from experience that his eyesight is poor. You can walk up without taking any special precautions until, under ordinary conditions of light, you are within two hundred and fifty or three hundred yards. Then you have to begin to be more careful. You move ahead while he is asleep, and when he wakes up you stop motionless. You can safely proceed on all fours until within something less than two hundred yards, but after that you will have to play more faithfully. Your method of locomotion will then have to be that of the seal, which does not differ very materially from that of a snake, and which therefore has its disadvantages at a season of the year when the surface of the ice is covered with puddles of water anywhere from an inch to twenty inches in depth, as it is in spring and early summer. You must not only crawl ahead, seal-fashion, but you must be careful to always present a side view of your body to the seal, for a man coming head-on does not look particularly like a seal.

Until you are within a hundred yards or so the seal is not likely to notice you, but somewhere between the hundred yards and the seventy-five yard mark his attention will suddenly be attracted to you, and instead of going to sleep at the end of his ordinary short period of wakefulness, he will remain awake and stare at you steadily. The seal knows, exactly as well as the seal hunter knows, that no seal in this world will sleep continuously for as much as four minutes at a time. If you lie still that long, he will know you are no seal, and up will go his tail and down he will slide into the water in the twinkling of an eye. When the seal, therefore, has been watching you carefully for twenty or thirty seconds, you must raise your head twelve or fifteen inches above the ice, look around seal-fashion, so that your eyes will sweep the whole circle of the horizon, and drop your head again upon the ice. By the time he has seen you repeat this process two or three times in the space of five or six minutes he will be convinced that you are a seal, and all his worries will be gone. From then on you can proceed more rapidly, crawling ahead while he sleeps and stopping while he remains awake, never doing anything unbecoming a seal. In this way you can crawl within five or ten yards of him if you like, and as a matter of fact I have known of expert seal hunters who under emergencies would go after a seal without any ordinary weapon and crawl so near him that they could seize him by a flipper, pull him away from his hole, and club or stab him. My Eskimo companions generally used to crawl within about fifteen or twenty yards; but I have found under ordinary circumstances that fifty yards is close enough for a man with a rifle. The animal lies on a slippery incline beside his hole, so that the shot that kills him must kill him instantly. It must shatter the brain or break the spinal cord of the neck; the slightest quiver of a muscle will send him sliding into the water and all your work will have been to no purpose.

Seals were not common in this locality, and although we got a few we were anxious also to get some caribou. The second day after our enforced halt Natkusiak and I accordingly went off in different directions looking for caribou. It was a long hunt for both of us. I returned in about eighteen hours with a young fawn for a back-load, which was one of two animals I had seen, while Natkusiak returned six or eight hours later with the story of having killed two caribou out of three that he saw. Evidently this was no paradise for big game. Ducks, however, were very abundant.

As our main food supply at this time was waterfowl, we expected our dogs as well as ourselves to live on ducks, but this did not suit them very well at first. Our experience with dogs shows that their food prejudices are very much like those of men. It is the common opinion of those who keep hotels and boarding schools that they can tell much about a man's bringing up from the things he objects to eating. The son of wealthy parents who is used to eating fifty different articles of food in a week will take readily to the fifty-first; but a farmer's son who from one year's end to another has lived on nothing but fat pork, potatoes, bread, and tea, is likely to be so wedded to the idea that nothing but pork and potatoes is fit to eat that when he meets with a new dish, the fifth or sixth one of his experience, it strikes him as an unheard-of thing and unfit for food. It is common knowledge among guides in such out of the way places as Iceland that the wealthy travelers who visit the country will readily and with enjoyment adapt themselves to the food of the peasant, while the servants who accompany their wealthy masters have to be especially looked after by the guides and insist on being fed on provisions such as they are used to having in their own country.

The same principle applies to our house dogs, which are used to eating all the varied things that we eat. They are used to so many different flavors that they take readily to one more that happens to be strange. The white man's dog that comes to the Arctic is likely to eat seal meat or any other meat of local growth the first time it is offered him; but take an Indian's dog, that has been brought up inland on nothing but caribou meat, and bring him to the coast, and he will starve for a week before he is willing to swallow the first mouthful of seal. Similarly, I have known Eskimo dogs brought up on seal meat, which when taken inland would have to be starved for a week or more before they would eat the first mouthful of caribou.

We now had with us dogs which we had brought from the Mackenzie River and which it had taken several days of starvation to teach to eat seal; we also had with us dogs of Eskimo bringing up which had similarly been forced to eat caribou meat; but now all of these were simultaneously brought face to face with a new diet (ducks), and it took long periods of abstinence from food to enable them to get up an appetite for the new dish. An interesting observation in this connection is that we have invariably found the conservatism of the females to be greater than that of the males. Out of any pack of dogs that are compelled to learn to eat a new kind of food, the last to give in are the female dogs.

Numerous travelers have pointed out that dogs will not eat dog meat, and have considered this a proof that dogs have an

inherent aversion to cannibalism. We have seen nothing to sub-
stantiate this view, for a dog that has been brought up on seal
meat will eat dog meat quite as readily as he will caribou, and a
dog brought up on caribou meat will learn to eat dog meat
quite as readily as he will learn to eat seal or duck. There is
prejudice against the new but no disinclination to cannibalism.

Alone

—RICHARD E. BYRD

I stood at the trapdoor and watched the two Citroëns move away. Their red hoods and rounded canvas superstructures made a jaunty picture. June headed due north into the noon sun, so big and swollen, and so low in the sky, that it could well have passed for a setting sun. In the cold air (the temperature was 50° below zero) the exhaust vapor puffed up like a smoke screen, which a gentle northerly wind fanned out until much of the eastern horizon was obscured. I went below, intending to busy myself with the wind-speed records; but the errand was a piece of self-deception which I could not quite bring off. For perhaps the only moment in my adult life I was conscious of being utterly at loose ends. The shack, which had seemed bright and cheery, now was neither. And, obeying an impulse which I had no time to be ashamed of, I rushed up the hatch ladder. Just why, I don't know even now; perhaps for a last look at something alive and moving. Although the cars were by then some distance away, I could still hear the *beep-beep* of the horns and the clatter of the treads, so clearly do sounds carry in that crystal air.

About 1 o'clock in the morning, just before turning in, I went topside for a look around. The night was spacious and fine.

Numberless stars crowded the sky. I had never seen so many. You had only to reach up and fill your hands with the bright pebbles. Earlier, a monstrous red moon had climbed into the northern quadrant, but it was gone by then. The stars were everywhere. A sailor's sky, I thought, commanded by the Southern Cross and the wheeling constellations of Hydrus, Orion, and Triangulum drifting ever so slowly. It was a lovely motion to watch. And all this was mine—the stars, the constellations, even the earth as it turned on its axis. If great inward peace and exhilaration can exist together, then this, I decided my first night alone, was what should possess the senses.

No, it wasn't going to be half bad. A man had no need of the world here—certainly not the world of commonplace manners and accustomed security. The Barrier, austere as platinum, was world enough; and onto it I had trespassed but little. The only things of mine that showed were the radio antenna, the twelve-foot anemometer pole surmounted by the silver weather vane, and the aluminum wind cups, the beehive instrument shelter for the thermometers and recording barograph, and the ventilator pipes and stovepipe sticking above the shack roof. Without taking more than a few steps, I could touch them all; and a traveler on a darkish night might pass at twenty yards and miss them entirely. Yet, wasn't this really enough? It occurred to me then that half the confusion in the world comes from not knowing how little we need.

That night, anyway, I had no consciousness of missing conventional sounds and stirrings. I was as methodical as any family man follownig his ordinary routine. I turned off the valve in the stove and put out the fire. Then I undressed, draping my clothes over a chair. I remember cussing inwardly when my bare feet touched the floor, and certainly I stepped lively in crossing the shack to open the door for ventilation and in leaping into the sleeping bag before the inflowing cold blast overtook me. The bag at first was cold, as it always was, from accumulated body moisture. And, while I waited for it to warm up to a tolerable temperature and massaged the protesting shoulder and felt around to make sure that I hadn't forgotten the flashlight in case I had to get up, my mind was wondering whether my family was all right and about the things I'd do in the morning. But, most of all, it kept dropping back to the tractor crew somewhere between me and Little America, and I couldn't help reproaching myself for having kept them so long.

Cold—even April's relatively moderate cold—gave me plenty to think about. The novocaine in my medical kit froze and shattered the glass tubes. So did the chemicals in the fire bombs. Two cases of tomato juice shattered their bottles. Whenever I brought canned food inside the shack I had to let it stand all day near the stove to thaw. On very cold days the kerosene and Stoddard solvent flowed like cylinder oil; I dug a deep hole in the tunnel floor for my can to lengthen the drop in the rubber hose which I used as a siphon. Frost was forever collecting on the electrical contact points of the wind vane and wind cups. Some days I climbed the twelve-foot anemometer pole two and three times to clean them. It was a bitter job, especially on blustery nights. With my legs twined around the slender pole, my arms flung over the cleats, and my free hands trying to scrape the contact point clean with a knife and at the same time hold a flashlight to see, I qualified for the world's coldest flagpole sitter. I seldom came down from that pole without a frozen finger, toe, nose, or cheek.

The shack was always freezingly cold in the morning. I slept with the door open. When I arose the inside temperature (depending upon the surface weather) might be anywhere from 10° to 40° below zero. Frost coated the sleeping bag where my breath had condensed during the night; my socks and boots, when I picked them up, were so stiff with frozen sweat that I first had to work them between my hands. A pair of silk gloves hung from a nail over the bunk, where I could grab them the first thing. Yet, even with their protection, my fingers would sting and burn from the touch of the lamp and stove as I lighted them. The old flesh had sloughed off the tips, and the new flesh for a while was insufferably tender. So I had my troubles. Some came from my own inadequacies. At first I had a devil of a time with the weather instruments. The traces became horribly blotched, the pens stuck, and the instruments themselves stopped without rhyme or reason. But, one way or another, I usually managed to contrive a cure. I learned how to thin the ink with glycerine to keep it from freezing, and how to cut the oil in the instruments with gasoline and rub the delicate parts with graphite, which wasn't affected so much by the cold.

The coming of the polar night is not the spectacular rush that some imagine it to be. The day is not abruptly walled off; the night does not drop suddenly. Rather, the effect is a gradual accumulation, like that of an infinitely prolonged tide. Each day the darkness, which is the tide, washes in a little farther and stays a little longer; each time the day, which is a beach, contracts a little more, until at last it is covered. The onlooker is not conscious of haste. On the contrary, he is sensible of something of incalculable importance being accomplished with timeless patience. The going of the day is a gradual process, modulated by the intervention of twilight. You look up, and it is gone. But not completely. Long after the horizon has interposed itself, the sun continues to cast up a pale and dwindling imitation of the day. You can trace its progress by the glow thrown up as it makes its round just below the horizon.

These are the best times, the times when neglected senses expand to an exquisite sensitivity. You stand on the Barrier, and simply look and listen and feel. The morning may be compounded of an unfathomable, tantalizing fog in which you stumble over sastrugi you can't see, and detour past obstructions that don't exist, and take your bearings from tiny bamboo markers that loom as big as telephone poles and hang suspended in space. On such a day, I could swear that the instrument shelter was as big as an ocean liner. On one such day I saw the blank northeastern sky become filled with the most magnificent Barrier coast I have ever seen, true in every line and faced with cliffs several thousand feet tall. A mirage, of course. Yet, a man who had never seen such things would have taken oath that it was real. The afternoon may be so clear that you dare not make a sound, lest it fall in pieces. And on such a day I have seen the sky shatter like a broken goblet, and dissolve into iridescent tipsy fragments—ice crystals falling across the face of the sun. And once in the golden downpour a slender column of platinum leaped up from the horizon, clean through the sun's core; a second luminous shadow formed horizontally through the sun, making a perfect cross. Presently two miniature suns, green and yellow in color, flipped simultaneously to the ends of each arm. These are parhelia, the most dramatic of all refraction phenomena; nothing is lovelier.

April 14. Took my daily walk at 4 P.M. today, in 89° of frost. The sun had dropped below the horizon, and a blue—of a richness I've never seen anywhere else—flooded in, extinguishing all but the dying embers of the sunset.

Due west, halfway to the zenith, Venus was an unblinking diamond; and opposite her, in the eastern sky, was a brilliant twinkling star set off exquisitely, as was Venus, in the sea of blue. In the northeast a silver-green serpentine aurora pulsed and quivered gently. In places the Barrier's whiteness had the appearance of dull platinum. It was all delicate and illusive. The colors were subdued and not numerous; the jewels few; the setting simple. But the way these things went together showed a master's touch.

I paused to listen to the silence. My breath, crystallized as it passed my cheeks, drifted on a breeze gentler than a whisper. The wind vane pointed toward the South Pole. Presently the wind cups ceased their gentle turning as the cold killed the breeze. My frozen breath hung like a cloud overhead.

The day was dying, the night being born—but with great peace. Here were the imponderable processes and forces of the cosmos, harmonious and soundless. Harmony, that was it! That was what came out of the silence—a gentle rhythm, the strain of a perfect chord, the music of the spheres, perhaps.

It was enough to catch that rhythm, momentarily to be myself a part of it. In that instant I could feel no doubt of man's oneness with the universe. The conviction came that that rhythm was too orderly, too harmonious, too perfect to be a product of blind chance—that, therefore, there must be purpose in the whole and that man was part of that whole and not an accidental offshoot. It was a feeling that transcended reason; that went to the heart of man's despair and found it groundless. The universe was a cosmos, not a chaos; man was as rightfully a part of that cosmos as were the day and night.

May 12. The silence of this place is as real and solid as sound. More real, in fact, than the occasional creaks of the Barrier and the heavier concussions of snow quakes. . . . It seems to merge in and become part of the indescribable *evenness*, as do the cold and the dark and the relentless ticking of the clocks. This evenness fills the air with its mood of unchangeableness; it sits across from me at the table, and gets into the bunk with me at night. And no thought will wander so far as not eventually to be brought up hard by it. This is timelessness in its ultimate meaning. Very often my mood soars above it; but, when this mood goes, I find myself craving change—a look at trees, a rock, a handful of earth, the sound of foghorns, anything belonging to the world of movement and living things.

But I refuse to be disconcerted. This is a great experience. The despondency which used to come after supper—probably because that is the hour when we expect companionship—seems to have disappeared. Incidentally, I have mastered the business of waking myself in the morning; it has returned as mysteriously as it disappeared. Every morning for the last fortnight I've awakened within five minutes of the time I set in my mind.

I'm getting absent-minded. Last night I put sugar in the soup, and tonight I plunked a spoonful of corn-meal mush on the table where the plate should have been. I've been reading stories from several old English magazines. I got started on a murder serial, but I'll be damned if I can find two crucial installments. So I've had no choice but to try the love stories, and it is queer to reflect that beyond the horizon the joyful aspects of life go on. Well, this is the one continent where no woman has ever set foot; I can't say that it is any better on that account. In fact, the stampede to the altar that took place after the return of my previous expedition would seem to offer strong corroboration of that. Of the forty-one men with me at Little America, thirty were bachelors. Several married the first girls they met in New Zealand; most of the rest got married immediately upon their return to the United States. Two of the bachelors were around fifty years old, and both were married shortly after reaching home. There are only a few left, and I suspect their lonesome state is not entirely their fault.

May 16. It's just a week since the last after-supper depression. I don't want to be overconfident, but I believe I have it licked.
. . .

June 1st was a Friday. A black Friday for me. The nightmare left me, and about 9 o'clock in the morning I awakened with a violent start, as if I had been thrown down a well in my sleep. I found myself staring wildly into the darkness of the shack, not knowing where I was. The weakness that filled my body when I turned in the sleeping bag and tried to throw the flashlight on my wrist watch was an eloquent reminder. I was Richard E. Byrd, United States Navy (Ret.), temporarily sojourning at Latitude 80° 08′ South, and not worth a damn to myself or anybody else. My mouth was dry and tasted foul. God, I was thirsty. But I had hardly strength to move. I clung to the sleeping bag, which was the only source of comfort and warmth left to me, and mournfully debated the little that might be done.

Two facts stood clear. One was that my chances of recovering were slim. The other was that in my weakness I was incapable of taking care of myself. These were desperate conclusions, but my mood allowed no others. All that I could reasonably hope for was to prolong my existence for a few days by hoarding my remaining resources; by doing the necessary things *very slowly* and with *great deliberation.* So long as he did that and maintained the right frame of mind, even a very ill man should be able to last a time. So I reasoned, anyway. There was no alternative. My hopes of survival had to be staked on the theory.

But you must have *faith*—you must have faith in the outcome, I whispered to myself. It is like a flight, a flight into another unknown. You start and you cannot turn back. You must go on and on, trusting your instruments, the course you have plotted on the charts, and the reasonableness of events. Whatever goes wrong will be mostly of your own making; if it is to be tragedy, then it will be the commonplace tragedy of human vulnerability.

My first need was warmth and food. The fire had been out about twelve hours; I had not eaten in nearly thirty-six. Toward providing those necessities I began to mobilize my slender resources. If there had been a movie camera to record my movements, the resulting picture could have been passed off as slow motion. Every act was performed with the utmost patience. I lifted the lantern—and waited. I edged out of the sleeping bag—and rested on the chair beside the stove. I pulled on my pants, hiking them up a little bit at a time. Then the shirt. Then the socks. And shoes. And finally the parka. All this took a long time. I was shaking so from the cold that, when my elbow struck the wall, the sound was like a peremptory knock at the door. Too miserable to stick it out, I retreated to the sleeping bag; half an hour later the chill in my body drove me into a fresh attempt to reach the stove.

Faintness seized me as I touched foot to the floor. I barely made the chair. There I sat for some minutes, not moving, just staring at the candle. Then I turned the valve, and with the stove lids off waited for the wick to become saturated with the cold, sluggish oil. Thirst continued to plague me. Several inches of ice were in the water bucket. I dropped it on the floor, bottom up. A sliver of ice fell out, which I sucked until my teeth rattled from the cold. A box of matches was on the table. I touched one to the burner. A red flame licked over the metal ring; it was a beautiful thing to see. I sat there ten or fifteen minutes at least, absorbing the column of warmth. The flame burned red and smoky, when it should have been blue and clear; and, studying it, I knew that this was from faulty combustion and was one source of my misfortunes. This fire was my enemy, but I could not live without it.

Thus this never-ending day began. To describe it all would be tedious. Nothing really happened; and yet, no day in my life was more momentous. I lived a thousand years, and all of them were agonizing. I won a little and lost a lot. At the day's end —if it can be said to have had an end—all that I could say was that I was still alive. Granting the conditions, I had no right to expect more. Life seldom ends gracefully or sensibly. The protesting body succumbs like a sinking ship going down with the certificate of seaworthiness nailed fast to the wheelhouse bulkhead; but the mind, like the man on the bridge, realizes at last the weakness of the hull and ponders the irony. If the business drags out long enough, as mine did, the essence of things in time becomes pitifully clear; except that by then it is wadded into a tight little scrap ready to be thrown away, as the knowledge is of no earthly use.

My thirst was the tallest tree in a forest of pain. The Escape Tunnel was a hundred miles away, but I started out, carrying the bucket and lantern. Somewhere along the way I slipped and fell. I licked the snow until my tongue burned. The Escape Tunnel was too far. But in the food tunnel my boots had worn a rut eighteen inches wide and six inches deep, which was full of loose snow. The snow was dirty, but I scraped the bucket along until it was nearly full, then pulled it into the shack, a foot or so at a time.

Snow took a long time to melt in the bucket, and I could not wait. I poured a little into a pan and heated it with alcohol tablets. It was still a soggy mass of snow when I raised it to my lips. My hands were shaking, and the water spilled down the front of my parka; then I vomited, and all that I had drunk came up. In a little while I tried again, taking sips too small to be thrown up. Then I crawled on top of the sleeping bag, drawing a heavy blanket over my shoulders, hoping I should somehow regain strength.

Nevertheless, I was able to do a number of small things, in a series of stealthy, deliberate sorties from the bunk. I attended to the inside thermograph and register, changing the sheets, winding the clocks, and inking the pens. The outlet ventilator was two-thirds filled with ice; I could just reach it from the bunk with a stick which had a big nail in the end. After every exertion I rested; the pain in my arms and back and head was almost crucifying. I filled a thermos jug with warm water, added powdered milk and sugar, and carried the jug into the sleeping bag. My stomach crawled with nauseous sensations; but by taking a teaspoonful at a time, I finally managed to get a cupful down. After a while the weakness left me, and I felt strong enough to start for the instrument shelter. I reached the hatch and pushed it open, but could go no farther. The night was a gray fog, full of shadows, like my mood. In the shack I lost the milk I had drunk. On the verge of fainting, I made for the bunk.

June 8. I am endeavoring to set forth, day by day, the way I live. I am steadfastly holding to a routine designed to give me the best chance of pulling through. Though the mere thought of food is revolting, I force myself to eat—a mouthful at a time. It takes me two or three minutes just to get down a single mouthful. Mostly I eat dehydrated vegetables—dried lima beans, rice, turnip tops, corn, and canned tomatoes—which contain the necessary vitamins—occasionally cold cereals slaked with powdered milk. When I feel up to it, I cook fresh seal meat.

The uncertainty of my existence rises from the realization, when I blow out the candles at night, that I may lack the strength to get up on the morrow. In my stronger moments I fill the oil tank supplying the stove. I use kerosene exclusively now. Its fumes seem less injurious than those from the solvent. I no longer carry the tank into the tunnel as at first. My only container holds just one gallon, and I must make four trips into the tunnel to fill the tank and supply fuel for my lantern. I creep a bit, then rest a bit—over an hour at the job this morning. I froze my hand rather badly. Little by little I've added to the food stores on the shelves within reach of my bunk. They are my emergency cache. The last thing I do when I turn in is to make sure that the lantern is full of oil. If some morning I cannot get out of my bunk, I shall have enough food and light at hand to carry on for a while.

What baffles me is that I have no reserve strength whatever. Climbing the ladder to go topside, I must rest at every other rung. The temperature today was only 40° below zero; but, though I was clad in furs, the cold seemed to shrivel my bones. It's been blowing pretty steadily from the southeast, and I can't seem to keep any heat in the shack. At night the pains in my body nag incessantly. Sleep is what I need most, but it seldom comes. I drift into a torpor, lighted up by fearful nightmares. Mornings it's a tough job to drive myself out of the sleeping bag. I feel as if I had been drugged. But I tell myself, over and over again, that if I give in—if I let this stupor claim me—I may never awaken.

July 1. It is getting cold again—65° below zero today by the minimum thermometer. I have a feeling that it is going to be a very cold month, to make up for June. It was a great piece of luck that June was relatively so warm. I could not have survived otherwise. Now, when the stove is going, I keep the door cracked as wide as I can stand it; and, when it has been out long enough for the fumes to dissipate, I stuff rags (worn-out shirts and underwear, to be exact) up the engine ventilator in the tunnel and into the intake ventilator, so that the tunnel and shack won't get too cold. As a matter of fact, I do without the stove anywhere from twelve to fourteen hours a day. Believe me, it is a strain on the fortitude. Last night I froze an ear in the sleeping bag.

I'm worried about drift. Ever since I've been unable to attend to it, the drift has been deepening over the roof. This morning, when I went topside for the observations, I noticed how high the ridges were over the Escape Tunnel and the tunnels west of the shack. However, I may be able to do something about this before long. Advancing the radio schedules to the afternoon has been an immense help in bringing me back to my feet. With more time to prepare, the drain on me is not quite so heavy. Today's schedule, though tiring, did not knock me out as the others did.

There was no news to speak of from Little America. Hutcheson said that Charlie and John Dyer were out skiing, and that "Doc" Poulter was with the meteor observers. Lord, how I envy them the multitudinous diversions of Little America; even, I suppose, as they must on their side envy the people home with whom they chat on the radio.

I sent a message approving the meteor journey, subject to its being made with full regard for its hazards.

July 15. Even now, after four years, the whole business sounds fantastic. I was lying, because there was nothing else for me to do. But at Little America they were lying, too. The difference was that *they* were coming to suspect that I was lying, and even as they divined that I was concocting a fiction to mislead them, so *they* in turn concocted their own brand to mislead me.

It seems that some time in the last week in June Charlie Murphy began to feel that something was wrong at Advance Base. He had nothing tangible upon which to hang his suspicions—"nothing but my imagination and intuitions and, paradoxically, the absence of news from you," as he put the matter later. But the suspicion was there; and sitting at the other end of the radio channel, watching my messages take shape on Dyer's typewriter, he was like a doctor with a finger on a man's pulse. The loss of communications in July gave Murphy's suspicions something tangible to feed upon; and they grew as he noted my floundering with the hand-cranked set, the all but unintelligible code, and the long waits between the words, which to him were not easily explained except by physical weakness.

However, the rest of the men at Little America refused at first to take him seriously. It was argued that he was no psychic, and that my deficiencies with the radio were only to be expected. Yet, this notwithstanding, the idea that I was in trouble would not be downed in Murphy's mind.

Although Poulter has always insisted that he was not influenced by Murphy's intuitions when he took up the proposal for the meteor trip to Advance Base, I have my doubts; knowing his gallantry, I have come to suspect increasingly as time has gone on that he told me this to spare my feelings. But I do know that, when he and Murphy started making plans for the meteor trip to Advance Base, they ran into a stone-wall opposition. Under what might be considered the constitutional government which I had set up in Little America, they were obliged to take up all important propositions with the group of sixteen officers who constituted the staff and who had veto power by a two-thirds vote over any act of the executive officers. The struggle was close and, from what I've been told, rather heated. The argument went on for days; the caves at Little America seethed with dissension. The crux of the opposition was the lack of any specific permission from me to come to Advance Base before daylight. It was argued that my original strict instructions had forbidden just such a night journey under any conditions; and it was pointed out that in authorizing the early base-laying trip, I had specifically cautioned Poulter not to start until there was ample light.

But Murphy stood on his intuitions and insisted upon decisive action, even though he admitted before the staff that he had nothing concrete to go on. "I grant you," he told them, "that an intuition is pretty poor stuff to allow men to take risks on; but if I am right and you are wrong, we'll never forgive ourselves." On his side, Poulter argued earnestly on behalf of the sheer worth of the meteor observations. But, to certain of the men, many of them navy or ex-navy ratings habituated to arbitrary orders, the proposed trip was a deliberate evasion of an explicit command; a reckless dash supported merely by a hunch; and a potential disaster which might bring disgrace upon the leader and themselves. If, as they surmised, this was to be a relief journey, common sense and the leader's instructions required that the man supposedly in need of assistance first be asked directly whether he needed it.

This Murphy would not do, on the ground that the man at Advance Base, if these facts were laid before him, would have no alternative but to veto the journey. His argument was that they could do two things in one throw: provide Poulter with the base line he needed for his observations, and at the same time find out whether I was all right. It was on this basis that he and Poulter finally persuaded the staff to approve.

August 4. Poulter has started. This afternoon I was told that he had taken departure five hours earlier with two months' rations aboard and a big reserve of gasoline. The weather looks good, for there's practically no wind, and the temperature is steady in the minus thirties. Also, the fact that Poulter is actually headed south again has pierced my torpor, and hope is once more quickening in my heart.

August 8. When next I peered from the hatch, I saw the searchlight very clearly—so clearly, in fact, that I was able to decide that it was fixed to the side of the cabin. Even then, I decided, they were still about five miles off. It would take them another hour to run out the journey. So I sat down in the snow to await the conclusion of this wonderful event. In a little while I could hear on the clear, vibrant air the rumble of the treads, then the *beep-beep-beep* of the horn. But the car was not appreciably nearer. Feeling cold, I went below and huddled beside the fire for a little while. It was hard to sit still when a miracle was being contrived overhead; yet, I compelled myself to do so lest I collapse completely. I looked around the shack and thought how different it would be in a few minutes. It was a filthy mess, and I remember being ashamed that Poulter and the others should find me in such a state; but while I did make a few feeble passes at the untidy heaps, I was too weak to do much about them.

A few minutes before midnight I went topside again. They had come very close. I could see the bulking shadow of the tractor. As a greeting I set off the last can of gasoline and the last flare. They were just dying when the car stopped about a hundred yards away. Three men jumped out, with Poulter in the center, looming doubly big in furs. I stood up, but I did not dare to walk forward. I remember shaking hands all around, and Waite insists that I said, "Hello, fellows. Come on below. I have a bowl of hot soup waiting for you." If that is really so, then I can only plead that no theatricalism was intended. The truth is that I could find no words to transport outward what was really in my heart. It is also said that I collapsed at the foot of the ladder. I have only a muddled impression of that, and a slightly clearer one of trying to hide my weakness. Nevertheless, I do remember sitting on the bunk, watching Poulter and Demas and Waite gulp down the soup and the biscuits; and I do remember what their voices were like, even if I am not sure of what they said. And I do remember thinking that much of what they said was as meaningless as if it were spoken in an unfamiliar tongue; for they had been together a long time, occupied with common experiences, and in their talk they could take a good deal for granted. I was the stranger.

All this happened a little after midnight, August 11, 1934. Two months and four days passed before I was able to return to Little America—which was all to the good, since it enabled us to extend the meteorological recordings that much longer. This second wait was also a long one, but I was in no shape to leave earlier than I did. I could not possibly have survived a trip back in the tractor; and I hesitated to risk an airplane until I had enough endurance to withstand the rigors of a forced landing, always a possibility in that part of the world. It is a tribute to Poulter's self-restraint that he never once brought up the question of my returning. Neither, until toward the end, did Charlie Murphy, who continued to act as buffer, relaying only those expedition matters which required my final decision. "We are all happy beyond words over the way things have turned out," he radioed Poulter. "Tell him that he will find an expedition ready to go when he throws the switch."

The two months that followed the tractor's coming were as pleasant as the others had been miserable. True, with four of us in the shack, we couldn't move without getting in each other's way. At night the three of them used to spread their sleeping bags on the deck and sleep shoulder to shoulder like three Musketeers. Demas and Waite took turns at cooking and cleaning house; Poulter looked after the instruments, and observed meteors as long as the darkness lasted. For a long time they wouldn't allow me to do anything; and, to tell the truth, I didn't insist beyond the requirements of simple courtesy. For it was wonderful not to have to do anything for a change. The darkness lifted from my heart, just as it presently did from the Barrier, with a tremendous inrush of white light. I was a long time regaining my strength, but little by little it came back, and with it some of my lost weight.

Yet, for a reason that I can't wholly explain, except in terms of pride, I concealed from these men, as best I could, the true extent of my weakness. I never mentioned and, therefore, never acknowledged it. On their side, the men never pressed me to tell what had happened before they came. They must have had their own ideas when they cleaned up the mess, but whatever they thought they kept to themselves. The self-preservation instinct of leadership and a sense of shame over my flimsiness drove me to wall off the immediate past. I wanted no one to be able to look over the wall; also, something deep inside me demanded that I close my mind to the notion that I had been rescued.

Lives of the Hunted

NO DOUBT it was while killing animals that man first learned to love them. They were game before they were pets or even objects of disinterested observation, and to this day the sportsman is often an animal lover as well. Others may often wonder how he can regard the duck or the rabbit with affection yet prefer that any given individual should be dead rather than alive. Nevertheless, the paradox is a fact. Thoreau believed that the boy naturally began as a hunter and he regretted only that the process of discovering what other game he was after should so commonly be arrested in ambiguous midway. If our government raises pheasants in cages and then sets them free—tame by now as chickens—to be shot at, at least the inconsistency is one which runs through a good many communal practices besides that of wildlife protection.

Ernest Thompson Seton's *Lives of the Hunted*, from which the first selection in this section is taken, was an epoch-making book. Like several of the author's later works in the same manner, it was a best-seller for a whole generation and more than any other single book it aroused an interest in animals for their own sake on the part of those more robustious children and adults to whom the earlier New England cult had seemed precious and tame. Mr. Seton was an unmistakably manly man who could talk the hunter's own language, and he stirred their imaginations by a direct appeal to the fellow feeling of the huntsman rather than by the scientific or the philosophical approach. In so doing he also provoked the whole "nature-faking" controversy in which John Burroughs and Theodore Roosevelt took part, and which has left nature writers still sensitive—perhaps almost too sensitive—to the charge of anthropomorphism.

The extent to which animals think and feel may be as easily under- as over-estimated. They do have some kind of conscious life; they are not machines; and we may be no further wrong when we make them too much like us than when denying them all awareness of their motives or their actions. We cannot prove that they are aware of what they do or of what they want. But neither can we prove that any human creature, except ourselves, thinks or feels as we do. By limiting themselves to what is objectively verifiable, the behaviorists have made man himself almost as much an automaton as Descartes made the animals, and it is only by introspection that we can arrive at the probability that our own mental processes are not unique, even among humankind. We have as good evidence that animals know not only pleasure and pain but also some kind of gladness and some kind of sorrow as we have that our human companions know them. It seems no rash assumption that even their instinctive actions have some sort of mental accompaniment and that is as much as a really thoroughgoing mechanist will grant *Homo sapiens.*

The selection from *The Wise One*, by Frank Conibear and J. L. Blundell, naturally follows *Lives of the Hunted*, since Mr. Conibear, for more than thirty years a trapper in the Canadian Northwest, writes from a point of view not essentially different from that of Ernest Thompson Seton.

In conclusion I offer Alan Devoe's bloodcurdling account of what happened to a sea beast recently washed up on the savage coast of New Jersey, and the late Will Cuppy's account of the fate of the last of the Great Auks—taken from his *How to Become Extinct*. Mr. Cuppy's handling of natural history is like nothing which ever existed before, and it is the joy of many professional biologists. This little piece is calculated to make some bird lovers squirm.

Johnny Bear

—ERNEST THOMPSON SETON

Johnny was a queer little Bear cub that lived with Grumpy, his mother, in the Yellowstone Park. They were among the many Bears that found a desirable home in the country about the Fountain Hotel.

The steward of the Hotel had ordered the kitchen garbage to be dumped in an open glade of the surrounding forest, thus providing throughout the season a daily feast for the Bears, and their numbers have increased each year since the law of the land has made the Park a haven of refuge where no wild thing may be harmed. They have accepted man's peace-offering, and many of them have become so well known to the Hotel men that they have received names suggested by their looks or ways. Slim Jim was a very long-legged thin Blackbear; Snuffy was a Blackbear that looked as though he had been singed; Fatty was a very fat, lazy Bear that always lay down to eat; the Twins were two half-grown, ragged specimens that always came and went together. But Grumpy and Little Johnny were the best known of them all.

Grumpy was the biggest and fiercest of the Blackbears, and Johnny, apparently her only son, was a peculiarly tiresome little cub, for he seemed never to cease either grumbling or whining.

From *Lives of the Hunted*, by Ernest Thompson Seton, Copyright 1901 by Charles Scribner's Sons, New York, Copyright 1929 by Ernest Thompson Seton. Reprinted by permission of the publishers.

This probably meant that he was sick, for a healthy little Bear does not grumble all the time, any more than a healthy child. And indeed Johnny looked sick; he was the most miserable specimen in the Park. His whole appearance suggested dyspepsia; and this I quite understood when I saw the awful mixtures he would eat at that garbage-heap. Anything at all that he fancied he would try. And his mother allowed him to do as he pleased; so, after all, it was chiefly her fault, for she should not have permitted such things.

Johnny had only three good legs, his coat was faded and mangy, his limbs were thin, and his ears and paunch were disproportionately large. Yet his mother thought the world of him. She was evidently convinced that he was a little beauty and the Prince of all Bears, so, of course, she quite spoiled him. She was always ready to get into trouble on his account, and he was always delighted to lead her there. Although such a wretched little failure, Johnny was far from being a fool, for he usually knew just what he wanted and how to get it, if teasing his mother could carry the point.

II

It was in the summer of 1897 that I made their acquaintance. I was in the Park to study the home life of the animals, and had been told that in the woods, near the Fountain Hotel, I could see Bears at any time, which, of course, I scarcely believed. But on stepping out of the back door five minutes after arriving, I came face to face with a large Blackbear and her two cubs.

I stopped short, not a little startled. The Bears also stopped and sat up to look at me. Then Mother Bear made a curious short *Koff, Koff,* and looked toward a near pine tree. The cubs seemed to know what she meant, for they ran to this tree and scrambled up like two little monkeys, and when safely aloft they sat like small boys, holding on with their hands, while their little back legs dangled in the air, and waited to see what was to happen down below.

The Mother Bear, still on her hind legs, came slowly toward me, and I began to feel very uncomfortable indeed, for she stood about six feet high in her stockings and had apparently never heard of the magical power of the human eye.

I had not even a stick to defend myself with, and when she gave a low growl, I was about to retreat to the Hotel, although previously assured that the Bears have always kept their truce with man. However, just at this turning-point the old one stopped, now but thirty feet away, and continued to survey me calmly. She seemed in doubt for a minute, but evidently made up her mind that, "although that human thing might be all right, she would take no chances for her little ones."

She looked up to her two hopefuls, and gave a peculiar whining *Er-r-r Er-r*, whereupon they, like obedient children, jumped, as at the word of command. There was nothing about them heavy or bear-like as commonly understood; lightly they swung from bough to bough till they dropped to the ground, and all went off together into the woods. I was much tickled by the prompt obedience of the little Bears. As soon as their mother told them to do something they did it. They did not even offer a suggestion. But I also found out that there was a good reason for it, for had they not done as she had told them they would have got such a spanking as would have made them howl.

This was a delightful peep into Bear home life, and would have been well worth coming for, if the insight had ended there. But my friends in the Hotel said that that was not the best place for Bears. I should go to the garbage-heap, a quarter-mile off in the forest. There, they said, I surely could see as many Bears as I wished (which was absurd of them).

Early the next morning I went to this Bears' Banqueting Hall in the pines, and hid in the nearest bushes.

Before very long a large Blackbear came quietly out of the

woods to the pile, and began turning over the garbage and feeding. He was very nervous, sitting up and looking about at each slight sound, or running away a few yards when startled by some trifle. At length he cocked his ears and galloped off into the pines, as another Blackbear appeared. He also behaved in the same timid manner, and at last ran away when I shook the bushes in trying to get a better view.

At the outset I myself had been very nervous, for of course no man is allowed to carry weapons in the Park; but the timidity of these Bears reassured me, and thenceforth I forgot everything in the interest of seeing the great, shaggy creatures in their home life.

Soon I realized I could not get the close insight I wished from that bush, as it was seventy-five yards from the garbage-pile. There was none nearer; so I did the only thing left to do: I went to the garbage-pile itself, and digging a hole big enough to hide in, remained there all day long, with cabbage-stalks, old potato-peelings, tomato-cans, and carrion piled up in odorous heaps around me. Notwithstanding the opinions of countless flies, it was not an attractive place. Indeed, it was so unfragrant that at night, when I returned to the Hotel, I was not allowed to come in until after I had changed my clothes in the woods.

It had been a trying ordeal, but I surely did see Bears that day. If I may reckon it a new Bear each time one came, I must have seen over forty. But of course it was not, for the Bears were coming and going. And yet I am certain of this: there were at least thirteen Bears, for I had thirteen about me at one time.

All that day I used my sketch-book and journal. Every Bear that came was duly noted; and this process soon began to give the desired insight into their ways and personalities.

Many unobservant persons think and say that all Negroes, or all Chinamen, as well as all animals of a kind, look alike. But just as surely as each human being differs from the next, so surely each animal is different from its fellow; otherwise how would the old ones know their mates or the little ones their mother, as they certainly do? These feasting Bears gave a good illustration of this, for each had its individuality; no two were quite alike in appearance or in character.

This curious fact also appeared: I could hear the Woodpeckers pecking over one hundred yards away in the woods, as well as the Chickadees chickadeeing, the Blue-jays blue-jaying, and even the Squirrels scampering across the leafy forest floor; and yet I *did not hear one of these Bears come.* Their huge, padded feet always went down in exactly the right spot to break no stick, to rustle no leaf, showing how perfectly they had learned the art of going in silence through the woods.

I I I

All morning the Bears came and went or wandered near my hiding-place without discovering me; and, except for one or two brief quarrels, there was nothing very exciting to note. But about three in the afternoon it became more lively.

There were then four large Bears feeding on the heap. In the middle was Fatty, sprawling at full length as he feasted, a picture of placid ursine content, puffing just a little at times as he strove to save himself the trouble of moving by darting out his tongue like a long red serpent, farther and farther, in quest of the tidbits just beyond claw reach.

Behind him Slim Jim was puzzling over the anatomy and attributes of an ancient lobster. It was something outside his experience, but the principle, "In case of doubt take the trick," is well known in Bearland, and settled the difficulty.

The other two were clearing out fruit-tins with marvelous dexterity. One supple paw would hold the tin while the long tongue would dart again and again through the narrow opening, avoiding the sharp edges, yet cleaning out the can to the last taste of its sweetness.

This pastoral scene lasted long enough to be sketched, but

was ended abruptly. My eye caught a movement on the hilltop whence all the Bears had come, and out stalked a very large Blackbear with a tiny cub. It was Grumpy and Little Johnny.

The old Bear stalked down the slope toward the feast, and Johnny hitched alongside, grumbling as he came, his mother watching him as solicitously as ever a hen did her single chick. When they were within thirty yards of the garbage-heap, Grumpy turned to her son and said something which, judging from its effect, must have meant: "Johnny, my child, I think you had better stay here while I go and chase those fellows away."

Johnny obediently waited; but he wanted to *see*, so he sat up on his hind legs with eyes agog and ears acock.

Grumpy came striding along with dignity, uttering warning growls as she approached the four Bears. They were too much engrossed to pay any heed to the fact that yet another one of them was coming, till Grumpy, now within fifteen feet, let out a succession of loud coughing sounds, and charged into them. Strange to say, they did not pretend to face her, but as soon as they saw who it was, scattered and all fled for the woods.

Slim Jim could safely trust his heels, and the other two were not far behind; but poor Fatty, puffing hard and waddling like any other very fat creature, got along but slowly, and, unluckily for him, he fled in the direction of Johnny, so that Grumpy overtook him in a few bounds and gave him a couple of sound slaps in the rear which, if they did not accelerate his pace, at least made him bawl, and saved him by changing his direction. Grumpy, now left alone in possession of the feast, turned toward her son and uttered the whining *Er-r-r Er-r-r Er-r-r-r*. Johnny responded eagerly. He came "hoppity-hop" on his three good legs as fast as he could, and joining her on the garbage, they began to have such a good time that Johnny actually ceased grumbling.

He had evidently been there before now, for he seemed to know quite well the staple kinds of canned goods. One might almost have supposed that he had learned the brands, for a lobster-tin had no charm for him as long as he could find those that once were filled with jam. Some of the tins gave him much trouble, as he was too greedy or too clumsy to escape being scratched by the sharp edges. One seductive fruit-tin had a hole so large that he found he could force his head into it, and for a few minutes his joy was full as he licked into all the farthest corners. But when he tried to draw his head out, his sorrows began, for he found himself caught. He could not get out, and he scratched and screamed like any other spoiled child, giving his mother no end of concern, although she seemed not to know how to help him. When at length he got the tin off his head, he revenged himself by hammering it with his paws till it was perfectly flat.

A large sirup-can made him happy for a long time. It had had a lid, so that the hole was round and smooth; but it was not big enough to admit his head, and he could not touch its riches with his tongue stretched out its longest. He soon hit on a plan, however. Putting in his little black arm, he churned it around, then drew out and licked it clean; and while he licked one he got the other one ready; and he did this again and again, until the can was as clean inside as when first it had left the factory.

A broken mousetrap seemed to puzzle him. He clutched it between his forepaws, their strong inturn being sympathetically reflected in his hind feet, and held it firmly for study. The cheesy smell about it was decidedly good, but the thing responded in such an uncanny way when he slapped it that he kept back a cry for help only by the exercise of unusual self-control. After gravely inspecting it, with his head first on this side and then on that, and his lips puckered into a little tube, he submitted it to the same punishment as that meted out to the refractory fruit-tin, and was rewarded by discovering a nice little bit of cheese in the very heart of the culprit.

Johnny had evidently never heard of ptomaine poisoning, for nothing came amiss. After the jams and fruits gave out he turned his attention to the lobster and sardine-cans, and was not appalled by even the army beef. His paunch grew quite balloon-like, and from much licking his arms looked thin and shiny, as though he was wearing black silk gloves.

I V

It occurred to me that I might now be in a really dangerous place. For it is one thing surprising a Bear that has no family responsibilities, and another stirring up a bad-tempered old mother by frightening her cub.

"Supposing," I thought, "that cranky little Johnny should wander over to this end of the garbage and find me in the hole; he will at once set up a squall, and his mother, of course, will think I am hurting him, and without giving me a chance to explain, may forget the rules of the Park and make things very unpleasant."

Luckily, all the jam-pots were at Johnny's end; he stayed by them, and Grumpy stayed by him. At length he noticed that his mother had a better tin than any he could find, and as he ran whining to take it from her he chanced to glance away up the slope. There he saw something that made him sit up and utter a curious little *Koff Koff Koff Koff*.

His mother turned quickly, and sat up to see "what the child was looking at." I followed their gaze, and there, oh, horrors! was an enormous Grizzly Bear. He was a monster; he looked like a fur-clad omnibus coming through the trees.

Johnny set up a whine at once and got behind his mother. She uttered a deep growl, and all her back hair stood on end. Mine did too, but I kept as still as possible.

With stately tread the Grizzly came on. His vast shoulders sliding along his sides, and his silvery robe swaying at each tread, like the trappings on an elephant, gave an impression of power that was appalling.

Johnny began to whine more loudly, and I fully sympathized with him now, though I did not join in. After a moment's hesitation Grumpy turned to her noisy cub and said something that sounded to me like two or three short coughs—*Koff Koff Koff*. But I imagine that she really said: "My child, I think you had better get up that tree, while I go and drive the brute away."

At any rate, that was what Johnny did, and this what she set out to do. But Johnny had no notion of missing any fun. He wanted to *see* what was going to happen. So he did not rest contented where he was hidden in the thick branches of the pine, but combined safety with view by climbing to the topmost branch that would bear him, and there, sharp against the sky, he squirmed about and squealed aloud in his excitement. The branch was so small that it bent under his weight, swaying this way and that as he shifted about, and every moment I expected to see it snap off. If it had been broken when swaying my way, Johnny would certainly have fallen on me, and this would probably have resulted in bad feelings between myself and his mother; but the limb was tougher than it looked, or perhaps Johnny had had plenty of experience, for he neither lost his hold nor broke the branch.

Meanwhile, Grumpy stalked out to meet the Grizzly. She stood as high as she could and set all her bristles on end; then, growling and chopping her teeth, she faced him.

The Grizzly, so far as I could see, took no notice of her. He came striding toward the feast as though alone. But when Grumpy got within twelve feet of him she uttered a succession of short, coughy roars, and charging, gave him a tremendous blow on the ear. The Grizzly was surprised; but he replied with a left-hander that knocked her over like a sack of hay.

Nothing daunted, but doubly furious, she jumped up and rushed at him.

Then they clinched and rolled over and over, whacking and pounding, snorting and growling, and making no end of dust and rumpus. But above all their noise I could clearly hear Little Johnny, yelling at the top of his voice, and evidently encouraging his mother to go right in and finish the Grizzly at once.

Why the Grizzly did not break her in two I could not understand. After a few minutes' struggle, during which I could see nothing but dust and dim flying legs, the two separated as by mutual consent—perhaps the regulation time was up—and for a while they stood glaring at each other, Grumpy at least much winded.

The Grizzly would have dropped the matter right there. He did not wish to fight. He had no idea of troubling himself about Johnny. All he wanted was a quiet meal. But no! The moment he took one step toward the garbage-pile, that is, as Grumpy thought, toward Johnny, she went at him again. But this time the Grizzly was ready for her. With one blow he knocked her off her feet and sent her crashing on to a huge upturned pine-root. She was fairly staggered this time. The force of the blow, and the rude reception of the rooty antlers, seemed to take all the fight out of her. She scrambled over and tried to escape. But the Grizzly was mad now. He meant to punish her, and dashed around the root. For a minute they kept up a dodging chase about it; but Grumpy was quicker of foot, and somehow always managed to keep the root between herself and her foe, while Johnny, safe in the tree, continued to take an intense and uproarious interest.

At length, seeing he could not catch her that way, the Grizzly sat up on his haunches; and while he doubtless was planning a new move, old Grumpy saw her chance, and making a dash, got away from the root and up to the top of the tree where Johnny was perched.

Johnny came down a little way to meet her, or perhaps so that the tree might not break off with the additional weight. Having photographed this interesting group from my hiding-place, I thought I must get a closer picture at any price, and for the first time in the day's proceedings I jumped out of the hole and ran under the tree. This move proved a great mistake, for here the thick lower boughs came between, and I could see nothing at all of the Bears at the top.

I was close to the trunk, and was peering about and seeking for a chance to use the camera, when old Grumpy began to come down, chopping her teeth and uttering her threatening cough at me. While I stood in doubt, I heard a voice far behind me calling:

"Say, Mister! You better look out; that ole B'ar is liable to hurt you."

I turned to see the cowboy of the Hotel on his Horse. He had been riding after the cattle, and chanced to pass near just as events were moving quickly.

"Do you know these Bears?" said I, as he rode up.

"Wal, I reckon I do," said he. "That there little one up top is Johnny; he's a little crank. An' the big un is Grumpy; she's a big crank. She's mighty onreliable gen'relly, but she's always strictly ugly when Johnny hollers like that."

"I should much like to get her picture when she comes down," said I.

"Tell ye what I'll do: I'll stay by on the pony, an' if she goes to bother you I reckon I can keep her off," said the man.

He accordingly stood by as Grumpy slowly came down from branch to branch, growling and threatening. But when she neared the ground she kept on the far side of the trunk, and finally slipped down and ran into the woods, without the slightest pretence of carrying out any of her dreadful threats. Thus Johnny was again left alone. He climbed up to his old perch and resumed his monotonous whining:

Wah! Wah! Wah! ("Oh, dear! Oh, dear! Oh, dear!")

I got the camera ready, and was arranging deliberately to take his picture in his favorite and peculiar attitude for threnodic song, when all at once he began craning his neck and yelling, as he had done during the fight.

I looked where his nose pointed, and here was the Grizzly

coming on straight toward me—not charging, but striding along, as though he meant to come the whole distance.

I said to my cowboy friend: "Do you know this Bear?"

He replied: "Wal I reckon I do. That's the old Grizzly. He's the biggest B'ar in the Park. He gen'relly minds his own business, but he ain't scared o' nothin'; an' today, ye see, he's been scrappin', so he's liable to be ugly."

"I would like to take his picture," said I; "and if you will help me, I am willing to take some chances on it."

"All right," said he, with a grin. "I'll stand by on the Horse, an' if he charges you I'll charge him; an' I kin knock him down once, but I can't do it twice. You better have your tree picked out."

As there was only one tree to pick out, and that was the one that Johnny was in, the prospect was not alluring. I imagined myself scrambling up there next to Johnny, and then Johnny's mother coming up after me, with the Grizzly below to catch me when Grumpy should throw me down.

The Grizzly came on, and I snapped him at forty yards, then again at twenty yards; and still he came quietly toward me. I sat down on the garbage and made ready. Eighteen yards—sixteen yards—twelve yards—eight yards, and still he came, while the pitch of Johnny's protests kept rising proportionately. Finally at five yards he stopped, and swung his huge bearded head to one side, to see what was making that aggravating row in the treetop, giving me a profile view, and I snapped the camera. At the click he turned on me with a thunderous

G--R--O--W--L!

and I sat still and trembling, wondering if my last moment had come. For a second he glared at me, and I could note the little green electric lamp in each of his eyes. Then he slowly turned and picked up—a large tomato-can.

"Goodness!" I thought, "is he going to throw that at me?" But he deliberately licked it out, dropped it, and took another, paying thenceforth no heed whatever either to me or to Johnny, evidently considering us equally beneath his notice.

I backed slowly and respectfully out of his royal presence, leaving him in possession of the garbage, while Johnny kept on caterwauling from his safety-perch.

What became of Grumpy the rest of that day I do not know. Johnny, after bewailing for a time, realized that there was no sympathetic hearer of his cries, and therefore very sagaciously stopped them. Having no mother now to plan for him, he began to plan for himself, and at once proved that he was better stuff than he seemed. After watching, with a look of profound cunning on his little black face, and waiting till the Grizzly was some distance away, he silently slipped down behind the trunk, and despite his three-leggedness, ran like a hare to the next tree, never stopping to breathe till he was on its topmost bough. For he was thoroughly convinced that the only object that the Grizzly had in life was to kill him, and he seemed quite aware that his enemy could not climb a tree.

Another long and safe survey of the Grizzly, who really paid no heed to him whatever, was followed by another dash for the next tree, varied occasionally by a cunning feint to mislead the foe. So he went dashing from tree to tree and climbing each to its very top, although it might be but ten feet from the last, till he disappeared in the woods. After perhaps ten minutes, his voice again came floating on the breeze, the habitual querulous whining which told me he had found his mother and had resumed his customary appeal to her sympathy.

V

It is quite a common thing for Bears to spank their cubs when they need it, and if Grumpy had disciplined Johnny this way, it would have saved them both a deal of worry.

Perhaps not a day passed that summer without Grumpy getting

into trouble on Johnny's account. But of all these numerous occasions the most ignominious was shortly after the affair with the Grizzly.

I first heard the story from three bronzed mountaineers. As they were very sensitive about having their word doubted, and very good shots with the revolver, I believed every word they told me, especially when afterward fully endorsed by the Park authorities.

It seemed that of all the tinned goods on the pile the nearest to Johnny's taste were marked with a large purple plum. This conclusion he had arrived at only after most exhaustive study. The very odor of those plums in Johnny's nostrils was the equivalent of ecstasy. So when it came about one day that the cook of the Hotel baked a huge batch of plum tarts, the telltale wind took the story afar into the woods, where it was wafted by way of Johnny's nostrils to his very soul.

Of course Johnny was whimpering at the time. His mother was busy "washing his face and combing his hair," so he had double cause for whimpering. But the smell of the tarts thrilled him; he jumped up, and when his mother tried to hold him he squalled, and I am afraid—he bit her. She should have cuffed him, but she did not. She only gave a disapproving growl, and followed to see that he came to no harm.

With his little black nose in the wind, Johnny led straight for the kitchen. He took the precaution, however, of climbing from time to time to the very top of a pine-tree lookout to take an observation, while Grumpy stayed below.

Thus they came close to the kitchen, and there, in the last tree, Johnny's courage as a leader gave out, so he remained aloft and expressed his hankering for tarts in a woebegone wail.

It is not likely that Grumpy knew exactly what her son was crying for. But it is sure that as soon as she showed an inclination to go back into the pines, Johnny protested in such an outrageous and heartrending screeching that his mother simply could not leave him, and he showed no sign of coming down to be led away.

Grumpy herself was fond of plum jam. The odor was now, of course, very strong and proportionately alluring; so Grumpy followed it somewhat cautiously up to the kitchen door.

There was nothing surprising about this. The rule of "live and let live" is so strictly enforced in the Park that the Bears often come to the kitchen door for pickings, and on getting something, they go quietly back to the woods. Doubtless Johnny and Grumpy would each have gotten their tart but that a new factor appeared in the case.

That week the Hotel people had brought a new Cat from the East. She was not much more than a kitten, but still had a litter of her own, and at the moment that Grumpy reached the door, the Cat and her family were sunning themselves on the top step. Pussy opened her eyes to see this huge, shaggy monster towering above her.

The Cat had never before seen a Bear—she had not been there long enough; she did not know even what a Bear was. She knew what a Dog was, and here was a bigger, more awful bobtailed black dog than ever she had dreamed of, coming right at her. Her first thought was to fly for her life. But her next was for the kittens. She must take care of them. She must at least cover their retreat. So, like a brave little mother, she braced herself on that doorstep, and spreading her back, her claws, her tail, and everything she had to spread, she screamed out at that Bear an unmistakable order to

STOP!

The language must have been "Cat," but the meaning was clear to the Bear; for those who saw it maintain stoutly that Grumpy not only stopped, but she also conformed to the custom of the country and in token of surrender held up her hands.

However, the position she thus took made her so high that the Cat seemed tiny in the distance below. Old Grumpy had faced a Grizzly once, and was she now to be held up by a miserable little spike-tailed skunk no bigger than a mouthful? She was ashamed of herself, especially when a wail from Johnny smote on her ear and reminded her of her plain duty, as well as supplied his usual moral support.

So she dropped down on her front feet to proceed.

Again the Cat shrieked, "STOP!"

But Grumpy ignored the command. A scared mew from a kitten nerved the Cat, and she launched her ultimatum, which ultimatum was herself. Eighteen sharp claws, a mouthful of keen teeth, had Pussy, and she worked them all with a desperate will when she landed on Grumpy's bare, bald, sensitive nose, just the spot of all where the Bear could not stand it, and then worked backward to a point outside the sweep of Grumpy's claws. After one or two vain attempts to shake the spotted fury off, old Grumpy did just as most creatures would have done under the circumstances: she turned tail and bolted out of the enemy's country into her own woods.

But Puss's fighting blood was up. She was not content with repelling the enemy; she wanted to inflict a crushing defeat, to achieve an absolute and final rout. And however fast old Grumpy might go, it did not count, for the Cat was still on top, working her teeth and claws like a little demon. Grumpy, always erratic, now became panic-stricken. The trail of the pair was flecked with tufts of long black hair, and there was even bloodshed (in the fiftieth degree). Honor surely was satisfied, but Pussy was not. Round and round they had gone in the mad race. Grumpy was frantic, absolutely humiliated, and ready to make any terms; but Pussy seemed deaf to her cough-like yelps, and no one knows how far the Cat might have ridden that day had not Johnny unwittingly put a new idea into his mother's head by bawling in his best style from the top of his last tree, which tree Grumpy made for and scrambled up.

This was so clearly the enemy's country and in view of his reinforcements that the Cat wisely decided to follow no farther.

She jumped from the climbing Bear to the ground, and then mounted sentry-guard below, marching around with tail in the air, daring that Bear to come down. Then the kittens came out and sat around, and enjoyed it all hugely. And the mountaineers assured me that the Bears would have been kept up the tree till they were starved, had not the cook of the Hotel come out and called off his Cat—although this statement was not among those vouched for by the officers of the Park.

V I

The last time I saw Johnny he was in the top of a tree, bewailing his unhappy lot as usual, while his mother was dashing about among the pines, "with a chip on her shoulder," seeking for someone—anyone—that she could punish for Johnny's sake, provided, of course, that it was not a big Grizzly or a Mother Cat.

This was early in August, but there were not lacking symptoms of change in old Grumpy. She was always reckoned "onsartain," and her devotion to Johnny seemed subject to her characteristic. This perhaps accounted for the fact that when the end of the month was near, Johnny would sometimes spend half a day in the top of some tree, alone, miserable, and utterly unheeded.

The last chapter of his history came to pass after I had left the region. One day at gray dawn he was tagging along behind his mother as she prowled in the rear of the Hotel. A newly hired Irish girl was already astir in the kitchen. On looking out, she saw, as she thought, a Calf where it should not be, and ran to shoo it away. That open kitchen door still held unmeasured terrors for Grumpy, and she ran in such alarm that Johnny caught the infection, and not being able to keep up with her, he made for the nearest tree, which unfortunately turned out to be a post; and soon—too soon—he arrived at its top, some seven feet from the ground, and there poured forth his woes on the chilly morning air, while Grumpy apparently felt justified in continuing her flight alone. When the girl came near and saw that she had treed some wild animal, she was as much frightened as her victim. But others of the kitchen staff appeared, and recognizing the vociferous Johnny, they decided to make him a prisoner.

A collar and chain were brought, and after a struggle, during which several of the men got well scratched, the collar was buckled on Johnny's neck and the chain made fast to the post.

When he found that he was held, Johnny was simply too mad to scream. He bit and scratched and tore till he was tired out. Then he lifted up his voice again to call his mother. She did appear once or twice in the distance, but could not make up her mind to face that Cat, so disappeared, and Johnny was left to his fate.

He put in the most of that day in alternate struggling and crying. Toward evening he was worn out, and glad to accept the meal that was brought by Norah, who felt herself called on to play mother, since she had chased his own mother away.

When night came it was very cold; but Johnny nearly froze at the top of the post before he would come down and accept the warm bed provided at the bottom.

During the days that followed, Grumpy came often to the garbage-heap, but soon apparently succeeded in forgetting all about her son. He was daily tended by Norah, and received all his meals from her. He also received something else; for one day he scratched her when she brought his food, and she very properly spanked him till he squealed. For a few hours he sulked; he was not used to such treatment. But hunger subdued him, and thenceforth he held his new guardian in wholesome respect. She, too, began to take an interest in the poor motherless little wretch, and within a fortnight Johnny showed signs of developing a new character. He was much less noisy. He still expressed his hunger in a whining *Er-r-r Er-r-r Er-r-r*, but he rarely squealed now, and his unruly outbursts entirely ceased.

By the third week of September the change was still more marked. Utterly abandoned by his own mother, all his interest had centered in Norah, and she had fed and spanked him into an exceedingly well-behaved little Bear. Sometimes she would allow him a taste of freedom, and he then showed his bias by making, not for the woods, but for the kitchen where she was, and following her around on his hind legs. Here also he made the acquaintance of that dreadful Cat; but Johnny had a powerful friend now, and Pussy finally became reconciled to the black, woolly interloper.

As the Hotel was to be closed in October, there was talk of turning Johnny loose or of sending him to the Washington Zoo; but Norah had claims that she would not forgo.

When the frosty nights of late September came, Johnny had greatly improved in his manners, but he had also developed a bad cough. An examination of his lame leg had shown that the weakness was not in the foot, but much more deeply seated, perhaps in the hip, and that meant a feeble and tottering constitution.

He did not get fat, as do most Bears in fall; indeed, he continued to fail. His little round belly shrank in, his cough became worse, and one morning he was found very sick and shivering in his bed by the post. Norah brought him indoors, where the warmth helped him so much that thenceforth he lived in the kitchen.

For a few days he seemed better, and his old-time pleasure in *seeing things* revived. The great blazing fire in the range particularly appealed to him, and made him sit up in his old attitude when the opening of the door brought the wonder to view. After a week he lost interest even in that, and drooped more and more each day. Finally not the most exciting noises or scenes around him could stir up his old fondness for seeing what was going on.

He coughed a good deal, too, and seemed wretched, except when in Norah's lap. Here he would cuddle up contentedly, and whine most miserably when she had to set him down again in his basket.

A few days before the closing of the Hotel, he refused his usual breakfast, and whined softly till Norah took him in her lap; then he feebly snuggled up to her, and his soft *Er-r-r Er-r-r* grew fainter, till it ceased. Half an hour later, when she laid him down to go about her work, Little Johnny had lost the last trace of his anxiety to see and know what was going on.

Adventure with Indians

—FRANK CONIBEAR AND
J. L. BLUNDELL

The Young Black Beaver had no qualms about tackling life singlehanded. The caution that he habitually practiced sprang not from fear but from necessity, for to survive he must pit his intelligence and nerve against the carnivores—the swift, the supple, the cunning, and the tireless. With his bodily limitations, restricted range, and nonpredatory inclinations, caution was his best defense.

Although up to the time he left the lodge he had been, theoretically, subject to parental control, in accordance with racial tradition and filial inclination; actually he was independent of such. He had been well grounded in forest and beaver lore by his painstaking parents, and in addition he felt the greater power of knowledge from within. Experience alone would prove him, if indeed he was fated to survive.

Like a cocksure and inquisitive young pup, inclined to run in all directions, he yearned for experience, and opportunity, to which likewise he had hitherto been a stranger, seemed a gift of the gods.

From *The Wise One*, by Frank Conibear and J. L. Blundell, Copyright 1949 by Frank Conibear and J. L. Blundell. Published by William Sloane Associates, Inc., New York.

Yet something seemed to be missing. From babyhood he had been one of a family of ten, accustomed to the companionship of brothers and sisters of varying ages. Never before had he been out of hearing range of tail slaps on the water, summoning him to participate in whatever juvenile diversions might be in progress. In fact, he was lonely. This was odd, for at the same time he felt no special urge to see either his parents or his brothers again. Well, whatever it was that was missing, he would search for it and would not rest until he found it.

It was this undefined want that kept him traveling downstream, farther and still farther from home, till just as the sun began to rise he came to a larger stream. Here he spent the next hour or two feeding, leaving several little mats of peeled white sticks half in, half out of the water. Having satisfied his hunger, drowsiness descended upon him, but he fought it off and swam a little way downstream before climbing onto the bank to look for a bed. It would be dangerous to sleep near the telltale little mats.

During the nights that followed, the Young Black Beaver continued his travels along the newly discovered stream, the whitely gleaming mats recording the distance he had made. But they were not very far apart, for like all vegetarian creatures he had a large and cavernous stomach, and it took a long time to fill it. But filled it must be, and that twice during his waking hours; once in the late afternoon or evening, before he resumed his travels, and again after the sun rose, before he took his sleeps.

Normally he would have slept again during the deep twilight that is the short northland night, but so keen was he to know what was round each bend, and what life had in store for him, that he continued his journeying. Yet although he swam eagerly throughout the nights, he made little headway, for after swimming upstream along one bank for a while he would come back down the other, stopping to investigate the little white mats that he sometimes found, or any spot where a beaver had been, clambering onto the bank at such places, and often crossing from one side to the other on the return journey, to make sure that he had missed nothing when he had looked before.

On warm days he slept in the sun and on rainy or stormy ones he took shelter under the willows that overhung the bank. Now and again he was fortunate enough to come upon an old beaver lodge, the previous occupants of which had either abandoned it for fresh quarters or had been killed, perhaps by hunters. Here he would swim up into the lodge by one of the underwater entrances, and though the roof had usually sunk low and the interior was damp and musty, and dark as midnight, he felt safe, and slept soundly.

Thus far one day had been very like another, but even within the fortnight changes had taken place about him. On the sunny exposures of the hillsides low flowers had come into bloom. Parents in the bird world were occupied now not with one another, but in providing for and protecting their young. The eagles carried fish and rabbits to their eyrie high on the cliff, the robins dug worms for their nestlings; among the willows the red-winged blackbirds brought insects to theirs, and in the grass the peewees collected seeds and insects for their downy chicks. Both parents united in this daylong task, and only the oncoming of twilight put a stop to their activities.

But this unity of purpose was by no means universal in the forest. In the bird world the hen partridge, for one, elected to bring up her precocious chicks, as the ducks brought up their ducklings, independent of paternal assistance. The young picked up food with veteran competence almost as they emerged from the shell, and such slight training as they needed in self-protection they received from their mothers. And the mothers who now no longer needed the guardianship of a mate as they did when sitting on the nest, with maternal pride, feeling themselves solely responsible for the birth of their young and selfishly wishing to keep all the pleasures of parenthood entirely to themselves, willfully drove their mates away.

In the animal world matriarchy was rife. The cow moose and

the caribou had suffered their mates to remain with them no longer than a month or so after the close of the rutting season, and had then forsaken them. The she-bears had remained with theirs no longer than to assure motherhood. Only a few among the carnivores, perhaps a weak vixen and a wolf mother, feeling unequal to bringing down big game alone, permitted their mates to stay with them a while longer so that they might bring back food for themselves and their offspring.

But the Young Black Beaver, born into a tribe in which unity was the mainspring of existence, heeded not the seasonal infelicities in the lives of such of his neighbors as he passed by the way. Untroubled by emotion, he lived from day to day, enjoying the freedom, the delights of day, the fascination of the night, the drowsy abandon of rest, and the awakening to a world that awaited him.

A flock of bluebills, victims of the epidemic seasonal revolt, quacked animatedly in the shallows. Drakes all, companions in misfortune, if domestic discord be misfortune, they had banded together to discuss their several variations of this time-worn but absorbing theme. Time was when each had succeeded in engaging the admiration and attentions of an apparently docile mate, plumed with the restraint becoming her sex, implying an appealing feminine diffidence conducive to a happy domesticity.

And in the beginning it had been so. Each had wanted none but the other. Indeed, after the shock of the first thrust of her scolding bill, her mate, with the astounding long-suffering of the domestic male, had returned to her side again and again. But often and more often she had left him, to sit solitarily on her nest, in which presently olive-brown eggs appeared. To these she devoted herself extravagantly, even pulling the soft down from her breast for their protection.

The discomfited drakes compared grounds for indignation. One had outmaneuvered a fox, at great personal inconvenience, one had led astray a too-inquisitive mink. A few, it was feared, had encountered foes too strong for them, and had fallen to the unsuspected range of an Indian gun or been borne aloft in the talons of an eagle. Yet others had kept unremitting and monotonous vigil, without molestation of any kind, till the ducklings were hatched. But all this chivalry went unrewarded. The mothers arrogated the duty of guardianship and the disgruntled drakes drifted together for lack of occupation.

"Look out, drakes all," quacked the sentry. " 'Ware water!"

It was the splashing sound of their sudden uprising and swift onrush that had roused the Young Black Beaver. It was unusual for ducks to fly so fast. Raising his head to look upstream to see if there was reason for him to share their alarm, he saw none. Something there was that had not been there before, but nothing that seemed to him alarming, though it had the wind in its favor. It did not even seem to be alive, for it offered no resistance to the current. What could it be? Not a log, for too much of it showed abovewater.

A young moose, a young fox, or other young creatures that depended for their safety upon speed would have fled, putting a wide margin between themselves and any such startling novelty lest it mean danger. But the adventurous Young Black One, close to the water as he was, saw no reason why he should not remain. And remain he did, staring at the strange object with innocent curiosity.

Not till he heard the whine of the bullet that clipped a furrow across the fur of his back and heard the sharp report of the rifle that discharged it did he realize that he was in the presence of an enemy. He was in and under the water before the smoke had cleared.

But he could not remain underwater indefinitely. Moreover, it behooved him, if possible, to take stock of this enemy that spat at him from afar, for it was like none he had known. He must learn more of it lest again he be taken unawares.

Fortunately for his present predicament, he had always excelled in the games of hide-and-seek that he had played daily with his brothers and sisters, and when he was obliged to come up for air he did so with great caution and skill. Against the overhanging willows some floating mare's-tail reeds had drifted, and not the most watchful observer could have told from the almost imperceptible movement of these, a movement less noticeable than that caused by the gentle motion of the waves, that a clever two-year-old beaver was hiding there, immediately below them, with just the button-like tip of his black nose at the surface.

Filling his lungs with a good breath of air he submerged himself once more and swam to another place, this time farther back, behind overhanging bushes. Here he felt safe enough to risk raising the back of his head, thus permitting his eyes to come abovewater. Was it there still? Yes. The thing was still there. Out in the stream floating the small, well-laden birchbark canoe, in the center of which sat Tschon, eldest son of that renowned and skilled hunter, Chief Pierre Squirrel.

Tschon waited, gun in hand, his coarse features intently set as he scanned the choppy water for a sign of the beaver that he had missed only because the waves had rocked his canoe just enough to spoil his aim.

But the roughness of the water concealed the small air bubbles that floated to the surface as the beaver swam beneath it, which in calm weather would have given his presence away. Also, fortunately for the Young Black One, Tschon was on his way back to the trading post, having concluded a good spring hunt, as the bundles of beaver and muskrat pelts in the canoe bore witness, and was impatient to get there. He had shot merely from that irresistible urge to kill that characterizes the Indian, for he well knew that a beaver pelt at this time of year was almost valueless. He was far too good a hunter for a traveling beaver, once sighted, to escape him if he made up his mind to get it, but on second thought, practical consideration induced him to let it go.

Thus fate spared the Young Black One, who from his concealment watched Tschon lay his gun on the baggage before him and proceed upon his way.

For some days following this incident the Young Black One saw the canoes of other Indians, bound on the same errand as Tschon, using the river as a highway to the trading post, but they caught no more than a glimpse of the fugitive. He saw to that.

He was clever enough to recognize that these strange creatures, though able to strike from a distance, without beak or claws, could not smell him in the water, and that he had the advantage there, for he relied upon his nose, which might betray him to them at close range but which informed him of this while giving no clue to his enemies.

Each time he spied an Indian canoe he placed himself in a position where he could study it unobserved. He sniffed the strange yet somehow familiar smell of it—birchbark, which he knew, and the smell of the Indian—so that henceforth he could detect it without risk of discovery. And that other half-familiar yet strangely disquieting smell—the smell of death. It came from the pelts of beaver, mink, muskrat, and otter, or whomever among his neighbors the Indians had slain, which they bore in their canoes.

The unexpected report of Tschon's gun brought the Young Black One's carefree nonage to an abrupt conclusion. Gone, he realized, were the days of youthful pantomime bravado. With characteristic beaver courage and philosophy he adjusted himself to the realities of existence, resolved to maintain his rightful place in the universe against all comers.

The Brave Men of Brielle

—ALAN DEVOE

Yesterday (so the morning paper tells) a great soft-flippered sea beast nosed her way up the Manasquan River in New Jersey. She was a sea cow—kin to what in southern waters is called a manatee—a cumbersome, warm-blooded water-mammal of singular gentleness and a curiously human look. It is thought likely that manatees were the originals of those mermaids that fanciful old sailors used to see. This particular sea cow, yesterday, was in quest of sanctuary, for her sleek, salt-wet belly was big with young. What befell her, as she swam near to the town of Brielle, is briefly told. The first of the inhabitants to sight her, as she passed quietly upstream in search of haven, discharged both barrels of a shotgun and was successful in tearing a bloody hole in her.

She did not die, though, then. She did not die until a dozen, or a score, of additional citizens of Brielle had sunk as many iron-barbed gaffs into her warm flesh, had harried her inshore with blows of clubs and gun butts, and had at last, with grappling tackle, hauled her to dry land. Lying on the shore, blood-smeared and in an extremity of terror, she did that thing which made the *Herald Tribune* deem the episode worth recounting

for the breakfast-table amusement of its readers. While a group
of brave Briellemen were smashing her skull with clubs, and one
especially intrepid fellow was pushing with all his might against
her belly, she delivered from her convulsed womb the baby that
she had been seeking to spawn in some safe sanctuary. This
done, her clumsy blood-soaked body shuddered, and she was
dead.

This is not much of a story, as newspaper stories go. It contains no portent of communism or fascism, and is remote from
those sociological issues which alone are currently considered
worthy of scareheads. It is possible, nonetheless, to read in it an
implication quite as ghastly as any whisper that drifts from
Moscow, any dark tale out of Japan. For it must be clear to even
the most rudimentary moralist that there is a terrifyingly tiny difference between the willful butchery of a manatee and the willful
butchery of a man. In either case there is the same gross indifference to that attribute of life which used to be called its
sanctity; in either case there is the same grisly phenomenon of
human ears grown deaf to entreaty, human eyes grown blind to
the miracle of existence, human hearts grown heedless and un-
caring of those subtle and precious values which can inhere alike
in men and manatees and mice and millipedes. There is the
same deadly absence—to return to the starting-point—of that
simple ancient virtue which can be called by the name of natural
piety.

It is likely that many of us can never return to the old tribal
faiths, the particular theological orthodoxies of our fathers. But
it is one of the tragedies of our time that, in our enthusiastic
iconoclasm, our zeal to disavow the venerable dogmas of this
formal faith or that, we have disavowed all faith entirely. Because our science has cast doubt on this or that phrase of what
used to be our Holy Scriptures, we have been affrighted into
damning the whole of theocentric thinking; and because the religion of some men has been shown up as something of a joke,
we have been persuaded to fancy that religiousness itself is only

a kind of humorous delusion. Piety, in the sense of the stiff-necked, thin-lipped piousness of the grim old sectarians, was never a very lovely or very admirable thing. But piety, in the sense of a humility, an exultant wonderment, a gentleness of tread when we are in the holy places of the earth, is not today a less lovely or less saving thing than it was when Francis knelt in a meadow of buttercups at Assisi.

There is an ancient stern injunction that men, to enter heaven, must become as little children. It is an advice rich with truth and full of deep wisdom; and it is an advice which, more than any other precept, we have steadfastly ignored. The tribal politicians have constructed their rigmaroles of projects; the questers after Truth have sought it in economics and social patterns; and plain men have everywhere overlaid their simple, natural, childlike awareness with a thousand kinds of solemn and obscurative nonsense. It is the childlike vision that we must bring back, the child-awareness of beauty and mystery and miracle that we must revive to succor us in this bleak time. We are equipped to see and smell and touch the loveliness of an anemone in spring woods, and our ears are not unable to hear the morning song of thrushes. No man, in childhood, is deaf and blind to things like these; the little children look out upon the world with eyes big with wonder, and are full of a consuming ecstasy in the presence of such simple miracles as budding sassafras twigs and running waters and the whorls of multicolored seashells. To the little child is given the keep of happiness, and the key, likewise, of wisdom. He trails his fingers in cool water, and it is enough to make him laugh and sing with the gladness of living. He breathes the spring wind, or watches snowflakes falling, or stares at the patterned lichen on a stone, and his heart is set singing with the glory and the wonder of the world.

It is quite possible to claim, I think, that the dazzled Negro who calls himself Father Divine may well, despite his zany vagaries, be closer to the truth than are, for example, those thinkers who expect to heal the sickened modern heart by abolishing the Standard Oil Company. Perhaps the crotchety messiahs whose advertisements now crowd the religious notices in the Sunday papers—the Swamis and New Thoughtists and Yogis and the rest—are not, after all, quite wholly wrong. For however fantastical the creeds they propose, this much, at least, they have acknowledged and recognized: that deep down below our economic woes and social troubles, there is a basic disorientation of our souls. There is a misery amongst us, and its wellsprings are in our spirit; there is an empty lack in our lives, and it is a lack of simple piety.

A man need be no cultist, no religious devotee, to agree that these are truths. He need only reflect a little, I think, on the day's newspaper headlines, and then look out from his window at a phoebe or a blade of grass. He need only call to mind, perhaps, a certain sea cow that swam up the Manasquan River in search of hospice; he need only ponder on The Brave Men of Brielle.

And I Ought to Know

—WILL CUPPY

The last two Great Auks in the world were killed June 4, 1844, on the island of Eldey, off the coast of Iceland. The last Passenger Pigeon, an old female named Martha, died September 1, 1914, peacefully, at the Cincinnati Zoo. I became extinct on August 23, 1934. I forget where I was at the time, but I shall always remember the date.

The two Great Auks were hit on the head by Jon Brandsson and Sigurdr Islefsson, a couple of Icelandic fishermen who had come from Cape Reykjanes for the purpose. A companion, Ketil Ketilsson, looked around for another Great Auk but failed to find one, naturally, since the species had just become extinct. Vilhjalmur Hakônarsson, leader of the expedition, stayed in the boat.

The main reason why these particular fishermen went birding that day is part of history. It seems that bird lovers and bird experts everywhere were upset over the disappearance of the Great Auk from its accustomed haunts and its extreme rarity even in its last refuge, the little island of Eldey. Since there was grave danger that it would soon become entirely and irrevocably extinct—as dead as the Dodo, in fact—it looked as though something would have to be done and done quickly.

Well, something was done. As always, one man rose to the occasion. Mr. Carl Siemsen, a resident of Reykjavik and quite an ornithologist on his own, hired Jon and Sigurdr and the rest of the boys to row over to Eldey and kill all the Great Auks they could find, in order that they might be properly stuffed and placed in various museums for which he acted as agent and talent scout. And of course that was one way of handling the situation. It was pretty tough on the Auks, though, wasn't it?

I don't say the museum people themselves would have hit the Great Auks on the head, or even that they would have approved such an act. I do say that ornithologists as a class, so far as I have been able to observe them, generally from a safe distance, do seem to suffer from a touch of split personality when faced with a dwindling species of bird. They appear to be torn between a sincere desire to bring that bird back to par, at any cost to themselves and to certain well-to-do persons whose names they keep in a little black book, and an uncontrollable urge or compulsion to skin a few more specimens and put them in a showcase at the earliest possible moment. I don't pretend to follow their line of reasoning, if such it may be called. To do that you have to be a Ph.D. in birdology. It takes years of hard study, and I guess you have to be that way in the first place.

Right here I might offer a word of advice to the Ivory-billed Woodpecker, now the rarest bird on the North American continent and one that is going to come in for more and more attention. Keep away from bird lovers, fellows, or you'll be standing on a little wooden pedestal with a label containing your full name in Latin: *Campephilus principalis*. People will be filing past admiring your glossy blue-black feathers, your white stripes and patches, your nasal plumes in front of lores, your bright red crest and your beady yellow eyes. You'll be in the limelight, but you won't know it. I don't want to alarm you fellows, but there are only about twenty of you alive as I write these lines, and there are more than two hundred of you in American museums and in collections owned by Ivory-billed Woodpecker enthusiasts. Get it?

Yes, I know that many ornithologists are gentle, harmless souls without a murderous thought in their whole field equipment. I should like to remind them, though, that even a bird has a nervous system, and I am thinking especially of the Roseate Spoonbill, one of our few native birds with a bill shaped like a soup ladle. It can't help the Roseate Spoonbill much to go chasing over hill and dale practically twenty-four hours a day, aiming binoculars at it from behind every bush—as if it didn't know you were there!—clicking your cameras, watching every move and that sort of thing. There must be Roseate Spoonbills who haven't had a decent night's rest in years. No sleep, no nothing. And you wonder why they're neurotic.

I should like to add that the habit of climbing up into trees and rubber-stamping the eggs of birds threatened with extinction in order to warn wandering collectors away from the nests might well be abandoned in the interests of whatever remnants of sanity may still be left among our feathered friends.

Coming back to the Great Auk, if I may, I am rather surprised that I brought up the subject at all, for it is not one of my favorite birds of song or story. I lost interest some years ago when I learned that it was only as large as a tame Goose, and some say smaller—the Great Auk, mind you! When I think of the precious hours I once wasted thinking how wonderful it would be to see a Great Auk, I could sue.

Besides, it was one of those birds that lost the power of flight through long disuse of their wings, and surely that is no fault of mine, to put it no closer home. I am always a bit impatient with such birds. Under conditions prevailing in the civilized world, any bird that can't make a quick get-away is doomed, and more so if it is good to eat, if its feathers are fine for cushions, and if it makes excellent bait for Codfish when chopped into gobbets. Such a bird, to remain in the picture, must drop everything else and develop its wing muscles to the very limit. It does seem as though that should be clear even to an Auk.

Flightlessness alone, however, does not explain the fate of this species to my satisfaction, since it is a well-known fact that fish do not fly, either—that is, most fish. By the way, there are grounds for believing that the Great Auk regarded itself as more of fish than a bird, for it made its annual migrations to Florida by water, and largely beneath the surface at that. Still and all, it didn't work out in the long run. I cannot avoid the feeling that birds migrating under water is something Mother Nature will stand just so long and no longer.

I'm afraid the Great Auks were pretty foolish in other ways, too. Like Dodos, they had a tendency to pal with just anybody. Whenever they noticed some one creeping up on them with a blunt instrument, they would rush to meet him with glad little squawks of welcome and stick out their necks. Both species did this once too often. Maybe you never heard that duodo, the earliest version of Dodo, is Portuguese for simpleton. You didn't know the Portuguese had a word for that, eh?

We should now be in a position, if we're ever going to be, to form some opinion on why the Great Auk became extinct. It would be too easy, and not very scientific, to say that it happened merely because Jon Brandsson and Sigurdr Islefsson were running amuck on the morning of June 4, 1844. But why were there only two Great Auks left on Eldey? What had been going on in this species? Just how far had *Alca impennis* evolved, whether rightly or wrongly? As Richard Swann Lull states in *Organic Evolution*, "Extinction in phylogeny has two aspects, each of which has its equivalent in ontogeny." And two aspects is putting it mildly.

Let's not be too quick to blame the human race for everything. We must remember that a great many species of animals became extinct before man ever appeared on earth. At the same time it is probably true that when two husky representatives of *Homo sapiens*, with clubs, corner the last two birds of a species, no matter how far they have or have not evolved, both the phylogeny and the ontogeny of those birds are, to all intents and purposes, over. For the present I shall have to leave it at that.

Since I mentioned two other extinct individuals in the first paragraph of this article, my readers may expect me to bring them into the story. To the best of my knowledge and belief, Martha, last of the Passenger Pigeons, is now one of the treasures of the Smithsonian Institution. After life's fitful fever she can do with a good rest. No more of those incredible, sky-darkening flights amid general uproar and pandemonium. No more dodging bullets. No more roup. Martha was far from a Squab when she left us in 1914, having reached the age of twenty-nine. Her name, by the way, is no whimsical invention of mine. She was really Martha, as anybody will tell you who knew his Cincinnati around the turn of the century.

We are not quite sure why the Passenger Pigeon became extinct as a species. Some say that all the Passenger Pigeons in the world—except Martha, presumably—were caught in a storm and perished during their last migration southward over the Gulf of Mexico. The weakness of this theory is that Passenger Pigeons never went near the Gulf of Mexico on any pretext, let alone made a habit of flying over it in a body. I grant you there have been some bad storms over the Gulf, but that also holds true of other bodies of water.

My own view is the economic one. The food supply of these birds probably gave out, and there they were. Only the other day I came across the statement that the chief food of the Passenger Pigeon was beech-mast, a commodity which could never have been abundant enough in this country to last them forever. I never even heard of it myself except in this connection. I do think our scientists, instead of spinning picturesque yarns about the disappearance of the Passenger Pigeon, mere guesswork for the most part, might well devote themselves to the question:

Whatever became of the beech-mast? Then we might get somewhere.

So much for *Ectopistes migratorius*. Nevermore, alas, will they alight in our forests by the billion, breaking down and killing the trees for miles around by the weight of their untold numbers, destroying the crops for thousands of acres in every direction, wreaking havoc and devastation upon whole counties and leaving the human population a complete wreck from shock, multiple contusions, and indigestion. People miss that sort of thing, but you needn't look for any more Passenger Pigeons. They have gone to join the Great Auk, the Labrador Duck, the Eskimo Curlew, the Carolina Parakeet, the Heath Hen, and the Guadalupe Flicker. You won't find any of them. They're through.

What is more, sooner than we think we may see the last of the California Condor, the Everglade Kite, the Trumpeter Swan, the Whooping Crane and the Limpkin, not to mention some of the Godwits, which haven't been doing any too well here lately. It's enough to make Donald Culross Peattie go and hang himself.

But look, Mr. Peattie, only last June a thing called a Cahow, supposed to be extinct, turned up in Bermuda as chipper as ever. It wasn't extinct at all. Does that help any? And I honestly don't think we need worry about the Whooping Crane. There will always be people who will see to it, if it's the last thing they do, that there are plenty of Whooping Cranes around. Life has taught me that much at least.

If I may close on a personal note, I'm sorry but there seems to be some doubt whether I became extinct on August 23, 1934, or whether the date will have to be moved ahead a few years. That day was one of my birthdays and it was not my twenty-first or my thirtieth—or even, I am afraid, my fortieth. And it got me to thinking. Since then I have had more birthdays, so things haven't improved much in that respect. I find, however, that it is technically incorrect to call anybody extinct while he is still at large. I must have made a mistake in one of the minor details. Some day that can be fixed in a jiffy by changing a numeral or two, and then everything will be right as rain.

Anyway, you can see how the thoughts of a person who fully believed himself to be extinct, even if he had talked himself into it, could be a bit on the somber side. Yet I had my moments, for I assure you that becoming extinct has its compensations. It's a good deal like beating the game. I would go so far as to say that becoming extinct is the perfect answer to everything and I defy anybody to think of a better. Other solutions are mere palliatives, just a bunch of loose ends, leaving the central problem untouched. But now I must snap out of all that. According to our leading scientists, I am not yet extinct, and they ought to know. Well, there's no use crying about it.

As I look back over the period since 1934, I guess I didn't go into the thing quite thoroughly enough. I never really classed myself with the Dodo, a bird we always think of as the ultimate in extinction, though I suppose the Dodo is no more extinct than anything else that is extinct, unless it's the Trilobite. Maybe I'm more like the Buffalo, which seems to be coming back now in response to no great popular demand that I can see. Did I ever tell you what happened to the Buffaloes that time? The moths got into them.

Small Deer

ORIGINAL genius is as rare among nature writers as among writers of any other kind. The number of those who have combined scientific competence and the gift of sympathy with a literary style capable of communicating the flavor of a unique personality is small indeed. But Gustav Eckstein is certainly one of that small number.

Being a professor of Physiology at the University of Cincinnati Medical School, he knows the animal body as that combined machine and chemical laboratory which, in one aspect, it is. Being endowed as few men have been with the gift of empathy, he can also feel his way into the existence of any living creature until that creature lives in his imagination an intense and poignant life. But that is not all. He was granted also a way with words which serves to communicate undimmed the fresh originality of his thought and feeling. His way of writing, like his way of feeling, is like that of no one else. One cannot say of it as one can of Thoreau that it obviously owes much to this or that predecessor. It fits into no rhetorical classification. Sometimes it is not even what anyone who applied the test of rules or principles would call good writing. But it is an instrument which no one else could handle. Sometimes colloquial, sometimes tangential, sometimes, perhaps, not quite in accord with the laws of English syntax, it is at once informal and mannered; or, rather, it would be mannered if it were not so obviously natural to Eckstein, if to him alone. One is tempted to fall back on Samuel Johnson's half-puzzled, half-resentful commendation of the style of Dryden, whose apparently casual rightness he could not fathom: "Every word seems to drop by chance, though it falls into its proper place."

Any chapter from any of his books deserves a place in some anthology. I was tempted to choose the astonishing account of the cockroach in which he describes with the subtlety of a psychological novelist how the sense of something unutterably alien turned into horror the wondering admiration with which he first contemplated the cockroaches' busy, efficient possession of a universe fitted into the interstices of a laboratory building. But that piece is a tour de force and less characteristic than the cat portraits from his *Four Lives*.

Perhaps one does not immediately think of Samuel L. Clemens as an animal lover. Perhaps, indeed, even the tremendously vivid and comic description of the coyote from *Roughing It* here included is not irrefutable evidence. And perhaps, therefore, it is worth while to cite the following monologue recorded by Samuel Stevens Hood:

* "Take this fellow, Harry Orchard, out West. Now I like a fellow like that: straightforward, downright honest. He blew up the house of an enemy and then shot to death the only eye-witness of the crime. When interrogated by the police captain after the capture, as to why he had killed the eyewitness, Orchard coolly replied; 'Why, Cap., it stands to reason. I had to *shoot the evidence.*'

"Now I can't help but like that fellow Orchard. You must hand it to him: he's honest. . . .

"On the other hand, take Teddy Roosevelt. Just read, if you please, this horrible brutal book about shooting deer and other wild game. *Game!* Teddy is not content with stalking those poor

* From *Archibald Henderson*, by Samuel Stevens Hood, Copyright 1949 by Samuel Stevens Hood. Reprinted by permission of Beechhurst Press, Inc., New York, publishers.

beasts and mercilessly shooting down the lovely defenseless creatures from ambush—*from ambush!* . . . If I had to choose between, *give me Harry Orchard every time.*"

The virtues of the other two essays in the present section are of a very different kind. The first is from *Wilderness Wanderers,* by Wendell and Lucie Chapman—two amateur adventurers who passed a winter in Yellowstone Park. The second is from *Antarctic Penguins,* by G. Murray Levick, a scientist by profession, who has here the advantage of dealing with a creature whose almost human appearance has made it appealing even to many who normally find little in animals to interest them. But he studied soberly the penguin in its native habitat and he discovered that its quaintness does not lie merely on the surface. Truth is both funnier and more touching than fiction.

Seven Cats

—GUSTAV ECKSTEIN

A cat had followed Joe up the path and round the road and to the back of the building, and Joe fed her and drove her away. Next day she followed again, was fed again, was driven again, was harder to drive, and harder still on the day after that. It worried Joe. A medical college is no place for a cat. So he took to walking to the other side of the dump to feed her there, but she followed just the same. He tried chasing her with his dog, the dog having plain directions to chase the cat but not to harm her—and the cat understood the directions. Finally, exasperated, he came to me, and the upshot was that I had the cat. She was the alley kind, gaunt, young, looking middle-aged.

I had her, but could not make her eat. I thought it hurt feelings, but Joe thought her ill, and it went so a number of days. She still had no fever and the whites of her eyes were clear, yet by the end of the week I could not doubt that something serious was the matter with her, and by the end of another week I knew I must help her die.

On the top of the radiator is a marble slab. It is warm on the slab, so I laid her on it, then sat myself in front of her and watched her. Her chin, her neck, her belly, the whole of her

From *Lives*, by Gustav Eckstein, Copyright 1932 by Harper & Brothers, New York. Reprinted by permission of the publishers.

· 262 ·

flat body seemed sunk into the marble. Her respirations also had changed, had taken the rhythm of death. Mr. Kupka came into the laboratory. He knows animals, and I asked him if he thought I ought to chloroform her. He thought not, thought she had only the slimmest chance, but need not die immediately.

He went, and maybe I dozed, because it was with a shock I realized that some queer change had passed over that cat. Something seemed to have run out into that limp left front leg and made it rigid, and she drew back the leg and planted the paw squarely on the marble. But, what was more queer, she opened the left eye, though she kept the right tight shut. It was an unnatural, a fantastic, almost a frightful behavior. That left eye appeared not looking at me, but beyond me; appeared to be seeing something I could not, something possibly not even materially in the room. At the thought of that I leaped quickly up and looked quickly behind me, and there, leisurely crossing my desk on her way to her drawer, went mother rat. It was mother rat the dying cat had seen, had imagined, no doubt, she was in heaven already where rats disport at random. Anyway, something remarkable happened to her, touched her soul or her psyche, or a doctor might say her secretions, because when I brought her milk she drank, and in a few days was her own old self.

I took her to the house, and soon she was staying out nights and I knew she had a lover. There were others, admirers; and my neighbor said they were killing the chickens. Funny eyes my neighbor has—the kind of man likes to finger a gun, would have made a good huntsman or a great soldier, but danger in those professions, and shooting cats has its interest too. He would open his window, settle in his chair, and every time he hit he laughed. You would hear the shot, then the laugh. A mad laugh. More than the eyes of my neighbor was mad. He killed those admirers one by one and after each laughed. Mine took hers up the windowless side of the house to the roof. Nights you could hear the two discussing.

A little after dark I would see the lover come from behind his barrel, and he looked hungry, yet when I tried to feed him fled. He was afraid of the window, but afraid also of her, who did not allow him near the house, preferred to go out to her friends, did not like this hanging about of males. Nevertheless, one evening as I came in through the lower door I stumbled over him, talked to him, which he did not like, but in spite of that began with me to mount the steps. We were about half up when I saw a head push out above through the open door. And he saw the head. And the head saw him. It was as two antique swordsmen see each other through the tear in an arras, and the instant that followed had also that speed. Not that she moved, but there was such movement in the way she did not. And he, he went at one bound back to the bottom, then wanted to go straight on through the door, beat his head into its again and again, and when I opened it rushed into the night.

One small matter more was hard on my neighbor. A 3 P.M. she would go to her sand, would go at other times, too, but always at 3 P.M., and the sand was just under the window, and there she would sit, aware of where she sat, and of who sat, and of the divine right of who sat to sit where she sat.

In July she and I drove to Elkhart. She was used to driving, but on this trip was nervous from the start. We slept the first night in Connersville, then next morning went up through the sandier parts of Indiana. To me sand is sand, but to her there are distinctions, and I could get no interest for any sand I showed her. Then in the restaurants they began not to want her, and that made me apologetic, and then they wanted her less. Then I began letting her eat on the seat of the automobile, but a dog barked, and after that she was forever prowling on the floor.

By the second night we entered Chicago. I stuck her under my coat, registered at the Palmer House, and no one found us out, but it was not a happy night. The room was long, with expensive carpet and a low bed, and she was perpetually going about under the bed and making me uneasy for what she might do, especially as she liked the carpet in exactly the same way that she did not like the sand, kept pressing her paws rhythmically in and out, as a cat does, a female cat particularly, and more at one period of her life than at any other. Unexpectedly her purr would swell through the night and she would seem in an orgy of content.

At Elkhart she showed something new. She never had hunted beetles or mice or other living things, but at Elkhart one afternoon I caught her watching a frog. The frog was playing dead. She tapped him. He went on playing dead. She tapped him more energetically, and he leaped, and instantly she was on him and I on her. I scolded her and took her in. Half an hour afterward she was out again, and I scolded her and took her in. But the huntress was roused, and late that day when I saw him he was dead.

She and I got back from Elkhart in September. Her nervousness was gone and she was quite at the other extreme. Whatever I did for her she thanked me disproportionately; then toward seven o'clock one evening I knew the hour had arrived, so got a rag-lined basket and went with her round the room to find what would be the most suitable place. I hoped it might not be the clothes-closet, and kept that shut and did not refer to it, but there she stood and stuck. It was a first labor and hard. She knew just what to do—bit off the cords, licked away the blood, licked the bodies, and all the while pressed her paws rhythmically into the rags as she had into the carpet at the Palmer House, and at each accomplished birth was more tired till, with the last, the third, I helped her. She rubbed my leg and purred when I changed the soiled rags.

By noon the next day she was asking for a woolen blanket—the room had got cold. And all that day she warmed the three with the blanket and with her body, and all the next day, but on the evening of the third day disappeared. I found her far from the house, tripping along like an irresponsible kitten, and the lover I saw slipping behind his barrel. I snatched her up and carried her home and pointed severely to her three, and as soon as she saw them she was wholly absorbed in them again. That night she brought them into my bed. She herself always liked to lie in the hollow between my feet and the wall, but now it was she and three, so I lugged them back to the basket. Each time I waked they were in the bed again. She simply waited till I slept.

On the tenth day she brought a rat, and in the following days all species of living things, but when she began with birds I strung a bell round her neck. Any sudden move must warn every bird for a quarter of a mile. Consequently there were no sudden moves. She would put out one paw, then one paw, then one paw, infinitely cautiously approach a tree, infinitely cautiously climb the trunk, creep out a branch, and when she was at the end of the branch turn round, and all without once ringing the bell. And she would stay there hours, seemed to expect a bird to fly precisely into her mouth, which, to judge by the quiet of her, may sometimes have occurred. Once, however, she was in that tree for a different reason—was chased there by a dog who made himself comfortable below, and had to wait till a policeman came and got her down.

On a Sunday—she in the tree—I left the room at four o'clock, and when I got back at five o'clock two of the kittens were gone. Two were gone and the third crouched in a corner and could not be made to come out. I looked everywhere. Everybody looked. The policeman, a big-bodied, healthy man, was so simply concerned when I told him, also looked. I knew it was no use. How the two had been done away with I did not know, but done away with they were. Of course they could not have been shot from the window, because it was a quiet Sunday and people would have heard. And they were not out-of-doors where they could have been shot. They were in the closed room.

The third, who crouched in the corner and could not be made to come out, was so tiny when he was born that it was hard to see how he could live. Hence his name, Tiny. But so soon as he had his name, so soon as the baptism was over, he began to grow, and grew and grew and grew, prodigiously, till in a few months he was twice as big as Mother, and more beautiful than any other kitten I have ever known.

He never would go down into the dump, but would sit poised in the window, and from the window watch most carefully everything that went on in the dump and in the street beyond the dump. One afternoon there was a crowd in the street. He would like to have known what drew that crowd. The wish got him restless, and I heard the thud as he dropped to the floor, then his complaint that the outer door was locked. I got up and unlocked the outer door. He proceeded down the steps and round the road and to the edge of the crowd, then went round the crowd, wary of the feet, saw what he went to see, which was all there was to see, merely a wreck, and immediately came back round the road and up the steps, returned to his window, and at his leisure followed what further unfolded below.

With evening he deserted his window for the shadow at the end of the room. He did that every evening. He moved to and fro in the shadow. One sometimes wonders what an old cat thinks when he blinks that way, but it is more a question what a young cat thinks, for an old cat, after all, has his past. Tiny in the blue-black on this particular evening was like a figure on a basalt etching, and it may be he was thinking of Egypt and ancestors. At least it was far he came to be aware for the first time of the music. With one spring he was up beside me on the piano bench, and with a second on the books at the end of the piano, was peering in on the hammers, his imagination caught by some problem of the mechanism, his head darting back and forth as the hammers leaped up here or there. With a shrewd quiet he glided now to where he could look instead at the keys. I struck the keys slowly. He glided once more, back a little to where he could at one time see both hammers and keys, and in the next moment it was plain in his face that he had grasped the principle and was staying only long enough to establish experimentally how tone is made. With a shrug he deserted the books and went again to blink in the shadow.

April came and with it three more, two gray, and the third the boy who does the chores named, Little Black. And Little Black is what her name just had to be. Again the difficulty about the bed, but no curing Little Black. I would burst from sleep because some villain was choking me. Paws! But impossible to be angry with Little Black.

It was Little Black too tried to undermine the laws of the high-chair, despite the high-chair was an old institution. I had bought it when Mother was the only one, my idea being to lift her where she could be part of the room's principal activities—dinners, table conversations, newspapers. When Tiny was weaned, Mother gave him the seat of the chair, took for herself the board where I up to then had set her warmed plates. This was not for comfort, but for justice. It raised her above Tiny. It placed her in front of Tiny. It brought Tiny's food a measurable interval late. In short, it put rank where you could see it, and every distinction was minutely kept up. When the new kittens came and were weaned, Mother ruled there was no more free space on the chair, and the two gray ones obeyed. But Little Black simply couldn't. She simply had to climb up now and then where Tiny was, Tiny always moving over and giving her room, but Mother always ordering her down. Some kind of discipline Mother must maintain, with Tiny getting so big and the kittens every day growing. It was all the happy time of kitten life, a glass over everything that spring, Tiny so beautiful,

Mother so wise, Little Black so quaint, the gray ones so snub-nosed and dear.

As for the meat, the first piece went to Mother, the second to Tiny, the third to Little Black, the fourth to the one gray one, the fifth to the other gray one, each in turn raising a paw. This was Tiny's idea. He thought he ought to take his food like the human being, ought to take it in his paw, and ought to sit. For this he was much praised, and therefore, when hunger was not too pressing, the others tried it too, and they were much praised, and soon all were doing it regularly. After meat came milk, which was preferred warm but not hot, and if hot, was fanned cool with paws.

Then on a Tuesday night when I came to feed them Tiny would not eat. He seemed so quiet. And perhaps he glistened more than otherwise. After a while we all went to bed, he under the piano bench, Mother and the kittens in the corner by the book-closet.

I had slept an hour when I waked with the feeling that some-one had waked me, but there was utter quiet. I got right up and went to find Tiny. He was not asleep. He was under the bench just where I had left him, sitting, and the fact that he was sitting was somehow appalling. He was like a huge, beautiful woman with a fever, but when I touched him he was cold. I was stricken with fear at that touch, and lifted him quickly into my arms and hurried with him to the radiator. His eyes shone so. I knew what it meant, and yet it was not like death, but more like the end of some sublime imagined thing. He took one long quiet breath, and that was all.

A terrible night, Tiny dead, something plainly wrong with Mother, something plainly wrong with the kittens. About dawn I went for a few moments into the air, and when I came back through the lower door I saw Little Black above me on the steps. She was wanting to greet me as she always had when she heard my keys; but her legs were too weak, and down she rolled, catching herself and failing to catch herself, like an awkward bag. Before I got her to the room she was dead. Then the one gray one died. Then the other. Then Mother. Mother I helped a bit. She did not want me to, poor Mother. Poison. May God understand it. I do not.

Father of Eight

—GUSTAV ECKSTEIN

A crash against the laboratory window, and in the same instance a shadow. A hawk—has got my female canary. She was standing on the top of the lower sash, and he drove at her, and at the sight of him she fell like lead between the panes.

Father canary is quiet. He saw. The very way he does **not** search for her proves that he saw.

So I go to the birdstore and get another bird, a plain one who enters the laboratory as if she had had a call to be father's wife. Father cuffs her and pushes her. Father is all fire, and she is a woman, and I do not know whether he means to, but after a month he has put it into my head that probably he is too much for her; that probably he would be too much for any one woman. And that is why in March I am again at the birdstore to get another bird—the striped one. When the striped one enters the laboratory father comes quickly; but the striped one only flies past father on to his cage, and when father also would enter his cage she drives him out.

Then months have passed. Eleven canaries now, the striped one having had a family, one child striped like herself and two plain like father; and the wife having had a second family, a family of two.

It is evening, and not an unusual evening. I have just pushed from the wall the heavy glass case that is all but concreted in, and there, blinking in the unexpected light, was standing the owl —father's last son. And he would have stood there till he rotted. He is gloomy. He looks gloomily around, then shoves himself into the air, lands in front of his mother, demands food. She hesitates. He beats her. This baby beats his mother. Father comes and perches on the lowest branch of the tree that I have brought into the laboratory, is not sure whether he ought to take a hand or not.

The striped one is thinking she needs a bath and goes to the rim of the black bath-bowl, but the water is so cold. It is hard for her to make up her mind. She wets her face. She hops to the other side of the rim. She prances all round the rim. She wets her feet. Billy, but the water is too cold.

She goes to the pan of ashes and eats ashes. Everybody goes to the pan of ashes and eats ashes. Two bump, and stop eating, and two mouths go wide open and terrible threats come from the bottom of two throats. The owl's first sister gets ashes all over her, tries to clean herself by rubbing herself against the pan. The owl sees her and chases her, but the owl's second sister sees him and chases him, and the striped baby chases her, and soon everybody is chasing everybody, and everybody is chirping— then the telephone rings and everybody is still.

Then the striped one uncovers a mystery—a fuzzy coat left on the piano. She goes to the fuzzy coat and picks fuzz, red fuzz, a striped yellow bird with a red fuzzy beard. Everybody watches her. Then everybody picks fuzz and everybody has a red beard. Fuzz does not much interest father. Something else begins to, and the striped one knows what it is, and flies. Father is all fire. Round the laboratory they go. I hurry, play a few notes in the treble, and wonderful as beautiful the way he changes the direction of his flight, from her toward me, alights on my Beethoven sonatas, his little chest already flat.

Then everybody starts to the window to look at the rain, and the babies put the tips of their bills where they think the drops are and flap their wings as if they were actually out in the shower.

Then the striped one uncovers another mystery—the seed-bag left open. What she would like would be to jump into the seed-bag, but it would be dangerous in such a half-dark hole. She jumps. Everybody knows it is dangerous, and when I rise everybody flees, something guilty in their tails.

Then everybody gets ready for the night. Four transom rods are not many for eleven birds. One rod has four birds on it, so one gets shoved off, flies to the next rod and shoves off someone else, who flies to the next rod and shoves off someone else. Then three birds have their heads tucked under. Then five birds have their heads tucked under. Then father has his head tucked under, is a fluffy ball that you could not tell from the rest.

A whole year passes. Many things happen in that year, but the common things of common life, the kind of year that slips back and loses itself in a line of years. Father's feelings toward the wife are what they were, and toward the striped one what they were. Where they have changed is toward his art. At the bird-store they said father would be a fine singer; but he is more, is a great singer, has power with frailty, like Mozart. And father does by no means sing only for his women, but for the song, practices many hours of every day. He likes a broad platform. The top of the book-closet is very good. He comes out to the edge of that, chases everybody else off, wants the platform to himself, plants his feet, fills his throat, flattens his chest, and begins. Or he comes to the piano, perches on the Beethoven sonatas, ever so often reaches down and eats of the Beethoven, on some pages has eaten as far as the first printed staff, then suddenly remembers again he is practicing. He selects a few notes of the theme I am playing and repeats them over and over. When the theme modulates he modulates, feels his way note for note from one key to the other in the same quick yet half-groping fashion that the human singer does. And he sings true. Last evening he was imitating a bobwhite, repeating the call as he would a theme, the result not at all like a bobwhite, but never any doubt what he was meaning to do.

This afternoon, while father was singing, without announcement the striped one rose from her nest. I am struck by this, partly because it is too soon after the last time she rose, partly because I have been worried about her, and partly because of something in the way she rises. Father is struck, too. She has alighted on the lowest branch of the tree, and father has come quickly and alighted beside her. Something is wrong! He flattens his chest and begins vigorously to sing. She drops to the floor, dead. Father's voice is broken. He keeps right there on the branch in front of me. Then he leaves the branch, flies to the piano, calls up to the nest, but it is in the gentlest pianissimo. And he does not look into the nest. He does not look at the body either. Striped baby goes right past the body and does not look. None of them looks.

All yesterday father did not sing, and not the day before, and this morning tried and broke down, then did not try again all morning, but now, as if he had made up his mind he would, he does, and forces his way through, a viciousness about it. Absent-mindedly the owl breaks in. The owl thinks father is going to give a lesson, but father is only singing because the world must go on, so sidles over and delivers the owl a whack, from which the owl scoots but returns. A son of the second generation comes, too, stands at the other end of the chair, father now between them. Neither son is making a noise, but their nearness is annoying and father is not happy. Then presently he is sorry for them, invites them to sing, gives them one of his extraordinary lessons, works with them as with himself, puts an excitement into the teaching that few human teachers would understand.

The sons flat their notes and their trills are uneven. When father sings it is as if he were letting the whole earth come up through him. The sons, on the contrary, are so careful, but they try. If father moves a step the owl moves a step, keeping right in front of father, facing father. The owl has been singing on one tone, and father takes that tone up an octave and trills on it and keeps trilling till it seems something inside him must break. The owl cannot. The owl has not the muscles yet. This singing is work. The song of birds is not what some people think, fully formed in nature; but a deliberate art passed from bird to bird round the world and through time.

Father gives, gives, gives, when he is teaching and when he is not. This morning as dawn came along the edges of the green window shade I lay awake, and father flew from his transom rod, and kept up a long low warbling. Then I saw the strangest instance of his giving. In the night I keep open one window and there was father at that window, pushing rape seeds through the screen into the mouths of the sparrows who were also awake and waiting outside.

Winter has come and snow has blown through the screen, and late this afternoon the ten were playing in the snow. They are used to cold. They are big almost as the younger of the sparrows, and heavily feathered, and generally equal to their world. And the laboratory being dirty, they are dirty—dirty, big, ready for weather, and free.

Tonight there has been a turn in the weather. This afternoon was unnatural, balmy as spring, but with evening snow fell, and with darkness icy winds began to blow. It is eight o'clock. It is the 30th of January—and six of them are gone. Out there in that night! Yes, and father among them. It is the boy who does the chores opened a screen, and when one bird slipped through, left open the screen so that the one might come back. Six of them—more than half my little family—in that dark, in this changed weather, no knowledge of how to find food, of how to find water. If it were summer or autumn—but better not to think. Better simply to do what we can do.

A number of us go down to the lot with lights, and soon see the owl's first sister perching on a branch. Perhaps if I were to drive those still in the room away from the windows and snapped on the lights, perhaps she would fly in. The reverse happens. The lights only frighten her, and she flies off in the direction of the engine-house, perches on another branch. It is dark, and I can come very near now. Carefully I throw a rope over the branch, carefully draw down the branch, but again something frightens her, and this time she disappears into the night. I should not have done that.

In the laboratory the music has kept uninterruptedly on. If there is music, surely father must stay near, and if father stays near, probably the others will too. But as well not to hope for much for tonight. As well for tonight to try not to think, to sleep instead, to get up with the dawn and begin the playing then. Father will be wanting his breakfast, and that ought to help.

Toward three o'clock Wiggles barks and I am awake. Then Wiggles is still. Then on the roof I hear steps—a cat. Could she have been seeing something in the trees?

With dawn the playing begins, and father's ears save his life. As soon as he hears the music he comes closer and closer, tree by tree, almost a quarter of a mile, till he is out on the sill among the sparrows. The Piper of Hamelin is no fancy. He was real, that man. The sparrows are disturbed by father, do not know what to make of him, but do not hurt him, perhaps remember the rape seeds. Or perhaps when father hears the music it is so plain he knows what he is about that the sparrows feel his decision and let him alone. Anyway, they are quiet, and when I open the screen he comes right in. And immediately he is in he joins in the music, sings as hard as ever I have heard him sing, understands just what has taken place and helps in the work. Downstairs they are saying that two more are around the house now. Meanwhile across the street the owl is saving himself with his voice, sings outside a window and is let in. Then one of the two downstairs comes up to the screen and is let in. And another. And another. All come in but her I drove into the night with my bad thinking.

In the room there is such an excitement, and it keeps up for hours. Everybody is telling everybody. They were outside! The whole night long! In the trees! Secretly they are glad to be in, but they have some right to brag. Every now and then the excitement gets so high that father cannot sing, but must listen a little to what they are saying, then nervously goes to work again.

By noon the first sister has not returned. I have gone in all directions. She is a female and can only chirp and is not apt to save herself with her voice as the owl saved himself, and her ears are not so good, either. By night she still has not returned. *Le bon Dieu te garde!* The snow is beginning again.

Roughing It

—SAMUEL L. CLEMENS

Along about an hour after breakfast we saw the first prairie-dog villages, the first antelope, and the first wolf. If I remember rightly, this latter was the regular *coyote* (pronounced ky-o-te) of the farther deserts. And if it *was*, he was not a pretty creature, or respectable either, for I got well acquainted with his race afterward, and can speak with confidence. The coyote is a long, slim, sick and sorry-looking skeleton, with a gray wolf-skin stretched over it, a tolerably bushy tail that forever sags down with a despairing expression of forsakenness and misery, a furtive and evil eye, and a long, sharp face, with slightly lifted lip and exposed teeth. He has a general slinking expression all over. The coyote is a living, breathing allegory of Want. He is *always* hungry. He is always poor, out of luck and friendless. The meanest creatures despise him, and even the fleas would desert him for a velocipede. He is so spiritless and cowardly that even while his exposed teeth are pretending a threat, the rest of his face is apologizing for it. And he is *so* homely!—so scrawny, and ribby, and coarse-haired, and pitiful. When he sees you he lifts his lip and lets a flash of his teeth out, and then turns a little out of the course he was pursuing, depresses his head a bit, and strikes a long, soft-footed trot through the sage-brush, glancing over his shoulder at you, from time to time, till he is about out of easy pistol range, and then he stops and takes a deliberate survey of you; he will trot fifty yards and stop again—another fifty and stop again; and finally the gray of his gliding body blends with the gray of the sage-brush, and he disappears. All this is when you make no demonstration against him; but if you do, he develops a livelier interest in his journey, and instantly electrifies his heels and puts such a deal of real estate between himself and your weapon, that by the time you have raised the hammer you see that you need a minie rifle, and by the time you have got him in line you need a rifled cannon, and by the time you have "drawn a bead" on him you see well enough that nothing but an unusually long-winded streak of lightning could reach him where he is now. But if you start a swift-footed dog after him, you will enjoy it ever so much— especially if it is a dog that has a good opinion of himself, and has been brought up to think he knows something about speed. The coyote will go swinging gently off on that deceitful trot of his, and every little while he will smile a fraudful smile over his shoulder that will fill that dog entirely full of encouragement and worldly ambition, and make him lay his head still lower to the ground, and stretch his neck further to the front, and pant more fiercely, and stick his tail out straighter behind, and move his furious legs with a yet wilder frenzy, and leave a broader and broader, and higher and denser cloud of desert sand smoking behind, and marking his long wake across the level plain! And all this time the dog is only a short twenty feet behind the coyote, and to save the soul of him he cannot understand why it is that he cannot get perceptibly closer; and he begins to get aggravated, and it makes him madder and madder to see how gently the coyote glides along and never pants or sweats or ceases to smile; and he grows still more and more incensed to see how shamefully he has been taken in by an entire stranger, and what an ignoble swindle that long, calm, soft-footed trot is; and next he notices that he is getting fagged, and that the coyote actually has to slacken speed a little to keep from running away from him—and *then* that town-dog is mad in earnest, and he begins to strain and weep and swear, and paw the sand higher than ever, and reach for the coyote with concentrated and desperate energy. This "spurt" finds him six feet behind the gliding enemy, and two miles from his friends. And then, in the instant that a wild new hope is lighting up his face, the coyote turns and smiles blandly upon him once more, and with a something about it which seems to say: "Well, I shall have to tear myself away from you, bub—business is business, and it will not do for me to be fooling along this way all day"—and forthwith there is a rushing sound, and the sudden splitting of a long crack through the atmosphere, and behold that dog is solitary and alone in the midst of a vast solitude!

It makes his head swim. He stops, and looks all around; climbs the nearest sand-mound, and gazes into the distance; shakes his head reflectively, and then, without a word, he turns and jogs along back to his train, and takes up a humble position under the hindmost wagon, and feels unspeakably mean, and looks ashamed, and hangs his tail at half-mast for a week. And for as much as a year after that, whenever there is a great hue and cry after a coyote, that dog will merely glance in that direction without emotion, and apparently observe to himself, "I believe I do not wish any of the pie."

The coyote lives chiefly in the most desolate and forbidding deserts, along with the lizard, the jackass-rabbit and the raven, and gets an uncertain and precarious living, and earns it. He seems to subsist almost wholly on the carcasses of oxen, mules, and horses that have dropped out of emigrant trains and died, and upon windfalls of carrion, and occasional legacies of offal bequeathed to him by white men who have been opulent enough to have something better to butcher than condemned army bacon. He will eat anything in the world that his first cousins, the desert-frequenting tribes of Indians, will, and they will eat anything they can bite. It is a curious fact that these latter are the only creatures known to history who will eat nitroglycerine and ask for more if they survive.

Wilderness Wanderers

—WENDELL AND LUCIE CHAPMAN

All through the night we could hear the faint plop, plop, of heavy animal feet in the mud on the banks of the stream, and at dawn we lay listening to the small noises of wood folk breaking the hushed stillness of the forest.

The following evening our cooking dinner sent an odorous invitation into the forest. We were watching the casserole of canned meat simmer and the corn bread brown in the reflector oven before the flames, when claws rattled in the bark of a tree close behind us. All at once a small brown animal with glossy fur jumped in a flowing leap to a limb over our heads. Large feet of black velvet rested easily on the limb; bushy tail draped down; and bright eyes gleamed at us as a black nose wriggled sensitively in appreciation of the food in the open oven. All at once the gorgeous creature ran down the tree, head first, its hind feet swiveling back in the descent until the toes pointed upward as do those of a squirrel. Eager and excited, we set up the motion-picture camera and caught the rare marten running out on the limb, leaping its length to the branch of another tree, to disappear into the forest.

We were just ready to sit down to our evening meal when back he bounded across a clearing, his body arching like a measuring worm. We stood breathless as he hopped gracefully from the ground to a stool, then to the camp table to sample first the currant jelly, next, the butter. Then he tried to run away with the corn bread, but the pan, tipping at the edge of the table, wrenched away from his tooth hold, plopped upside down on the grass. Savagely the marten sprang upon the slippery pan, growling and mauling it. But when the pan failed to struggle, he lost interest in it. Lucie offered the plate of meat. At the smell of this he was willing to give up the bread, which pleased us because we had more of the meat in the oven but no more bread. By the time our visitor was ready to leave his long willowy form bulged under the glistening fur.

Before we fell asleep we heard something moving about on a tree outside, then in the tent. Rising, I set up the camera, and operating the trigger with one hand and touching off a flash bulb with the other, took the marten's picture. Apparently he mistook the photo flash bulb for lightning for he did not mind it, but did seem to be disturbed by the flashlight. He looked more gorgeous than before, his orange neck more brilliant, and he was ravenously hungry for graham crackers, raisins, canned milk, bacon. As our eggs had become unreliable, the result of a combination of warm weather and jolting in the boat, we gave them to the marten. By switching the flashlight on and off we watched him open his jaws and carefully slide his slender canine teeth over an egg until he had it firmly in his mouth, although his head was scarcely larger than the egg itself. With this prize he ran to the tree, and the second flashlight picture caught him on a limb, puncturing the shell with his sharp teeth, lapping the contents as it flowed out. Undoubtedly the deft handling of the eggs was the result of practice at bird nests.

The marten returned so often during the night that we wondered how a three-pound animal with a body only fourteen inches long could possibly hold so much food. Although he was carrying some away, we saw him eating most of it. Not until morning did the mystery clear. Not one marten, but several had been visiting us. We distinguished at least three, but as martens are not sociable with one another, only one at a time visited us. We saw a small one run to the very top of a tree and lie quietly concealed all the time a larger one was in camp.

The pine squirrel, on whose homestead we were camping, came each day to collect her rental in raisins, nuts, crackers, and scraps. Before long she grew quite tame, drinking from our water bucket instead of going to the spring a few yards farther on. The nuts she carried to an underground cache, the raisins to a hole in the tree, and the crackers to various branches overhead, apparently knowing they would mildew if stored underground. The sharp-eyed Canada jays profited most from these tree-top caches, often flying away with the crackers before the squirrel had reached the ground. By so doing, they acquired a taste for our food, and learned to swoop to our table, when our backs were turned, and fly away with whatever they could snatch. As the squirrel was running through the grass with a cracker after breakfast, a jay hopped from limb to limb above her. When she rested the cracker on the grass for a moment in order to get a better grip, the jay swooped and whisked it into the air. Too dumbfounded even to scold, the squirrel gazed up at the vanishing cracker. All day she berated the jays for robbing her branches, or chased other squirrels from her territory, tackling them in rough-and-tumble fights whenever she could overtake them, and went into spasms of rage at gleaning chipmunks, which dodged about too rapidly to be caught. Considering her unwillingness to share her homestead with native neighbors, we felt fortunate to have her approval, although, of course, we were paying for it.

The idea that we might be playing traitor to her by encouraging the visits of the martens did not occur to us until at daybreak one morning a marten came to the tent. While eating at the base of the tree outside, he froze—a furry statue as immobile as a cat stalking a mouse. Crouched, tense, he watched the squirrel come within a yard of him. Like lightning he leaped! Screaming, the squirrel dodged and sprang for the tree. Up she tore, flaking off bark with her claws, the marten in close pursuit. Our heads swam at the speed of the brown bodies. Wildly they circled up and down the trunk, head first, then leaped from branch to branch, flashed in and out of sight among the foliage. Like a shot the squirrel dropped through the air in a fifteen-foot leap and dashed across the meadow. Down jumped the marten from the same take-off, his fluffy tail extended stiffly to break the fall. When he hit the ground he hesitated to watch the speeding squirrel, who by now was twenty-five feet in the lead. Giving up the chase, he turned toward the tent.

"Oh, I'm glad he didn't catch her," Lucie said, breathlessly. "I'd have felt that we were to blame."

"She'll probably take care of herself if she has lived this long in marten territory," I assured her, recalling the squirrel at the Norris cabin which, despite winter lethargy, had likewise escaped these enemies.

Again the marten froze. His fluffy tail a train on the ground, his cat-like ears pointed forward, he began to stalk. Three chipmunks were scurrying around the base of another tree a hundred feet away. Little by little the marten stole closer, head and long body low. Creeping up behind the tree he approached to within ten feet of the nearest chipmunk. With a rush he charged. The tiny creature jumped to the tree, circling as it climbed. Racing round and round, spiralling up and down the tree trunk, both chipmunk and marten seemed flattened to the bark as if they were lizards. In less than five seconds the marten jumped to the ground holding the limp chipmunk as a cat would a mouse.

Later one of the martens became friendly with us. At first we fed him honey, bread soaked in sweetened canned milk, raisins, bacon or canned meat from a spoon. In accepting them he growled, exposing his long white teeth, but his snarling thanks seemed to be a bluff. Eventually Lucie handed him a morsel of raw bacon from her fingers. He looked up into her face and growled. With a jump, as if he feared the food would vanish, he grabbed her thumb in his teeth. In a flash he realized that he had hold of her. Growling again, he relaxed his jaws without hurting her, stuck up his tongue in place of his lower teeth and with it and his upper teeth, carefully pulled away the bacon. Then he growled again.

"He thinks he has to keep us intimidated," I said as he sat back licking his whiskers before resuming his feast.

"He's going to lose his willowy form and turn into a marmot, if we don't stop stuffing him." Lucie smiled as he ran with sides as round as those of a gorged puppy.

He disappeared into some brush and slept for a couple of hours. His nap finished, he came out, stretched and yawned. We called and he came loping over with arched back to take some more food from our hands. For several days we hardly left camp. It was not possible to keep from growing sentimental about him.

Antarctic Penguins

—G. MURRAY LEVICK

The penguins of the Antarctic regions very rightly have been termed the true inhabitants of that country. The species is of great antiquity, fossil remains of their ancestors having been found which showed that they flourished as far back as the eocene epoch. To a degree far in advance of any other bird, the penguin has adapted itself to the sea as a means of livelihood, so that it rivals the very fishes. The proficiency in the water has been gained at the expense of its power of flight, but this is a matter of small moment, as it happens.

In few other regions could such an animal as the penguin rear its young, for when on land its short legs offer small advantage as a means of getting about, and as it cannot fly, it would become an easy prey to any of the carnivora which abound in other parts of the glove. Here, however, there are none of the bears and foxes which inhabit the North Polar regions, and once ashore the penguin is safe.

The reason for this state of things is that there is no food of any description to be had inland. Ages back, a different state of things existed: tropical forests abounded, and at one time, the seals ran about on shore like dogs. As conditions changed, these latter had to take to the sea for food, with the result that their four legs, in course of time, gave place to wide paddles or "flippers," as the penguins' wings have done, so that at length they became true inhabitants of the sea.

When seen for the first time, the Adelie penguin gives you the impression of a very smart little man in an evening dress suit, so absolutely immaculate is he, with his shimmering white front and black back and shoulders. He stands about two feet five inches in height, walking very upright on his little legs.

His carriage is confident as he approaches you over the snow, curiosity in his every movement. When within a yard or two of you, as you stand silently watching him, he halts, poking his head forward with little jerky movements, first to one side, then to the other, using his right and left eye alternately during his inspection. He seems to prefer using one eye at a time when viewing any near object, but when looking far ahead, or walking along, he looks straight ahead of him, using both eyes. He does this, too, when his anger is aroused, holding his head very high, and appearing to squint at you along his beak.

After a careful inspection, he may suddenly lose all interest in you, and ruffling up his feathers, sink into a doze. Stand still for a minute till he has settled himself to sleep, then make sound enough to wake him without startling him; and he opens his eyes, stretching himself, yawns, then finally walks off, caring no more about you.

The Adelie penguin is excessively curious, taking great pains to inspect any strange object he may see. When we were waiting for the ship to fetch us home, some of us lived in little tents which we pitched on the snow about fifty yards from the edge of the sea. Parties of penguins from Cape Royds rookery frequently landed here, and almost invariably the first thing they did on seeing our tents was at once to walk up the slope and inspect these, walking all round them, and often staying to doze by them for hours. Some of them, indeed, seemed to enjoy our companionship. When you pass on the sea-ice anywhere near a party of penguins, these generally come up to look at you; and wc had great trouble to keep them away from the sledge dogs when these were tethered in rows near the hut at Cape Evans. The dogs killed large numbers of them in consequence, in spite of all we could do to prevent this.

The Adelies are extremely brave, and though panic occasionally overtakes them, I have seen a bird return time after time to attack a seaman who was brutally sending it flying by kicks from his sea-boot, before I arrived to interfere.

The Adelie penguins spend their summer and bring forth their young in the far South. Nesting on the shores of the Antarctic continent, and on the islands of the Antarctic seas, they are always close to the water, being dependent on the sea for their food, as are all Antarctic fauna; the frozen regions inland, for all practical purposes, being barren of both animal and vegetable life.

Their requirements are few: they seek no shelter from the terrible Antarctic gales, their rookeries in most cases being open wind-swept spots. In fact, three of the four rookeries I visited were possibly in the three most windy regions of the Antarctic. The reason for this is that only wind-swept places are so kept bare of snow that solid ground and pebbles for making nests are to be found.

When the chicks are hatched and fully fledged, they are taught to swim; and when this is accomplished and they can catch food for themselves, both young and old leave the Southern limits of the sea, and make their way to the pack-ice out to the northward; thus escaping the rigors and darkness of the Antarctic winter, and keeping where they will find the open water which they need. For in the winter the seas where they nest are completely covered by a thick sheet of ice which does not break out until early in the following summer. Much of this ice is then borne northward by tide and wind, and accumulates to form the vast rafts of what is called "pack-ice," many hundreds of miles in extent, which lie upon the surface of the Antarctic seas.

When young and old leave the rookery at the end of the breeding season, the new ice has not yet been formed, and their long journey to the pack has to be made by water; but they are wonderful swimmers and seem to cover the hundreds of miles quite easily.

Arrived on the pack, the first year's birds remain there for two winters. It is not until after their first molt, the autumn following their departure from the rookery, that they grow the distinguishing mark of the adult, black feathers replacing the white plumage which has hitherto covered the throat.

The spring following this, and probably every spring for the rest of their lives, they return South to breed, performing their journey, very often, not only by water, but on foot across many miles of frozen sea.

For those birds who nest in the southernmost rookeries, such as Cape Crozier, this journey must mean for them a journey of at least four hundred miles by water, and an unknown but considerable distance on foot over ice.

The first Adelie penguins arrived at the Ridley Beach rookery, Cape Adare, on October 13. A blizzard came on then, with thick drift which prevented any observations being made. The next day, when this subsided, there were no penguins to be seen.

By the morning of October 19 there had been a good many more arrivals, but the rookery was not yet more than one-twentieth part full. All the birds were fasting absolutely. Nest building was now in full swing, and the whole place waking up to activity. Most of the pebbles for the new nests were being taken from old nests, but a great deal of robbery went on nevertheless. Depredators when caught were driven furiously away, and occasionally chased for some distance, and it was curious to see the difference in the appearance between the fleeing thief and his pursuer. As the former raced and ducked about among the nests, doubling on his tracks, and trying by every means to get lost in the crowd and so rid himself of his pursuer, his feathers lay close back on his skin, giving him a sleek look which made him appear half the size of the irate nest-holder who sought to catch him, with feathers ruffled in indignation. This at first led me to think that the hens were larger than the cocks, as it was generally the hen who was at home, and the cock who was after the stones, but later I found that sex makes absolutely no difference in the size of the birds, or indeed in their appearance at all, as seen by the human eye. After mating, their behavior as well as various outward signs serve to distinguish male from female. Besides this, certain differences in their habits are to be noted.

The consciousness of guilt, however, always makes a penguin smooth his feathers and look small; while indignation has the opposite effect. Often when observing a knoll crowded with nesting penguins, I have seen an apparently undersized individual slipping quietly along among the nests, and always by his subsequent proceedings he has turned out to be a robber on the hunt for his neighbors' stones. The others, too, seemed to know it, and would have a peck at him as he passed them.

At last he would find a hen seated unwarily on her nest, slide up behind her, deftly and silently grab a stone, and run off triumphantly with it to his mate who was busily arranging her own home. Time after time he would return to the same spot, the poor depredated nest-holder being quite oblivious of the fact that the side of her nest which lay behind her was slowly but surely vanishing stone by stone.

Here could be seen how much individual character makes for success or failure in the efforts of the penguins to produce and rear their offspring. There are vigilant birds, always alert, who seem never to get robbed or molested in any way: these have big high nests, made with piles of stones. Others are unwary and get huffed as a result. There are a few even who, from weakness of character, actually allow stronger-natured and more aggressive neighbors to rob them under their very eyes.

In speaking of the robbery which is such a feature of the rookery during nest building, special note must be made of the fact that violence is never under any circumstances resorted to by the thieves. When detected, these invariably beat a retreat, and offer not the least resistance to the drastic punishment they receive if they are caught by their indignant pursuers. The only disputes that ever take place over the question of property are on the rare occasions when a bona-fide misunderstanding arises over the possession of a nest. These must be very rare indeed, as only on one occasion have I seen such a quarrel take place. The original nesting sites being, as I will show, chosen by the hens, it is the lady, in every case, who is the cause of the battle; and when she is won her scoop goes with her to the victor.

As I grew to know these birds from continued observation, it was surprising and interesting to note how much they differed in character; though the weaker-minded who would actually allow themselves to be robbed were few and far between, as might be expected. Few, if any, of these ever could succeed in hatching their young and winning them through to the feathered stage.

When starting to make her nest, the usual procedure is for the hen to squat on the ground for some time, probably to thaw it, then working with her claws to scratch away at the material beneath her, shooting out the rubble behind her. As she does this she shifts her position in a circular direction until she has scraped out a round hollow. Then the cock brings stones, performing journey after journey, returning each time with one pebble in his beak which he deposits in front of the hen, who places it in position.

Sometimes the hollow is lined with a nest pavement of stones placed side by side, one layer deep, on which the hen squats, afterwards building up the sides about her. At other times the scoop would be filled up indiscriminately by a heap of pebbles, on which the hen then sat, working herself down into a hollow in the middle.

Individuals differ, not only in their building methods, but also in the size of the stones they select. Side by side may be seen a nest composed wholly of very big stones, so large that it is a matter of wonder how the birds can carry them, and another nest of quite small stones.

Different couples seem to vary much in character or mood. Some can be seen quarreling violently, whilst others appear most affectionate, and the tender politeness of some of these latter toward one another is very pretty to see.

I may here mention that the temperatures were rising considerably by October 19, ranging about zero F.

During October 20 the stream of arrivals was incessant. Some mingled at once with the crowd; others lay in batches on the sea-ice a few yards short of the rookery, content to have got so far, and evidently feeling the need for rest after their long journey from the pack. The greater part of this journey was doubtless performed by swimming, as they crossed open water, but I think that much of it must have been done on foot over many miles of sea-ice, to account for the fatigue of many of them.

On the ice they have two modes of progression. The first is simple walking. Their legs being very short, their stride amounts at most to four inches. Their rate of stepping averages about one hundred and twenty steps per minute when on the march.

Their second mode of progression is "tobogganing." When wearied by walking or when the surface is particularly suitable, they fall forward on to their white breasts, smooth and shimmering with a beautiful metallic luster in the sunlight, and push themselves along by alternate powerful little strokes of their legs behind them.

When quietly on the march, both walking and tobogganing produce the same rate of progression, so that the string of arriving birds, tailing out in a long line as far as the horizon, appears as a well-ordered procession. I walked out a mile or so along this line, standing for some time watching it tail past me and taking photographs. Most of the little creatures seemed much out of breath, their wheezy respiration being distinctly heard.

First would pass a string of them walking, then a dozen or so tobogganing. Suddenly those that walked would flop on their breasts and start tobogganing; and conversely strings of tobogganers would as suddenly pop up on to their feet and start walking. In this way they relieved the monotony of their march, and gave periodical rest to different groups of muscles and nerve-centers.

The surface of the snow on the sea-ice varied continually, and over any very smooth patches the pedestrians almost invariably started to toboggan, whilst over "bad going" they all had perforce to walk.

On October 21 many thousands of penguins arrived from the northerly direction and poured on to the beach in a continuous stream, the snaky line of arrivals extending unbroken across the sea-ice as far as the eye could see.

Although squabbles and encounters had been frequent since their arrival in any numbers, it now became manifest that there were two very different types of battles; first, the ordinary quarreling consequent on disputes over nests and the robbery of stones for these, and secondly, the battles between cocks who fought for the hens. These last were more earnest and severe, and were carried to a finish, whereas the first-named rarely proceeded to extremes.

In regard to the mating of the birds, the following most interesting customs seemed to be prevalent.

The hen would establish herself on an old nest, or in some cases scoop out a hollow in the ground and sit in or by this, waiting for a mate to propose himself. She would not attempt to build while she remained unmated. During the first week of the nesting season, when plenty of fresh arrivals were continually pouring into the rookery, she did not have long to wait as a rule. Later, when the rookery was getting filled up, and only a few birds remained unmated in that vast crowd of some three-quarters of a million, her chances were not so good.

For example, on November 16 on a knoll thickly populated by mated birds, many of which already had eggs, a hen was observed to have scooped a little hollow in the ground and to be sitting in this. Day after day she sat on looking thinner and sadder as time passed and making no attempt to build her nest. At last, on November 27, she had her reward, for I found that a cock had joined her, and she was busily building her nest in the little scoop she had made so long before, her husband steadily working away to provide her with the necessary pebbles. Her forlorn appearance of the past ten days had entirely given place to an air of occupation and happiness.

As time went on I became certain that invariably pairing took place after arrival at the rookery. On October 23 I went to the place where the stream of arrivals was coming up the beach, and presently followed a single bird, which I afterwards found to be a cock, to see what it was going to do. He threaded his way through nearly the whole length of the rookery by himself, avoiding the tenanted knolls where the nests were, by keeping to the emptier hollows. About every hundred yards or so he stopped, ruffled up his feathers, closed his eyes for a moment, then "smoothed himself out" and went on again, thus evidently struggling against desire for sleep after his journey. As he progressed he frequently poked his little head forward and from side to side, peering up at the knolls, evidently in search of something.

Arrived at length at the south end of the rookery, he appeared suddenly to make up his mind, and boldly ascending a knoll which was well tenanted and covered with nests, walked straight up to one of these on which a hen sat. There was a cock standing at her side, but my little friend either did not see him or wished to ignore him altogether. He stuck his beak into the frozen ground in front of the nest, lifted up his head and made as if to place an imaginary stone in front of the hen, a most obvious piece of dumb show. The hen took not the slightest notice nor did her mate.

My friend then turned and walked up to another nest, a yard or so off, where another cock and hen were. The cock flew at him immediately, and after a short fight, in which each used his flippers savagely, he was driven clean down the side of the knoll away from the nests, the victorious cock returning to his hen. The newcomer, with the persistence which characterizes his kind, came straight back to the same nest and stood close by it, soon ruffling his feathers and evidently settling himself for a doze; but, I suppose because he made no further overtures, the others took no notice of him at all, as, overcome by sheer weariness, he went to sleep and remained so until I was too cold to await further developments. On my way back to our hut I followed another cock for about thirty yards, when he walked up to another couple at a nest and gave battle to the cock. He, too, was driven off after a short and decisive fight. Soon there were many cocks on the war-path. Little knots of them were to be seen about the rookery, the lust of battle in them, watching and fighting each other with desperate jealousy, and the later the season advanced the more "bersac" they became. The roar of battle and thuds of blows could be heard continuously, and of the hundreds of such fights, all plainly had their cause in rivalry for the hens.

When starting to fight, the cocks sometimes peck at each other with their beaks, but always they very soon start to use their flippers, standing up to one another and raining in the blows with such rapidity as to make a sound which, in the words of Dr. Wilson, resembles that of a boy running and dragging his hoop-stick along an iron paling. Soon they start "in-fighting," in which position one bird fights right-handed, the other left-handed; that is to say, one leans his left breast against his opponent, swinging in his blows with his right flipper, the other presenting his right breast and using his left flipper. My photographs of cocks fighting all show this plainly. It is interesting to note that these birds, though fighting with one flipper only, are ambidextrous. Whilst battering one another with might and main they use their weight at the same time, and as one outlasts the other, he drives his vanquished opponent before him over the ground, as a trained boxing man when "in-fighting" drives his exhausted opponent round the ring.

Desperate as these encounters are, I don't think one penguin ever kills another. In many cases blood is drawn. I saw one with an eye put out, and that side of its beak (the right side) clotted with blood, while the crimson print of a blood-stained flipper across a white breast was no uncommon sight.

Hard as they can hit with their flippers, however, they are also well protected by their feathers, and being marvelously tough and enduring, the end of a hard fight merely finds the vanquished bird prostrated with exhaustion and with most of the breath beaten out of his little body. The victor is invariably satisfied with this, and does not seek to dispatch him with his beak.

It was very usual to see a little group of cocks gathered together in the middle of one of the knolls squabbling noisily. Sometimes half a dozen would be lifting their raucous voices at one particular bird, then they would separate into pairs, squaring up to one another and emphasizing their remarks from time to time by a few quick blows from their flippers. It seemed that each was indignant with the others for coming and spoiling his chances with a coveted hen, and trying to get them to depart before he went to her.

It was useless for either to attempt overtures whilst the others were there, for the instant he did so, he would be set upon and a desperate fight begin. Usually, as in the case I described above, one of the little crowd would suddenly "see red" and sail into an opponent with desperate energy, invariably driving him in the first rush down the side of the knoll to the open space surrounding it, where the fight would be fought out, the victor returning to the others, until by his prowess and force of character, he would rid himself of them all. Then came his overtures to the hen. He would, as a rule, pick up a stone and lay it in front of her if she were sitting in her "scoop," or if she were standing by it he might himself squat in it. She might take to him kindly, or, as often happened, peck him furiously. To this he would submit tamely, hunching up his feathers and shutting his eyes while she pecked him cruelly. Generally after a little of this she would become appeased. He would rise to his feet, and in the prettiest manner edge up to her, gracefully arch his neck, and with soft guttural sounds pacify her and make love to her.

Both perhaps would then assume the "ecstatic" attitude, rocking their necks from side to side as they faced one another, and after this a perfect understanding would seem to grow up between them, and the solemn compact was made.

It is difficult to convey in words the daintiness of this pretty little scene. I saw it enacted many dozens of times, and it was wonderful to watch one of these hardy little cocks pacifying a fractious hen by the perfect grace of his manners.

This antic is gone through by both sexes and at various times, though much more frequently during the actual breeding season. The bird rears its body upward and stretching up its neck in a perpendicular line, discharges a volley of guttural sounds straight at the unresponding heavens. At the same time the clonic movements of its syrinx or "sound box" distinctly can be seen going on in its throat. Why it does this I have never been able to make out, but it appears to be thrown into this ecstasy when it is pleased; in fact, the zoologist of the *"Pourquoi Pas"* expedition termed it the *"Chant de Satisfaction."* I suppose it may be likened to the crowing of a cock or the braying of an ass. When one bird of a pair starts to perform in this way, the other usually starts at once to pacify it.

On November 3 several eggs were found, and on the 4th these

were beginning to be plentiful in places, though many of the colonies had not yet started to lay.

Let me here call attention to the fact that up to now not a single bird out of all those thousands had left the rookery once it had entered it. Consequently not a single bird had taken food of any description during all the most strenuous part of the breeding season, and as they did not start to feed till November 8, thousands had to my knowledge fasted for no fewer than twenty-seven days. Now of all the days of the year these twenty-seven are certainly the most trying during the life of the Adelie.

With the exception, in some cases, of a few hours immediately after arrival (and I believe the later arrivals could not afford themselves even this short respite), constant vigilance had been maintained; battle after battle had been fought; some had been nearly killed in savage encounters, recovered, fought again and again with varying fortune. They had mated at last, built their nests, procreated their species, and, in short, met the severest trials that Nature can inflict upon mind and body; and at the end of it, though in many cases blood-stained and in all caked and bedraggled with mire, they were as active and as brave as ever.

By November 7, though many nests were still without eggs, a large number now contained two, and their owners started, turn and turn about, to go to the open water leads about a third of a mile distant, to feed, and as a result of this a change began gradually to come over the face of the rookery. Hitherto the whole ground in the neighborhood of the nests had been stained a bright green. This was due to the fasting birds continually dropping their watery, bile-stained excreta upon it. (The gall of penguins is bright green.) These excreta practically contained no solid matter except epithelial cells and salts.

The nests themselves are never fouled, the excreta being squirted clear of them for a distance of a foot or more, so that each nest has the appearance of a flower with bright green petals radiating from its center. Even when the chicks have come and are being sat upon by the parents, this still holds good, because they lie with their heads under the old bird's belly and their hindquarters just presenting themselves, so that they may add their little decorative offerings, petal by petal! Now that the birds were going to feed, the watery-green stains upon the ground gave place to the characteristic bright brick-red guano, resulting from their feeding on the shrimp-like euphausia in the sea; and the color of the whole rookery was changed in a few days, though this was first noticeable, of course, in the region of those knolls which had been occupied first, and which were now settled down to the peaceable and regular family life which was to last until the chicks had grown.

During the fasting season, as none of the penguins had entered the water, they all became very dirty and disreputable in appearance, as well may be imagined considering the life they led; but now that they went regularly to swim, they immediately got back their sleek and spotless state.

From the ice-foot to the open water, the half mile or so of sea-ice presented a lively scene as the thousands of birds passed to and fro over it, outward bound parties of dirty birds from the rookery passing the spruce bathers, homeward bound after their banquet and frolic in the sea. So interesting and instructive was it to watch the bathing parties, that we spent whole days in this way.

As I have said before, the couples took turn and turn about on the nest, one remaining to guard and incubate while the other went off to the water.

On leaving their nests, the birds made their way down the ice-foot on to the sea-ice. Here they would generally wait about and join up with others until enough had gathered together to make up a decent little party, which would then set off gaily for the water. They were now in the greatest possible spirits, chattering loudly and frolicking with one another, and playfully chasing each other about, occasionally indulging in a little friendly sparring with their flippers.

Arrived at length at the water's edge, almost always the same procedure was gone through. The object of every bird in the party seemed to be to get one of the others to enter the water first. They would crowd up to the very edge of the ice, dodging about and trying to push one another in. Sometimes those behind nearly would succeed in pushing the front rank in, who then would just recover themselves in time, and rushing round to the rear, endeavor to turn the tables on the others. Occasionally one actually would get pushed in, only to turn quickly under water and bound out again onto the ice like a cork shot out of a bottle. Then for some time they would chase one another about, seemingly bent on having a good game, each bird intent on finding any excuse from being the first in. Sometimes this would last a few minutes, sometimes for the better part of an hour, until suddenly the whole band would change its tactics, and one of the number start to run at full tilt along the edge of the ice, the rest following closely on his heels, until at last he would take a clean header into the water. One after another the rest of the party followed him, all taking off exactly from the spot where he had entered, and following one another so quickly as to have the appearance of a lot of shot poured out of a bottle into the water.

A dead silence would ensue till a few seconds later, when they would all come to the surface some twenty or thirty yards out, and start rolling about and splashing in the water, cleaning themselves and making sounds exactly like a lot of boys calling out and chaffing one another.

So extraordinary was this whole scene, that on first witnessing it we were overcome with astonishment, and it seemed to us almost impossible that the little creatures whose antics we were watching were actually birds and not human beings. Seemingly reluctant as they had been to enter the water, when once there they evinced every sign of enjoyment, and would stay in for hours at a time.

As may be imagined, the penguins spent a great deal of time on their way to and from the water, especially during the earlier period before the sea-ice had broken away from the ice-foot, as they had so far to walk before arriving at the open leads.

As a band of spotless bathers returning to the rookery, their white breasts and black backs glistening with a fine metallic luster in the sunlight, met a dirty and bedraggled party on its way out from the nesting ground, frequently both would stop, and the clean and dirty mingle together and chatter with one another for some minutes. If they were not speaking words in some language of their own, their whole appearance belied them, and as they stood, some in pairs, some in groups of three or more, chattering amicably together, it became evident that they were sociable animals, glad to meet one another, and like many men, pleased with the excuse to forget for a while their duties at home, where their mates were waiting to be relieved for their own spell off the nests.

After a variable period of this intercourse, the two parties would separate and continue on their respective ways, a clean stream issuing from the crowd in the direction of the rookery, a dirty one heading off towards the open water; but here it was seen that a few who had bathed and fed, and were already perhaps half-way home, had been persuaded to turn and accompany the others, and so back they would go again over the way they had come, to spend a few more hours in skylarking and splashing about in the sea.

In speaking of these games of the penguins, I wish to lay emphasis on the fact that these hours of relaxation play a large part in their lives during the advanced part of the breeding period. They would spend hours in playing at a sort of "touch last" on the sea-ice near the water's edge. They never played on the ground of the rookery itself, but only on the sea-ice and the ice-foot and in the water; and I may here mention another favorite pastime of theirs. Small ice-floes are continually drifting past in the water, and as one of these arrived at the top of the ice-foot, it would be boarded by a crowd of penguins, sometimes until it could hold no more. This "excursion boat," as we used to call it, would float its many occupants down the whole length of the ice-foot, and if it passed close to the edge, those that rode on the floes would shout at the knots of penguins gathered along the ice-foot who would shout at them in reply, so that a gay bantering seemed to accompany their passage past the rookery.

Arrived at the farther end, some half a mile lower down, those on the "excursion boat" had perforce to leave it, all plunging into the tide and swimming against this until they came to the top again, then boarded a fresh floe for another ride down. All day these floes, often crowded to their utmost capacity, would float past the rookery. Often a knot of hesitating penguins on the ice-foot, on being hailed by a babel of voices from a floe, would suddenly make the plunge, and all swim off to join their friends for the rest of the journey, and I have seen a floe so crowded that as a fresh party boarded it on one side, many were pushed off the other side into the water by the crush.

Once, as we stood watching the penguins bathing, one of them popped out of the water onto the ice with a large pebble in its mouth, which it had evidently fetched from the bottom. This surprised me, as the depth of the sea here was some ten fathoms at least. The bird simply dropped the stone on the ice and then dived in again, so that evidently he had gone to all the trouble of diving for the stone simply for the pleasure of doing it. Mr. J. H. Gurney in his book on the gannet, says they (gannets) are said to have got themselves entangled in fishing-nets at a depth of 180 ft. and that their descent to a depth of 90 ft. is quite authentic, so that perhaps the depth of this penguin's dive was not an ususual one.

The tide at the open water leads where they bathed ran a good six knots, but the Adelies swam quite easily against this without leaving the surface.

In the water, as on the land, they have two means of progression. The first is by swimming as a duck swims, except that they lie much lower in the water than a duck does, the top of the back being submerged, so that the neck sticks up out of the water. As their feet are very slightly webbed, they have not the advantages that a duck or gull has when swimming in this way, but supplement their foot-work by short quick strokes of their flippers. This they are easily able to do, owing to the depth to which the breast sinks in the water.

The second method is by "porpoising."

This consists in swimming underwater, using the wings or "flippers" for propulsion, the action of these limbs being practically the same as they would be in flying. As their wings are beautifully shaped for swimming, and their pectoral muscles extraordinarily powerful, they attain great speed, besides which they are as nimble as fish, being able completely to double in their tracks in the flash of a moment. In porpoising, after traveling thirty feet or so underwater, they rise from it, shooting clean out with an impetus that carries them a couple of yards in the air, then with an arch of the back they are head first into the water again, swimming a few more strokes, then out again, and so on.

Perhaps the most surprising feat of which the Adelie is capable is seen when it leaps from the water onto the ice. We saw this best later in the year when the sea-ice had broken away from the ice-foot, so that open water washed against the ice cliff bounding the land. This little cliff rose sheer from the water at first, but later, by the action of the waves, was undercut for some six feet or more in places, so that the ledge of ice at the top hung forwards over the water. The height of most of this upper ledge varied from three to six feet.

Whilst in the water, the penguins usually hunted and played in parties, just as they had entered it, though a fair number of solitary individuals were also to be seen. When a party had satisfied their appetites and their desire for play, they would swim to a distance of some thirty to forty yards from the ice-foot, when they might be seen all to stretch their necks up and take a good look at the proposed landing-place. Having done this, every bird would suddenly disappear beneath the surface, not a ripple showing which direction they had taken, till suddenly, sometimes in a bunch, sometimes in a stream, one after the other they would all shoot out of the water, clean up on to the top of the ice-foot. Several times I measured the distance from the surface of the water to the ledge on which they landed, and the highest leap I recorded was exactly five feet. The "take-off" was about four feet out from the edge, the whole of the necessary impetus being gained as the bird approached beneath the water.

The most important thing to note about this jumping from the water was the accuracy with which they invariably rose at precisely the right moment, the exact distance being judged during their momentary survey of a spot from a distance, before they dived beneath the water, and carried in their minds as they approached the ice. I am sure that this impression was all they had to guide them, as with a ripple on the water, and at the pace they were going, they could not possibly have seen their landing place at all clearly as they approached it, besides which, in many cases, the ledge of ice on which they landed projected many feet forwards from the surface, yet I never saw them misjudge their distance so as to come up under the overhanging ledge.

During their approach they swam at an even distance of about three or four feet beneath the surface, projecting themselves upwards by a sudden upward bend of the body, at the same time using their tail as a helm.

Their quickness of perception is shown very well as they land on the ice. If the surface is composed of snow, and so affords them a good foothold, they throw their legs well forward and land on their feet; but should they find themselves landing on a slippery ice-surface, they throw themselves forward, landing on their breasts in the tobogganing position.

The Adelies dive very beautifully. We did not see this at first, before the sea-ice had gone out, because to enter the water they had only to drop a few inches; but later, when entering from the ice terraces, we constantly saw them making the most graceful dives.

At the place where they most often went in, a long terrace of ice about six feet in height ran for hundreds of yards along the edge of the water, and here, just as on the sea-ice, crowds would stand near the brink. When they had succeeded in pushing one of their number over, all would crane their necks over the edge, and when they saw the pioneer safe in the water, the rest followed.

When diving into shallow water they fall flat, but into deep water and from any considerable height, they assume the most perfect positions and make very little splash. Occasionally we saw them stand hesitating to dive at a height of some twenty feet, but generally they descended to some lower spot, and did not often dive from such a height; but twelve feet was no uncommon dive for them.

The reluctance shown by each individual of a party of intending bathers to be the first to enter the water may partly have been explained when, later on, we discovered that a large number of sea-leopards were gathered in the sea in the neighborhood of the rookery to prey on the penguins. These formidable animals used to lurk beneath the overhanging ledges of the ice-foot, out of sight of the birds on the ice overhead. They lay quite still in the water, only their heads protruding, until a party of Adelies would descend into the water almost on top of them, when with a sudden dash and snap of their great formidable jaws, they would secure one of the birds.

It seemed to me then that all the chivvying and preliminaries which they went through before entering the water arose mainly from a desire on the part of each penguin to get one of its neighbors to go in first in order to prove whether the coast was clear or not, though all this maneuvering was certainly taken very lightly, and quite in the nature of a game. This indeed was not surprising, for of all the animals of which I have had any experience, I think the Adelie penguin is the very bravest. The more we saw of them the fonder we became of them and the more we admired their indomitable courage. The appearance of a sea-leopard in their midst was the one thing that caused them any panic. With dozens of these enemies about they would gambol in the sea in the most light-hearted manner, but the appearance of one among them was the signal for a stampede; but even this was invariably gone through in an orderly manner with some show of reason, for, porpoising off in a clump, they at once spread themselves out, scattering in a fan-shaped formation as they sped away, instead of all following the same direction.

As far as I could judge, however, the sea-leopards are a trifle faster in the water than the Adelies, as one of them occasionally would catch up with one of the fugitives, who then, realizing that speed alone would not avail him, started dodging from side to side, and sometimes swam rapidly round and round in a circle of about twelve feet diameter for a full minute or more, doubtless knowing that he was quicker in turning than his great heavy pursuer; but exhaustion would overtake him in the end, and we could see the head and jaws of the great sea-leopard rise to the surface as he grabbed his victim. The sight of a panic-stricken little Adelie tearing round and round in this manner was a sadly common sight late in the season.

When the sea-ice had gone out, leaving open water right up to the ice-foot, a ledge of ice was left along the western side of the rookery, forming a sort of terrace or "front," with its sides composed of blue ice, rising sheer out of the water to a height of some six feet or more in places. From this point of vantage it was possible to stand and watch the penguins as they swam in the clear water below, and some idea was formed of their wonderful agility when swimming beneath the surface. As they propelled themselves along with powerful strokes of their wings, they swerved from side to side to secure the little prawn-like euphausia which literally swam everywhere in the

Antarctic seas, affording them ample food at all times. Their gluttonous habits here became very evident. They would gobble euphausia until they could hold no more, only to vomit the whole meal into the water as they swam, and so lightened, start to feast again. As they winged their way along several feet beneath the surface, a milky cloud would suddenly issue from their mouths and drift slowly away downstream, as without the slightest pause in their career they dashed eagerly along in the hunt for more.

When a penguin returned to his mate on the nest, after his jaunt in the sea, much formality had to be gone through before he was allowed to take charge of the eggs. This ceremony of "relieving the guard" almost invariably was observed.

Going up to his mate, with much graceful arching of his neck, he appeared to assure her in guttural tones of his readiness to take charge. At this she would become very agitated, replying with raucous staccato notes, and refusing to budge from her position on the eggs. Then both would become angry for a while, arguing in a very heated manner, until at last she would rise, and standing by the side of the nest, allow him to walk onto it, which he immediately did, and after carefully placing the eggs in position, sink down upon them, afterwards thrusting his bill beneath his breast to push them gently into a comfortable position. After staying by him for a little while, the other at length would go off to bathe and feed.

When the chicks began to appear all over the rookery, a marked change was noticed in the appearance of the parents as they made their way on foot from the water's edge to the nests. Hitherto they had been merely remarkable for their spotless and glistening plumage, but now they were bringing with them food for the young, and so distended were their stomachs with this, that they had to lean backward as they walked, to counterbalance their bulging bellies, and in consequence frequently tripped over the inequalities of the ground which were thus hidden from their gaze.

What with the exertion of tramping with their burden across the rookery, and perhaps on rare occasions one or two little disputes with other penguins by the way, frequently they were in some distress before they reached their destination, and quite commonly they would be sick and bring up the whole offering before they got there. Consequently, little red heaps of mashed-up and half-digested euphausia were to be seen about the rookery. Once I saw a penguin, after he had actually reached the nest, quite unable to wait for the chick to help itself in the usual manner, deposit the lot upon the ground in front of his mate. When this happens the food is wasted, as neither chick nor adult will touch it however hungry they may be, the former only feeding by the natural method of pushing his head down the throat of a parent, and so helping himself direct from the gullet.

When the chicks are small they are kept completely covered by the parent who sits on the nest. They grow, however, at an enormous rate, gobbling vast quantities of food as it is brought to them, their elastic bellies seeming to have no limit to their capacity; indeed, when standing, they rest on a sort of tripod, formed by the protuberant belly in front and the two feet behind.

To see an Adelie chick of a fortnight's growth trying to get itself covered by its mother is a most ludicrous sight. The most it can hope for is to get its head under cover, the rest of its body being exposed to the air; but the downy coat of the chick is close and warm, and suffices in all weathers to protect it from the cold.

Some way back I made allusion to the way in which many of the penguins were choosing sites up the precipitous sides of the Cape at the back of the rookery. Later I came to the conclusion that this was purely the result of their love of climbing. There was one colony at the very summit of the Cape, whose inhabitants could only reach their nests by a long and trying climb to the top and then by a walk of some hundred yards across a steep snow slope hanging over the very brink of a sheer drop of seven hundred feet onto the sea-ice.

During the whole of the time when they were rearing their young, these mountaineers had to make several journeys during each twenty-four hours to carry their enormous bellyfuls of euphausia all the way from the sea to their young on the nests—a weary climb for their little legs and bulky bodies. The greater number who had undertaken this did so at a time when there were ample spaces unoccupied in the most eligible parts of the rookery.

Large masses of ice were stranded by the sea along the shores of the rookery. These fragments of bergs, some of them fifteen to twenty feet in height, formed a miniature mountain range along the shore. All day, parties of penguins were to be seen assiduously climbing the steep sides of this little range. Time after time, when halfway up, they would descend to try another route, and often when with much pains one had scaled a slippery incline, he would come sliding to the bottom, only to pick himself up and have another try.

Generally, this climbing was done by small parties who had clubbed together, as they generally do, from social inclination. It was not unusual for a little band of climbers to take as much as an hour or more over climbing to the summit. Arrived at the top they would spend a variable period there, sometimes descending at once, sometimes spending a considerable time there, gazing contentedly about them, or peering over the edge to chatter with other parties below.

Again, some half a mile from the beach, a large berg some one hundred feet in height was grounded in fairly deep water, accessible at first over the sea-ice, but later, when this had gone, surrounded by open water. Its sides were sheer except on one side, which sloped steeply from the water's edge to the top.

From the time when they first went to the sea to feed until the end of the season, there was a continual stream of penguins ascending and descending that berg. As I watched them through glasses I saw that they had worn deep paths in the snow from base to summit. They had absolutely nothing to gain by going to all this trouble but the pleasure they seemed to derive from the climb, and when at the top, merely had a good look round and came down again.

Two Legs Too Many

TO MAN, insects are the most amazing of all the lesser creatures, but they are also the most difficult to love—one may almost say the most difficult to believe in. That, the biologist will tell us, is because they took so long ago an evolutionary path which branched away from the road followed by all other living things. At every point where a choice was possible, their ancestors made one choice and ours another. Where we developed a hard skeleton inside, they developed it outside; where we made our blood run red, they made theirs white; where we evolved a central brain, they chose a wholly different nervous system. Some of them, at least, have ears on their legs, and all of them breathe through tubes which ramify throughout their bodies, instead of circulating oxygen through the blood. Most important of all, they chose to face the world equipped with instincts which resist almost absolutely adaptation or change, instead of with intelligences which are prepared to experiment and to make adjustments.

Something of all this the most uninstructed of men seem somehow to feel. Whatever walks on four legs can easily come to seem capable not only of being comprehended, but also of returning some comprehension. Whatever walks on six—as insects invariably do—has two legs too many and seems to warn us thereby that he is not one of us. It does not surprise us to be told that such creatures are possibly without consciousness at all,

even more probably incapable of feeling pain. There seem to be
no individuals, only members of a species; and man recoils in
a sort of incomprehension from a creature who is so devoid of
personality that nothing seems to be lost when any number of
individuals cease to be. We almost wonder whether they ought
to be called alive at all—whether anything except a biologist's
definition can call them living, either in our sense or, even, in
the sense that the most cold-blooded of the reptiles and amphibians is alive. Perhaps the sense of distaste with which the
average person regards the very word "bug" is the product of
this sense of a being so completely alien. Perhaps it is a sort
of ultimate xenophobia. Of all the foreigners with whom we come
in contact, no other in all the universe is so foreign as any
member of the insect tribe.

The writer about the beaver and the deer may fear that he
will make them too human, but anthropomorphism is not the
danger here. The difficulty, instead, is the difficulty of discovering
a nexus between us and those who go on six legs instead of on
two or four. Their strangeness must be the dominant theme;
the fact that their ways are workable and their extraordinary
mores acceptable to nature must be the moral.

No one before or since ever equaled the Frenchman Henri
Fabre in making their doings literature. His dramatic, highly
personal accounts of insect behavior are probably the most
completely achieved specimens in any language of their particular genre. By comparison his great predecessor Réaumur was
almost too plain, as Maeterlinck is much too fancy and too
fanciful. Fabre never forgot that his business was equally to convey information and the excitement of discovering it. He drama-
tized not only himself and the insects but also God, nature, and
the desire for knowledge. The result is something very nearly
unique both as science and as literature. But the personality
which is revealed is always his, not his subject's, and the two
are never confused. A lifetime of observation and loving study
never deluded him into supposing that he ever so much as

glimpsed the universe from an insect's point of view. Some scientists have quarreled with his theology, with his stubborn insistence that the insect can know nothing and want nothing and that his intricate techniques are therefore proof that only God's will and intelligence makes him move at all. But that is, as a figure of speech, something which ought to be acceptable even to those to whom it is no more. It is at least a way of saying that the insect's ego, if he has one, is incomprehensible to us and that his libido is discontinuous with ours.

For this section I have chosen three very different American approaches to the insect world. The first piece is taken from *A Multitude of Living Things* by Lorus and Marjorie Milne, two young college teachers of biology. In this essay they have described clearly and simply some of the insect inhabitants of the surface film of a New England pond, and managed, at the same time, to do something more. They have reminded us of the fact that for the insect, as for various other living creatures, the world is divided into exploitable and non-exploitable regions according to principles of division which have little to do with those which are supremely important to man. One group finds its Eden in a dry, clay bank; another under the bark of a rotting log; still another moves in to colonize the elastic surface of quiet water. The "haunts of life," as one British biologist liked to call them, are various, and there are few which are not for some race ideal.

Second, by way of curiosity, comes a fanciful little piece written in the nineteenth century by Langstroth, the theologian turned beekeeper who revolutionized the whole honey-growing industry by observing how a peculiar fixed habit of the bee might be taken advantage of and the modern demountable hive be invented. A truly obsessed monomaniac, he was suddenly seized in adult life with the irresistible need to study bees and he alternated between manic periods during which nothing else interested him, and periods of depression when everything connected with his obsession was so distasteful that the mere sight of the letter "B" was, by association, intolerable. But in apiculture he was the one great revolutionist because of whose genius a whole modern industry became practicable.

Charles D. Stewart, whose volume *Fellow Creatures* supplies the third selection, is also something of an eccentric. He began his professional career as a walking dictionary who spelled and defined technical and other out-of-the-way words to dime-museum audiences, and varied the performance by writing backwards from dictation. Later he became a draftsman for newspapers until photoengraving destroyed his trade. Still later he wrote familiar essays on nature and other subjects, some of which were published in the *Atlantic Monthly*. Spiders, the subject of the present paper, have interested him, but so has everything else odd in one way or another.

A Multitude of Living Things

—L. J. AND M. J. MILNE

When you sit by a pond or a slowly winding stream, the city's impatient tempo drains away, and from the corners of the mind, thoughts come out and sun themselves. Before you on the water surface, bugs and beetles skip about. They stay afloat because the liquid's surface tension acts as a skin, elastic and smooth, preventing them from falling in. Yet this animal activity on the water seems to contradict all human experience. That "water is wet" is one of the first facts learned by every child. In more mature years this wetness is so taken for granted that any exceptions to the rule arouse great interest. Thus the sewing needle that can be lowered gently onto the surface of a tumblerful of water, there to float completely dry, is a startling paradox. But to a large number of animals and plants, this problem of wetness and dryness is a matter of life or death. Many of them find the "dry" surface of water a place on which to live, albeit precariously. Suspended between the air above and the depths below, they inhabit the surface film of ponds, streams, lakes and even oceans. Theirs is an almost two-dimensional realm—a special niche in nature for use of which certain requirements must be met.

When a substance attracts water molecules more strongly than water molecules attract each other, the water wets the surface. The liquid creeps along, invading every crevice, clinging tightly to each irregularity. But some materials such as waxes and oils, attract water molecules so little that the water draws away, pulling back into itself and leaving the surfaces dry. Aquatic birds take advantage of these differences by regularly adding oil to their outer plumage, thereby keeping their feathers from becoming water-soaked. The many creatures that walk on water do so by means of well-waxed, hair-booted feet that the water cannot wet.

Best known of all the animals that walk dry-shod on ponds and streams are the water striders—insects with four long legs stretching out to the sides and a shorter pair held under the head. Texans call them "Jesus bugs," while in Canada they are "skaters." Their slender feet are covered with a short pile of greasy hairs that the water fails to invade. Each foot presses the water surface and makes a dimple there, but the water does not let the foot fall through the surface film as it would if the fine waxy bristles were absent. Instead the insect's weight is supported, partly by the buoyant force of the water displaced from the dimples, partly by the surface tension that tends to erase the depressions and bring all the water film to the same level. The strider stands chiefly on its hind- and foremost legs, while with the middle pair as oars it sculls along, its body well above the smooth and slippery surface of the pond. Mirrored in the water film below the bug is its image—a reflected "double" seldom seen except by small creatures close to the water surface. Below the strider, on the bottom of a shallow stream, are dark shadows cast not only by the insect, but also by the dimples in the surface film where its feet press downward. Sometimes, on sunny days, these shadows on a sandy bottom are more conspicuous than the insect making them. They drift along and follow every movement of the rowing strider on the film above.

L. J. and M. J. Milne

A considerable *length* of surface must be called upon to support an insect as heavy as a full-grown water strider. If its hair-booted feet pressed on the film at only six small points, the bug would penetrate into the water and sink at once. But the strider's legs are spread so widely as to be almost parallel to the surface, and its feet make elongated dimples which are really furrows in the water film. So secure is the insect on a quiet pond or stream that it can shift its weight freely among its feet. Most spectacular are the demonstrations of this when a strider cleans itself. Drawing its rowing legs far back, it stands with its head almost in the water, while its hind legs are raised well above the surface and rubbed one on the other much in the manner of a housefly. Then the insect rests on forefeet and one hind foot, with the rowing leg on that side as an outrigger, while the middle and rear feet of the opposite side are elevated into the air and rubbed free of clinging particles by a similar fiddling movement. To accomplish this contortion the bug practically lies down on its side. The water film stands the strain, but the shadows cast on the bottom shift and spread as the pressures on the fewer surface furrows are increased. Finally the strider stands on rowing feet and rear pontoons while its body and forelegs are raised high above the water. The insect washes itself much as a kitten does, transferring dust particles from feelers, beak and body to the forefeet. Then it rubs these together until they are satisfactorily clean. If uninterrupted, such a complete toilet operation may take ten minutes, and the bug seems to give great care to every detail. At last, with antennae brushed, the insect rows forth alertly to seek its fortune.

Water striders dive upon occasion, but only under threat of serious danger. They have difficulty breaking through the film, but once below they sink to the bottom. Afterwards they crawl out, wet and obviously miserable, to dry and comb themselves into respectability. All active stages in a water strider's life are spent on the water surface, but for winter they fly or crawl (some are wingless even as adults) under leaves on the shore.

Other animals that spread their weight on outstretched feet may rest with safety on the water film. Small gnats and midges flit from place to place on ponds, alighting with equal equanimity on film or foliage. Even large craneflies settle with surprising grace upon the water's skin, and rise again with their long legs trailing after. Each foot combines the advantages of waxed hair covering and slender length that can distribute the insect's weight along the surface film. But Jesus bugs are not adverse to live meat when they can catch it. Many of their dashes over the pond surface are rewarded with small flies that fail to take to flight in time. Occasionally, too, a cranefly dies of unknown causes while resting on the water surface. Without muscular effort to hold its body well above the water, the insect sags into the pond, sinking in or barely floating. Water striders gather around it to salvage such nourishing juices as remain. It is but one of the many types of food they seek as they push their way along the transparent but rubbery surface film. Some of their sustenance floats up to them from below; each dead fish attracts a crowd of striders. But most of the food of these insects falls into the water from the air above. Ants tumble from leaves overhanging the water. Beetles close their wings and drop or blunder into ponds and streams where the water wets them and renders them helpless prey for the predacious bugs. Striders investigate every particle, often making great leaps over the water to reach some newly fallen object. A green leaf floating down a small stream draws the attention of these bugs, one after the other, as it passes through each quiet stretch. Small articles such as drowning ants are picked out of the surface film and held on a slender black beak while the liquid contents are drained away. Often a strider is seen carrying with it a gnat or other carcass as it glides along the water surface. Occasionally other striders chase the food-bearing relative across the pond, just as chickens do a hen fortunate enough to find a large grub. But when not in the act of feeding, each strider defends some section of shoreline or creek surface, driving away invaders that trespass on the unmarked watery hunting ground.

Only on quiet days do striders venture far from shore. If a breeze springs up they hurry to reach calm water near the bank before the surface becomes ruffled. Rain and winter drive the striders from the water, to crawl out upon the bank. In spite of these precautions, the insects do get wet at times. Although they show great ability in navigating streams, and can spring ahead to make progress against the current, an occasional bug is swept through a riffle and fails to stay afloat. Air clinging to its body usually keeps the creature just below the surface film, where it rows to shore to crawl out, dry and clean itself.

There is also a sea-going water strider—a small gray form common in tropical and subtropical lagoons and mangrove swamps, where it congregates in large groups. These same water striders are found too at great distances from land, riding the waves like the best sailors. No one knows what they do during a storm at sea or when it rains there. They must get wet, and where is there to creep out upon to dry? To add to the problem, these sea-going striders often crawl down into the water during calm weather, and row along to feed there, back downward on the under side of the water film! Many of them live out their lives hundreds of miles from shore and raise their families at sea. The eggs are laid on seaweed at the surface of the ocean or on the infrequent feathers dropped by a sea gull.

Spiders and mites of several kinds frequent the water film, in pursuit of the insects there. They have the same means of staying dry as do the striders, and they scamper about on ponds picking up food wherever they can find it. Most of the water spiders are tan colored with dark stripes; many of the females lay their eggs in a creamy sphere of silk, and drag their precious ball after them wherever they go, even out upon the water film. One of these ball-making spiders is a giant called *Dolomedes*. A full-grown mother may spread two inches or more between the tips of outstretched legs; her egg sphere may be half an inch in diameter and contain hundreds of potential spiders. Even after they hatch, the spiderlets stay with their parent, and the adult is seen often with a fuzzy covering—mostly legs—which can scurry off, like goslings from a mother goose. Such a family group is quite a prize for a hungry fish, and those spiders that hesitate while running on the water film may lose their lives. However, spiders seldom stop on the surface. They run from shore to plant or leaf to lily pad, carrying their prey with them to a safe spot. But fish in ponds and streams follow walkers on the water to profit from occasional unwariness. Sometimes a fish makes a mistake too, and seizes a spider's ghost—the empty, cast-off skin. Often these skins float downstream, casting on the bottom a shadow much like that of the spider itself. But the skin rests on the water like a dead cranefly, while the living spider walks well above the surface with only its eight feet furrowing the film and making silhouettes on the sand below.

Nor are water spiders restricted by the surface film. Sometimes they creep down the side of a stone or stump and walk about warily below the water's skin. Bubbles of air, glistening like jewels in the light, cling to their bodies where they are trapped below arching bristles and hairs. On such aquatic hunting trips a spider often catches a small fish or some water animal that would be entirely beyond reach from the air above. Other spiders live in coral rock between high and low tide along the sea coast. When the sea threatens them, these creatures close their crevices with a water-tight silk door and wait in the enclosed air until the tide recedes enough to liberate them. But most spectacular of all the water spiders is one that, while still breathing from its envelope of air, weaves a web under water and in it provides an air-tight umbrella of silk. Then the spinner makes trip after trip to the surface, each time capturing a bubble to take below and stock its air-bell. From this artificial haven the spider goes out into the surrounding water to catch truly aquatic animals, only to retire again to the safety of its air-filled bell. Even courtship, mating, and incubation of the young take place in this chamber, and many of the adults close off the bottom too and spend the winter there.

Most conspicuous of the water mites is a common one with a ball-like body of brilliant, velvety red. When full-grown, these mites reach a diameter of a quarter of an inch. They run so smoothly on their very short legs that they seem to glide over the surface film rather than move on distinct feet. The females leave solitary brown eggs on floating vegetation, to hatch into immature mites with six legs instead of the characteristic eight. These larval mites spend a few weeks as parasites on some insect. They lie in wait for water striders or diving beetles—anything that comes their way. Sometimes they ride on damsel flies; more often they catch the striders. One strider may carry several of these clinging mites, each sucking some nourishment yet seeming to do little harm to its host. Eventually they drop off, molt to gain another pair of legs and the spherical form of the adult body, and forage for themselves as their parents do. The mites not only run along the surface; frequently they climb down plant stems into the water and swim about. Their eight short legs give them an even motion by which they may be distinguished easily from all other aquatic animals.

Very small insects with waxy feet can stand upon the water film without the additional precaution of spreading their legs widely. The smallest mites have this advantage. So do the several kinds of springtails and the many leafhoppers that jump over the surface. These animals are so very light that even when they press down sharply on the water film to throw themselves into the air and escape some threatening danger, they do not produce any sizable dimple in the surface. Leafhoppers have leaping legs like a locust's or a katydid's, but the springtails have a much more ingenious way of catapulting themselves into the air. They are grotesque insects, with an elongated tail. Some merely keep their tail curved under them, almost resting on the water film, between their six short legs. To jump they simply straighten out, but do so suddenly. Others carry the tip of the underturned tail in a special catch, like the notched trigger of a mousetrap. The tail is strained against the catch just as is the mousetrap spring. When the insect is frightened (or sometimes seemingly just for fun!) the catch is slipped, the tail whacks the water film, and the springtail is thrown high in the air, to land somewhere else. For a creature so minute, air has an excellent cushioning effect, so that the springtail settles without damage, usually on its feet.

Two types of springtails are common on fresh water and one on quiet bays of the ocean. The more abundant of the lake and pond forms is bluish black, about an eighth of an inch long, and congregates in enormous numbers, often conspicuous as a band along the water's edge. These individuals walk about among their fellows, but at the slightest disturbance, the group flings itself into the air like tiny corn kernels popping on a hot griddle. They alight many inches away and no longer in association with each other. To all intents and purposes they have vanished. Many springtails have a ventral tube extending from the under side, near the catch for the springing organ, by which they can hold themselves to the water surface. The tube tip can be wet by the water, and forms a sort of anchor for the insect. The sea-going springtail, like the sea-going strider, is an interesting exception to the rule that almost every insect is terrestrial or found only in fresh water. The sea-going springtail is found all over the world along sandy and muddy coasts and on tidal pools of rocky shorelines. No one knows what happens to them either, during storms and showers at sea. Not all of them can come ashore for such occasions.

There is no scarcity of water surface on our earth, so that there should be room for all the animals that can live in this special niche. Almost three-quarters of the area of the globe is ocean—nearly a hundred and forty million square miles of it.

Yet relatively few creatures make any use of its surface film. Instead they are crowded on a single million square miles of lakes and rivers, ponds and streams, finding in these smaller bodies of fresh water far better living conditions than over the great depths of the sea. The oceans are interconnected and it would be easy to see how similar plants and animals could spread over these great reaches. Fresh waters, on the other hand, are often isolated. They seem peppered over the land area of the earth in little spots and streaks. Yet the similarity of living creatures on their surfaces is far greater than that of animals and plants along their banks. Showy orchids and howling monkeys do not run wild in Alaska, nor caribou and tundra plants in the jungles of Panama. But a water strider, a diving beetle and a lily pad from these two regions are indistinguishable except to a specialist. Belt, the great English naturalist, once commented on the similarity between fresh-water creatures of Nicaragua and those familiar to him in Europe. It is so everywhere. Conditions of life are much more uniform over the freshwater surfaces of the globe than on the land areas surrounding them. For this reason, a naturalist in a foreign and unfamiliar land can feel very much at home once he rows a boat out on a pond or stream and examines the animals and plants beside this floating craft.

The inside (or under side) of the water surface is used by a surprising number of aquatic creatures. Now and again a pond snail crawls up a plant stem as far as the water surface, there to roll over and glide out under the water film. Its flat foot pulses with slow waves of movement from aft to fore along its length. In this position, many of the snails apply to the water surface a part of the body between foot and shell, and there open up the single hole that leads into the lung. They breathe in a load of air to take below again. In very shallow water, a flat sole similar to that of the pond snail, but much smaller, shorter and narrower, turns out to belong to a worm that is all sole, with almost no thickness. This flatworm, a free-living scavenger related to the liver flukes and tapeworms, is commonly a "planarian" with seemingly crossed eyes spotted on its speckled head. It is a source of never-ending delight to all biology students, and a laboratory pet whose life is hard to take. Planarian pieces cut from a single animal are so elementally constructed that each can reorganize to form a whole. Biologists have worried out the philosophies of "self" in terms of many-headed, several-tailed planarians, which crept along the sides and water surface in laboratory jars to mock their captors.

Another animal capable of remarkable regeneration is *Hydra*, named two centuries ago by a man who discovered its power of head multiplication when mutilated and remembered the Greek mythical monster of that name. *Hydra* looks like a discarded umbrella without any cloth covering—merely a stalk with long arms from one end to represent the parasol's ribs. The arms are tentacles with nettling cells for catching microscopic life, and between the arms is an opening into the animal's interior, through which the prey is thrust for digestion. The opposite end of the stalk is armed with a sticky disk, the stickiness of which is under the animal's control. Often *Hydra* reaches upward with a few tentacles to attach them to some plant stem, then lets go with the sticky disk, to somersault in slow motion and glue its body to a higher point. Repetition of this process or a gradual gliding of the sticky disk may bring the animal almost to the water's surface. There *Hydra* often hangs, foot stuck to the underside of the water film, body pendent, tentacles outstretched for an inch or two beyond, waiting for unwary water animals to bump into a battery of stinging cells. *Hydra's* weight upon the water surface forms a dimple there, but the depression is not like the furrow under a water strider's foot. It is more similar to that around the snail or flatworm, and *Hydra* can creep along the water as they do, although with no visible waves of movement. These submerged creatures produce a water-repelling material from the flat area applied to the surface film. The water draws away, clinging wetly only to the rim of *Hydra's* disk or of the sole of snail or worm.

Two types of minute crustaceans upon which *Hydra* feeds have odd relationships to the under side of the water film. One of these, called *Scapholeberis*, is associated habitually with the surface and has special waxy bristles with which to puncture the water film from below and lay hold upon it. Since these bristles are on the under side of the crustacean, the creature rests back downward, supported by the film. For purposes of camouflage, its body coloring is related to its upside-down position. Instead of being dark-backed and light-bellied like fish and most other animals, *Scapholeberis* is just the opposite. As it faces the air in this position, the crustacean rows itself about with its long antennae, browsing on single-celled plants that float upward from below, and upon pollen and other flotsam accumulated on the water surface from above. A gust of wind tows the surface and *Scapholeberis* attached to it—a "sort of submarine sailing" as some have aptly called it.

The other type of crustacean is typified by *Bosmina*, a tiny creature that is trapped often by accidentally breaking through the water film as it swims along below the surface. Unless a wave or similar disturbance knocks the helpless animal below the film again, it must wait in this position—partly in and partly out of the water—until it can molt its skin and slip out of the old covering into the lake below. The difficulties encountered when a small underwater creature is caught by the "dry" upper surface of water are similar to those experienced by animals of similar bulk and strength when they fall into the water from the air and get wet. Unless a branch is nearby, upon which they can crawl out, they usually drown or are picked up by water striders and other carnivores that make this queer realm their home. Even water striders have difficulties; readers of Lutz's fieldbook are cautioned to carry home their striders in a dry pail, not in water, lest they drown.

The many insect adults and the young of some that live in ponds and streams must have atmospheric air to breathe, and remarkable provisions have been made for reaching through the surface film. The mosquito wriggler, being heavier than the water, must writhe and toss itself upward through the liquid to the surface. There it can push against the film a special breathing tube near its posterior end. The tube tip opens out a crown of pointed flaps that repel the water and support the insect at the surface. Air is carried in through an opening surrounded by the flaps, and transported through tubes to the various organs of the animal's interior. The dreaded malaria-carrying *Anopheles* mosquito produces a wriggler that lies parallel to the surface while breathing. The other kinds of biting mosquitoes have wrigglers that hang head downward—a difference in habit that the mosquito-control man is quick to learn. The pupae or "bullheads," however, are all lighter than water and float just below the surface with a pair of little tubes like soda straws extending through to breathe the air above. When done with breathing for a time, the wriggler closes up its crown of flaps and sinks down into the pond or rain barrel. The bullhead, however, must jerk itself below when danger threatens, only to rise again as soon as its writhing ceases. When the mosquito is about to emerge from the bullhead, it uses the skin as a dry-topped raft through which to rise, avoiding all the surface difficulties. When its legs are dry, the insect can stand upon the water to let its wings expand and harden before flying off. Many other insects emerge from their larval or pupal skins at the surface of the water, and fly away in even shorter time—midges, blackflies, mayflies, caddisflies, alderflies—to name a few.

Swimming insects, from the giant "electric light bugs" to the smaller water boatmen, backswimmers, and various water beetles, come to the surface from time to time to thrust through the water film some tubular mechanism whereby they may replenish the air stores beneath their wings or in their internal breathing tubes. Only by such frequent restocking can they carry on their precariously submarine existence. Some of the fly young, maggot-like and of other peculiar shapes, have telescoping segments at their hinder ends, that they can extend to and through the surface film for gathering air continually while the creatures burrow busily to find food in the mire. Some of the water beetle larvae not only come up to get their air but they drag living or freshly killed prey to the surface and thrust it out into the air, where it can give less resistance to being swallowed and where gravity can be of more help.

One of the common water beetles has a greasy back that repels all moisture like the feathers of a duck. This is the whirligig beetle that spends much of its life at the surface of ponds and streams. Actually it is a double animal—dry above and wet below, with paddle-like feet to propel it rapidly through the water. Even its eyes are divided into an upper portion for vision into air and a lower part with which to watch the water's depths. These shiny black beetles zigzagging in groups draw attention to themselves by their hurried movements. They fascinate a small boy standing dry-shod at the bank. He wants to catch one, but the insects are safe from cupped hands as they dart and spin. Thoreau watched them from the high banks of Walden Pond, "ceaselessly progressing over the smooth surface a quarter of a mile off; for they furrow the water slightly, making a conspicuous ripple bounded by two diverging lines . . ." —little V's of waves like speedboat wakes.

Whirligigs often climb out on floating logs or lily pads to bask like turtles in the sun, but at the slightest movement within sight, they are off into the surrounding film. If alarmed beyond their gyrating system of escape, the beetles tip their tail ends up to grasp a bubble of air as they dive to the bottom. There they swim around or hide a while, and later surface like a submarine some distance off, their glossy backs shedding every speck of water. In winter the whirligigs hide under fallen leaves along the banks or in nearby woods. Warm spring days bring them out to seek their fellows on little pools or in quiet bays along the river. Female beetles lay their eggs just above the water's surface. There the young hatch as hungry, worm-like, aquatic larvae that hunt for smaller animals within the pond.

The water film forms a definite barrier for those insects that must lay their eggs in the water itself. An almost endless variety of solutions to the problem has been observed. Perhaps the simplest is that of the Water-lily Leaf-beetle, which cuts a small, circular hole through the dry top of its lily pad, pushes its abdominal tip through the hole into the water below, and while standing high and dry on a familiar surface, lays two rows of eggs on the under side of the lily leaf in close concentric arcs. Many dragonflies, caddisflies, mayflies and others extrude a single egg or a group of them from the abdominal tip while soaring over the water. They fly down close and suddenly flick the abdomen through the surface film and liberate the egg. Pulling quickly out, they zoom away to repeat the process when the next egg is ready. The insect's momentum insures it against being caught in the surface film and dragged down to drown. Much more careful are the ordinary biting mosquitoes, which lay a raft (literally) of eggs, the raft floating upon the water film with only its lower surface wet. The eggs hatch through their lower ends and the young wrigglers emerge into the water directly, many only to be eaten at once by hungry beetle larvae and by fish. The malaria mosquito, in contrast, lays her eggs singly in the water.

Another little fly stands on the surface like a water strider while she deposits an extruded wet mass of eggs suspended by a strand of gelatine. As the egg mass is let down into the water, the fly adds to the supporting filament a circular, transparent disk that repels water. The disk catches on the surface film and pulls down a dimple as the strand below lengthens out and the suspended eggs sink farther into the water. The fly leaves, but the eggs with their little float drift around as the water surface is blown, or as currents move the water itself. The eggs may become stuck to some vegetation or break their mooring and sink to the bottom, there to hatch.

Some other insects, when ready to lay their eggs in the water, wrap their wings around their bodies like a cloak, enclosing a bubble of air, and crawl down stones or stems through the surface film and into the depths below. Those that succeed in laying their eggs and escaping capture in the water may later crawl back into the air, dry off and fly away. Damselflies co-operate in this. The male uses a pair of claspers at the end of his long abdomen to hold the female by her slender neck. After her eggs are fertilized and seem ready for laying, the pair alight at the water's edge and the female backs into the water down a stem. The male holds on and remains above the surface at least as far as his wings. When the eggs have been deposited the female starts upward and the male pulls, fluttering his wings so that between the efforts of the two of them the female is brought out of the water again, to dry off and fly away. But the male is very particular how far he will back into a pond or stream. Some females insist on going deeper before they lay their eggs. When the male has been pulled down as far as seems right, he lets go of his mate and either hovers over the spot until she reappears or settles on some nearby twig to keep watch. This is a dangerous practice for the female, for if she takes too long, her mate may leave to court another damselfly, leaving his first spouse to drown.

The many special abilities and difficulties related to the water film are based on the very high surface tension that is so characteristic of this commonest liquid. Each adaptation in form or behavior is a means of either using or of circumventing the strong surface forces involved. None of them do anything to change the surface tension itself. Yet this is possible, and is the basis of some classical parlor magic and of much modern industrial chemistry. Ever since someone first dropped a piece of camphor into a dish of water, people have been amused to see the chip of waxy white gum dash here and there over the water surface. It spins around and sails in erratic courses like a whirligig beetle, propelled not by paddles but by a mysterious force. Actually the camphor is dissolving in the water faster at some parts of its perimeter than at others, and since camphor greatly reduces the surface tension of water, the surface forces are weakest where the gum is dissolving most rapidly. The chip moves because of inequality of surface forces pulling it from all sides. The weakest forces are those behind the moving chip; there the camphor is dissolving fastest. The water opposite yanks the chip away.

A similar experiment may be performed with two toothpicks or wooden matches floated in a dish of water. After a few moments they will cling together in the center of their pond. If a slender, pointed stick of soap is pushed down to touch the water surface between the two toothpicks, the surface tension there is suddenly reduced and the water film beyond the toothpicks jerks them apart. If a cube of sugar can be spared, dip it into the water between the spread picks. Back together they come. The soap film climbs quickly into the spaces of the sugar cube, leaving pure water between the floating sticks. With the soap removed, this water can compete once more with the surface tensions beyond the toothpicks. The current of water following the soap into the cube brings the picks together in its wake.

All this is entertaining parlor magic, but there is a little rove beetle, *Stenus* by name, that actually uses this trick. Like its relatives, *Stenus* is an active little beetle, running or flying around much of its time in search of carrion or prey small enough to overcome and eat. Sometimes *Stenus* falls into a puddle or a pond. It has no waxed hair to keep its feet dry and the insect sinks into the surface film, its legs and underparts thoroughly wetted by the water. But *Stenus* merely expels from its anal glands a substance that makes the water wetter—reducing the surface tension at its posterior end. Undiminished surface forces in front of the beetle promptly draw it forward. As long as the insect continues to emit this magic substance, it sails along with no apparent effort. Often the beetle reaches some dry object upon which it can crawl to dry off and take to flight again. This rove beetle can keep up its speedboating for many minutes, but if it is deprived of the abdominal tip with the anal glands, the insect is quite helpless in the water.

Even vertebrate animals may cross the water surface if they are quick about it. Barbour tells of small lizards in Central America, the basilisks, that are common around streams and ponds. When disturbed they rush across the water surface on their hind legs, with the forefeet folded against their sides and the tail raised to counterbalance them. Related lizards in Cuba do this too, but instead of hurrying to the opposite bank or some solid refuge, they run over the water merely to some quiet spot where they stop, sink quickly out of sight to the bottom, and remain until they believe the danger to have passed. Some of our native salamanders and newts can scamper across the water film in much the same way, although they use all four feet and must touch the water along their bellies too. In all of these instances the animal is kept from sinking by its nimble action. The feet press down on the water and are away again so quickly that the water cannot flow around. The liquid's inertia is no match for the speed of the animal. There is no true walking on water for creatures too heavy for the surface film to support when standing still.

Some of our pond plants are like the whirligig beetles, with a water-shedding top to their leaves, while the lower surface rests in and is wet by the water. Lily pads are of this sort, anchored to their log-like roots by long, slender, ropy stems. Their two surfaces support two different types of clinging life, one wet, one dry, while in between the water lily gathers up the sunshine energy to make it grow. Duckweeds too, small flakes of green, are always at the water surface. The larger kinds rest in the surface with rootlets dangling into the pond below. One of these duckweeds is our smallest flowering plant, floating freely just below the water film among the lily pads. Contrast with this the largest water leaf of the Victoria lily, whose six-foot disk with turned-up rim will float a human child of medium size, all safe and dry.

When spring comes to the lake or pond surrounded by pine-clad hills, the water film takes on a golden yellow cast with squandered pollen grains. The wind makes patterns of the driven dust, while through it the whirligigs push on and raise a wake like tiny boats, rocking all the water bugs and giving rise to quiet lappings on the nearby shore. Though spent and useless to the trees around, this pollen dies and sinks below. Throughout the years it may build up a layered record of the past. From just such fossil pollen piles we know many of the plants from ancient times, that lived and passed away but left no other mark. Each pollen grain bears in its surface markings a microscopic signature of the plant from whose flower it came. Pollen, wind and water film combine to make a fossil trail of bygone trees and herbs.

The Life of Langstroth

—FLORENCE NAILE

V irgil, who was a great poet, but not enough of a practical beekeeper to know a laying from a virgin queen, was the first writer of much note to have his fling at me. To him I was only an idle knave, born to consume the fruits of others' labors, and deserving no better fate than death, by ignominious expulsion from the industrious commonwealth. Ever since he so grossly libeled me, to compare one to a drone is the most orthodox form of denunciation for laziness, gluttony, and what has been called "general cussedness."

Now, I am proud to say to this court that I can disprove every charge brought against me, by simply proving that, to the best of my ability, I fulfill the express purpose for which I was born. Surely no creature can do any better than this, and excuse me for thinking that few men do as well.

If any of my enemies had authority to call the roll of my demerits, he would surely begin by accusing me of being too *lazy* to gather any honey. But an expert in points of this kind could remind him that if he examines my proboscis, he will see that it is much too short for sipping nectar from the opening flowers. I am free to admit that I make no wax; but even

Cheshire himself, whose microscopes have fairly turned me inside-out, will tell you that I have not a single wax-secreting gland, and am also without those plastic, trowel-like jaws which enable the worker-bee to mold the wax into such delicate combs.

Now, do not insinuate that I might at least employ some of my leisure time in gathering pollen! Can you not see that my thighs have no basket-like grooves in which it could be packed, and are quite destitute of the bristles by which the workers hold the pollen in place?

No doubt you have often denounced me as a big, hulking coward that leaves to the women the whole defense of the state. Are you not aware that I have nothing to fit me for acting on the offensive? Would that I had one proportioned to my bulk! If only that I might make proof of it upon all who berate me for not accomplishing impossibilities! I am not at all ashamed to admit that I spend the most of my time, not given to eating, either in sleeping or what you are pleased to call listless moping about the hive. Has it never occurred to you that if I should try to assume the restless activity of the worker-bee, I could be nothing better than a meddlesome busybody, perpetually interfering with the necessary business routine? I guess the silly meddler who put me up to such nonsense ought more than once to have had a dishcloth pinned to him, to teach him not to bother the women in their work!

I am sorry to number Shakespeare among those who have misconceived me, by calling me "the lazy, yawning drone"; but as one of my maligners has likened me to Falstaff, I may be allowed to quote, in my own defense, what this great braggart, when accused of cowardice, says of himself to the prince: "Was it for me to kill the heir-apparent? should I turn upon the true prince? why, thou knowest I am as valiant as Hercules: but beware instinct; the lion will not touch the true prince. Instinct is a great matter; I was now a coward on instinct. I shall think the better of myself and thee during my life; I for a valiant lion, and thou for a true prince." I lie not, like the false knight, when I say that what you call my laziness is a matter of pure instinct.

With all your boasted reason, you seem to have overlooked the doctrine of conservation of forces. You upbraid me with consuming so much of the precious honey, to the gathering of which I contribute nothing! Well! if I made a single uncalled-for motion, would not that necessitate an extra consumption of food? What better can I do, then, than to keep as quiet as possible? There is nothing either outside or inside of the hive which calls for any other line of conduct, until the young queens are on the wing; and as they do not sally forth until long after noon, why should I go abroad any earlier? I can assure you that if bridal excursions were in order as many hours in the day as the flowers secrete honey, no worker would ever be earlier to rise, or later to go to bed than myself.

I an idle, lazy, listless lounger, forsooth! Does anyone wish to witness the most perfect embodiment of indefatigable activity? Let him then look at me, when, at the proper time, with an eager, impetuous rush, and a manly, resonant voice, I sally from the hive! See with what amazing speed I urge what our old friend Samuel Wagner called my "circumvoluting" flights! For aught you know, I may cover greater distances in describing these vast circles than the busiest worker in the longest summer day. There is great need, then, that I should be abundantly provisioned for such exhausting excursions; and it is only a law of nature that on my return from them, all that I carried out with me should be found to have been used up. If you taunt me either for the full or the empty stomach, I merely ask you if you have never heard of honeymoon trips among your own people, which began with extra-full purses, to end only with uncomfortably light ones.

To cap the climax of your abuse, what savage delight you take in seeing the worker drive me from my pleasant home! and how glibly you can moralize over what you call a righteous judgment upon a life spent in gluttony and inglorious ease! Just as if you did not know that the whole economy of the beehive is founded upon the strictest principles of utilitarianism! Is not a worker-bee, when disabled by any accident, remorselessly dragged out to die, because it can no longer contribute to the general good? Even so exalted a personage as the queen mother herself, as soon as it is plain that her fertility is too much impaired, has a writ of *supersedeas* served upon her, in favor of one of her own daughters.

Knowing well the law under which I was born, I urge nothing against being put to death when Shakespeare's "pale executioners" deem the day of my prospective usefulness to be over. Truly, the sword of Damocles is suspended over my head; and from the hour of my birth till that of my death it may fall at any moment. Many bitters are thus mingled with my sweets.

I have time to mention only one more. While I know that most of the young queens come safely back from their wedding excursions, I cannot help foreboding the worst when I see that no drone ever returns to tell of his experience.

I will close my defense by reminding you how the good father of the great Scotch beekeeper, Bonner, showed his appreciation of our persecuted race. It was his custom to watch every year for the first flying drone. Its cheerful hum so filled him with delight, as the happy harbinger of approaching swarms, with their generous harvests of luscious sweets, that he called an instant halt on the work of his busy household, and devoted the rest of the day to holiday feasting. The patron of the drones ought forever to bear the honored name of "Saint Bonner."

The Decision Of The Court. This court having heard the defense of Sir Drone, pronounces him to be innocent of each and every one of the misdeeds alleged against him. It only regrets that it cannot inflict adequate punishment upon his slanderers. Alas, my poor fellow! the lies against which you protest have had so many centuries the start of your true story that you may well despair of ever overtaking them in your short lifetime.

Morals. From the plea of the drone, many good morals might be drawn; for, "As he is guilty, that shooteth arrows and lances unto death, so is the man that hateth his friend deceitfully, and, when he is taken, saith, 'I did it in jest.'"

Chicago Spiders

—CHARLES D. STEWART

Being a spider in Chicago is a very satisfactory vocation. In the evening, when it is time to take down the old web and put up the new, a spider will gather a section into a ball or skein that is positively black, and kick it out behind him into the street below as if he were disgusted with such a grimy mess. It is so bulky with dirt that a small piece of web makes a large armful for him. And after the new one has been spread for an hour or two, its sticky filaments are so coated with particles of atmosphere that it will hardly catch anything else. Only by going through a sort of jumping-jack performance can a Chicago spider manage to make a fly stick.

Whether a country spider, with a whole garden fence at his disposal, takes down his old web, I do not know, though it would seem that there he could, by merely moving a foot or two, save himself all the work; but in Chicago, where corner locations are the most valuable—especially the corners of windows where houseflies long to enter—and where each corner is pre-empted by a particular spider, the taking down of the old web is necessary to the greatest daily profit. It pays better than to move.

Charles D. Stewart

A Chicago spider can take down a web and put up another in about twenty minutes—and from this I am anxious to have the reader infer that the daily presence of a great number of them does not mean a neglected window. If anyone thinks his household guiltless in this regard, let him observe his own window closely. I dare say he will find this story sumptuously illustrated.

Before I was laid on a bed by a window and tied down as firmly as any Gulliver by Chicago pygmies, most of whom belonged to the tribe of Typhus, I would have considered it poor employment for any man to enter into the affairs of creatures so much smaller than himself. But they did shrewd things before my eyes every day, and when I began to understand, I became interested; and thus, for three weeks, I found myself bound out to the trade.

It was the jumping-jack trick that I first discovered and appreciated. The spider, sitting patiently at the focus of his elastic wheel with all legs on the lines, is in telegraphic communication with every part of it; now let a fly so much as flutter a filament, and the spider jumps up and down as if he were trying to shake the whole structure from its moorings. This bounces the fly till he has his feet solidly on the line, and perhaps tangled in other lines. After taking this precaution, the spider, if he has been lucky, runs out and ties up his victim in the usual bundle, ready to carry. He does up a fly like a turkey trussed and ready for the table.

To one who has had a motionless and half-forgotten spider in his eye for an hour or so, this sudden exhibition of vigor in jumping up and down is startling. He does it as if he were in a great fit of temper. From this practice it is evident that he cannot depend upon the web alone to catch the prey, and hold it long enough for him to get out to it. The web is not merely a stationary snare, like a tree with birdlime on it, but a contrivance that may be operated personally by the spider as a trap. The structure, being elastic, works up and down when he jumps, so that each row of lines traverses at least the distance between it and the next row of lines. Thus, despite the open spaces between them, he is virtually in possession of the whole plane of space, for anything with air-disturbing wings can hardly pass through it without sending in an alarm and being caught. All spiders, I suppose, know this trick of the trade; but a Chicago spider must stick to his post and practice it in every case. If he did not, his daily catch would be all soot and no flies.

The same spiders did not occupy the window throughout the three weeks; but with the exception of one red spider who came along and seemed very doubtful about setting to work, they were all of one kind, big and little. This auburn-hued spider was more slender and shapely—not so fat and commercial-looking as the others. There were little spiders who spun little webs of such fineness that they were visible only when the sun fell just right on the glinting new gossamer; and for over a week a very big fellow, with a yellow hieroglyph on him like gold bullion on the back of a priest, held sway in webs a foot across. He sat with his back toward the room, whereas most of them made a practice of keeping their under sides toward the window. In this, there seems to be a difference in practice; but all of them sit up-side-down, head-downwards, invariably.

I discovered, to my own satisfaction at least, why a spider sits in his web upside-down. A spider has eight legs, besides a very short pair in front which are more like arms; but in truth a spider's legs are all fingers, and he needs as many as possible to handle his prey. Were he to support himself right side up in grappling with a victim, it would require four of the legs merely to hold him in that position, for he would have to grasp more than one thread; but he can hang head-downwards with only the one hind pair of legs, and have all the rest free to handle the prey before him. His hind pair of legs extend almost straight behind him for the purpose of being his sole support in such cases; and because he is built in this way, in order to cope successfully with other insects, the upside-down attitude is his easiest way of staying on watch. It is his most restful position.

One of the big spiders was one day surprised by a chrysalis that fell down from some place into his web. It turned out to be a very windfall of fortune, for the luscious larva was quite to his taste. At least, he examined it thoroughly, and kept it, as if he were satisfied with what he found inside of the cocoon. It was almost as long as himself, and he showed great dexterity in turning it about and examining it in all positions with his six free legs, holding it before him as he hung head-downwards. A spider can handle himself in all positions with equal facility, and when he is surprised he will suddenly turn head-upward as he surveys the web, and keep that position for a while. But when all is quiet on the Potomac, he turns upside-down again and takes his ease.

I read in a book review that the male spider is said to dance in order to please his inamorata. I have seen such a performance, and would describe it as follows. One of the spiders retreats backward an inch or two from the other; he pauses there a moment and advances; and when the two are face to face, they go through certain antics, both of them, with their front legs. It is exactly as if one were to interlock his fingers loosely and then twiddle them. After this twiddling of legs, the visitor backs up, pauses, and comes forward again; and they will keep up this performance for quite a while. Whether this is flirtation I do not know; much less do I understand the code. And whether it is dancing or not depends upon—the figure of speech.

These spiders, according to the dictionary, are geometrical or garden spiders; but the ones with whom I was personally acquainted saw nothing more verdant than a rubber plant and one smoke-blasted tree. This ailing tree was the only survivor in those parts, and so its twiggery had to accommodate the sparrows of a large territory every evening; it was little more than a community perch or convention tree, and it had more sparrows on it than leaves. Regularly they would come home to Bedlam at night, and they would seem much excited over the return to nature. As to the spiders, they were garden spiders in the sense that Chicago is the Garden City.

Before proceeding further, I must explain that this comment on the secrets of the craft is merely by way of introducing the reader to a particular spider, who had an admirable adventure. I shall come to him later on. I should confess that I do not know spiders anatomically or microscopically, but only personally; I know only that about a spider which he knows himself —namely, his trade. This, I think, is worth describing, step by step.

It will be best to take a Chicago spider who is building in the upper corner of a window, for here is a set of conditions which are uniform throughout the country, and which everyone is familiar with. The spider, having found this unoccupied place, walks on the window frame away from the corner and stops at the right distance for the size of the web, which depends upon the size of the spider. The corner of the window frame offers the foundation, or outline, for two sides of his web; but he must himself complete the circumference within which to spread his work. Now, a line stretched from where he stands, on the top frame, to a point on the side frame will give him a triangle; and he must project this line transversely through the air.

This is easily done. Pressing the end of the line to the window frame, he takes hold of it with one hind leg and runs along with it to the corner, spinning it out as he goes; and he holds the line out with his hind leg like a boy flying a kite. He must hold it well out and keep it taut, for it must not touch the wood anywhere along its length. Having reached the corner, he turns and runs down the side frame; and now it is as if the kite were going up in the air. As he runs downward from the corner, paying out the line, it opens, fanwise, from the upper frame; and when it has formed the triangle he stops and fastens that end.

This is to be his main cable, which must, on that side, support the ends of all the lines. And these inner lines are to be stretched with considerable tension. For such a heavy strain the single strand is not enough, so he now runs back and forth along its length and keeps paying out till he has augmented it with several plies of filament—a cable. It is now strong enough, but as the tension on it is to be sidewise it is not rigid enough; it would bow inwards as he stretched the web from it, and so it needs a few small guy lines, or stays, to brace it. These stays he fastens farther out on the wood, or to points on the glass itself. He could, in fact, as far as his abilities are concerned, fasten every line of his web to the glass; but the wind would blow it against the pane and interfere with its workings. Therefore he makes the cable to stretch it to, a little distance from the window.

The outline or foundation is now done. Inside this triangular circumference he has now to make the spokes of his wheel before stretching upon them the circular lines. In like manner as he put up the main cable, he runs a single line across this triangular space, about the middle of it. Having this line stretched, he climbs to the middle of it and there stops, for this is to be the center of his wheel. In stretching this diametrical line he has really made two spokes at one operation; but now he must pursue a different method, making one spoke at a time. If he were to try to keep up this way of making two spokes at a time, fastening a line at one side and running around the circumference to the opposite side to fasten it there, his line would become entangled with the one stretched before; it would stick, and he could not raise the new line to the middle of the other where it ought to cross. Therefore he must now work from the middle outwards, stretching one spoke at a time. He fastens the end of the spoke he is about to spin to the middle of this diametrical line, takes this new line in his hind leg in order to hold it free of the other as he climbs it, and thus he gets the spoke to the window frame. Then he proceeds with it along the window frame a short distance, the second line opening out, fanwise, from the first; and when it has opened to the proper angle he fastens it down to the wood. He then descends the new one and repeats the operation; and so he keeps on, always using the one he stretched last to return upon and bring out another, and always holding the new line clear and taut as he pays it out, exactly like a boy flying a kite. It must not touch and tangle. And, like the boy, he runs along at a good gait as if he had no time to lose.

By this simple method, the spokes are all put in; and it is very easy according to his system. It is worth considering, however, that he is always very fortunate in coming out so nearly uniform in the spacing of his spokes—and this is an irregular triangle upon which the spokes must fall at all sorts of distances in order to be equally spaced. He seems to be an expert in division. But it is not the *outside* of his space that he can measure off in an automatic way, for there the distances are not uniform. I think he must accomplish it all by watching the new line open fanwise from the middle, and so I regard him as a sort of surveyor with a good eye for angles. The wheel part is now done, and he has to weave on it the circling strands.

He takes his place at the middle of the wheel, and keeping his head always toward the center, he steps sidewise from spoke to spoke, fastening the thread to a spoke, drawing it across to the next one at the right tension, dabbing it down to fasten it, and so on, round and round. And he works with considerable speed.

But this mode of operation cannot be kept up to the end. When he has worked out a short distance from the center, the radiating spokes are too far apart for him to straddle across. Here he changes the method. Instead of straddling across, he goes out on a single spoke, fastens his thread to it, comes in and crosses to the next spoke by means of the line that he stretched on his last trip around. He then goes out on the next spoke, carrying the line in his hind leg, and fastens it—and he always handles it with his leg, so that there is no surplus spun out, and it has the right tension. Thus he continues till his wheel is big enough, always using his last circle as a bridge from spoke to spoke as he adds the next surrounding circle. This part, when done, is really a spiral.

The garden spider, in making a web that fulfills the ideal, puts in this spiral I have just described with the lines very far apart —very open. He then starts at the circumference and fills it in finer, working round and round toward the middle. This first spiral may be considered his scaffold. As we see, it was constructed under certain drawbacks; but now that he has so much put in coarsely, he can walk round and round with more footing, and work with less trouble.

When the web seems finished, one thing yet remains to be done. Where the spokes have each been fastened to the center, there is a mass of fiber, the tag-ends of the whole job, which would be in his way as he sat in the middle of the web. He takes this out neatly, leaving a hole. Had he taken this out before the spiral was put on, the whole wheel would, of course, have collapsed. He throws the fiber into the street below, and takes his place over the hole with his legs holding the lines around him; and now it is time for Providence to send a fly.

The spider does his work behind his back, as it were; he cannot see what he is doing; and yet in certain of his operations he must make strokes that are instantly accurate and "to the point." This would call for some miraculous knowledge of location—which he has not; and his way of meeting the problem is interesting. In that division of his work which consists in stretching the cable and spokes, his problem is simple; it is merely the fastening of sticky threads to the window frame, a surface which is firm and flat. As it is flat, he does not need to strike a fine particular point on it; and as it is perfectly stable, he simply presses the line down firmly behind him as it comes from his spinneret. But in stretching the spiral from spoke to spoke of the web itself, he must strike a certain point on his line against a particular point on the web, in order to have the right tension; he must unite them firmly at that point and do it at a dab. It is a fine point to find; and to do such work behind him, against a yielding, air-blown filament, is quite a different matter from pressing his line to a flat, firm surface. He proceeds, accordingly, on the same principle, but takes it another way about. Instead of merely dabbing down the line he is spinning, he seizes with a hind leg the line *to which* he wishes to make a fastening and presses that against a particular part of *himself*; that is, he raises the spoke and touches it firmly to the point where the new line is spinning out. Thus the spiral is put in. The whole extraneous difficulty is transmuted into a mere matter of self-knowledge—like finding one's mouth in the dark.

During this part of the work he does not need to use one leg to prevent entanglement, the parallel spans being shorter and more widely separate from the beginning; and it is lucky for him that he can now spare that member, for in the operations of putting in the spiral his multitude of legs are busy indeed. One is seizing the spoke and dabbing it to his spinneret; one is pressing on the new-spun line, as if to regulate the tension; the others are stepping about lively in order to accommodate his body to the advancing work—and altogether it is as rapid and unobservable as the flight of knitting needles. But once it is caught by the eye, the mystery of his accuracy is small, and its ingenuity is great. But the very fact that he has to descend to mere ingenuity, in lieu of instinct, which can perform miracles, presents him to us as a humble spinner, and human. I think it is a person of little promise who can look through his web and not find that this display of window work, spread out between us and the universe, is a sort of trap for the mind, tending to keep it within bounds.

The large spiders, so far as I have observed, are the most careless workmen. In some of their webs the geometrical design could hardly be perceived were it not for the radiating spokes; and these are not straight, but drawn to this side and that by the connecting lines. And these lines, that ought to be the spiral, have been put in any way at all, as if one at a time, here and there; and moreover they have been put in loosely and then tightened to the spoke with other little guy lines, so that they have the shape of a Y. The web seems to be not only patched, but all patchwork from the start. It has the wheel shape in it, however, and the same principles are employed throughout; in fact, there is more individuality and a greater display of mechanical science in such a web than in one that conforms to the ideal. It takes a better mechanic to patch a job than to follow specifications to a successful conclusion. The little spiders do the most perfect work, strikingly geometrical, with the lines of the spiral exactly parallel. I once picked from a bush a withered leaf that had curled up at the end, and in this space, smaller in extent than a quarter of a dollar, was a spider's web perfect in every detail.

Other webs would differ from this window web; but the difference would not be in the web proper so much as in the outrigging or foundation for it. In truth, the most interesting part of a spider's work is not in the geometrical part that excites our first wonder, but in his ways of devising the irregular circumference, the making use of vantage points, the solving of problems peculiar to each set of surroundings. Here is individual work, separate planning to suit each case, the application of principles rather than automatic and uniform procedure—the work of a mechanic.

The opportunities for studying nature in a city apartment are growing every day. The renaissance of Colonial architecture, with the small windowpanes, allows the spiders to cultivate the whole field of glass. A spider soon learns all about glass; a fly never. The spider works with it familiarly; he even uses its surface to moor the stays of his cable; but the fly buzzes and butts his head against it, utterly unable to learn that the invisible can have existence. The invention of glass was a godsend to spiders, and a sorry thing for flies.

There is much more to the trade of building a web, but so technical in detail that it would have to be considered at much length in order to arrive at the ultimate mechanical reasons. A thing superficially perceived or half explained might as well not be explained at all. Much "nature study" consists in these mere semblances of explanations—incomplete perceptions. The most profitable work in this line, I think, would be the work of the skilled mechanic, rather than the poetic "nature student" or the mere microscopic observer; for this shrewd stealing of secrets, by both observation and basic reasoning, has been his lifelong attitude in filching his own trade from others, as well as from nature. And as to the writing of it, the simple and luminous expression of such things calls for the very highest and completest set of mental faculties. Contrary to the popular notion, the creation of so-called "atmospheric" impression in literature is much easier, and of a lower order of intellect, than to convey in familiar words exactly what was done, and why. This also takes imagination.

But, as I have said, it was not my intention in writing this to record all that I learned of the trade so far as I advanced, but rather to make public a tragi-comedy that was enacted in spider life. To recount all that I observed would be robbing the reader of his privilege of discovering things for himself—even denying him the right to look out of his own window—which is one of the things I protest against. I have told this much because it was necessary thus to introduce, in their proper persons, the two characters of the play.

It was drawing on toward evening. The day had been—simply another day; a wilderness of roofs in a soft-coal mist, a turbid patch of sky, and the people below moving monotonously past like cattle in a canyon. The street nearby became darker with the stream of people hurrying home from store and factory; Chicago had let out. The worn-out tree was receiving back the sparrows, and every twig was a perch. I was tired of all this;

there was nothing interesting about it; and so from trying to see something *out* of the window I turned again to look *at* it, for it was time for the spiders to go to work.

The corner nearest me, which had to be renovated of its dusty and damaged web, belonged to a medium-sized spider; and promptly he came forth to the work. Another corner was held—I cannot say occupied—by a set of legs on a very old web. A spider, with all his skill in taking down a web, moves away and leaves his dirt behind him. Not only this, but he has a habit, when he has his new set of legs, of leaving the old ones on the web; and there they remain, occupying the position that he last held. They do not come off him singly, but in a complete set, like a truck that has been removed from a car. And it is wonderful how long a web will withstand the weather and bear this grisly semblance of a spider with each leg set on a line. This particular set of sere and yellowish legs danced in every breeze, and seemed even more active than when they had a spider to operate them. I often wished that some enterprising spider would come along and take it all down; but none ever did. From watching to see whether this would happen, I turned my attention to the medium-sized spider as he cleared his space. Finally, he had his old web all down and disposed of; and the new one was put up with "neatness and dispatch."

When the web was seemingly done, the spider spent a little while on the window frame among his guy lines—possibly making things still more taut. There now appeared suddenly on the top of the frame, at the opposite corner of the web, a big able-bodied spider. He was much larger than the other—let us call them David and Goliath. He stopped short at the edge of the web as if pausing to look across at the owner and make up his mind. The other spider stopped work suddenly, as if looking back at him. I immediately suspected that here was a situation, and so I watched closely; there seemed to be spider thinking going on. The big spider stepped deliberately on the web, and then, with a sudden dash, went out on it. He had no more than reached the middle when he was snapped back to where he came from, and thrown against the upper frame of the window as if he had been shot from a rubber sling—and the web was gone. In that instant, the smaller spider had cut the main cable. David's elastic sling had not only thrown Goliath back where he belonged, but had knocked him against the frame and slapped him in the face for his impudence.

The big spider, we can only conclude, meant harm—either robbery or bodily injury—and the other spider knew it. But this does not explain what we like always to see in nature—an object in everything. What was the beneficent object? It was not a provision on the part of instinct to enable the spider to save its web from the robber, for the web was utterly sacrificed. As to the loss of property, the little spider might just as well have run away and let the big one have it. And as to the little spider saving its life, it might as well have run at once, for a spider can pursue another anywhere, even if there is no web. To me it seemed to be a pure case of "You won't get the best of me." Does Nature, in her wise regard for the needs of all her creatures, make provision for the satisfaction of transcendental justice?

It looked like an original act of thought—the presence of mind of a good mechanic who understands his machine. I have often wondered, on the theory that it might have been a way of saving the smaller spider's life, whether the big spider was injured; and if the smaller spider had simply run away and left his web, would not the other have been satisfied with it, and not bothered to pursue him? Why this provision of instinct—if it was mere instinct?

I am sorry to say that I was not myself in a condition to look into the physical state of Goliath and see whether he was disabled. I was so taken up with the tragi-comic view, the human phase of it, that I did not even think of these other things. In fact I was so delighted over the victory that, weak as I was, and bound down as by cords made of my own tendons, I raised myself up and inwardly exclaimed—*Foiled!*

Spiders are interesting companions—under conditions. And the outcome of all one's observations is finally a question—Is it God that is doing these things, or is it a spider?

Majesty of the Inanimate

THE most important of all distinctions is the distinction between that which is alive and that which never was and never can be. Yet man has never been entirely willing to accept the absolute deadness of the dead world. He must get into some sort of relation with it as well as with the world of living things. In primitive societies mountains and streams are personified so that they become, indistinguishably, either the dwelling places of supernatural beings or those beings themselves. For more sophisticated societies poetry keeps the thought alive as a figure of speech, but even that is not, for long, sufficient; and the earth itself then becomes again, in romantic eras, what Goethe called "the living garment of God." Even those not explicitly mystical are moved in mysterious ways by the majestic manifestations of inanimate nature, which seem necessarily to have some human meaning. To many, indeed, the fellowship of mountains or forests or rivers or seas seems, paradoxically, more intimate and real than the fellowship of other living creatures.

Henry Beston's *Outermost House*, from which the first selection is taken, has quietly become a classic, reprinted year after year. In the selection chosen, the hero is the beach and surf of eastern Long Island.

Mary Austin developed a mystical philosophy peculiarly her own. She believed in the supreme importance of geography and developed the queer doctrine that the dominant influence on American culture was not the imported European tradition but the rhythm of the American landscape itself. That doctrine is not explicit in the chapter here reprinted from *The Land of Little Rain,* but it is perhaps implicit. In any event, there are few other examples in literature where the personality of a region has been so successfully communicated. Vegetation plays a part, but the real subject is the dry earth itself.

As for the final piece in this section, the present compiler's immodesty is no doubt too patent to admit apology. He is simply unwilling to miss what may be his only chance to be included in an anthology of nature writers. The selection is from his book *The Twelve Seasons.*

The Headlong Wave

—HENRY BESTON

This morning I am going to try my hand at something that I do not recall ever having encountered either in a periodical or in a book, namely, a chapter on the ways, the forms, and the sounds of ocean near a beach. Friends are forever asking me about the surf on the great beach and if I am not sometimes troubled or haunted by its sound. To this I reply that I have grown unconscious of the roar, and though it sounds all day long in my waking ears, and all night long in my sleeping ones, my ears seldom send on the long tumult to the mind. I hear the roar the instant I wake in the morning and return to consciousness, I listen to it a while consciously, and then accept and forget it; I hear it during the day only when I stop again to listen, or when some change in the nature of the sound breaks through my acceptance of it to my curiosity.

They say here that great waves reach this coast in threes. Three great waves, then an indeterminate run of lesser rhythms, then three great waves again. On Celtic coasts it is the seventh wave that is seen coming like a king out of the gray, cold sea. The Cape tradition, however, is no half-real, half-mystical fancy, but the truth itself. Great waves do indeed approach this beach by threes. Again and again have I watched three giants roll in one after the other out of the Atlantic, cross the outer bar, break, form again, and follow each other in to fulfillment and destruction on this solitary beach. Coast guard crews are all well aware of this triple rhythm and take advantage of the lull that follows the last wave to launch their boats.

It is true that there are single giants as well. I have been roused by them in the night. Waked by their tremendous and unexpected crash, I have sometimes heard the last of the heavy overspill, sometimes only the loud, withdrawing roar. After the roar came a briefest pause, and after the pause the return of ocean to the night's long cadences. Such solitary titans, flinging their green tons down upon a quiet world, shake beach and dune. Late one September night, as I sat reading, the very father of all waves must have flung himself down before the house, for the quiet of the night was suddenly overturned by a gigantic, tumbling crash and an earthquake rumbling; the beach trembled beneath the avalanche, the dune shook, and my house so shook in its dune that the flame of a lamp quivered and pictures jarred on the wall.

The three great elemental sounds in nature are the sound of rain, the sound of wind in a primeval wood, and the sound of outer ocean on a beach. I have heard them all, and of the three elemental voices, that of ocean is the most awesome, beautiful, and varied. For it is a mistake to talk of the monotone of ocean or of the monotonous nature of its sound. The sea has many voices. Listen to the surf, really lend it your ears, and you will hear in it a world of sounds: hollow boomings and heavy roarings, great watery tumblings and tramplings, long hissing seethes, sharp, rifle-shot reports, splashes, whispers, the grinding undertone of stones, and sometimes vocal sounds that might be the half-heard talk of people in the sea. And not only is the great sound varied in the manner of its making, it is also constantly changing its tempo, its pitch, its accent, and its rhythm, being now loud and thundering, now almost placid, now furious, now grave and solemn-slow, now a simple measure, now a rhythm monstrous with a sense of purpose and elemental will.

Every mood of the wind, every change in the day's weather, every phase of the tide—all these have subtle sea musics all their own. Surf of the ebb, for instance, is one music, surf of the flood another, the change in the two musics being most clearly marked during the first hour of a rising tide. With the renewal of the tidal energy, the sound of the surf grows louder, the fury of battle returns to it as it turns again on the land, and beat and sound change with the renewal of the war.

Sound of surf in these autumnal dunes—the continuousness of it, sound of endless charging, endless incoming and gathering, endless fulfillment and dissolution, endless fecundity, and endless death. I have been trying to study out the mechanics of that mighty resonance. The dominant note is the great spilling crash made by each arriving wave. It may be hollow and booming, it may be heavy and churning, it may be a tumbling roar. The second fundamental sound is the wild seething cataract roar of the wave's dissolution and the rush of its foaming waters up the beach—this second sound *diminuendo*. The third fundamental sound is the endless dissolving hiss of the inmost slides of foam. The first two sounds reach the ear as a unisonance—the booming impact of the tons of water and the wild roar of the up-rush blending—and this mingled sound dissolves into the foam-bubble hissing of the third. Above the tumult, like birds, fly wisps of watery noise, splashes and counter splashes, whispers, seething, slaps, and chucklings. An overtone sound of other breakers, mingled with a general rumbling, fills earth and sea and air.

Here do I pause to warn my reader that although I have recounted the history of a breaker—an ideal breaker—the surf process must be understood as mingled and continuous, waves hurrying after waves, interrupting waves, washing back on waves, overwhelming waves. Moreover, I have described the sound of a high surf in fair weather. A storm surf is mechanically the same thing, but it *grinds*, and this same long, se-pulchral grinding—sound of utter terror to all mariners—is a development of the second fundamental sound; it is the cry of the breaker water roaring its way ashore and dragging at the sand. A strange underbody of sound when heard through the high, wild screaming of a gale.

Breaking waves that have to run up a steep tilt of the beach are often followed by a dragging, grinding sound—the note of the baffled water running downhill again to the sea. It is loudest when the tide is low and breakers are rolling beach stones up and down a slope of the lower beach.

I am, perhaps, most conscious of the sound of surf just after I have gone to bed. Even here I read myself to drowsiness, and, reading, I hear the cadenced trampling roar filling all the dark. So close is the Fo'castle to the ocean's edge that the rhythm of sound I hear oftenest in fair weather is not so much a general tumult as an endless arrival, overspill, and dissolution of separate great seas. Through the dark, mathematic square of the screened half window, I listen to the rushes and the bursts, the tramplings, and the long, intermingled thunderings, never wearying of the sonorous and universal sound.

Away from the beach, the various sounds of the surf melt into one great thundering symphonic roar. Autumnal nights in Eastham village are full of this ocean sound. The "summer people" have gone, the village rests and prepares for winter, lamps shine from kitchen windows; and from across the moors, the great levels of the marsh, and the bulwark of the dunes re-sounds the long wintry roaring of the sea. Listen to it a while, and it will seem but one remote and formidable sound; listen still longer and you will discern in it a symphony of breaker thunderings, an endless, distant, elemental cannonade. There is beauty in it, and ancient terror. I heard it last as I walked through the village on a starry October night; there was no wind, the leafless trees were still, all the village was abed, and the whole somber world was awesome with the sound.

I I

The seas are the heart's blood of the earth. Plucked up and kneaded by the sun and the moon, the tides are systole and diastole of earth's veins.

The rhythm of waves beats in the sea like a pulse in living flesh. It is pure force, forever embodying itself in a succession of watery shapes which vanish on its passing.

I stand on my dune top watching a great wave coursing in from sea, and know that I am watching an illusion, that the distant water has not left its place in ocean to advance upon me, but only a force shaped in water, a bodiless pulse beat, a vibration.

Consider the marvel of what we see. Somewhere in ocean, perhaps a thousand miles and more from this beach, the pulse beat of earth liberates a vibration, an ocean wave. Is the original force circular, I wonder? and do ocean waves ring out from the creative beat as they do on a quiet surface broken by a stone? Are there, perhaps, ocean circles so great and so intricate that they are unperceived? Once created, the wave or the arc of a wave begins its journey through the sea. Countless vibrations precede it, countless vibrations follow after. It approaches the continent, swings into the coast line, courses ashore, breaks, dissolves, is gone. The innermost waters it last inhabited flow back in marbly foam to become a body to another beat, and to be again flung down. So it goes night and day, and will go till the secret heart of earth strikes out its last slow beat and the last wave dissolves upon the last forsaken shore.

As I stand on my dune top, however, I do not think of the illusion and the beat of earth, for I watch the waves with my outer rather than my inner eye. After all, the illusion is set off by an extraordinary, an almost miraculous thing—the embodiment of the wave beat in an almost constant shape. We see a wave a quarter of a mile off, then a few hundred yards nearer in, then just offshore; we seem to have been watching the same traveling mass of water—there has been no appreciable change in mass or in shape—yet all the while the original beat has taken on a flowing series of liquid bodies, bodies so alike, so much the same, that our eye will individualize them and follow them in—the third wave, we say, or the second wave behind the great wave. How strange it is that this beat of earth, this mysterious undulation of the seas, moving through and among the other forces stirring the waters close off the continent, should thus keep its constancy of form and mass, and how odd a blend of illusion and reality it all is! On the whole, the outer eye has the best of it.

Blowing all day long, a northwest wind yesterday swept the sky clear of every tatter and wisp of cloud. Clear it still is, though the wind has shifted to the east. The sky this afternoon is a harmony of universal blue, bordered with a surf rim of snowiest blue-white. Far out at sea, in the northeast and near the horizon, is a pool of the loveliest blue I have ever seen here —a light blue, a petal blue, blue of the emperor's gown in a Chinese fairy tale. If you would see waves at their best, come on such a day, when the ocean reflects a lovely sky, and the wind is light and onshore; plan to arrive in the afternoon so that you will have the sun facing the breakers. Come early, for the glints on the waves are most beautiful and interesting when the light is oblique and high. And come with a rising tide.

The surf is high, and on the far side of it, a wave greater than its fellows is shouldering out of the blue, glinting immensity of sea.

Friends tell me that there are certain tropic beaches where waves miles long break all at once in one cannonading crash; a little of this, I imagine, would be magnificent; a constancy of it, unbearable. The surf here is broken; it approaches the beach in long intercurrent parallels, some a few hundred feet long, some an eighth of a mile long, some, and the longest, attaining the quarter-mile length and perhaps just over. Thus, at all times and instants of the day, along the five miles of beach visible from the Fo'castle deck, waves are to be seen breaking, coursing in to break, seething up and sliding back.

But to return to the blue wave rolling in out of the blue spaciousness of sea. On the other side of the world, just opposite the Cape, lies the ancient Spanish province of Galicia, and the town of Pontevedra and St. James Compostela, renowned of pilgrims. (When I was there they offered me a silver cockle shell, but I would have none of it, and got myself a seashell from some Galician fisherfolk.) Somewhere between this Spanish land and Cape Cod the pulse of earth has engendered this wave and sent it coursing westward through the seas. Far off the coast, the spray of its passing has, perhaps, risen on the windward bow of some rusty freighter and fallen in rainbow drops upon her plates; the great liners have felt it course beneath their keels.

A continent rises in the west, and the pulse beat approaches this bulwark of Cape Cod. Two-thirds of a mile out, the wave is still a sea vibration, a billow. Slice it across, and its outline will be that of a slightly flattened semicircle; the pulse is shaped in a long, advancing mound. I watch it approach the beach. Closer and closer in, it is rising with the rise of the beach and the shoaling of the water; closer still, it is changing from a mound to a pyramid, a pyramid which swiftly distorts, the seaward side lengthening, the landward side incurving—the wave is now a breaker. Along the ridge of blue forms a rippling crest of clear, bright water; a little spray flies off. Under the racing foam churned up by the dissolution of other breakers the beach now catches at the last shape of sea inhabited by the pulse— the wave is *tripped* by the shoaling sand—the giant stumbles, crashes, and is pushed over and ahead by the sloping line of force behind. The fall of a breaker is never the work of gravity alone.

It is the last line of the wave that has captured the decorative imagination of the world—the long seaward slope, the curling crest, the incurved volute ahead.

Toppling over and hurled ahead, the wave crashes, its mass of glinting blue falling down in a confusion of seething, splendid white, the tumbling water rebounding from the sand to a height almost always a little above that of the original crest. Out of the wild, crumbling confusion born of the dissolution of the force and the last great shape, foamy fountains spurt, and ringlets of spray. The mass of water, still all furiously a-churn and seething white, now rushes for the rim of the beach as it might for an inconceivable cataract. Within thirty-five feet the water shoals from two feet to dry land. The edge of the rush thins, and the last impulse disappears in inch-deep slides of foam which reflect the sky in one last moment of energy and beauty and then vanish all at once into the sands.

Another thundering, and the water that has escaped and withdrawn is gathered up and swept forward again by another breaking wave. Night and day, age after age, so works the sea, with infinite variation obeying an unalterable rhythm moving through an intricacy of chance and law.

I can watch a fine surf for hours, taking pleasure in all its wild plays and variations. I like to stand on my beach, watching a long wave start breaking in many places, and see the curling water run north and south from the several beginnings, and collide in furious white pyramids built of the opposing energies. Splendid fountains often delight the eye. A towering and deep-bellied wave, toppling, encloses in its volute a quantity of air, and a few seconds after the spill this prisoned and compressed vapor bursts up through the boiling rush in feathery, foamy jets and geyser plumes. I have seen fountains here, on a September day, twenty and twenty-five and even thirty feet high. Sometimes a curious thing happens. Instead of escaping vertically, the rolled-up air escapes horizontally, and the breaker suddenly blows, as from a dragon's mouth, a great lateral puff of steamy spray. On sunny days, the toppling crest is often mirrored in the glassy volute as the wave is breaking. One lovely autumn afternoon, I saw a beautiful white gull sailing along the volute of a breaker accompanied by his reflection in the wave.

I add one curious effect of the wind. When the wind is directly offshore or well offshore, the waves approach fighting it; when the wind is offshore but so little off that its angle with the coast line is oblique—say an angle never greater than twenty-two degrees and never less than about twelve—the waves that approach the coast do not give battle, but run in with their long axis parallel to the wind. Sitting in the Fo'castle, I can often tell the exact quarter of an offshore wind simply by looking at this oblique alignment of the waves.

The long miles of beach are never more beautiful than when waves are rolling in fighting a strong breeze. Then do the breakers actually seem to charge the coast. As they approach, the wind meets them in a shock of war, the chargers rear but go on, and the wind blows back their manes. North and south, I watch them coursing in, the manes of white, sun-brilliant spray streaming behind them for thirty and even forty feet. Sea horses do men call such waves on every coast of the world. If you would see them at their best, come to this beach on a bright October day when a northwest wind is billowing off to sea across the moors.

The Land of Little Rain

—MARY AUSTIN

E AST away from the Sierras, south from Panamint and
Amargosa, east and south many an uncounted mile, is the Country of Lost Borders.

Ute, Paiute, Mojave, and Shoshone inhabit its frontiers, and
as far into the heart of it as a man dare go. Not the law, but
the land sets the limit. Desert is the name it wears upon the
maps, but the Indian's is the better word. Desert is a loose term
to indicate land that supports no man; whether the land can be
bitted and broken to that purpose is not proven. Void of life it
never is, however dry the air and villainous the soil.

This is the nature of that country. There are hills, rounded,
blunt, burned, squeezed up out of chaos, chrome and vermilion
painted, aspiring to the snow-line. Between the hills lie high
level-looking plains full of intolerable sun glare, or narrow valleys drowned in a blue haze. The hill surface is streaked with
ash drift and black, unweathered lava flows. After rains water
accumulates in the hollows of small closed valleys, and, evaporat-
ing, leaves hard dry levels of pure desertness that get the local
name of dry lakes. Where the mountains are steep and the
rains heavy, the pool is never quite dry, but dark and bitter,

rimmed about with the efflorescence of alkaline deposits. A thin crust of it lies along the marsh over the vegetating area, which has neither beauty nor freshness. In the broad wastes open to the wind the sand drifts in hummocks about the stubby shrubs, and between them the soil shows saline traces. The sculpture of the hills here is more wind than water work, though the quick storms do sometimes scar them past many a year's redeeming. In all the Western desert edges there are essays in miniature at the famed, terrible Grand Canyon, to which, if you keep on long enough in this country, you will come at last.

Since this is a hill country one expects to find springs, but not to depend upon them; for when found they are often brackish and unwholesome, or maddening, slow dribbles in a thirsty soil. Here you find the hot sink of Death Valley, or high rolling districts where the air has always a tang of frost. Here are the long heavy winds and breathless calms on the tilted mesas where dust devils dance, whirling up into a wide, pale sky. Here you have no rain when all the earth cries for it, or quick downpours called cloudbursts for violence. A land of lost rivers, with little in it to love; yet a land that once visited must be come back to inevitably. If it were not so there would be little told of it.

This is the country of three seasons. From June on to November it lies hot, still, and unbearable, sick with violent unrelieving storms; then on until April, chill, quiescent, drinking its scant rain and scanter snows; from April to the hot season again, blossoming, radiant, and seductive. These months are only approximate; later or earlier the rain-laden wind may drift up the water gate of the Colorado from the Gulf, and the land sets its seasons by the rain.

The desert floras shame us with their cheerful adaptations to the seasonal limitations. Their whole duty is to flower and fruit, and they do it hardly, or with tropical luxuriance, as the rain admits. It is recorded in the report of the Death Valley expedition that after a year of abundant rains, on the Colorado desert was found a specimen of Amaranthus ten feet high. A

year later the same species in the same place matured in the
drought at four inches. One hopes the land may breed like qualities in her human offspring, not tritely to "try," but to do. Seldom does the desert herb attain the full stature of the type. Extreme aridity and extreme altitude have the same dwarfing effect, so that we find in the high Sierras and in Death Valley related species in miniature that reach a comely growth in mean
temperatures. Very fertile are the desert plants in expedients to
prevent evaporation, turning their foliage edgewise toward the
sun, growing silky hairs, exuding viscid gum. The wind, which
has a long sweep, harries and helps them. It rolls up dunes
about the stocky stems, encompassing and protective, and above
the dunes, which may be, as with the mesquite, three times as
high as a man, the blossoming twigs flourish and bear fruit.

There are many areas in the desert where drinkable water
lies within a few feet of the surface, indicated by the mesquite
and the bunch grass (*Sporobolus airoides*). It is this nearness
of unimagined help that makes the tragedy of desert deaths.
It is related that the final breakdown of that hapless party that
gave Death Valley its forbidding name occurred in a locality
where shallow wells would have saved them. But how were they
to know that? Properly equipped it is possible to go safely across
that ghastly sink, yet every year it takes its toll of death, and
yet men find there sun-dried mummies, of whom no trace or
recollection is preserved. To underestimate one's thirst, to pass
a given landmark to the right or left, to find a dry spring where
one looked for running water—there is no help for any of these
things.

Along springs and sunken watercourses one is surprised to find
such water-loving plants as grow widely in moist ground; but the
true desert breeds its own kind, each in its particular habitat.
The angle of the slope, the frontage of a hill, the structure of
the soil determines the plant. South-looking hills are nearly
bare, and the lower tree line higher here by a thousand feet.
Canyons running east and west will have one wall naked and

one clothed. Around dry lakes and marshes the herbage preserves a set and orderly arrangement. Most species have well-defined areas of growth, the best index the voiceless land can give the traveler of his whereabouts.

If you have any doubt about it, know that the desert begins with the creosote. This immortal shrub spreads down into Death Valley and up to the lower timber line, odorous and medicinal, as you might guess from the name, wandlike, with shining fretted foliage. It vivid green is grateful to the eye in a wilderness of gray and greenish white shrubs. In the spring it exudes a resinous gum which the Indians of those parts know how to use with pulverized rock for cementing arrow points to shafts. Trust Indians not to miss any virtues of the plant world!

Nothing the desert produces expresses it better than the unhappy growth of the tree yucca. Tormented, thin forests of it stalk drearily in the high mesas, particularly in that triangular slip that fans out eastward from the meeting of the Sierras and coastwise hills where the first swings across the southern end of the San Joaquin Valley. The yucca bristles with bayonet-pointed leaves, dull green, growing shaggy with age, tipped with panicles of fetid, greenish bloom. After death, which is slow, the ghostly hollow network of its woody skeleton, with hardly power to rot, makes the moonlight fearful. Before the yucca has come to flower, while yet its bloom is a creamy cone-shaped bud of the size of a small cabbage, full of sugary sap, the Indians twist it deftly out of its fence of daggers and roast it for their own delectation. So it is that in those parts where man inhabits one sees young plants of *Yucca arborensis* infrequently. Other yuccas, cacti, low herbs, a thousand sorts, one finds journeying east from the coastwise hills. There is neither poverty of soil nor species to account for the sparseness of desert growth, but simply that each plant requires more room. So much earth must be pre-empted to extract so much moisture. The real struggle for existence, the real brain of the plant, is underground; above there is room for a rounded perfect growth. In Death Valley, reputed the very core of desolation, are nearly two hundred identified species.

Above the lower tree line, which is also the snow line, mapped out abruptly by the sun, one finds spreading growth of piñon, juniper, branched nearly to the ground, lilac and sage, and scattering white pines.

There is no special preponderance of self-fertilized or wind-fertilized plants, but everywhere the demand for and evidence of insect life. Now where there are seeds and insects there will be birds and small mammals, and where these are will come the slinking, sharp-toothed kind that prey on them. Go as far as you dare in the heart of a lonely land, you cannot go so far that life and death are not before you. Painted lizards slip in and out of rock crevices, and pant on the white hot sands. Birds, humming-birds even, nest in the cactus scrub; woodpeckers befriend the demoniac yuccas; out of the stark, treeless waste rings the music of the night-singing mockingbird. If it be summer and the sun well down, there will be a burrowing owl to call. Strange, furry, tricksy things dart across the open places, or sit motionless in the conning towers of the creosote. The poet may have "named all the birds without a gun," but not the fairy-footed, ground-inhabiting, furtive, small folk of the rainless regions. They are too many and too swift; how many you would not be-lieve without seeing the footprint tracings in the sand. They are nearly all night workers, finding the days too hot and white. In mid-desert where there are no cattle, there are no birds of carrion, but if you go far in that direction the chances are that you will find yourself shadowed by their tilted wings. Nothing so large as a man can move unspied upon in that country, and they know well how the land deals with strangers. There are hints to be had here of the way in which a land forces new habits on its dwellers. The quick increase of sun at the end of spring sometimes overtakes birds in their nesting and effects a reversal of the ordinary manner of incubation. It becomes nec-essary to keep eggs cool rather than warm. One hot, stifling spring in the Little Antelope I had occasion to pass and repass frequently the nest of a pair of meadowlarks, located unhappily in the shelter of a very slender weed. I never caught them sitting except near night, but at midday they stood, or drooped above it, half fainting with pitifully parted bills, between their treasure and the sun. Sometimes both of them together with wings spread and half lifted continued a spot of shade in a temperature that constrained me at last in a fellow feeling to spare them a bit of canvas for permanent shelter. There was a fence in that country shutting in a cattle range, and along its fifteen miles of posts one could be sure of finding a bird or two in every strip of shadow; sometimes the sparrow and the hawk, with wings trailed and beaks parted, drooping in the white trace of noon.

If one is inclined to wonder at first how so many dwellers came to be in the loneliest land that ever came out of God's hands, what they do there and why stay, one does not wonder so much after having lived there. None other than this long brown land lays such a hold on the affections. The rainbow hills, the tender bluish mists, the luminous radiance of the spring, have the lotus charm. They trick the sense of time, so that once inhabiting there you always mean to go away without quite realizing that you have not done it. Men who have lived there, miners and cattle-men, will tell you this, not so fluently, but emphatically, cursing the land and going back to it. For one thing there is the divinest, cleanest air to be breathed anywhere in God's world. Some day the world will understand that, and the little oases on the windy tops of hills will harbor for healing its ailing, house-weary broods. There is promise there of great wealth in ores and earths, which is no wealth by reason of being so far removed from water and workable conditions; but men are bewitched by it and tempted to try the impossible.

You should hear Salty Williams tell how he used to drive eighteen- and twenty-mule teams from the borax marsh to Mojave, ninety miles, with the trail wagon full of water barrels.

Hot days the mules would go so mad for drink that the clank of the water bucket set them into an uproar of hideous, maimed noises, and a tangle of harness chains, while Salty would sit on the high seat with the sun glare heavy in his eyes, dealing out curses of pacification in a level, uninterested voice until the clamor fell off from sheer exhaustion. There was a line of shallow graves along that road; they used to count on dropping a man or two of every new gang of coolies brought out in the hot season. But when he lost his swamper, smitten without warning at the noon halt, Salty quit his job; he said it was "too durn hot." The swamper he buried by the way with stones upon him to keep the coyotes from digging him up, and seven years later I read the penciled lines on the pine headboard, still bright and unweathered.

But before that, driving up on the Mojave stage, I met Salty again crossing Indian Wells, his face from the high seat, tanned and ruddy as a harvest moon, looming through the golden dust above his eighteen mules. The land had called him.

The palpable sense of mystery in the desert air breeds fables, chiefly of lost treasure. Somewhere within its stark borders, if one believes report, is a hill strewn with nuggets; one seemed with virgin silver; an old clayey water bed where Indians scooped up earth to make cooking pots and shaped them reeking with grains of pure gold. Old miners drifting about the desert edges, weathered into the semblance of the tawny hills, will tell you tales like these convincingly. After a little sojourn in that land you will believe them on their own account. It is a question whether it is not better to be bitten by the little horned snake of the desert that goes sidewise and strikes without coiling, than by the tradition of a lost mine.

And yet—and yet—is it not perhaps to satisfy expectation that one falls into the tragic key in writing of desertness? The more you wish of it the more you get, and in the meantime lose much of pleasantness. In that country which begins at the foot of the east slope of the Sierras and spreads out by less and less lofty hill ranges toward the Great Basin, it is possible to live with great zest, to have red blood and delicate joys, to pass and repass about one's daily performance an area that would make an Atlantic seaboard State, and that with no peril, and according to our way of thought, no particular difficulty. At any rate, it was not people who went into the desert merely to write it up who invented the fabled Hassayampa, of whose waters, if any drink, they can no more see fact as naked fact, but all radiant with the color of romance. I, who must have drunk of it in my twice seven years' wanderings, am assured that it is worth while.

For all the toll the desert takes of a man it gives compensations, deep breaths, deep sleep, and the communion of the stars. It comes upon one with new force in the pauses of the night that the Chaldeans were a desert-bred people. It is hard to escape the sense of mastery as the stars move in the wide clear heavens to risings and settings unobscured. They look large and near and palpitant; as if they moved on some stately service not needful to declare. Wheeling to their stations in the sky, they make the poor world-fret of no account. Of no account you who lie out there watching, nor the lean coyote that stands off in the scrub from you and howls and howls.

The Twelve Seasons

—JOSEPH WOOD KRUTCH

Even in New England, August creates what I assume to be a pretty good imitation of the jungle I have never seen; January certainly suggests the most wide-open and most arid regions of our own West, through which I have often wandered in automobile, on horseback, and afoot. Walking through snow a few inches deep is a good deal like walking through sand, and driving a car through a drift is even more like driving off the roads in New Mexico and Arizona. The same tricks will serve to negotiate what looks unnegotiable and they bring the same sense of triumph. The contrast between piercing cold and blazing heat is not sufficient to dispel the effect of similarity both in respect to mere physical form and, more importantly, in respect to a certain spiritual quality. Emptiness, loneliness, the sense that man is a mere accidental intruder, are as characteristic of the one as of the other.

The biologist might sum it up with inhuman detachment by saying that neither is an environment very favorable to life. But we are not, thank God, necessarily limited to analyses so detached that either winter or the desert need have no emotional significance, and "an environment not very favorable to life" may be translated into a sense of awe not untinged by fear. For that reason a desert or a winter landscape can be for us "sublime." Temporarily in the one, permanently in the other, the forces of death—or more properly the forces of the non-living—have got the upper hand; and those of us, be we plants or animals or human beings, who have managed to survive have managed only by taking the most elaborate precautions. In winter we wrap ourselves up and lie low; in the desert, where no waiting will ever be long enough to witness any change, the permanent dwellers have adopted strange devices and deformed themselves in strange ways so that they and their kind may hang on a little longer, may continue to live in regions which would need to be only a little hotter or a little drier to defeat the last of life's ingenuities.

There are some to whom winter and desert alike are nothing except distasteful hardship. For them the one cannot be over, nor the other got out of, soon enough. And perhaps to feel either as awesome or sublime one must have some power of entering into that aspect of Nature, that intention one might almost say, of which desert and winter are the freest embodiments. To be part of summer one must feel a part of life, but to be part of winter one must feel a part of something older than life itself. Here is beauty which is more literally, or at least more indubitably, its own excuse for being than is even the beauty of a flower. Perhaps the last is really only a flower's way of attracting an insect. Perhaps the song of the bird is intended for the ears of another bird, if not for ours. In one way or another, life is calling out to life, and beauty's excuse for being is the other living thing which will be in some way aware of it. But the snowflake cannot be *intended* for anything. It serves no purpose, it is not observed—not even by another crystal of ice. It is proof that inanimate Nature, by the very physical laws of her being, creates comeliness and symmetry.

Thus winter serves to remind us that the world would be beautiful even though there were no consciousness, no awareness, which could ever acknowledge that it was. And if it be objected that to say this is only to play with words—since "the beautiful" is something that exists only in the human mind— then I can only answer that it all merely comes down to the same thing as the ancient question whether the fall of a tree would make a sound when there was no one there to hear it. Beauty would exist without an eye to see it in precisely the same degree and precisely the same way that sound would exist even though there were no ear it could fall upon.

Traditionally—and properly—winter is for human beings the season of festivities. In the very middle of it are "the holidays," when we become gay by acting as though we were, and when there is something defiantly human about the deliberate, conscious triviality of the Christmas tree which substitutes for beauty the most childish kind of prettiness, as if we were determined to show what we can do in the way of frivolous decoration at the very time when Nature renounces everything of the sort. On these festive occasions we make sorties into the out-of-doors but they are sorties only from which we return from the world we did not make to the world of artificial light and artificial heat which we have made for ourselves. No time is "cozier," but coziness means the sense of successful withdrawal from the great world into a little one of our own.

Summer knows no such contrasts. We open wide the windows and the doors to let the outside in. In the country, at least, we abolish as far as possible the distinction between the two. The lawn is a drawing-room, the woods a conservatory. There is no change of mood as we move from the indoors to the out. Nature and we are in the same frame of mind, we speak the same language. But in January there is much more than the mere physical chill to which we must adjust ourselves when we leave the fireside. It is almost literally like being transplanted to the moon where we must learn to appreciate a new kind of landscape.

Joseph Wood Krutch

All about us now is beauty in its most inhuman form, or at least its most completely nonhuman. History is not ancient enough to tell us when mankind first discovered that smiling fields make glad the heart, but it is within the period of the more recent recorded time that Western civilization began generally to recognize as beautiful the more awesome aspects of Nature; and ice or snow must have waited even longer than mountains to be celebrated in prose or verse. In winter it is the sublime which takes over, and the sublime is something which requires for its appreciation more detachment than the very young or the very simple find it easy to achieve.

There is nothing else in Nature which seems so pure as a winter landscape and there is a curiously complex set of ideas connected with that adjective when it is so applied. A snowscape is white of course, and of course white is the universal symbol of "purity." But its beauty is also a matter of "pure" form, without color and without accent. Most important of all, perhaps, it is "pure" after a fashion peculiar to that which is not alive, since all life is "impure" both in the sense of being mixed and in the sense of being warm in various ways, including the sexual. Passions imply movement and movement implies change, the breaking of the line, the shifting of the form. Only what is not alive can be in so many different fashions "pure."

Surely, too, it is curious that what is actually one of the most transient things in Nature, the one that vanishes like a dream and leaves nothing behind, should also be the one which most strongly suggests permanence. For when the earth is covered with snow it looks as though it had come to rest at last; as though these stretches and these hillocks were as enduring as granite. It is almost as though Nature were exhibiting to us for a few brief weeks what eternity will be like.

I am, I think, rather less a transcendentalist than even the average man is. No voice has ever spoken to me in unmistakable, unambiguous terms. I have never simply "felt" that anything was and must be absolutely true. Neither have I ever believed in the authenticity of the communications which others are convinced that they have received from some source beyond humanity and beyond Nature. A stubborn rationality has always had for me the last word. There are, I say, far too many instances when the mechanism is obvious for me not to suspect that some all-too-human mental quirk is responsible for what I tend to regard as only less gross examples of self-deception. Awake or asleep, I insist, you dreamed. It was you who spoke to yourself, not something outside which addressed itself to you.

I must confess, however, that silence, and solitude, and snow, provide the conditions under which I come closest to feeling myself open to transcendental communication. I am not, mind you, speaking now of nothing more than the sense of intimacy with living things, the sense of being in the same fellowship with them. That is, to me, no more transcendental than friendship or human sympathy. It is merely an extension of that solidarity with one's own kind which very few indeed have never felt at least in connection with some members of their family or of their immediate circle of associates. It is based upon an identity of fundamental interests with what is essentially like one's self and it is either purely rational or but little beyond rationality. What I do mean is the half conviction that one has been spoken to by, or that one has to some extent penetrated into the meaning of, something which is neither the self nor anything like the self. And there is no time when one seems so surrounded by or so immersed in that which is not even remotely like the self as when one is out alone in a night of snow.

He who would feel the earth spin and the planets circle must get away from human beings and all other living things; even from whatever suggests them. Just as in human company one can hardly be properly aware of the other manifestations of animate Nature, so in the presence of animate Nature herself one cannot properly be aware of what is older and perhaps more enduring than animate Nature; with what was before her and will perhaps continue to be, time without end, after the last restless protozoan is dead and the last lichen shriveled on the surviving rock. It should not be on a night of storm, for that is something which must be struggled against and resistance to anything is fatal. But if it be a night of quiet and moonlight and snow, the physical place need not be remote. All the worlds except the white, dead, gleaming one can disappear twenty-five feet from a warm, cozy house.

I remember very vividly one such evening. It was the unghostly hour of eight P.M. and I had gone down the path shoveled across my lawn toward the garage, only a few dozen yards away. Suddenly I was alone with the universe. The realest things besides myself in all existence were not either human beings nor any other living things. I seemed about to grasp what the earth, the suns, and the stars meant to themselves as distinguished from what they mean to any of us creatures—from the simplest to the most complex—who live and grow and then die; who seem to have to purchase our kind of awareness at the price of the agreement that it shall be brief.

Then, at that very moment, came the far-away hoot—bark, it had better be called—of one of the great owls. There are few lonesomer sounds made by any living thing, but no living thing can be lonesome as the stars and the snow are lonesome. I remembered once having heard that the owl hoots in order to frighten the cowering mice into betraying by a start their secret whereabouts. What I saw now in my mind's eye was the sudden pounce of the great bird, the shrill scream of the mouse, and then—after aggressor and victim had disappeared together—the tiny spot of blood staining the inhuman purity of the snow. In an instant I was back among my own kind. The communication from space was never received. Sometimes I wonder whether God, the only time He ever began to speak to me, was interrupted by one of His own owls.

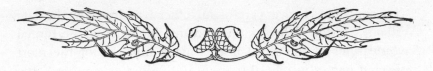

Mystery of Creation

ALL writing—or at least all literature—about living things is, of course, also about the mystery of creation. But for his last section I have reserved four very different authors who are, nevertheless, alike in that each has written something in which the real subject, clearly perceived behind the special subject, is that over-all mystery.

The first of the selections is from *Adventures with a Texas Naturalist,* in which Roy Bedichek considers the general question of man's feeling for the animals with whom he comes in contact during the ordinary course of his life.

William Beebe, from whose volume *Jungle Peace* the selection called "A Yard of Jungle" has been taken, scarcely needs introduction. To one world he is known as a distinguished technical scientist; to another as the author of popular works which draw upon his knowledge and observation for the purpose of communicating to the reader something of his sense of the wonder of life.

The next selection is from Donald Culross Peattie, perhaps the most widely read of all contemporary American nature writers. He first attracted widespread attention with *An Almanac for Moderns,* from which the passages which follow were selected. Each was originally assigned a day in the year and each constitutes a sort of lesson for that day—a meditation on one or another of the numberless mysteries.

To conclude, I give part of an official address by the late William Morton Wheeler, an academic biologist whose formal investigations of the social insects made him one of the most respected names in official science. But Wheeler combined the scientific impeccability required by his profession with a comprehensive imagination and a playful humor. In the general introduction to this collection a few sentences from another public address were quoted as summing up, perfectly and completely, the basic attitude of the student who goes to Nature fully aware of what it means to say that to study her is to study a great whole of which we are only a part. The portion of another speech reprinted here to close the whole anthology reveals the same mind approaching the subject from a different angle.

His innocent-sounding title, "On the Organization of Biological Research" suggests only a dry and formal problem. Quietly, however, it proceeds from some doubts about the desirability of "organizing" too thoroughly the work of university laboratories, to a consideration on the biological level of the meaning of freedom and of "organization." Without raising his voice above the level appropriate to the drone of a learned society's formal meeting he offers as fundamental a defense as it is possible to imagine of the individual's right and duty to follow his own bent. The address might have been called "On the indispensable Function of the Maverick in Nature."

Adventures with a Texas Naturalist

—ROY BEDICHEK

Farm machinery is pushing farm animals out of the picture. Restrictive codes in urban communities are breaking age-old animal ties. Since we have become largely a nation of apartment dwellers and housing has become scarcer and scarcer, the landlord can enforce more stringently his edict, "no children, no pets." This deprivation has come on so gradually that we fail to realize the deeper tragedy of it. Not only are we brought into unhealthy propinquity with our own species, but at the same time we are divorced from other species with which we have enjoyed intimacy for ages.

When I was a boy living on a small acreage near a rural village, the safety bicycle was just appearing, but there were no smooth roads, much less anything that resembled a pavement. I was brought, therefore, into daily contact with a sentient being as a means of transportation. It had moods, just as I had. It responded to caresses, and to scoldings or ill-treatment. This animal knew my voice and reflected its intonations by quick changes in behavior. In short, my pony was my pal. At the same time I associated on terms of a flea-exchanging familiarity with anywhere from one to half-a-dozen dogs. I got my milk from a cow the hard way—not out of a bottle.

Well do I remember the sense of companionship with which in the deeper darkness just before dawn, a Texas norther howling about the barn, I settled down in a comfortable stall, my forehead pressed firmly into the flank of the great beast, to do the milking, talking soothingly to her as every good milkman does.

While in this intimate contact with the cow, I heard around me the soft, guttural complaints of the hogs; also the protesting sniffs of the tied-off calf. Presently the rooster quit crowing, and began gently clucking to the sluggish hens, which communication I faithfully translated as, "Come on, come on, come on now—time to get up—cluck, cluck, cluck"; and of course my translation was shortly verified, for the hens did follow their lord and master off the roost.

This cluster of animals, or biotic colony, as the biologist calls it, was then and still is a big part of the rural child's life on the small, unmechanized farm. There are fewer rural children, however, every year, and fewer animals for them to associate with.

Another thing that the rural child experiences every day of his life is maternal love as exhibited in domestic animals—that is, the care, solicitude, tenderness, and the infinite pains as well as the evident satisfactions, of sow with brood, bitch with litter, hen with chicks, ewe with lamb, goat with kid, mare with foal, and cow with calf. The concept of maternity, thus daily enriched, sinks in and becomes a part of the developing child and affects his thoughts and emotions deeply and for all time. Bergson comments with a striking figure of speech on the significance of maternal love. He conceives of all life as motion which possesses the consciousness most convincingly as the operation of maternal love is observed in nature. "It shows each generation," he says, "leaning over the generation that shall follow. It allows us a glimpse of the fact that the living being is above all a thoroughfare, and that the essence of life is in the movement by which life is transmitted."

Our contacts with the animal world in pioneer periods were even more intimate and more extensive since many wild animals were included. It was not the sympathy of the animal for man, but certainly man's belief in that sympathy, which was largely responsible for domestication. How many ages and how firm a faith it took for the human being to coax into life a genuine inter-species affection between himself and the jackal, one of the most disgusting of beasts, we shall never know. But faith and infinite patience finally accomplished the miracle. The transformed beast now licks man's hand or face, while man on his part accepts these lingual caresses with evident satisfaction.

The caves of prehistoric man are decorated with drawings, ninety per cent of which are animal representations. The human community of towns and cities and the isolated family group as well, rich or poor, have always associated with them a cluster of animals: the sacred geese of Rome, doves of Venice, sparrows of London, vultures of Calcutta; parrots and magpies in the mansions of the nobility; cats, dogs, and other commensals in the hovels of the poor. These, and their like, affection alone detains, to say nothing of that vast horde of parasites, dependents, sneak thieves, and so on, which have, time out of mind, invaded or hovered about in the vicinity of human habitations. Refuse heaps of Romano-British London "have yielded bones of oxen, pigs, sheep, horses, goats, and dogs among the domestic; red and roe deer, hares, and birds among the wild animals." The bones of the raven, a favored scavenger, are second in quantity only to those of domestic fowl in kitchen middens of ancient Silchester. An excavation of a stone wall in Crete (1500 B. C.)

shows a mass of sculptured leaves in the center of which a cat is crouched to pounce upon a bird which is joyfully unaware of the danger.

Our kinship with animate nature is so deep and our sympathetic ties are so strong and of such long standing that a sudden break with them is more serious than is generally supposed. Indeed, it requires some such historical conception of the relationship to account for the irrational fondness for lower animals and for our determination, whether or no, to have them constantly around us. I wonder why even the most scientifically trained and unsentimental of parents permit Junior to sacrifice the peace and cleanliness of the whole apartment in order to gratify a passion for pups! Is it not astonishing that we, a scientific generation, ignore studies proving the dangers of psittacosis, and still keep parrots; and not only keep, but kiss them! Despite the warnings by competent epidemiologists against the dangers of pneumonitis and other dreadful consequences, pigeon lofts abound in residential sections of all our cities. We hold the gratifications of contact with animals above considerations of health and convenience. This is not irrational; quite the contrary. We have come to our present state as a part of nature, and we have an instinctive fear of the isolation which now threatens. Emotional ties of long standing bind us to the animal world, and we would rather risk germ diseases and other physical ills and inconveniences, in maintaining animal associations, than the nervous disorders of isolationism. The cat which carries dangerous germs may bring much-needed psychological repose to the household; and if she has kittens, all the better.

Natural history subjects have a fascination for old and young, wise and foolish. Theodore Roosevelt and Viscount Grey, during their only personal contact, spent the daylight hours of the twenty allotted to them near the little village of Tichborne in Hampshire, and in New Forest, listening to the songs of birds and discussing them with the enthusiasm of a couple of schoolboys.

A large percentage of Mother Goose rhymes and other kindergarten verses have to do with the antics of imaginary animals or with the behavior, appearance, or characteristics of real ones. Aesop's Fables after 2,500 years are still read with relish and quoted almost as frequently as the Bible. A spontaneous cheer bursts from the youngsters in the theater as the animal cartoon is announced.

The swift advance of technology redistributing our population into huge clots, called cities, and the rapid mechanization of the farm have broken the rhythm of life. We have been dissociated too suddenly from the placidity of rural or village life. We have been expelled from an environment in which we were part and parcel of the other life about us.

> Though inland far we be
> Our souls have sight of that immortal sea
> Which brought us hither.

That startling novelist, Aldous Huxley, follows out this break with nature in his extravaganza, *This Brave New World*, caricaturing the specialization and regimentation toward which we are tending under the monitorship of "pure intellect."

The attraction of beast for beast within a given species is still another matter, and one which more readily commands human understanding and sympathy. Being gregarious ourselves, we actually experience the same gravitational tug that holds the individual within the flock, herd, or other group of his kind.

Shortly after taking up my residence here, the owner of the pasture gave temporary refuge to a cow pony belonging to a friend of his. There were no other horses about at that time. Spike was restless. I ran across him first in one corner of the pasture and then in another, always on the move. After a rain his tracks were everywhere. They showed that he had crossed and recrossed Bear Creek dozens of times, night and day. He became noticeably leaner, although grass was plentiful.

But within two weeks he changed his habits, settled down, and began acting as a normal pony should. I missed him for a day or two, and after some looking about, I found him grazing contentedly in a glade bordering a division fence which separates this place from a pasture just to the south of it. I concluded that the buffalo grass in that part of the pasture was maybe a little more flavorsome, and thought nothing more of it.

One morning, however, I heard a sharp whinnying and went to investigate. With breast leaning hard against the barbed-wire fence, Spike was launching his calls with great vigor. Presently, from far down in the woods of the other pasture, I heard an answer. Soon two disreputable-looking ponies, both geldings, came in sight. Then over the fence was much nosing, and playful nibblings, neighings, ecstatic little squeals, greetings, and felicitations.

Thus by spying upon him, I discovered his secret. His long search had been for company, just the company of his kind, and nothing else. His gregariousness was completely satisfied with the knowledge that by uttering a call he could soon have two of his own species feeding just across the fence from him. It would be as unscientific to say that Spike was lonesome as it would be to refer to my own desire for company as a frustrated gregariousness, but the two terms are interchangeable. They mean exactly the same thing and either one may be applied with equal relevance to this particular variety of hungry-heartedness, whether it occurs in me or in Spike.

So it was with a snowy egret which spent the night in a tree among the white leghorn chickens of a coastal farm not so long ago. It was just after sundown when the farmer happened to notice a white bird sailing far above in the clear sky. He came lower in downward spirals until he was circling the tree in which the white leghorns were just going to roost. Alighting on one of the topmost branches he carefully folded his wings, adjusted his plumes, and stretched out his long neck, peering down suspiciously at the company he had chosen for the night. He shifted his position several times, but finally settled down on his stilts, heronwise, neck folded in sleeping posture.

"Next morning," said the big Norwegian farmer to me, apparently delighted to find someone interested in the occurrence, "the chickens flew down to the ground and the white bird flew up again into the sky."

This incident has stayed in my memory for months. I sometimes resort to it in bed when I can't go to sleep. The vision of that bird, the beauty of whose plumes fifty years ago spread a fierce rivalry among all the best-dressed women of the world—the picture of this, the most delicate and lovely of all the egrets, sailing down out of the blue sky to spend the night in a tree with dung-scratching fowls of the farmyard, and, come dawn, taking off again—really, the details of this evidence of a yearning for his kind are so quieting, the folding of the egret's wings is so suggestive, and the whole idyl is so clothed in sedative colors, white and blue, that I usually lose consciousness just as the bird disappears into the depths of the clear morning sky. I recommend it to others troubled with insomnia.

The bird was lonesome.

What means this roaming with a hungry heart? Spike searching ceaselessly until he calls up two disreputable ponies to provide himself across a barbed-wire barrier with a sense of companionship; an egret descending to consort for the night with earthbound creatures because they happened to remind him of his own kind—mere white spots in a tree, they must first have appeared, but suggestive of the rookery for which he was longing, as he saw from his great altitude the fast-approaching shadows of the night.

What does it mean? Simply that Spike and the egret were both lonesome.

Many observers record touching instances of sacrifices made or offered by one animal for another. The squeal of a pig caught in a crack will bring to the rescue every member of the herd within hearing. Waterfowl often linger near a wounded member of the flock at their own peril. It was this instinct, also, which was largely responsible for the extermination by man in the last century of the Carolina parakeet, the only species of the genus *Conurus* which ever extended its range far into the United States. "This fatal habit of hovering over their fallen companions," says Bent, "has helped, more than any one thing, to bring about their extermination. Their social disposition has been their undoing." He then quotes C. J. Maynard: "This is not a mere liking for company, as they are actually fond of one another, for if one out of the flock be wounded, the survivors, attracted by its screams, will return to hover over it and even if constantly shot at, will not leave it as long as their distressed friend calls for assistance."

This is the power which gives the decoy its effectiveness. Here is a deadly device literally baited with love. When, deep in some woodland by a quiet stretch of water, alert and expectant, hoping to surprise some wild thing in its secret maneuvers, I come suddenly upon a bunch of decoy ducks bobbing and leering like manikins, I am filled with resentment. There is something especially hateful to me about these painted dummies, representing, as they do, a malignant cunning whereby man ranges against another species its own altruistic impulses and puts devotion itself to perfidious use. A trap set with food catches the unwary animal in his effort to satisfy an egoistic appetite; so also with the wolf trap baited with the rutting odor of the female, although the method often used to secure this lure is too ghastly to describe in print; but the decoy derives its attraction from the gregarious instinct, parent of those moral motives which induce in man a regard for the interests of others— "spark of the divine," and placed by general consent on a pedestal above every other human virtue.

In cases of mutual advantage, or of even one-way benefits, association and amicability between or among entirely different species are easily explained. Along Bear Creek this spring I have found small sandpipers in association with killdeer. They fly when the killdeer flies and settle down with him, because the killdeer act as sentinels for the smaller birds who keep their bills plunged down into mud and water up to their eyes, so busy feeding in this posture that they have no time to look around for possible enemies, and trust to their associate with his high-pitched voice to give any necessary alarm. There are many instances of one animal's standing guard—unintentionally, of course—for another species. There are two vegetarian ducks of different species in constant association in our southern waters, one an underwater feeder and another a surface feeder, because the underwater feeder grabbles aquatic plants, pieces of which float to the surface to be snapped up in the greedy bills of the species that doesn't like to dive for his dinner.

Down in the pasture I see at this moment cowbirds at the nose of a grazing cow, feeding along on insects which the beast is flushing from their hide-outs in the grass. I once found myself in association with hundreds of swallows on this same unilateral basis. The birds swarmed about me, darting uncomfortably close to my head in their ambition to be on really intimate terms with an animal of another species. When I stopped, they stopped; when I moved on, they played along with me. I was flattered by this attention, but a prosaic explanation of it arose when I noticed that my feet moving in the high grass started thousands of small and, to my eyes, almost invisible insects flying over the bluff. Since the swallow is not equipped to go after his insects in the grass, he welcomes assistance from any lumbering, big-footed land animal that happens to come along, man included.

Outside my window at the present moment, a solitary mockingbird sits on the topmost branch of a huge live oak and charges furiously down at any intruder, bird or other animal, that dares approach this particular tree. The browsing goat shuns his wrath, robins dodge, jays fly screaming away, while the ill-tempered isolationist returns from each foray to his perch, his spleen purged, apparently quieted in the consciousness of successful self-assertion.

This solitary outlaw has never surrendered his will to man, beast, or even a group of his own kind. Being now undisturbed for a little while, having for a moment or two experienced the feeling of mastery and of unchallenged lordship, this mocker has broken into song.

On the lawn fifty yards away is a "charm of goldfinch," as the English say, feeding amicably together. Occasionally, as one starts for a nearby tree, all rise, as at a given signal, and group themselves in an elm to feed upon the tender buds. These tiny birds, still in winter plumage, move together, feed together, rest together. They live in cohesion, in an atmosphere of complete sociability. They diffuse good will and mutual toleration. In sustained flight, however, the goldfinch becomes less cohesive. Flocks have a tendency to divide, and individual members move in an erratic manner inside the flock, darting here and there about the edges, as if the individual birds were resisting but unable to overcome the will of the flock. Starlings and waxwings, on the other hand, surrender themselves completely, fly as a unit, apparently subservient to a single will.

A few weeks from now hundreds of chipping sparrows will occupy this same lawn. They, too, feed on the tender grass shoots but not so close together—they space themselves fully twice as far apart as the goldfinch do. When the chippies rise, startled by something, they, too, seem to move at a given signal, but not all together. A group takes off here, a moment later another, and another, until they have all left the lawn. They will go to the same trees, but in this short flight the course of one individual will cross that of another. You do not get the impression here, as you do with goldfinch making this short flight, of automata pulled by one string.

Again, the chippies do not cluster themselves so compactly in the trees as goldfinch do, but spread their perching order. In short, the flock will has a looser hold upon the individual. There's a trifle, but not much of a trifle, less freedom of enterprise.

From the ragged formations of grackles stringing across the country—hardly to be called a flock at all—ready to fall to pieces any time, anywhere, to the regimented, mathematical designs of migrating geese, there is every gradation of flock form, from pure anarchy yielding itself little at a time to this mysterious will of the group until something resembling a flock appears, and on by easy gradations until the individual will fades out completely, and the group, so far as the act of flying is concerned, becomes an organism.

Last fall, all one morning, I watched white-fronted geese, thousands and thousands of them, coming into the bay near Austell, Texas. There was a perfect discipline, not a feather out of line, until a flock descended to within about two hundred feet of a stretch of open water upon which it intended to alight. Then a curious thing occurs. The formation suddenly dissolves, and they all begin rolling over and over sideways until within a few feet of the water, where they straighten out and glide to rest as one expects normal geese to do.

It would seem to me that this tumbling, rolling, and cavorting in mid-air is an expression of the joy the individual feels in becoming once more a free agent. It may well be an expression of exhilaration in the recapture of his will from a domination to which he surrendered it in order to accomplish the long flight from the oncoming winter in his northern habitat to the safety of southern waters. It was like nothing else so much as a bunch of boys breaking out of school in late afternoon, freed from the day-long discipline, out in the open air at last for fun and frolic and the anarchy of individualistic expression.

Across the pasture I hear the raucous and continual cawing of crows. There is method in this apparently senseless cawing. It is not done just to irritate every man and beast within hearing distance, but for the purpose of maintaining contact among individuals widely separated. A crow becomes restive unless he can hear now and then the caw of another. Isolated and out of hearing, he soon seeks a perch within the sound of another's voice. If one crow finds food, he calls others to him, as jays do, participating share and share alike, until all appetites are satisfied or all the food is gone. They are just as sociable as the goldfinches, but their feeding habits compel, and the carrying power of their voices permits, dispersion over a wide area.

There is another bird on the Mexican border, the chachalaca, whose call permits an even wider dispersion. I have been told by credible observers that one of these birds will pick up another's call just as it ceases, carrying the same note on until another far away chimes in, thus making of the succession one continuous call stretching, so to speak, for miles and miles across the subtropical undergrowth in which the birds are hidden. It is thus co-operative, in a sense, and introduces between and among many individuals, secluded and lonesome, the fellowship of a game, like a party line relieving the tedium of the rural housewife's daily duties.

This is all a way of life worked out as a part of nature's plan. As in an individual life there is a principle of unity and symmetry always active, always harmonizing and constraining anarchic forces, bringing them into due subordination, so in the whole of nature, as diverse and contradictory as it may appear in any partial view, there is a "dark, inscrutable workmanship that reconciles discordant elements."

"Praise Allah," says the Arab proverb, "for the infinite diversity of his handiwork"—and also, we may add, for multitudinous evidences of design. We understand associations such as I have been describing only because we experience them. Alliances, mutual dependencies, parasitisms, preyer and preyed-on, linkages joining into one chain a dozen widely differentiated forms, and other relationships amazingly intricate weave all life, animal and vegetable, into the unity of one vast organism. It is exciting, especially when we of more mystical inclinations fancy we feel a pulse of sympathy beating through it all. "I could not," says Spinoza, "separate God from Nature."

An English professor whom I much admired in college days used to be fond of reading to his classes Browning's "An Epistle, Containing the Strange Medical Experience of Karshish, the Arab Physician." It was many years before I understood why his voice invariably broke and tears filled his eyes as he read the closing lines:

> "So, the All-Great were the All-Loving too—
> So, through the thunder comes a human voice
> Saying, 'O heart I made a heart beats here!'"

A Yard of Jungle

—WILLIAM BEEBE

Within five minutes the daily downpour of tropical rain would drench the jungle. At this moment the air was tense with electricity, absolutely motionless, and saturated with odorous moisture. The voices of all the wild creatures were hushed. The sense of mystery which is always so dominant in a tropical jungle seemed nearer, more vital, but more than ever a mystery. Its insistency made one oblivious of the great heat. The beating of one's heart became a perceptible sound, absurdly loud. All the swamp and jungle seemed listening to it.

Suddenly a voice came out of the heart of this mystery, and fittingly enough, the voice seemed something a little more or less than human, and also fittingly it uttered but a single word, and that word a question. And the listener realized that the answer to the question was the only thing which made life and work worth while. The throb of the blood in his veins was forgotten, and all his senses reached out to the sights and sounds and scents about him. And again the great black frog called from its slimy seat hidden in the still blacker water of the jungle swamp. Its voice was deep, guttural, and a little inhuman, but it asked as plainly as any honest man could ask, Wh—y? And after a minute, Wh—y?

I squatted in the center of a trail. Within walking distance behind me flowed the yellow waters of the Amazon, and the *igarapé* from which the frog had called was even now feeling the tidal heave of the ocean. Ahead, the jungle stretched without a break for three thousand miles or more. And here for a week I had suffered bodily torture, twisting into unhappy positions for hours at a time, watching the birds which crowded the berry-laden foliage of a single jungle tree. In the cool of early morning, throughout the terrible breathless heat of midday and the drenching downpour of afternoon, the frog and I put our questions. There was hope in our interrogation. And my five senses all gave aid, and my hand wrote down facts, and my mind pondered them.

In the very suburbs of Pará, at the mouth of the great Amazon and within a hundred miles of the equator, I found a Mecca of bird-life. It was a gastronomic Mecca to be sure, a tall, slender, wild cinnamon tree—*canella do matto* the natives called it. For a full week I invited torture by attempting to study the bird-life of this single tree. This thing had not been done before; it might not be worth the doing. But testing such possibilities are as important to a naturalist's work as following along the more conventional and consequently more certain lines of investigation. I had no time for exploration of the surrounding country; so I had determined to risk all my precious hours upon intensive observation in one spot.

The century before, a plantling had pushed up through the jungle mold and had won success in the terrible competition of the tropics—the helpless, motionless, silent strife of the vegetable folk. Year by year the lichen-sculptured trunk had pushed its way upward toward light and air, miraculously saved from the deadly embraces of the lianas which crawled forever through the jungle. Today it had gained an accepted place. Although no forest giant, with no great buttresses or masses of parasitic growths, it held up its branches and twigs in full sunlight a hundred feet or more above the ground. And its twiggy fingers were laden with a wonderful harvest of fruit, uncounted berries which attracted the birds from distant roosts and drinking places.

Here, then, a thousand combinations of fate had led me, and here I suffered day by day. Bound to the earth like other normal men, my eyes should have been directed forward. Now I forced them upward for hours at a time, and all the muscles of neck and shoulders revolted. Then eyestrain and headache and a touch of fever followed, and I cast about for means to ameliorate my bodily ills. I dragged a canvas steamer chair to my place of vigil and all my body was grateful.

In memory, there now remain only the high lights of new discoveries, the colorful moments of unalloyed realization of success. Nevertheless this new method of tropical work brought its own new delights and trials. One joy lay in the very difficulties to be overcome. Every sense came into play. Sight, first and foremost, had been put to the most severe of tests in attempting to record the happenings against the glare of the sky high up among the foliage of this bit of jungle. I strained through my high-power glasses until when I looked without them the world seemed withdrawn, dwarfed, as in the horrid imaginings of fever. The glasses gained in weight as I held them pointing vertically until they fairly dropped from my aching arms. My ears strove to catch every song, every note which might prove a character of worth. The jungle scents played upon my emotions and sometimes dominated my work; the faint aroma from some invisible orchid overhead, the telltale musk from a passing mammal, the healthful scent of clean jungle mold. As for taste, I had tested the aromatic berries and fruit of my canella tree, and for science's sake had proved two warningly colored insects. My sense of feeling had operated involuntarily and wholly aside from my scientific desires. Whether stimulated by dozens of mosquitoes, scores of ants, or hundreds of *bêtes rouges* or "mucuims," the insistency of discomfort never discouraged a primary desire to delve as deeply as possible into the secrets of this small area of tropical jungle.

As I walked slowly about beneath the tree or lay back resting in the chair, I seemed to be watching creatures of another world. Whether I ogled them with glasses or now and then brought one down with a charge of small shot, I was a thing of no account to the berry-eating flocks high overhead. A vulture soaring lower than usual passed over the tree, and the shadow of his partial eclipse of the sun froze every bird to instant silence and complete immobility. But my terrestrial activities wrought no excitement. The shot whistled through the foliage, one of their number dropped from sight, and life for the rest went on without a tremor. To ancestral generations, danger had come always from above, not below.

The very difficulty of observation rendered this mode of research full of excitement, and at the same time made my method of work very simple. Against the sky, green, blue, or black feathers all appear black, and the first two days my glasses helped but little. For several minutes I would watch some tiny bird which might have been a yellow warbler had I been three thousand miles farther north. After memorizing personal characters, scrutinizing its flight and method of feeding, striving to fix its individuality, I would secure the bird, and find in all probability that it was a calliste, or tanager of brilliant plumage. Tomorrow, if I were lucky, I might be able to tell off the numbers of this species, to watch them and to know that I was watching them. But recognition would not be by way of the cerulean or topaz or amethystine hues of plumage, but by the slight idiosyncrasies of flirting tail or wing or of general carriage.

Day by day, as I came to know better the jungle about me, I began to perceive a phase which did not change. Even when the sun shone most brightly, when the coolness of early morning had not yet passed, the mood of the Amazon jungle remained. It was consistent, this low swampy jungle, in its uniform, somber mystery. In spite of wholesale exaggeration it was the dangers which came to mind. Of all places in the world this was probably fullest of life, both in numbers and diversity. Yet it was death —or the danger of death—which seemed in waiting, always just concealed from view.

Beneath my tree I squatted silently. Just overhead the foliage might have been almost northern. The finely cut leaves were like willow, and at one side an oak, unusual but still an oak, reached out a thousand thousand motionless leaves, breaking the glare into innumerable patches. But ahead, the terrible interlacing of vines and thorny ropes, the strangle hold of serpentine lianas on every available trunk—all this could be only tropic.

The ground glistened here and there with a film of black water which revealed the swamp. Everywhere the mold and leaves of a hundred years lay scattered, the last fallen still green. Many feet above, great fans dangled, rayed fronds dry and crackling, fallen from high overhead, and suspended, waiting for the interfering twigs and foliage to die in turn and permit them to seek dissolution in the mold.

The jungle was bright with flowers, but it was a sinister brightness—a poisonous, threatening flash of pigment, set off by the blackness of the shadows. Heliconia spikes gleamed like fixed scarlet lightning, zigzagging through the pungent air. Now and then a bunch of pleasing, warm-hued berries reminded one of innocuous currants, but a second glance showed them ripening into swollen, liver-hued globes which offered no temptation to taste. One tree dangled hideous purple cups filled with vermilion fruits, and not far away the color sequence was reversed. A low-growing, pleasant-leaved plant lifted bursting masses of purple-black, all dripping like wounds upon the foliage below. Many flowers were unrecognizable save by their fragrance and naked stamens, advertised neither by color nor form of blossom. I despaired of flowers worthy of the name, until close by my foot I saw a tiny plant with a comely, sweet-scented blossom, grateful to the eye and beautiful as our northern blooms are beautiful. The leaf was like scores lying about, and I realized that this was a sproutling of the giant tree. Nothing but the death of this monster could give the light and air which the little plant needed. It was doomed, but it had performed its destiny. It had hinted that much of the beauty of the jungle lay far above the mold and stagnant water. And then I remembered the orchids high overhead. And the realization came that the low-growing blooms needed their glaring colors to outshine the dim, shadowy under-jungle, and their nauseous fumes to outscent the musky vapors of decay.

The plants of the jungle won success either by elbowing their neighbors and fighting their path up to sunlight, or else by adapting their needs to the starvation meed of air and light allotted to the lowly growths. The big-leaved churacas had found another means of existence. They lived like permanent rockets, bursting in mid-air. A long, curved stem shot up and reached far out into space. It was so slender as to be almost invisible in in the dim light. At its tip radiated a great burst of foliage, leaves springing out in all directions, and absorbing nutrition which a sapling growing amid the undergrowth could not possibly do.

From daybreak to dark the canella tree was seldom deserted. Usually a score or more birds fluttered and fed among its branches, and true to tropic laws, there were comparatively few individuals but a multitude of species. In the few hours I was able to devote to its study, I identified seventy-six different kinds, and together with those which I saw but could not name, I judge that more than a hundred species must have come to the berries during that week in early May. The first day I secured sixteen specimens, all different; and the following day yielded fourteen more, only one of which was a duplicate of the first day's results.

The bird visitors to the tree arrived in one of two characteristic ways. Many came direct and swiftly, singly or in pairs, flying straight and with decision. These came from a distance, with full knowledge of the berries. They fed quietly, and when satiated flew off. The second method of arrival was wholly casual—loose flocks drifting slowly from the neighboring jungle, sifting into the tree, and feeding for a time before passing on. When these left it was rather hastily, and in answer to the chirps and calls of the members of their flock who had not been beguiled by the berries and hence had forged steadily ahead.

These more or less well-defined flocks are very characteristic of all tropical jungles. Little assemblages of flycatchers, callistes, tanagers, antbirds, manakins, woodhewers, and woodpeckers are drawn together by some intangible but very social instinct. Day after day they unite in these fragile fraternities which drift along, gleaning from leaves, flowers, branches, trunks, or ground, each bird according to its structure and way of life. They are so held together by an intangible gregarious instinct that day after day the same heterogeneous flock may be observed, identifiable by peculiarities of one or several of its members. The only recognizable bond is vocal—a constant low calling; half unconscious, absent-minded little signals which keep the members in touch with one another, spurring on the laggards, retarding the overswift.

While I watched, there came to my tree a single species of pigeon, two hawks, and two parrots, four hummingbirds, and an equal number of toucans and woodpeckers. The remaining fifty-nine were all passerine birds, of which there were eight each of the families of flycatchers, manakins, and cotingas. Eleven were tanagers.

The greedy, noisy parakeets were always the center of commotion, wasting more berries than they ate. The toucans, those bizarre birds of whose lives we know so little, yelped and called and bathed in the water caught in the stubs of branches, and fed to repletion. All the flycatchers forgot their usual diet and took to berrying as ardently as the tanagers themselves. Not all the birds came to feed on the berries. A wren hunted insects among the branches, and a hawk found a giant snail crawling up the trunk and devoured it. The insect-eaters of the trunk numbered nine and showed no interest in the berries. Two were woodpeckers and seven woodhewers.

These latter are a strange tropical family four hundred strong, and all the very essence of protective coloring. Their habits of life make of them wandering bits of bark, easy to detect when they are in motion, but vanishing utterly when they are quiet. Their similarity in dress is remarkable. They may be large or small, short or long-tailed, with beaks blunt, sharp, straight, curved, thick, or needle-pointed. In these characters they differ; by these points they must know one another. But their colors are almost identical. Their olives or browns invariably warm into rich rufous on wings and tail, while over head and shoulders a shower of light streaks has fallen, bits of sunlight fixed in down.

Further details belong to the literature of ornithology. But the colors of the berry-hunters—these baffle description, yet we cannot pass them by in silence. The blood and orange splashed on black of the toucans, the scarlet and yellow of woodpeckers, the soft greens and buffs of flycatchers, all these paled when a flock of manakins or tanagers or honeycreepers came to the tree. Every precious stone found its counterpart in the metallic hues of these exquisite feathered folk.

The glory of all was the opal-crowned manakin, a midget in green coat and sulphur waistcoat, with a cap of scaly, iridescent, silvery mother-of-pearl plates, in no way akin to feathers. Until now the life of this Hop o' my Thumb, like those of all his ancestors, had gone smoothly on, with never a human to admire, to wonder, and vainly to echo the question of the great black frog, *Wh—y?*

On the last day of my stay I walked slowly up the trail toward the *canella do matto*. For the last time I strained upward at the well-known branches, and with the very movement there came the voice of the swamp. Its tone was insistent, with a tinge of accusation, a note of censure. W*h—y?* and after a little time, W*h—y?*

I looked about me despairingly. What had I learned after all? Was there any clearing up of the mystery of the jungle? Had my week of scrutiny brought me any closer to the real intimacies of evolution? Or—evading these questions for the time—was there nothing I could do in the few precious moments left?

In five minutes I should turn my back on all this wildness, this jungle seething with profound truths, and great solutions within arm's reach. I should pass to the ocean where monotony compels introspection, and finally to the great center of civilization where the veneer covers up all truths.

Even if my studies had taught only the lesson of the tremendous insurgence of life, could I not emphasize this, make it a more compelling factor to be considered in future efforts toward the frog's question and mine?

My eyes left the foliage overhead and sought the ground. Acting on impulse, I brought from my camping stores an empty war-bag, and scraped together an armful of leaves, sticks, moss, earth, mold of all sorts. Four square feet of jungle debris went into my bag, and I shouldered it.

Then I said adieu to my trail and my tree—a sorrowful leave-taking, as is always my misfortune. For the bonds which bind me to a place or a person are not easily broken. And, as usual when the trail passed from view, the ideal alone remained. The thoughts of mosquitoes, of drenchings, of hours of breathless disappointed waiting, all sank in the memory of the daily discoveries, the mental delights of new research.

A week later, when the sky-line was unbroken by land, when a long ground-swell waved but did not disturb the deep blue of the open sea, I unlaced my bag of jungle mold. Armed with forceps, lens, and vials I began my search. For days I had gazed upward; now my scrutiny was directed downward. With binoculars I had scanned without ceasing the myriad leaves of a great tree; now with lens or naked eye I sought for life or motion on single fallen leaves and dead twigs. When I studied the life of the great tree I was in the land of Brobdingnag; now I was verily a Gulliver in Lilliput. The cosmos in my war-bag teened with mystery as deep and as inviting as any in the jungle itself.

When I began work I knew little of what I should find. My vague thoughts visualized ants and worms, and especially I anticipated unearthing myriads of the unpleasant mucuims or *bêtes rouges*, whose hosts had done all in their power to make life in the jungle unhappy.

Day by day my vials increased. Scores of creatures evaded my search; many others, of whose kind I had captured a generous number, I allowed to escape.

My lilliputian census was far from the mere aggregation of ants and worms which I had anticipated, and a review of the whole showed that hardly any great group of living creatures was unrepresented.

As hinting of the presence of wild animals, a bunch of rufous hairs had in some way been tweaked from a passing agouti. Man himself was represented in the shape of two wads which had dropped from my gun-shots sometime during the week. One had already begun to disintegrate and sheltered half a dozen diminutive creatures. Five feathers were the indications of birds, two of which were brilliant green plumes from a calliste. Of reptiles there was a broken skull of some lizard, long since dead, and the eggshell of a lizardling which had hatched and gone forth upon his mission into the jungle. A third reptilian trace may have been his nemesis—a bit of shed snake-skin. The group of amphibians was present even in this square of four feet—a very tiny, dry, black, and wholly unrecognizable little frog. Fishes were absent, though from my knees as I scraped up the debris, I could almost have seen a little *igarapé* in which dwelt scores of minnows.

As I delved deeper and examined the mold more carefully for

the diminutive inhabitants, I found that this thin film from the floor of the jungle appeared to have several layers, each with its particular fauna. The upper layer was composed of recently fallen leaves, nuts, seeds, and twigs, dry and quite fresh. Here were colonies of small ants and huge, solitary ones; here lived in hiding small moths and beetles and bugs, awaiting dusk to fly forth through the jungle. The middle layer was by far the most important, and in it lived four-fifths of all the small folk. The lowest layer was one of matted roots and clayey soil and its animal life was meager.

Between the upper and the middle strata were sprouting nuts and seeds, with their blanched roots threaded downward into the rich dark mold, and the greening cotyledons curling upward toward light and warmth. Thus had the great bird-filled canella begun its life. In my war-bag were a score of potential forest giants doomed to death in the salt ocean. But for my efforts toward the Wh—y, their fate might have been very different.

Some of the half-decayed leaves were very beautiful. Vistas of pale, bleached fungus lace trailed over the rich mahogany-colored tissues, studded here and there with bits of glistening transparent quartz. Here I had many hints of a world of life beyond the power of the unaided eye. And here too the grosser fauna scrambled, hopped, or wriggled. Everywhere were tiny chrysalides and cocoons, many empty. Now and then a plaque of eggs, almost microscopic, showed veriest pin-pricks where still more minute parasites had made their escape. When one contracted the field of vision to this world where leaves were fields and fungi loomed as forests, competition, the tragedies, the mystery lessened not at all. Minute seeds mimicked small beetles in shape and in exquisite tracery of patterns. Bits of bark simulated insects, a patch of fungus seemed a worm, while the mites themselves were invisible until they moved. Here and there I discovered a lifeless boulder of emerald or turquoise—the metallic cuirass of some long-dead beetle.

Some of the scenes which appeared as I picked over the mold, suddenly unfolding after an upheaval of debris, were like Aladdin's cave. Close to the eye appeared great logs and branches protruding in confusion from a heaped up bank of diamonds. Brown, yellow, orange, and white colors played over the scene; and now over a steep hill came a horrid, ungainly creature with enormous proboscis, eight legs, and a shining, liver-colored body, spotted with a sickly hue of yellow. It was studded with short, stiff, horny hairs—a mite by name, but under the lens a terrible monster. I put some of these on my arm, to see if they were the notorious mucuims which tortured us daily. Under the lens I saw the hideous creature stop in its awkward progress, and as it it prepared to sink its proboscis I involuntarily flinched, so fearful a thing seemed about to happen.

The lesser organisms defy description. They are nameless except in the lists of specialists, and indeed most are of new, quite unnamed forms. The only social insects were small twigfuls of ants and termite colonies, with from five to fifteen members. All others were isolated, scattered. Life here, so far beneath the sunlight, is an individual thing. Flocks and herds are unknown; the mob has no place here. Each tiny organism must live its life and meet its fate single-handed.

Little pseudo-scorpions were very abundant, and I could have vialed hundreds. They rushed out excitedly, and unlike all the other little beings, did not seek to hide. Instead, when they were disturbed, they sought open spaces, walking slowly and brandishing and feeling ahead with their great pincer-tipped arms, as long as their entire body. When irritated or frightened, they scurried backwards, holding up their chelae in readiness.

Mites were the most abundant creatures, equaling the ants in number, always crawling slowly along, tumbling over every obstacle in their path and feeling their way awkwardly. Their kinds were numerous, all villainous in appearance. Ticks were less common but equally repellent. Small spiders and beetles were occasionally found, and hundred-legged wrigglers fled to shelter at every turn of a leaf. The smallest snails in the world crawled slowly about, some flat-shelled, others turreted. Tiny earthworms, bright red and very active, crept slowly through fungus jungles until disturbed, when they became an amazingly active tangle of twisting curves, dancing all about. Simple insects, which we shall have to call collembolas, were difficult to capture. They leaped with agility many times their own length, and when quiescent looked like bits of fungus. As for the rest, only Adam and a few specialists hidden in museums could call them by name. They were a numerous company, some ornamented with weird horns and fringes and patterns, others long of legs or legless, swift of foot or curling up into minute balls of animate matter.

One thing was evident early in my exploration: I was in a world of little people. No large insects were in any of the debris. The largest would be very small in comparison with a May beetle. And another thing was the durability of chitin. The remains of beetles, considering the rareness of living ones, were remarkable. The hard wing-cases, the thorax armor, the segments of wasps, eyeless head masks, still remained perfect in shape and vivid in color. Even in the deepest layers where all else had disintegrated and returned to the elements, these shards of death were as new.

And the smell of the mold, keen and strong as it came to my nostrils an inch away—it was pungent, rich, woody. It hinted of the age-old dissolution, century after century, which had been going on. Leaves had fallen, not in a sudden autumnal downpour, but in a never-ending drift, day after day, month after month. With a daily rain for moisture, with a temperature of three figures for the quicker increase of bacteria, and an excess of humidity to foster quick decay, the jungle floor was indeed a laboratory of vital work—where only analytic chemistry was allowed full sway, and the mystery of synthetic life was ever handicapped, and ever a mystery.

Before the vessel docked I had completed my task and had secured over five hundred creatures of this lesser cosmos. At least twice as many remained, but when I made my calculations I estimated that the mold had sheltered only a thousand organisms plainly visible to the eye.

And when I had corked my last vial and the steward had removed the last pile of shredded debris, I leaned back and thought of the thousand creatures in my scant four square feet of mold. Then there came to mind a square mile of jungle floor with its thin layer of fallen leaves sheltering more than six billion creatures. Then I recalled the three thousand straight miles of jungle which had lain west of me, and the hundreds of miles of wonderful unbroken forest north and south, and my mind became a blank. And then from the mist of unnamable numerals, from this uncharted arithmetical census, there came to memory a voice, deep and guttural—and this time the slow enunciation was jeering, hopeless of answer, W*h—y?* And soon afterwards, W*h—y?* And I packed up my last box of vials and went on deck to watch the sunset.

An Almanac for Moderns

—DONALD CULROSS PEATTIE

Comforting, sustaining, like the tea to the nursling, is Aristotle's beautiful idea that everything serves a useful purpose and is part of the great design. Ask, for instance, of what use is grass. Grass, the pietist assures us, was made in order to nourish cows. Cows are here on earth to nourish men. So all flesh is grass, and grass was put here for man.

But of what use, pray, is man? Would anybody, besides his dog, miss him if he were gone? Would the sun cease to shed its light because there were no human beings here to sing the praises of sunlight? Would there be sorrow among the little hiding creatures of the underwood, or loneliness in the hearts of the proud and noble beasts? Would the other simians feel that their king was gone? Would God, Jehovah, Zeus, Allah, miss the sound of hymns and psalms, the odor of frankincense and flattery?

There is no certainty vouchsafed us in the vast testimony of Nature that the universe was designed for man, nor yet for any purpose, even the bleak purpose of symmetry. The courageous thinker must look the inimical aspects of his environment in the face, and accept the stern fact that the universe is hostile and deathly to him save for a very narrow zone where it permits him, for a few eons, to exist.

Each year, and above all, each spring, raises up for Nature a new generation of lovers—and this quite irrespective of the age of the new votary. As I write this a boy is going out to the marshes to watch with field glasses the mating of the red-winged blackbirds, rising up in airy swirls and clouds. Or perhaps he carries some manual to the field, and sits him down on an old log, to trace his way through Latin names, that seem at first so barbarous and stiff. There is no explaining why the boy has suddenly forsaken the ball and bat, or finds a kite less interesting in the spring skies than a bird. For a few weeks, or a few seasons, or perhaps for a lifetime, he will follow this bent with passion.

And at the same time there will be a man who all his life has put away this call, or never heard it before, who has come to the easier, latter end of life, when leisure is his own. And he goes out in the woods to collect his first botanical specimen and to learn that he has much to learn for all his years.

They are never to be forgotten—that first bird pursued through thicket and over field with serious intent, not to kill but to know it, or that first plant lifted reverently and excitedly from the earth. No spring returns but that I wish I might live again through the moment when I went out in the woods and sat down with a book in my hands, to learn not only the name, but the ways and the range and the charm of the windflower, *Anemone quinquefolia.*

The tadpoles in the quiet bay of the brook are now far past the stage of inky black little wrigglers attached by their two little sticky pads to any stick or leaf, merely breathing through their gills, and lashing with their hair-fine cilia. A dark brown skin—really gold spots mottling the black—now proclaims the leopard frogs they will become. Now the hunger of the open mouths is insatiable; a tadpole, when not resting in sheer exhaustion, will not (and I suppose could not safely) cease for one moment to eat. They all scrape the slime from the sticks and stones; they nibble the water weeds; they are launched upon life with all its appetites and delights and perils.

And what perils! The water is now alive with treacherous, fiercely biting back-swimmers and their cousins the giant water bugs with ugly sucking mouths. The dragonfly nymphs emerge as if perfectly timed to live upon a banquet of frog larvae prepared for them, tigers of the ponds with legs that snatch, and jaws that devour. Fish, turtles, and water birds might all well die in early spring but for the monstrous fertility of the female leopard frog. She must spawn enough children to pay tribute to hundreds of merciless ogre overlords and still more, so that by good fortune June shall hear the marshes rattling with her children's hymns.

So already the contest has begun, not in reality the battle between death and life, but life locked naked with life, in a sort of terrible mating of substances, dissolving and fusing from one species into another, one instant palpitant batrachian jelly and the next the wry croak of a stilted shore-bird.

Upon the bottom of any pond in spring are pastured its tiny grazing animals, its pollywogs and snails, its microscopic flagellates, each one of which will produce a thousand descendants in a month, its rotifers of which each, seventy hours after hatching from the egg, becomes itself a spawning factory. Just above them wait and prowl the small creatures of prey, the crayfish and the tigerish dragonfly nymphs, the nymphs of the mayflies, agile as minnows. Voracity awaits these too; they are destined to vanish down greater jaws and bills and gullets. Life in the casual pond, like life in the sea or the jungle, is like a pyramid with the multiplex and miniform for the broad base.

A bucketful of water may support ten thousand copepods; but a water snake may require a marsh to himself, as a whale needs league upon league of sea, or a bear the half of a mountainside. It is a question if there be any biologic advantage in mastering your environment when you need such a quantity of it to support you. Necessity presses just as sternly on the great beasts as on the small. The problem of population and food is the same, and the increased consciousness of the so-called higher forms is hashly compensated for by their increased capacity for suffering. True, it were pleasanter to eat than be eaten, but in the end even kings must come to dust.

Mayflies emerge at that lush moment in the year when life brims over. Flowers are so many now that one has lost all count of the number of kinds. Birds arrive hourly each fine morning in such crowds that I have given up the resolve not to let an unidentified wing or song drift by. Ponds brim over their edges. Marshes send forth the multitudinous cacophony of song and croak and trill and call and scream. At this psychological moment the mayflies choose to emerge and pose the brief riddle of their whence and why. At times I really think of them as one organism too many.

The fact about mayflies that allures the philosopher is the shortness of their existence. The larval state is passed in water and at such a time one might mistake it for some sort of worm. Then the pre-adult emerges into aerial life. The air first rushes into its breathing pores. In a few minutes or at most twenty-four hours, the skin of the pre-adult is sloughed off and the wings burst forth and for the first time are lifted in flight. There will be a few days of fluttering—then death. Indeed, some species emerge in the morning, have mated before evening, and the next morning the female has laid the eggs in their glutinous covering. There being no further use for these parents, Nature allows them to die.

Was it worth while for a mayfly to have been born, to have been a worm for weeks and a bride or a bridegroom for one day, only to perish? Such is not a question to which Nature will give the human mind an answer. She thrusts us all into life, and with her hand propels us like children through the role she has allotted us. You may weep about it or you may smile; that matters only to yourself. The trees that live five hundred years, or five thousand, see us human mayflies grow and mate and die while they are adding a foot to their girth. Well might they ask themselves if it be not a slavish and ephemeral soft thing to be born a man.

At this season it used to be the custom, and I hope it still may be, for botanists everywhere to do honor to Linnaeus by meeting together for a light-hearted trip afield in search of plants, in the good old style. Formidable has grown that once gentle science of botany—a thing of laboratories and test tubes, of the complex mathematics of the geneticist. For such is the way of a science. It begins in medieval wonder and magic; then a door opens to the fields, it goes forth to its Lapland, to delight and describe and classify. Next come the lens, the laboratory, the investigation of structure, the experiment with function, and at last the mechanical control of the life processes themselves. Sometimes the youngsters of today look back upon the descriptive era as dry, dilettante, unworthy of the name of science.

But more seasoned men, conscious of the history of their science, still hold the name of Linnaeus in reverence. They remember that he did not foist Latin binomials on plants and animals, but pared the latinity down from some twenty words to two! To them the time of Linnaeus is an age of innocence and the true beginnings of modernism. Who would not, if he could, go back today and join Linnaeus and his pupils—so many of whom were to die for him at the ends of the earth—and march afield today to push the moss apart and find the little twin-flowers that he loved above all others, *Linnaea borealis*? Who would not be glad to come back with them, to the fluttering of banners, and the piping of hautboys, and unslinging his heavy case of plants, stand with Thunberg and Peter Kalm and Olaf Swartz and give the rousing *"Vivat Scientia! Vivat Linnæus!"*

They came very secretly, in the night, perhaps; or it may have been that for several days they had been assembling, emerging like bad, buried deeds, out of the earth. I realize now that for several days I had been seeing strange, transparent shards of insects upon the pavement, and on the steps down through the grass. But only today when the children came in, bright-eyed with excitement, and interrupting each other with a tale of enormous bugs everywhere, did I suspect of what they spoke.

I found that the cicadas were thick even upon the steps of the porch, huge, greenish and ruddy-brown heavy-bodied things with beautiful great wings, two very long forewings and a shorter hind pair, through which I could see the grass beneath as plainly as through a thin sheet of mica. I only needed to reach down and pick one up to capture him; he was so sluggish that he seemed like some sleeper awakened, dazed, after having been lost to the world for many years.

Even then, so sluggish was I myself, I did not instantly understand what an exciting discovery I had hit upon. The creature looked familiar, and yet I knew I had never seen him before. I thought of the common dog-day locust with his loud crackling sizzling song, but it was weeks before he would be due. No sound came from the creature in my hand, and I went to explore the grounds for more.

I bagged a dozen, and went into the city with them. Delightful old Dr. Howard was at his desk when I burst in. He opened the box and one of my captives crawled out upon his hand. "Why, man," he cried, "it's the seventeen-year cicada!" He seemed surprisingly pleased. "An old entomologist can never tell," he explained, "whether he will live to hear them again."

On this day, on which I have such good reason to be grateful to my mother, I may perhaps be permitted to put down the profession of one naturalist's faith. Whatever rudiments of religion are innate in me are what ordinarily pass as pantheism, though I am not really prepared to worship everything. I could take oaks as seriously as a druid, but I draw the line at any Hindu idolatry of animals, so that I am not exactly an animist. On this, the summer solstice, I would enjoy lighting bonfires to the sun; I have ever loved the morning best. I could easily find it in me to worship some madonna or any symbol of woman and child, but I do not like symbols as well as I like the thing itself.

A man's real religion is that about which he becomes excited, the object or the cause he will defend, the point at which, spontaneously, he cries out in joy over a victory, or groans aloud from an injury. In France I once startled my wife by bursting into the house with a loud cry of joy. She hastened downstairs to learn what good fortune had befallen us in our old farmhouse above the Lake of Annecy. It was only that fresh snow had fallen on the Alps and sheeted their heads in pure glittering hoods. They looked to me like gods, standing just behind our house. If they were not gods to her, that is because her religion is several degrees less icy and remote. That morning happened to be memorable in the history of science because it was the day on which the discovery of a new planet was announced. This too wrung a cheer from me, and to the joy of my little son and with the tender indulgence of my wife, I declared a holiday, with a trip by steamer around the turquoise lake.

The recognition between individual ants is not, apparently, really individual, but of the next only. It is not based on any sort of high-sign, since anesthetized ants are readily recognized by their sisters. Presumably its source is small; it might take the form of sound in some cases, but the most excited ant who has just discovered a store of honey cannot make itself heard an inch away. It must get at its fellows to communicate its intelligence.

I am more and more convinced that the ant colony is not so

much composed of separate individuals as that the colony is a sort of individual, and each ant like a loose cell in it. Our own blood stream, for instance, contains hosts of white corpuscles which differ little from free-swimming amoebae. When bacteria invade the blood stream, the white corpuscles, like the ants defending the nest, are drawn mechanically to the infected spot, and will die defending the human cell colony.

I admit that the comparison is imperfect, but the attempt to liken the individual human warrior to the individual ant in battle is even more inaccurate and misleading. The colony of ants with its component numbers stands halfway, as a mechanical, intuitive and psychical phenomenon, between our bodies as a collection of cells with separate functions and our armies made up of obedient privates. Until one learns both to deny real individual initiative to the single ant, and at the same time to divorce one's mind from the persuasion that the colony has a headquarters which directs activity (any more than we direct the activities of our white corpuscles), one can make nothing but petty fallacies out of the polity of the ant heap.

Thoreau in his generation, and Burroughs in the next, were the poets of Nature who brought us all closest to the purely natural way of thinking, the faith not so much in the ways of the wild as in what is nature in a man's self. Of the two I will take Thoreau any day; the difference is that between master and disciple. Burroughs had the art of popularizing himself. Thoreau is knotty, tough, difficult of access, solid grain from root to twig, that no dull hatchet can split. Like Sophocles and Christ, he stings complacency into discomfort, he prods us awake, and cherishes his doubts. The poem called "Conscience" is guaranteed to deal a slap on some very right reverend cheeks, in any age.

As a naturalist he discovered nothing new, I grant you; but he knew (as many men of the past and today, who have turned up fresh facts by the dozen, do not) what to make of what he saw. Fact finding is machine work. Unless the machine has a head there is little excuse for it. Had Thoreau but come under the influence of Darwin and Agassiz as he was under that of Pindar and Anacreon, he might have made an incomparable scientist.

Though we can all pronounce his name reverently, and read him with a steady and gentle glow of pleasure, his view of the natural world will not answer to our needs today. He has no sense of problem. But if he had known what we know—space expanding, elements no longer elemental, life a battle—he would, I venture, have come out of his thicket and joined the fight.

It is an old primitive instinct, I believe, to turn over stones, wondering what is under them. The legend of Theseus and the great stone that his mother made him try every day to pull out of the ground is a proof of the antiquity of this curiosity. I find no magic swords underneath the stones I turn. But after some blasting operations, a huge rock has rolled down the river bank, and I have discovered some large scarab beetles, *Anillus fortis*, where the rock had been. They showed none of the inclination to flee from the light which is exhibited by the grubs and silver fish and pill-box bugs that I sometimes find under stones. Not until I took one home and identified him did I learn that he was blind—he and all his race.

There are other examples of the riddle of life's complexity even more startling, but the beetle will serve well enough as a text for the topic of adaptation to environment. This theory was launched in the eighteenth century by Lamarck, a young officer stationed at Monaco. He spent his time botanizing in the strange Mediterranean vegetation and had the good sense to begin wondering why in dry climates plants have small tough leaves, in moist climates broad and filmy ones. An inheritance of acquired tendencies was the answer he evolved.

Lamarck would have explained the blind beetle in this fashion: living in the dark without use for his eyes, the beetle's optic nerve gradually atrophied; as this went on for thousands of generations the race at last became blind. So, everywhere, Lamarck believed, the great molding hand of environment has taken the plastic stuff of living matter and gradually but inexorably shaped it, until cave creatures are sightless, sun-bitten plants are chary of their foliage.

Star-gazing is a common name for harmless futility. But actually there is nobody in either the civilized or savage community, who is looked upon with more tolerance and awe than the man who professes to read the stars. I feel confident that if I were to go out and pass around two hats, one for a foundlings' home and one for a larger telescope than had ever been erected before, I would have my observatory long before I was prepared to tuck the first foundling into a pristine bed. Man is so eager about his great home of the universe, so eager about the secret behind all things, so certain that God is in the stars! That what the seer will tell the rich donor about such things will emerge in equations incomprehensible to him, troubles Mr. Midas not at all. He is rather tickled by the incomprehensibility of his oracle; it makes him certain that they are doing great things under the cyclopean dome.

I think Mr. Midas is a shade more conservative about endowing biological endeavor. Whatever the astronomer discovers— even if he foresees the end of the world—nothing he tells is intimately disquieting. It is all very grand and far away, and everything out there either happened long, long ago or will come to pass indefinite ages hence. But biology is strangely immediate and personal in all its applications, and there is no guaranteeing that its next discovery will be especially agreeable. The mind that would go along with it must have a certain toughness of fiber and a habit of thinking forward faster than prevailing beliefs.

The lichens, that appear the most gray and eventless of plants, are in reality a lively partnership. One member is some one of those little green algae that often stain emerald the north side of a creviced tree trunk, or collect between chinks of a garden walk, or fleck dark, sour, sunless soil. The other is one of certain fungi which half parasitize and half protect their green partners. Though the fungus feeds upon its algal captives, it benefits them too, by maintaining about them a perpetual moist, slimy film that defends them against desiccation, the alga's chief foe. On their side, the algae provide the parasite with that nutriment, manufactured in the mills of the sunlight, which the fungus, without chlorophyll, cannot obtain for itself.

Thus those elfin fructifications of the lichens, though they have the bright colors and often almost the delicacy of flowers, are not certainly sexual; they resemble fungoid pockets of spores, and yet they are not spores. They are not seeds or buds or slips, though they behave like all of them. Each one of them contains a small pellet of fungus matter to which the alga contributes, or is levied upon to contribute, a quota of its own strands. So together the two partners will roll or blow away, locked in each other's arms in a sort of love and hate, out of which a new lichen will be born, to scale mountain peaks and clothe the lonely forests in sage mourning. There seem to be no conditions that these strange plants will not endure except the fumes of our industrial civilization.

Only three explanations of the origin of life have ever been suggested by the mind of man.

Either it came into existence as the special creation of an omnipotent Providence whose dispositions are inscrutable, or else it reached this our earth in the form of spores or bacteria-like organisms from some other world, or else it was an act of spontaneous generation which took place long ago on the earth—in some instant when a pinch of dust and a drop of water became a living thing.

Each one of these explanations is accepted by groups of highly reputable scientists, as well as by a public at large. The scientific adherents of a special act of divine creation are recruited mainly among the astronomers, staggered by the immensities with which they deal. The physicists and chemists are prone to believe in spontaneous generation, for it is their instinct to proclaim the oneness of all things, and to explain all things in a purely mechanical way. Most reluctant to venture any hypothesis are the fellows who know most about the subject—the biologists. Some of them, with a rather grand simplicity, wave the question away to the stars, with the suggestion (by no means wholly fanciful) that life has reached our earth from very far afield in the cosmos.

On November 14, 1888, the Institut Pasteur was founded, Pasteur's greatest triumph. Now, all over the world, similar institutions carry on his work, lighthouses of safety for humanity. It was at the inauguration of this institute that Pasteur closed his oration with these prophetic and Christ-like words:

"Two opposing laws seem to me now in contest. The one, a law of blood and death, opening out each day new modes of destruction, forces nations to be always ready for battle. The other, a law of peace, work and health, whose only aim is to deliver man from the calamities which beset him. The one seeks violent conquests, the other the relief of mankind. The one places a single life above all victories, the other sacrifices hundreds of thousands of lives to the ambition of a single individual. . . . Which of these two laws will prevail, God only knows. But of this we may be sure, that science, in obeying the law of humanity, will always labor to enlarge the frontiers of life."

I often wish that that group of people who decry the progress of science—dilute orientalized mystics, fantastic Chestertonian Christians who imagine that life was gayer, more spiritual and clearer-headed in the Middle Ages, and others of that ilk—would recall that whatever chemistry and engineering may have done to make war horrible, the biological sciences have never done anything but render life nobler, and free man from his miseries.

Louis Pasteur died at St. Cloud in 1895. He awoke from one of his final torpors and gazed around at his students clustered at his bedside. *"Où en êtes vous?"* demanded this tireless admiral of the ship of humanity. *"Que faites-vous?"* And then, *"Il faut travailler!"* he said, and died.

The Organization of Research

—WILLIAM MORTON WHEELER

Everybody is so busy organizing something or inciting someone to organize something that the world's subtly concealed connotations of control and regulation appear to be overlooked. The purpose of organization is instrumental, as is shown by the derivation of the word, from *organon*, a tool, or implement, which is in turn derived from *ergo*, to work. It is one of those superb, rotund words which dazzle and hypnotize the uplifter and eventually come to express the peculiar spirit or tendency of a whole period.

These words, which for want of a better term I may call "high brow," and the conceptions they embody are so interesting that I will dwell on them for a moment. During the late Victorian period the most high-brow word was "progress." It disappeared and gave place to "organization" with the World War when we realized that the evolution of our race since the Neolithic Age was not nearly as substantial as we had imagined. Neither the Greeks nor the people of the Middle Ages seem to have had either of these words or their conceptions, though the Greeks, at least, did a fair amount of progressing and organizing. The medieval high-brow words were "chivalry," and "honor,"

From *Foibles of Insects and Men*, by William Morton Wheeler, Copyright 1928 by Alfred A. Knopf, Inc., New York. Reprinted by permission of the publishers.

the latter persisting down to the present day in Continental Europe in the German students' dueling code, as a living fossil, or what biologists would call a "relict." Schopenhauer remarked that the duel and venereal diseases were the only contributions to culture the race had made since the classical period, over-looking the fact that the Greeks and the Japanese had their own high-brow words and institutions. Gilbert Murray has shown that the word *aidos*, which the Achaean chiefs of the Homeric age so solemnly uttered, was applied to a peculiar kind of chivalry, and the *Bushido* of the Japanese was another similar though independent invention. All of these conceptions—progress, organization, chivalry, *aidos*, *Bushido*—seem to start among the intellectual aristocracy and all imply a certain *noblesse oblige*, for there is no fun in continually exhorting others to progress unless you can keep up with the procession, or organizing others unless you yearn to be organized yourself; just as there is no fun in getting up a dueling or *Bushido* code unless you are willing to fight duels or commit hara-kiri whenever it is required by the rules of the game.

Of course, the vogue of "organization" was abnormally stimulated by the mobilization of armies and resources for the World War. We acquired the organizing habit with a vengeance and have not since had time to reflect that there may be things in the world that it would be a profanation to organize—courtship, e.g. —or not worth organizing—a vacuum, e.g.—or things that cannot be organized, or if organizable, better left as they are—scientific research, perhaps.

There are at least three different types of organization. One of them we find ready to hand in individual animals and plants, in our own bodies and in animal colonies and societies, i.e., in complexes which organize themselves both onto- and phylogenetically. This is a self-contained type of organization, requiring much time and energy for its consummation, and though very intricate and profound, still sufficiently plastic and adaptable to trade with time and the environment and to resist a considerable amount of thwarting and meddling. For obvious reasons this type appears to us to be so admirable that it influences all our conceptions of organization. If the Greeks had coined a word for organization—the nearest word, *orgánosis*, seems not to appear till the twelfth century—they would probably have applied it to a second type of cases, in which an agent organizes a complex as an engine for accomplishing certain results. In this sense Mr. Ford would be an organizer of motor cars and in such a sense theologians might speak of the Deity as organizing the universe. This is organization imposed on inorganic or at any rate alien materials. At the present day the word is not used in this sense, since the notion of life in the materials to be organized seems to be so essential. There is, however, a third type, which is intermediate between the two preceding, one in which certain elements of a living complex are permitted or delegated or arrogate to themselves the right to organize the remaining elements, as is seen in innumerable human organizations from a state, church, or army to a band of robbers. This type of organization can often be swiftly accomplished, especially if reinforced by the first type, but is necessarily more or less of an artifact and prone to easy and unexpected disintegration. We have this type in mind when we speak of the organization of scientific research, or investigation. It is evident, moreover, that the organization of research up to the present time has developed according to the first type, through a natural division of labor and inclination among investigators and by means of such cooperative liaison agencies as learned societies and publications. Even the most pessimistic among us must be lost in admiration at the results thus accomplished during the past few centuries. But the organizers feel that we have been moving too slowly and have been wasting too much time and effort—and they also feel, apparently, that natural or organic organization of research, like that of the past, affords too little scope for the expression of those instincts of self-assertion and domination which are so evidently associated with the accumulation of hormones in the older males of all mammals. These hormones commonly produce such an obfuscation of the intellect that even our mature biologists seldom realize that they are headed for the fate of the old rogue elephants and bulls, which when they try to do too much organizing are promptly and unceremoniously butted out of the herd by the youngsters.

The phrase "organization of research" is nonsense if we take "research" in its abstract sense, for an abstraction, of course, is one of the things that cannot be organized. All we can mean by the term is the organization of the actual processes of research, or investigation; and since these processes are essentially nothing but the living, functioning investigators themselves, organization of research can mean only the organization of the investigators. It would seem desirable, therefore, before attempting such organization to make a behavioristic study of these creatures—either to catch and closely observe a number of them or to steal on them unawares while they are in the full ardor of research—in other words, to investigate the investigators. Unfortunately no one has made such a study, which should, of course, precede the making of a card catalogue of the various species, subspecies, varieties, mutations and aberrations of investigators and the enumeration of their genes and chromosomes. And as the investigators themselves seem to be so busy that they have no time to scrutinize their own behavior, or if they do, are either too proud or too bashful to tell us what they find, I am compelled, for the sake of my argument, to attempt such a study and hence to make a brief excursion into psychology. As this is one of the fields in which it is still possible to do a certain amount of loose thinking with impunity, I may hope to return sufficiently intact to proceed with the discussion.

It is often supposed that the investigator enters his laboratory full of instruments and glassware, and proceeds, with the use of this equipment, his sense organs, and his carefully controlled ratiocinative powers to excogitate the discoveries which our newspaper editors occasionally deign to distort for the benefit of the readers of their Sunday supplements. But every investigator who observes his own activities or those of other investigators knows that this is, to say the least, a very inadequate account of the process; and every psychologist knows that, while the proper employment of the senses and the reasoning powers is extremely important, the real "drives" are the instincts, emotions, and interests, or what some authors prefer to call in more anemic terms, the propensities, conative tendencies, sentiments, or dispositions. To the biologist, who takes a behavioristic view of the instincts, it is difficult to single out the various drives that initiate, determine, and sustain such intricate activities as those leading to scientific discovery and invention; and the psychologists themselves are far from unanimous on this matter.

To merit the designation of human instincts, in the conventional sense, tendencies or dispositions must be innate and purposive, common to all the normal individuals of our species, less overlaid or camouflaged by habits, and therefore more evident in the young than in the adult and represented by similar though more rudimentary tendencies in the higher mammals. Such instincts seem to be rather numerous and several of them are exhibited by the investigator in a highly specialized form or are at any rate evoked and conditioned by very specific objects or situations. We can recognize:

1. Curiosity, which seems to be clearly manifested in many mammals, like the cow which stares at us across the pasture, and in the open-mouthed wonder of the child. It is so characteristic not only of individuals but of whole peoples that the Germans often refer to it as a national peculiarity of the Saxons. In the investigator it is commonly insatiable and very intense, because restricted to certain objects and relations, particularly to the causal relations among phenomena. Its importance has been noticed by many writers. McDougall says that in men in whom curiosity is innately strong, "it may become the main source of intellectual energy and effort; to its impulse we certainly owe most of the purely disinterested labors of the highest types of in-

tellect. It must be regarded as one of the principal roots of both science and religion." It is perhaps worthy of note that "inquiry" is often used as a synonym of investigation, and that any problem is most naturally and most concisely stated in the form of an interrogatory sentence.

2. The hunting instinct, which is primarily nutritive in animals and remains so very largely in savages. In children and adults of civilized man it persists in the form of sport and the love of rapid movement in such intensity that it is leading to the extinction of our native faunas and an enormous development of the automobile industry; while in the investigators—the word itself means followers of an animal's spoor—such as zoologists, archaeologists and explorers it is too apparent to require discussion. It is not lacking, however, in other investigators, all of whom when too old or too lazy to hunt their accustomed prey in the open, delight to sit and hunt for the opinions of others and especially for confirmation of their own opinions, in comfortably heated libraries.

3. The acquisitive, collecting, or hoarding instinct, also primarily nutritive in animals and savages, but modified in children and adults of civilized peoples, in whom it manifests itself in the most extraordinary form of amassing all sorts of objects, from newspaper clippings and cigarbands to meerschaum pipes and shaving mugs. It is unnecessary to dwell on its truly monomaniacal manifestations among zoologists and botanists, who collect everything from mites to whales and from bacteria to sequoias. But even those who look down with contempt on the enthusiastic collectors of bird-lice or coprolites are themselves usually addicted to collecting so-called data or statistics. The significant difference between the mere magpie-like collector and the hamster-like investigator lies, of course, in the use made of the accumulated objects.

4. The instinct of workmanship, craftsmanship, or contrivance, which also has its phylogenetic roots in the constructive activities of very many animals. In man it begins ontogenetically

with the making of mud-pies and may lead to such achievements as the excavation of the Panama Canal or the construction of an airship. It is, as Veblen and others have shown, an instinct of the greatest importance. In the investigator it is seen in the inventing of methods and devices and the construction of apparatus and hypotheses, and reaches its highest manifestations in flights of the creative imagination.

The four instincts I have been very briefly considering might be called individual to distinguish them from four others which are more deeply rooted in the social life of the investigator. These are:

5. Emulation. The decision as to whether this may be traced among animals to competition for food or for mates may be left to Jung and Freud and their respective disciples. According to William James, emulation is "a very intense instinct, especially rife with young children or at least especially undisguised. Everyone knows it. Nine-tenths of the work of the world is done by it. We know that if we do not do the task someone else will do it and get the credit, so we do it." It is powerful and elaborately conditioned in investigators and perhaps the less said about it the better. The word "priority" will conjure up in your minds a sufficient number of emotionally toned ideas to meet the needs of this discussion.

6. What for lack of a better term I shall call the instinct of communication. It seems to have its roots in the behavior of those more or less gregarious or social animals which apprise one another by signs or sounds of the presence of danger, of food, or of certain sexual states. Its manifestations may be said to range from the chirping of crickets, tree frogs, and birds to the invention of language and the effusions of poetry and music, both vocal and instrumental. In both the old and the young of our species it appears also as the by no means sex-limited impulse to gossip and divulge secrets, to communicate news and rumors, much information and no little misinformation. It urges the investigator to communicate the results of his activities to

learned societies and to publish those results to the world or at least to a select coterie of specialists. The strength of this instinct might be tested by passing stringent laws forbidding certain investigators from attending scientific meetings or publishing anything for long periods of time or during their lifetime or even posthumously. The results of such experimental repression might be illuminating, but I refrain from speculating on their nature.

7. Closely connected with this instinct of communication is the craving for sympathy and appreciation so clearly exhibited by most highly social animals and so undisguisedly shown by children. Most investigators exhibit such a moderate development of this craving that they seem to be quite satisfied with the good opinion of the workers in their own specialties. But even if more appreciation were demanded, the individual investigator would stand little chance of obtaining it; for investigators have become so numerous and the field of their labors has been so vastly expanded through their own enthusiastic efforts and so thickly overgrown with a dense crop of technicalities of their own sowing and cultivation, that most of them can be known only to those who are working in the same or adjoining furrows.

8. The instinct of cooperation—also very evident and of far-reaching significance in gregarious and social animals, and manifested in the team-play of young human beings and the innumerable associations of adults. In many investigators this instinct seems to be rather feeble but may still appear at least in the ambition to figure in the role of an honest hod carrier in the erection of some small fragment of the great edifice of human knowledge. In others it may be sufficiently developed to constitute a powerful drive to the invention of labor-saving devices and machinery, methods of preventing disease and increasing longevity and mental and physical efficiency.

This list is probably incomplete, but I believe that it comprises at least the more important drives of the investigator. The special trend of his activities is, no doubt, further determined by his native capacities, but the psychological problem as to whether or not these also constitute drives, as Woodworth maintains and McDougall denies, I shall not attempt to discuss. The point I wish to emphasize is that the specific activities of the investigator depend primarily and pre-eminently on his instincts, emotions, interests, and native endowments.

If we turn now to a survey of investigators in general we find that they can be divided into two classes, usually called theoretical and practical, or pure and applied. The term "pure" is, to say the least, somewhat priggish, since it seems to imply that its alternative is more or less contaminated, and theoretical and practical are unsatisfactory because all investigation is necessarily both. I prefer, therefore, to designate the two classes as discoverers and inventors, since the former are primarily interested in increasing our knowledge of our environment and of ourselves, the latter in increasing our power over our environment and ourselves. From the very nature of this distinction it follows that the discoverer pursues more general, more theoretical and therefore more remote aims; whereas the inventor, in the very broad sense in which I am using the term, busies himself with more special, more practical, and therefore more immediate problems. As both types of investigation are equally essential to the fullest spiritual and economic exploitation of the universe, no society can attain to a high level of culture unless it provides impartially both for its discoveries and its inventors.

There is another classification of investigators which will be useful for the purposes of my argument—namely, into professionals and amateurs. I am, of course, using these words in their good sense, not with the evil connotations that have grown up around them. It is clear that both may suffer from certain disabilities, the professional from well-known guild restrictions, the amateur from lack of opportunity or equipment or of the lively interchange of ideas so necessary to the most fruitful type of investigation. Both, too, have their advantages, the professional in the support and advertisement of his guild-fellows, the amateur in the freedom to choose, and delimit his own problems, to work on them in his own way and to publish when he sees fit. These distinctions did not escape that clever old fox, Samuel Butler, who says:

"There is no excuse for amateur work being bad. Amateurs often excuse their shortcomings on the ground that they are not professionals, the professional could plead with greater justice that he is not an amateur. The professional has not, he might well say, the leisure and freedom from money anxieties which will let him devote himself to his art in singleness of heart, telling of things as he sees them without fear of what man shall say unto him; he must think not of what appears to him right and lovable, but of what his patrons will think and of what the critics will tell his patrons to say they think; he has got to square everyone all round and will assuredly fail to make his way unless he does this; if, then, he betrays his trust he does so under temptation. Whereas the amateur who works with no higher aim than that of immediate recognition betrays it from the vanity and wantonness of his spirit. The one is naughty because he is needy, the other from natural depravity. Besides the amateur can keep his work to himself, whereas the professional man must exhibit or starve."

Contrasting the professional and amateur, to the advantage of the latter, was also a favorite pastime with that irritable old bear, Schopenhauer. He compared the professionals with dogs, the amateurs with wolves, but he was not always consistent zoologically, for he sometimes thought of the professionals as cattle, as, e.g., when he says:

"On the whole, the stall-feeding of our professorships is most suitable for ruminants, but those who receive their prey from the hands of Nature live best in the open."

At present the terms "professional" and "amateur" seem to have fallen into disuse among scientists, for reasons that are not far to seek. We know that during the 18th and 19th centuries, when the books and apparatus necessary for the prosecution of research were so meager as to be within the reach of men of very moderate means, amateurs were able to do a vast amount of important work in all the departments of science. This was particularly true in England and America. In England we have a teacher of music, William Herschel, making great discoveries in astronomy; a stone-cutter, Hugh Miller, in geology; a Nottingham cobbler, George Green, in mathematics; a grocer of Ightham, Harrison, and a jeweler of St. Leonards, W. J. L. Abbott, in archaeology, and a country gentleman, Charles Darwin, in biology. There were men like John Hunter, Lyall, Wallace, Galton, Samuel Butler, Lubbock, Bates, and a host of other eminent investigators, who really belonged to the class of amateurs. Till very recently whole sciences, such as taxonomy and zoogeography, entomology and genetics were almost entirely in the hands of amateurs. Mendel was an amateur and all the wonderful varieties of our domestic animals and plants were developed— one might almost say invented—by amateurs. The change which has come over the situation is due to the great increase in our knowledge in more recent times and the exuberant growth of our universities, technical schools, museums, and research institutions. These have made investigation more and more difficult for the amateur, especially in the inorganic sciences and in physiology, which now demand an exacting preparation and elaborate apparatus, although there are even at the present time a few eminent amateur astronomers and geologists. Amateurs still abound, nevertheless, in zoology and botany, in which it is still possible to carry on much valuable research with very simple equipment. There must be thousands of them, and nothing is more extraordinary than the ignorance of their work on the part of many of our university professionals. I could give a long list of men in the most diverse professions, letter carriers, stage-coach drivers, hosiers, portrait-painters, engravers, parsons, priests, stockyard superintendents, engineers, bankers, country-grocers, country-doctors, army officers, mining prospectors, school teachers, and clerks, whose researches have greatly enriched entomol-

ogy and other departments of zoology. In such vast and complicated sciences as biology and archaeology the work of the amateur
is so much needed and so worthy of encouragement that we may
regard it as one of the greatest defects of our educational system
that a youth is ever able to leave the science courses of a high
school or college and take up the humblest calling without a
fixed determination to fill at least a portion of his leisure hours
with the joys of research.

The disuse of the words "professional" and "amateur" is also,
no doubt, due to the fact that the two kinds of investigators can
no longer be sharply distinguished. Not only are the biologists in
our universities and museums frequently recruited from the ranks
of the amateur, but as investigators in those institutions many
of them remain amateurs in spirit and merely exercise the teaching and curatorial professions because they can be more conveniently carried on in conjunction with research than more lu-
crative professions such as undertaking and plumbing. There is no
reason to suppose that the number of amateur investigators may
not greatly increase under a more favorable form of society. In
the ideal commonwealth of the future it may not be in the least
surprising to find that the communal furnace-man, after his four-
hour day, is conducting elaborate investigations in paleobotany,
and that the communal laundress is an acknowledged authority
in colloidal chemistry.

Now if the preceding very hasty behavioristic account is
accurate, we must admit that it would be difficult to find a body
of men more unfavorable for purposes of organization, even by a
committee of their own class, than the investigators. Many reasons might be given in support of this statement, but I shall
consider only the following four:

1. The activities of the investigator depend, as we have seen,
on an array of instincts, emotions, and interests, many of which
are so positive that their organization in the sense in which organizers are using the term is out of the question. It is possible,
of course, to overstimulate, repress, pervert, and exploit instincts,

and they are undoubtedly able to organize themselves by long processes of interplay, mutual adjustment and coordination, but even regulation of the *ab extra* is exceedingly difficult. In this matter the experience of the race in its age-long endeavors to regulate and organize such powerful drives as the sexual and parental instincts should be sufficiently illuminating, and the instincts of the typical inventor and discoverer seem to be every bit as imperative. The impossibility of organizing even a small body of investigators can be easily tested. Such bodies exist in our large universities, very small in comparison with the total number of investigators in the country, but large enough, if organized, to determine and control the whole policy of their respective institutions. But if any investigator attempts to organize such a body for such a purpose or for any other of mutual advantage, he will at once find his efforts frustrated, or at any rate circumvented, by a lot of individuals, turgid with peculiar instincts, emotions, and purely personal interests, and as blind to their collective interests as an equal number of soft-shell clams. Furthermore, it is important to note that the difficulties of organizing are greatly increased by the skeptical and critical attitude of mind which the investigator is bound to cultivate and the defective development of certain dispositions in his constitution, such as the gregarious instinct and the instinct of self-abasement and susceptibility to suggestion, propaganda, and leadership, which render other men so prone or at least so accessible to social, religious, and political organizaton.

2. Attempts at organizing investigators must fail because their highly specialized activities depend to such a great extent on their peculiar native aptitudes or capacities. The organizers are willing to admit that they are baffled by the geniuses, but these are dismissed as very rare birds, notwithstanding the fact that their influence on the trend of scientific research is out of all proportion to their numbers. The great majority of investigators appear on superficial acquaintance to be such commonplace, unassuming specimens of humanity that it would seem that they and

society in general could not be greatly benefited by having their problems "assigned" and their investigative efforts directed, controlled, and organized. This notion seems to me to be due to a singularly defective insight into the peculiar psychology of investigators. No one who has had long and intimate relations with these men can fail to be impressed with the extraordinary diversity of their aptitudes; and nothing is more evident than that these aptitudes must be permitted to express themselves not only with the greatest freedom, but even in the most whimsically personal manner. Nor can anyone who is running a laboratory fail to notice that he can secure the fullest enthusiasm, devotion, and team-play from all his men only on the condition that all considerations are absolutely subordinated to the ideals of research. He knows that some investigators can do their work best with a slow, uniform, and apparently never-tiring motion, others with a ravenous, carnivore-like onrush, accompanied by an expenditure of vitality so magnificent that they have to loaf for a considerable period before they can store sufficient energy for another onslaught on their problem; and that there are many others whose investigative activities are of an intermediate and more evenly rhythmical type. Yet men of such diverse aptitudes and habits of work can be easily induced to live in harmony and accomplish much valuable work if any suggestion of such things as punctuality, punching time-clocks, and other efficiency and factory devices are most carefully avoided. So sensitive is the investigator to the need of giving expression to his capacities and of doing his work in his own way that anyone who is enough of a martinet to insist on introducing any of the devices to which I have alluded will at once build up a defense reaction sufficiently powerful to vitiate or inhibit all the research activities of his laboratory. It is for this reason, I believe, that even the vague, tentative suggestions of the organizers are already creating a resentment, or at any rate a resistance, that would surprise no one who is not bent on behaving like the proverbial bull in a china shop.

3. Whatever may be the value of research to the individual investigator, it is certain that its only social value lies in the discoveries and inventions to which it may lead. The investigative genius may be defined as one who is in a chronic state of discovery or invention, whereas the ordinary investigator approximates genius more or less closely according to the frequency of his creative achievements. Now such essential achievements, both chronic and occasional, cannot be included in any scheme of organization, for they usually lie outside the purview of the investigator himself or depend on situations over which he has no control. Discovery and invention are in this sense fortuitous or accidental, and also involve a time factor which is equally unpredictable and unorganizable. The investigator, if you will pardon my emphatic language, can only do his damnedest and hope that the new truth will deign to ascend from the subconscious or descend from the lap of the gods. After long and tedious observation or experiment and many disappointments, he may or he may not find the discovery or invention flashing suddenly and more or less completely into consciousness, or emerging from some happy constellation of events. The plant-physiologist Sachs once told me that his best ideas suddenly entered his mind in the morning while he was lacing his shoes or brushing his teeth. I have noticed in my own case that the few unimportant ideas that strike me as unlike those which ordinarily infest my waking consciousness emerge suddenly while I am passing a certain vacant lot on my morning trip to my laboratory. Not improbably my single cup of breakfast coffee may be a stimulus so timed that the reaction coincides with the vacant lot. I hasten to confess, however, that the outline of this paper was not picked up in a vacant lot, as its miscellaneous contents might lead you to suppose, but came to me, probably after prolonged subconscious incubation, while I was wondering how much coal I could save by using as an "Ersatz" the literature received during the past three years from that noble superorganization of superorganizers, the National Research Council.

4. I have dwelt on the amateurs because they seem to me to form another insuperable obstacle to the organization of research, at least in the biological field, where they constitute a very large and important "bloc" of investigators. While one might be pardoned for supposing that some of the house-broken or domesticated investigators, who indulge in what is called "institutional" or "industrial" research, might be organized after a fashion, it would be unpardonable to suppose that the wild, untamable amateurs would ever submit to such an indignity. These seem to be described as "solitary workers" in some of the literature I have received—why, I cannot say. The amateur, as the word implies, is a lover, and all the world loves a lover, no matter how wild, or just because he is wild. Certainly the many members of our numerous natural history, ornithological, entomological, malacological, botanical, and mycological clubs, who hold monthly meetings and contribute modestly but effectively to the sum of our knowledge, regard themselves as anything but "solitary" workers. That designation would seem to be more applicable to some of the professionals in our universities and research institutions.

Of course, the organizer who has been stung by the efficiency bug is troubled by all this diffuse and elusive activity, and counters with the assertion that organization would save duplication of effort and direct it to problems of fundamental importance. This takes for granted a knowledge of the fundamental problems on the part of the organizer and a most enviable intuition of the means adapted to their solution, or at any rate seems to imply that working on fundamental problems means *eo ipso* making important discoveries and inventions. The contention that we must avoid duplication of effort must have had its origin in a machine shop or a canning plant, for it certainly never originated in the brain of any investigator worthy of the name. That the establishment of the simplest item of our knowledge not only requires duplication, but reduplication and re-reduplication of effort, is too obvious to require discussion; as is also the fact that we always regard the agreement in the results of two or more investigators working independently as presumptive evidence of truth. I would similarly pass over the further implication in the arguments of the organizers that the only value of an investigator's work lies in the scientific data and conclusions which it contains; and that we are not concerned with its unconscious revelations of habits of thought, personality, etc. The perusal of the works of the great amateur entomologists Réaumur and Fabre might be recommended for those whose minds are in such a ligneous, arenaceous, or argillaceous condition.

The suggestion that scientific research may be advantageously organized naturally leads one to consider those other great human activities, religion and art, which are also bound up with powerful instincts, emotions, and interests. Certainly religion, especially in the form of dogma and ritual, has been so superbly organized *semper ubique et omnibus*, since it first arose in the ghost-fear, daimonism and taboo of our savage ancestors, that it would seem to constitute a wonderful field for the study of both the blessings and curses of organization. It is, in fact, a field in which organization could be readily introduced and maintained owing to the proneness of so many human beings to suggestibility, credulity, the gregarious instinct, the instincts of self-abasement and fear, and of the sentiments of awe and reverence —all of which, be it noted, are singularly feeble or defective in the investigator. The same conclusion would seem to follow from the very different view of some of the Freudians who state that all religions are permeated by a subterranean feeling of guilt and that "this absolutely unfailing presence of the feeling of guilt shows us that the whole structure of religion is erected on a foundation of repression of instinct." That the perfection of organization so characteristic of religion may have been beneficent in other times may be admitted, but the more nearly perfect an organization the less it is able to adapt itself to changing conditions, and the World War has disclosed to all thinking men the same kind of hopeless, resourceless over-specialization in our ecclesiastical organizations as that with which the biologist is so familiar in archaic, moribund, and actually extinct species. At the present time the Church seems to be about as well adapted to piloting the great forces which are impelling society as a two-toed sloth to piloting an airplane, or a manatee the Twentieth Century Limited. Like the Edentate and the Sirenian, the Church exhibits such feebleness of volition and muscular tonus and such a low ebb of creative energy that one is inclined to find a modicum of truth in the aphorism which H. G. Wells saw posted by the bolsheviki on one of the houses in Moscow: "Religion is the opium of the people."

What a different picture is presented by that other great field of human activity, in which the instinct of workmanship and the creative imagination attain their finest and most un-restrained expression—the field of art! Its very life seems to depend on freedom from all imposed organization. Hence its plasticity and adaptability in all ages and places, its resilience and prompt resurgence after periods of conventionalization, or overspecialization. Unlike the religious person who seems always to be mistrusting his instincts, or the scientific investigator who is so sophisticated that he ignores them, the artist takes them to his bosom, so to speak, and in all his works tries to persuade the rest of the world to do the same. He thus becomes the ally of creative Nature herself, and while himself capable of such control and restraint as are demanded in the harmonious execution of his work, quickly resents the slightest suggestion of restraint or control from the outside. This is so well known that one would find it more entertaining than informing to hear the comments of a lot of painters, sculptors, composers, poets, novelists, and actors—and especially of a lot of actresses or prime donne—if some National Art Council had the temerity to suggest that their work could be greatly improved by organization.

The history of science and philosophy is not without significance in connection with the attempts of modern organizers.

It is well known that both, after their twin-birth and brilliant childhood among the Greeks, lived through a kind of stupid Babylonian captivity as hand-maidens to the medieval Church, which had been so successful in organizing itself that it naturally tried to organize everything else. But Science turned out to be such an obstreperous and incorrigible tomboy that she long since regained her freedom; and philosophy, though she had been treated with more consideration, and may still occasionally flirt, no longer, outside of our Jesuit colleges at least, sits down to spoon with theology as she did in the days of St. Thomas of Aquin.

Times have changed so greatly that at present we even have eminent amateurs, like the Rev. Erich Wasmann, S.J., who vie with Haeckel in the boldness of their evolutionary speculations. Scientific research is no longer concerned with the Church but with the two great forces which are contending for the mastery of the modern world, labor and capital. The present plight of the Russian investigators shows us, perhaps, what we may expect when certain communistic ideals of labor are put into practice; and Veblen's account of the evolution by atrophy of the creative artisan of former centuries into the modern factory operative, whose life has been reduced by capital, machinery, and efficiency experts to one long hideous routine in some overspecialized task, shows us, perhaps, what we may expect when nothing but money talks.

Even if the investigator could hold aloof and adopt a policy of watchful waiting, till the world is controlled by either labor or capital or, as seems more probable, by some compromise between them, he would still be in an unfortunate position. Since both labor and capital are primarily concerned with production, we should expect both to center their interests on applied research, or invention, and to neglect research which is fundamentally concerned with discovery. This would be unfortunate, because the two kinds of research can be most fruitful only in symbiosis; for the neglect of discovery must lead to impoverishment of the theoretical resources of the inventor, and purely theoretical research strongly tends to become socially ineffective. We have as yet, I believe, no concise information in regard to labor's attitude to so-called pure research. The attitude of the capitalist, or businessman, seems to be much more definite. His activities, like those of the investigator, are bound up with certain powerful, highly conditioned instincts, emotions, and interests, some of which have been elucidated by Taussig. He believes that the businessman is driven mainly by the acquisitive instinct, centered of course on pecuniary profits; the instinct of domination or predation; the instinct of emulation, in the special form of social emulation; and the instinct of devotion or altruism. Undoubtedly we must recognize also the importance of the instinct of workmanship as a powerful drive in many eminent businessmen, but both it and the instinct of devotion are, of course, apt to be directed to practical matters or to those which yield immediate returns, such as philanthropy, charity, medicine, etc. Apart from certain notable exceptions, businessmen may, therefore, be expected to favor invention and to take little interest in discovery, except when it relates to natural resources capable of exploitation.

These considerations lead me to the opinion that so long as our present society endures, adequate financial and other support for research in its most comprehensive form will be forthcoming only after the general community has thoroughly grasped the fact that of the four great fields of human endeavor, science, art, religion, and philosophy, science is of the most overwhelming social value in the sense that the welfare of every individual, physically, mentally and morally, absolutely depends on its developments, or in other words, on scientific research. To saturate the general public with this conviction is a formidable task and one that can be accomplished only by a slow process of education.

There is also another aspect of the subject which I can best make clear by returning to that form of organization which we

observe inhering in individual animals and plants and in the
societies of the former. Occasionally we find such organisms so
highly integrated, differentiated, or specialized as seriously to
impair their powers of adaptation. When such a condition is
reached, the organism either persists without phylogenetic
change, if its environment remains stable, or soon becomes
extinct, if its environment changes. Most organisms, however,
retain a lot of relatively unorganized or more or less generalized
structures and functions as reserves for prospective adjustments
to the changing environment. Our own bodies still contain many
such primitive elements, like the white blood corpuscles, the undifferentiated connective tissue, dermal and glandular cells, and
in larval insects we find even undifferentiated nerve cells. And we
all carry with us in our subconscious a great reservoir of very
primitive instincts and tendencies, many of which are as archaic
as those of our paleolithic and anthropoid ancestors. This whole
relatively undifferentiated and imperfectly organized equipment
must be of the greatest value as a source of future adaptations.

We are also beginning to see that as civilization advances it is
necessary to maintain a certain number of our activities in a
primitive, unorganized condition and for their exercise to set
aside hours of leisure and relaxation, vacations and holidays, so
that we can escape from the organized routine of our existence.
And as the earth becomes more densely covered with its human populations, it becomes increasingly necessary to retain
portions of it in a wild state, i.e., free from the organizing mania
of man, as national and city parks or reservations to which we
can escape during our holidays from the administrators, organizers, and efficiency experts and everything they stand for;
and return to a Nature that really understands the business of
organization. Why may we not regard scientific research, artistic
creation, religious contemplation, and philosophic speculation as
the corresponding reservations of the mind, great world parks to
which man must resort to escape from the deadening, over-
specializing routine of his habits, mores, and occupations, and

enjoy veritable creative holidays of the spirit? These world parks are in my opinion the best substitute we are ever likely to have for the old theological Heaven; and they have the great advantage that some of us are privileged to return from them with discoveries and inventions to lighten the mental and physical burdens of those whose inclinations or limitations leave them embedded in routine. This is the meaning of that stanza in the witch's song of Faust:

> The lofty skill
> Of Science, still
> From all men deeply hidden!
> Who takes no thought,
> To him 'tis brought,
> 'Tis given unsought, unbidden!

Like other members of society, the scientist, artist, and philosopher must always devote considerable time and energy to routine occupations; for their lives, with very rare exceptions, are not completely absorbed in research, speculation, and creative activity. They might therefore be expected to react rather unpleasantly to any suggestion of meddling with those occupations in which they feel that they can express their personalities with the greatest freedom and the greatest satisfaction to themselves if not to others. It seems to me that it can only be due to the modesty or indifference of scientific investigators that they have failed to voice their opinions of the organizers. The only utterances I have seen are an admirable paper by Professor Summer, and in another field, that of social theory, a few paragraphs by G. D. H. Cole.

Postscript

ONE word more. The reader should not be left with the impression that all men, or even all writers, since the seventeenth century have put their faith in Nature or taken pleasure in her manifestations. Charles Lamb declared roundly: "I shall not much care if I never see a mountain in my life; I have no passion for groves and valleys." Max Beerbohm's Happy Hypocrite (though he was, to be sure, a wicked fellow) confessed boastfully that it had been twenty years since he had seen a buttercup. And Saki's Eleanor Stringham will represent the attitude of the persistently worldly. From the circulating library Eleanor had expected a book of scandalous memoirs entitled *By Mere Chance* but she got instead, by mistake, one called *By Mere and Wold.*

* "The unwelcome substitute appeared to be a collection of nature notes contributed by the author to the pages of some Northern weekly, and when one had been prepared to plunge with disapproving mind into a regrettable chronicle of ill-spent lives it was intensely irritating to read the dainty yellowhammers are now with us, and flaunt their jaundiced livery from every bush and hillock.' Besides, the thing was so obviously untrue; either there must be hardly any bushes or hillocks in those parts or the country must be fearfully overstocked with yellow-

* From "The Jesting of Arlington Stringham," published in England by John Lane The Bodley Head, Ltd. In America this appeared in *The Short Stories of Saki,* by H. H. Munro, Copyright 1930 by The Viking Press, Inc., New York. Reprinted by permission of the publishers.

hammers. The thing scarcely seemed worth telling such a lie about.

"She turned at random to another paragraph. 'Lie quietly concealed in the fern and bramble in the gap by the old rowan tree, and you may see, almost every evening during early summer, a pair of lesser whitethroats creeping up and down the nettles and hedge-growth that mask their nesting place.'

"The insufferable monotony of the proposed recreation! Eleanor would not have watched the most brilliant performance at His Majesty's Theater for a single evening under such uncomfortable circumstances, and to be asked to watch lesser whitethroats creeping up and down a nettle 'almost every evening' during the height of the season struck her as an imputation on her intelligence that was positively offensive."

Obviously the Eleanor Stringhams will not be interested in this anthology. But there are, so the compiler hopes, others.